This book is due for return on or before the last date shown below.

Historical Materialism Book Series

The Historical Materialism Book Series is a major publishing initiative of the radical left. The capitalist crisis of the twenty-first century has been met by a resurgence of interest in critical Marxist theory. At the same time, the publishing institutions committed to Marxism have contracted markedly since the high point of the 1970s. The Historical Materialism Book Series is dedicated to addressing this situation by making available important works of Marxist theory. The aim of the series is to publish important theoretical contributions as the basis for vigorous intellectual debate and exchange on the left.

The peer-reviewed series publishes original monographs, translated texts, and reprints of classics across the bounds of academic disciplinary agendas and across the divisions of the left. The series is particularly concerned to encourage the internationalization of Marxist debate and aims to translate significant studies from beyond the English-speaking world.

For a full list of titles in the Historical Materialism Book Series available in paperback from Haymarket Books, visit:
www.haymarketbooks.org/category/hm-series

The Dimensions of Hegemony

Language, Culture and Politics
in Revolutionary Russia

by
Craig Brandist

Haymarket Books
Chicago, IL

First published in 2015 by Brill Academic Publishers, The Netherlands
© 2015 Koninklijke Brill NV, Leiden, The Netherlands

Published in paperback in 2016 by
Haymarket Books
P.O. Box 180165
Chicago, IL 60618
773-583-7884
www.haymarketbooks.org

ISBN: 978-1-60846-557-6

Trade distribution:
In the US, Consortium Book Sales, www.cbsd.com
In Canada, Publishers Group Canada, www.pgcbooks.ca
In the UK, Turnaround Publisher Services, www.turnaround-uk.com
In all other countries, Publishers Group Worldwide, www.pgw.com

Cover design by Jamie Kerry of Belle Étoile Studios and Ragina Johnson.

This book was published with the generous support of
Lannan Foundation and the Wallace Global Fund.

Printed in Canada by union labor.

10 9 8 7 6 5 4 3 2 1

Library of Congress Cataloging-in-Publication data is available.

Contents

If we had to express the essence of Bolshevism and its role in the Russian revolutionary movement in a phrase, and to name the main regulating idea of Bolshevism, we would say that this idea is the *hegemony of the proletariat.*[1]

GRIGORII ZINOV'EV, 1923

∴

---

1 Zinov'ev 1924 [1923], p. 304; Zinoviev 1973 [1923], p. 216.

Preface

The present study has been a long time in the making. It grew out of a project to study the development of Soviet sociological linguistics in the period 1917–38 hosted by the Bakhtin Centre at the University of Sheffield and funded by the Arts and Humanities Research Council between 2003 and 2007. This enabled me to collect a huge amount of published and archival materials and to meet with a number of people who were instrumental in helping me to track down this material. I was able to work on the monograph only intermittently between periods of research leave, and in this period the conception changed and the question of hegemony, which was a recurring theme in the early drafts, began to take a central position. This was strengthened by a small British Academy grant to work on the materials about Gramsci held in the Comintern archives. That research will be published separately, yet it could not but leave a trace on the present study.

In the course of the preparation of this book, I have accumulated a number of debts to scholars in a variety of ways. The formulation of the initial grant application was significantly aided by consultations with David Shepherd, while the research carried out on the basis of the grant owed much to my then research assistant Katya Chown, without whom the base material for the project would have been a good deal poorer. Vladimir Alpatov's encyclopaedic knowledge of the area was particularly helpful in helping to track down archival material, but credit must also go to the staff of a number of archives in Russia and the former USSR. Peter Thomas has been supportive and helpful at all stages. I was also fortunate to have the generous assistance of the late Natalia Iusova and her husband Sviatoslav Iusov on visiting Kiev for archival research. The grant application to research the Gramsci materials was supported by Alex Callinicos.

I have no doubt that the text bears marks of my valuable and constructive conversations with a number of extremely knowledgeable people, who are too great in number to enumerate in full. I must mention Vladimir Alpatov, Vera Tolz, Galin Tihanov, Mika Lähteenmäki, John Biggart, Dmitrii Iunov, Boris Gasparov, Ekatarina Velmezova, Viktoria Gulida, Iurii Kleiner, Galina Lilich, Jonathan Hall, Abbie Bakan, Patrick Sériot and Irina Ivanova.

A number of people provided me with copies of difficult-to-find materials, amongst whom I must mention John Biggart, Galin Tihanov and Evgeny Dobrenko, Gennadii Obatnin and Jukka Pietiläinen.

I am indebted to the comments on drafts, of the whole or parts of the text, by Mika Lähteenmäki, John Biggart, Evgeny Dobrenko, Peter Jones, Chris

Pawling, Alan Shandro and Galin Tihanov. Such help to overcome the conflations, incautious phrasing and misconceptions that ran throughout earlier drafts has made the current work, whatever its enduring flaws, considerably stronger than it would otherwise have been.

The following people were instrumental in allowing me to present preliminary versions of the materials that make up the current study and to benefit from the discussions that resulted: Ana Zandwais, Beth Brait, Renata Marchezan, João Vianney Cavalcanti Nuto, Maria Inês Batista Campos, Anderson Magalhães, Nikolai Vakhtin, Vladimir Feshchenko, Tat'iana Venediktova, Alessandro Carlucci, Tomi Huttunen, Ben Hellman, Tintti Klapuri, Liisa Steinby, Arja Rosenholm, Patrick Sériot, Ulla-Maija Peltonen, Danuta Ulicka, Juha Koivisto and the organisers of the *Historical Materialism* conferences over a number of years.

I am aware that a volume dealing with material of this nature has a potential audience with a number of specialisations. With this in mind I have provided a glossary of names of historical figures whose names appear throughout the book. Inevitably some such basic information will be quite superfluous to most readers, but I am confident that all readers will find something helpful here, especially given the blizzard of unfamiliar names any study of this nature inevitably generates. This is all the more important when dealing with the names of early Soviet institutions, the key ones of which have also been included, given that the period saw an almost constant renaming and reorganisation of the institutional structure.

A Note on Transliteration

Transliteration of Russian proper names has followed the Library of Congress system (without diacritics), except where there are well-established English conventions for well-known figures such as Trotsky, Gorky, Mayakovsky and so on. The reader is reminded that alternative transliterations may be found in other English-language texts.

Acknowledgements

The text includes reworked material originally included in the following publications, excerpted here with the permission of the publishers: (2003) 'The Origins of Soviet Sociolinguistics', *Journal of Sociolinguistics*, 7, 2: 213–33; (2006) 'The Rise of Soviet Sociolinguistics From the Ashes of *Völkerpsychologie*', *Journal of the History of the Behavioral Sciences*, 42, 3: 261–77; (2008) 'Sociological Linguistics In Leningrad: The Institute for the Comparative History of the Literatures and Languages of The West and East (ILJAZV) 1921–33', *Russian Literature* LXIII (II/III/IV): 171–200; (2010) *Politics and the Theory of Language in the USSR*, London: Anthem Press; (2012c) 'Rhetoric, Agitation and Propaganda: Reflections on the Discourse of Democracy (with Some Lessons from Early Soviet Russia)', in *Language, Ideology, and the Human*, eds. Sanja Bahun and Dušan Radunović with an Afterword by Ernesto Laclau (Farnham: Ashgate), 75–93, Copyright © 2012.

Introduction: The Multiple Dimensions of Hegemony

The concept of hegemony is so ubiquitous in social and cultural theory today that it is often difficult to remember that this is a relatively recent phenomenon. The term is used so freely to mean historically or socially dominant modes of thought or culture, and is employed so casually by writers of such a wide range of intellectual trends, that the critical force of the idea has become diluted to the point of banality. The reasons why one of the fundamental concepts of twentieth-century Marxism has lost so much of its substance and political traction in contemporary usage are matters that need to be addressed historically, since the issue pertains to the fate of Marxist theory in general over the last half-century. Yet such analysis needs a clear understanding of the concept of hegemony within Marxism itself, to understand how it arose, the various dimensions the concept acquired in concrete situations and analyses and how it came to be an idea that was invested with such critical power. This is a fascinating story that goes far beyond the work of any single individual into the revolutionary struggles of the first third of the twentieth century, which involved a reconsideration and reconceptualisation of large areas of socio-political and cultural thought. The very complexities and dynamics of social transformation compelled revolutionaries and intellectuals to develop penetrating, but largely now obscured, ideology critiques of dominant paradigms in the emerging academic disciplines, showing how they were bound up with the power of capital and the interests of imperialism. Recent characterisations of Marxism as inherently Eurocentric and wedded to a unilinear developmental paradigm, or blithely indifferent to questions of language and of democracy, have credibility only to the extent that critics have either ignored or have remained unaware of these crucial developments. The irony is that such critiques were often anticipated by Marxist thinkers of the 1900s–30s, and were, in some cases, directly indebted to the very tradition they caricatured. In this context it is hardly surprising to find the term 'hegemony' employed freely and unreflexively by critics of the very tradition they have unwittingly built upon.

The concept of hegemony became widespread in social, political and cultural theory in the 1970s after the prison writings of the former leader of the Communist Party of Italy, Antonio Gramsci, began to appear in translation in major European languages. Indeed, for a time many assumed Gramsci had coined the term itself and so it was viewed almost exclusively through the Gramscian lens.[1] In the wake of renewed mass struggles and ideological battles, the idea was seen to provide a valuable resource for Marxist intellectuals, enabling them to move beyond the pessimistic scenarios of total ideological domination that had been bequeathed by, for instance, the Frankfurt School. The struggles of the time clearly challenged analyses of the 'totally administered society', while the radical cultural movements that accompanied the struggles against the Vietnam War and for Civil Rights in the United States clearly questioned the validity of the all-too-homogenous analyses of 'mass culture' that had developed in the period immediately following World War II. As Perry Anderson argued in the mid-1970s, the experience of Stalinism and the separation of Marxist theory from political practice led most 'Western' Marxists to develop '*a priori* schemes for the understanding of history' which, while 'not necessarily inconsistent with empirical evidence', were 'always undemonstrated by it in their mode of presentation'.[2] Gramsci's writings on hegemony appeared as an exception to this trend, clearly conveying a sensitivity to the dynamics of struggles the author had been engaged in, but also centred on the presentation of empirical material, which was subjected to scientific analysis 'in the classic sense in which this was practised by the founders of historical materialism'.[3] However, this heritage from the period before the sundering of most Marxist theory from mass political practice was received largely by Marxist academics who remained (relatively) isolated from political practice or who were integrated into the Eurocommunist wings of Western Communist Parties.

Representative of the former trend was Raymond Williams, whose 1977 book, *Marxism and Literature*, presented hegemony in contrast to the prevalent notion of ideology. For Williams, the former goes beyond the commonly held notion of ideology as 'a relatively formal and articulated system of meanings, values and beliefs, of a kind that can be abstracted as a "worldview" or a "class outlook" '.[4] Instead, hegemony 'is a lived system of meanings and values – constitutive and constituting – which, as they are experienced as practices, appear as reciprocally confirming.... It is ... in the strongest sense a "culture", but a culture which has also to be seen as the lived dominance and subordination of particular classes'.[5] In foregrounding the endlessly contested and

---

1   Althusser was probably responsible for generating this myth, but it gained considerable currency for a time. On this see Brennan 2006, pp. 246–7.
2   Anderson 1979 [1976], p. 80.
3   Ibid.
4   Williams 1977, p. 109.
5   Williams 1977, p. 110.

constantly renewed aspects of bourgeois hegemony, and presenting culture as an arena of such contestation, Williams's discussion had much to commend it, but there was no historical discussion of the concept here and it facilitated the incorporation of hegemony into the lexicon of cultural analysis. The following year, Edward Said published his famous study *Orientalism*, in which hegemony was embraced as a 'form of . . . cultural leadership' operating in civil society, 'where the influence of ideas, of institutions, and of other persons works not through domination but by what Gramsci calls consent'.[6] European culture became 'hegemonic both in and outside Europe', with European identity seen as superior to all others, a 'flexible *positional* superiority'.[7] Like Williams, with whom he shared a significant amount, Said did not seek the intellectual roots of the idea, but employed it as a category for general cultural analysis. Unlike Williams, however, Said did not shrink from creating, in the words of Timothy Brennan, 'a patented eclectic amalgam in which the concepts of discursive network, hegemony, the homologies of Lucien Goldmann, and cultural materialism all mix'.[8] These appropriations were to prove extremely influential on the Anglophone reception of Gramsci's ideas. They also inadvertently launched contemporary cultural studies and post-colonial theory, both of which developed in such a way that Gramsci's terminology was used freely, in loose combinations with ideas quite alien to, and often incompatible with, Gramsci's own affiliations.

Williams was trying to promote a mode of analysis that would treat culture holistically, as the creation of meaning in, and as a formative part of, a 'whole way of life', examining the dynamics of cultural processes in a way that could incorporate social relations and culture in their totality.[9] Yet, as cultural studies developed into a budget-holding discipline under the leadership of Stuart Hall and his colleagues at the Centre for Contemporary Cultural Studies at the University of Birmingham in Britain, it tended to become shorthand for the study of forms of 'popular' culture. The Centre undoubtedly produced some significant studies, but most were no less one-sided than the tendency it sought to combat.[10] As Francis Mulhern argued in a trenchant critique of

---

6   Said 1995 [1978], p. 7.
7   Ibid. It should be noted that, subsequently, Said adopted a more rigorous approach to Gramsci's ideas, but the sheer popularity of *Orientalism* overshadowed these significant adjustments.
8   Brennan 2006, p. 111.
9   Williams first advanced this conception in his 1958 essay 'Culture is Ordinary', Williams 1997 [1958], pp. 5–14.
10   For an overview see Hall *et al.* (eds.) 1980.

the new discipline, the hierarchies of *Kulturkritik*, according to which forms of 'mass culture' could be dismissed as 'a mere opiate, successfully designed to induce passivity in a homogenised mass', were rejected, while its critical and potentially subversive aspects were highlighted.[11] Meanwhile, 'high' culture was largely removed from consideration.[12] This inversion of the Frankfurt School critique was based on a shift towards a 'treatment of the effectivity of language and discourse as *sui generis* and autonomous', coupled with a 'vehement opposition to "economism" and "class reductionism"'.[13] All manifestations of cultural difference were now treated as political. But more was at stake, for the proponents of cultural studies increasingly sought 'to subordinate the merely political (the old concepts "class", "state", "struggle", "revolution" and the like) to the higher authority of popular culture'.[14] 'Hegemony' now came to describe the formation of social subjects through the articulation of social relationships, but exclusively on ideological grounds, severed from painstaking analyses of the shifting relations between class forces of the type that permeate Gramsci's *Notebooks*.

Cultural Studies, as developed by Hall and his colleagues, was never simply one academic discipline among others. It was specifically linked to the project of the wing of the Communist Party of Great Britain (CPGB) that sought to develop a strategy broadly in conformity with that of Eurocommunism. What often became known as 'neo-Gramscianism' sought to reconstruct Gramsci's ideas and categories in a way that provided legitimacy for Eurocommunist objectives of building broad alliances that transcended divisions between the workers' movement and the liberal organisations of the bourgeoisie. The strategy pursued by the British journal *Marxism Today*, of building a 'broad democratic alliance' against the 'authoritarian populism' of the Thatcher government, was typical in this regard.[15] Hegemony now appeared as a general moral and intellectual leadership over allies, the choice of which was no longer limited by any class criteria. A series of works at the turn of the decade provided reconstructions of Gramsci's central categories in just such a way, presenting his *Notebooks* as incipient theoretical justifications of the Eurocommunist programme, as opposed to the 'class reductionism' that allegedly

---

11   Mulhern 1997, p. 45. See also Sparks 1996.

12   There were exceptions, however, such as Mellor *et al.* 1976. I am indebted to Chris Pawling for helping me to nuance this point.

13   Jessop *et al.* 1984, p. 37.

14   Mulhern 1997, pp. 47–8.

15   For good overviews and critical analyses see Jessop *et al.* 1984 and Callinicos 1985.

pervaded the Leninist tradition.[16] This mode of appropriation by influential Anglophone commentators provoked considerable opposition at the time. Significant works appeared showing that Gramsci never actually broke with Leninist politics.[17] While historical discussions of the way in which categories such as hegemony were embedded in the debates of the time, in which Gramsci was an active participant, appeared in Italian at this time, and some scholarship did appear in English too, they were often overlooked or perhaps ignored by those keen to appropriate Gramsci to the Eurocommunist agenda.[18]

Gramsci had discussed the linguistic and cultural dimensions of hegemony, which were key to the 'neo-Gramscian' reformulation. However, in the absence of detailed discussion of the bases of Gramsci's own treatment, his terminology was rendered opaque by being cut from its historical moorings and then employed in the construction of a 'post-Marxist' conception of hegemony. Brennan argues that the Italian Socialist parliamentary official, Norberto Bobbio, played a crucial role here, asserting that 'Gramsci represented a radical refinement of Marxism, that his work privileged the superstructure over the economy, held the war of position (that is, a reform-oriented or situational politics) to be the only viable strategy in the West, built a conceptual wall between state and civil society, located all effective political work within civil society's realm of cultural, nonparty activity, and warned of the penetration of the state into nonstate spheres'.[19] This line of argument was then developed in a semiotic direction by Ernesto Laclau and Chantal Mouffe in their influential 1985 book, *Hegemony and Socialist Strategy*, where Gramsci's own ideas about language were given little consideration and his concepts were linked directly to a poststructuralist theory of language.[20] Class now became a discursive construct, while the entire Marxist tradition was presented as essentialising class identity. Meanwhile, in Italy, Franco Lo Piparo presented path-breaking research on the linguistic sources of Gramsci's conception, ultimately concluding that the 'primitive matrix' of Gramsci's philosophy 'should not be searched

---

16   See, especially, Mouffe (ed.) 1979 and Simon 1982.

17   See, for instance, Harman 1977; Molyneux 1978.

18   Particularly important are Procacci 1974 and Paggi 1984. It is symptomatic that such valuable studies have never been made available to an Anglophone readership. Examples of valuable historical scholarship of the time that did appear in English and still rewards attention despite the passage of time, include Hoare and Smith 1971; Anderson 1976. A valuable but seldom-mentioned attempt to refute the neo-Gramscian case on the basis of a historical argument from this time is Gibbon 1983.

19   Brennan 2006, p. 239.

20   Laclau and Mouffe 1985. On the importance of Laclau (especially Laclau 1979) in gradually drawing Hall away from Marxism, see Sparks 1996.

for in Marx or in Lenin or in any other Marxist, but in the science of language
[*linguaggio*]'.[21] While Lo Piparo's research was undoubtedly very significant,
and provided an important corrective to the historically ungrounded appropriations of people like Hall, Laclau and Mouffe, his conclusions were unbalanced
and open to question. While acknowledging the value of such work, subsequent research by Giancarlo Schirru and others has provided an important critique of the presuppositions that run throughout Lo Piparo's work.[22] Gramsci's
theoretical reflections on the relationship between language and hegemony
were undoubtedly shaped in important ways by his time as a graduate student
working under the Italian 'neo-linguist' Matteo Bartoli, who discussed the way
in which word forms spread from one speech community to another as a result
of the relative cultural power of speakers. Bartoli had used the terms *fascino*
[fascination or attraction], *prestigio* [prestige] and *egemonia* [hegemony] to
discuss these matters, and Gramsci makes explicit reference to Bartoli when
discussing the same questions.[23] It is also clear that Gramsci's discussions of
political strategy in Italy were to a considerable extent affected by the issue
of the Italian national language and the dialects that were still widely spoken
among the masses.

   If cultural studies took little account of the intellectual sources of Gramsci's
linguistic ideas, many working within post-colonial theory compounded the
problem by attempting an even more radical separation of the idea of hegemony from Marxist theory. Said's characterisation of Marxism as an approach
at least compromised by the project he was trying to critique in *Orientalism*
played an important role here, for it suggested that, in order to oppose the
Eurocentric drift of theory in US universities, Marxist categories like hegemony
needed to be supplemented with, or rectified by, the inclusion of fundamentally non- or even anti-Marxist ideas, such as Foucault's notion of discourse.
Subsequently, commentators have shown that such arguments were based on
a highly debatable reading of Marx's views about India and a citation taken
out of context from Marx's *18th Brumaire* as an epigraph for the whole study.[24]
Orientalism now appeared to some of Said's epigones as, *fundamentally*, a

---

21   Lo Piparo 2010, p. 21. Lo Piparo's major work on the question was Lo Piparo 1979.
      Unfortunately this major work has never been translated into English and it was only in
      2004 that a significant summary of Lo Piparo's argument became available in Ives 2004a,
      pp. 16–52.
22   Schirru 2008, 2011; Gensini 2010.
23   Ives 2004b, pp. 44–7.
24   These issues were subject to penetrating critiques by Ahmad 1992, pp. 159–242 and Habib
      2005.

'hegemonic *discourse*' in the Foucauldian sense, '*a style of thought based on an ontological and epistemological distinction made between "the Orient" and (most of the time) "the Occident"*'.[25] Though Said's relationship to Marxism was complex, and became more nuanced over time, some post-structuralist thinkers sought to complete the separation of the notion of hegemony from Marxism in discussions of the relationship between culture and imperialism.[26] Perhaps the clearest example is Robert Young's 1990 book, *White Mythologies: Writing History and the West*, in which the author argues that, for all its emphasis on emancipation, Marxism's 'unifying narrative' embodies a conceptual imperialism that always involves the 'creation, subjection and final appropriation of Europe's "others"'.[27] Such categorical claims remained, however, unsupported by sustained historical analysis of political practice and the development of the concepts involved. What is most telling, however, and as we shall see below, is that Said's critique of Eurocentrism, and of conceptions of the orient that it involves, had a history that actually contradicted the assertions about Marxism that Young (and, at certain times, Said himself) advanced.[28]

In each case, what was missing was a systematic consideration of the history of the complex of ideas that came to be discussed under the term 'hegemony' in Russian Marxism. These not only extended well beyond the discussions found in Gramsci's *Notebooks*, but Gramsci's own formulations cannot be properly appreciated unless these debates are taken into consideration. The current study seeks to provide the reader with an insight into the Soviet background to Gramsci's formulations not, primarily, in order to elucidate Gramsci's thought (though this should be aided by the analysis here), but to show the way in which hegemonic considerations in revolutionary Russia pertained directly to

---

25   Said 1995 [1978], p. 2 (original emphasis). Said's enthusiasm for Foucault was, however, significantly qualified and certainly quite unlike that of subsequent popularisers of post-colonial theory, on which see Brennan 2006, pp. 93–125. As Brennan puts it at one point (p. 111), 'the greatest praise Said is able to give Foucault, and this despite what he describes as Foucault's "univocal assertions", is the French author's capacity to be a part of the "adversary epistemological current found in Vico, in Marx and Engels, in Lukács, in Fanon, and also in the radical political writings of Chomsky"'.

26   On Said's complex relationship to Marxism, see Jarah 1999; San Juan 2006; Howe 2007; McCarthy 2008.

27   Young 1990, p. 2.

28   Moreover, as Callinicos points out, the philosophical tradition which Young claims to be the basis for his own critique of Eurocentrism goes back to Nietzsche and Heidegger, who participated in the raising of classical Greece to the position of the pure origin of Modern Europe, while eliding the influence of Pharonic and Hellenic Egypt on Greek culture and of the Islamic world on medieval Christendom. See Callinicos 1995, pp. 179–203.

the problems that have become the focus of cultural studies and post-colonial theory. Before giving an outline of the study, we shall consider how some of the aspects of hegemony in Gramsci's work relate to those within Russian Marxism.

Gramsci and Russian Marxism

In his important 1976 article on Gramsci, Perry Anderson provided a careful discussion of the development of the idea of hegemony in Russian Marxism, illustrating how it arose in the last years of the nineteenth century to theorise the way in which the numerically small proletariat could lead the peasantry in overthrowing the tsarist autocracy in conditions where the bourgeoisie was too weak and cowardly to pursue a revolutionary transformation. He showed how Gramsci's conception drew upon and developed such formulations, but was also affected by the way the term was used in Comintern debates in the 1920s. Anderson noted the important cultural resonance the concept acquired in Gramsci's work and the way in which he developed it to theorise the specific features of bourgeois rule in the West that bolstered state power and class rule with mechanisms to secure levels of consent. All of this was true enough, but Anderson inadvertently encouraged the reader to assume, as we shall see, erroneously, that the concept of hegemony had no cultural or linguistic dimensions in Russian Marxism and consequently legitimised the search for the essential sources of these dimensions of Gramsci's thought elsewhere. Moreover, he asserted, again erroneously, that after the October Revolution, the term hegemony fell into 'relative disuse in the Bolshevik Party', since it had been forged to theorise the role of the working class in the bourgeois revolution and was 'rendered inoperative' by the advent of a socialist revolution.[29] In reality not only did hegemony remain a recurrent and vital issue in Russian Marxism throughout the 1920s, but language and culture constituted major dimensions in Russian Marxists' writings on hegemony both before and after the October Revolution of 1917. The present study is dedicated to unpacking some important dimensions of the relationship between language, culture and politics in Russian-Marxist thought. Among the important debates that took place during the 1920s, some occurred exactly when Gramsci was in Moscow in 1922–3 and in 1925, but the significance of these debates go beyond Gramsci's own limited engagement with them.

---

29   Anderson 1976, p. 17. These specific claims have, to some extent, been undermined by Buci-Glucksmann 1980, p. 7; Boothman 2008; Thomas 2009, pp. 232–4; McNally 2011.

The dearth of published information about Gramsci's time in Russia, coupled with testimony that he spent some of his time in Moscow in a sanatorium, has led to a widespread impression that this period of Gramsci's life is relatively insignificant. Archival documents show, however, that Gramsci was extremely active as PCI representative to the Comintern, serving on its Executive Committee (*Ispolnitel'nyi komitet Kommunisticheskogo Internatsionala*, IKKI) and meeting with leading Bolsheviks such as Lenin, Trotsky, Lunacharskii, Bukharin and Zinov'ev. Gramsci was meeting with Zinov'ev, the Chair of IKKI, several times a week at the very time the latter was giving his lectures on the history of the Party, which included a detailed history of the notion of hegemony.[30] For Zinov'ev, also anticipating certain aspects of Gramsci's idea of translatability:

> The word 'hegemonic' is a foreign one. Today the workers have translated it into Russian: the hegemony of the proletariat signifies, speaking in modern language, *power to the Soviets*, power to the working class. This slogan was prepared over years and tested in a decades-old crucible... That is why the idea of the hegemony of the proletariat is the basic ideological foundation of Bolshevism. It is one of the 'planks' upon which the Bolshevik Party stands.[31]

Gramsci also travelled to several other Russian cities, including Petrograd, and made considerable progress in learning Russian. The future publication of a detailed chronology of Gramsci's time in Russia, supplemented by archival documents, will necessitate a reappraisal of this period of Gramsci's life, and make it clear that the central concepts found in the *Notebooks* can only be understood with reference to Russian Marxism of the period.[32]

There is no sense in which highlighting some of the sophistication of the debates in Russia and the USSR more generally should be seen as an attempt to deny the importance of Italian linguistics and Italian intellectual history as sources of the specificity of Gramsci's formulations. The case for the significance of these sources seems beyond doubt. Rather, it significantly problematises attempts to split Gramsci's ideas about hegemony into political

---

30   Zinov'ev 1924 [1923] pp. 79–84, 111–12, 301–11; Zinoviev 1973 [1923] pp. 35–8, 60–1, 216–21.

31   Zinov'ev 1924 [1923] p. 111; Zinoviev 1973 [1923] p. 61. On Gramsci's notion of translatability, see Boothman 2010; Frostini 2010; Lacorte 2010.

32   The chronology is currently being prepared by Peter Thomas and me following research visits to Moscow supported by a grant from the British Academy. The most comprehensive account of Gramsci's time in Russia currently available is Grigor'eva 1998.

and cultural sections that can be developed independently of each other or reduced to one or the other. The development of ideas about the relationship between language, culture and hegemony within the USSR was much more significant than has generally been supposed, and Gramsci inherited a great deal from the theoretical and practical considerations of such questions that he was exposed to in Russia and subsequently. Yet Gramsci was removed from such close practical engagements at a decisive point, when he was arrested and imprisoned in 1926. Relatively insulated from the enormous distortions of not only political doctrine and practice but also of the very terminology and methodology of Russian Marxism that accompanied Stalin's so-called 'revolution from above', the first Five-Year Plan and after, Gramsci was able to reflect on the lessons of the political and cultural dimensions of hegemony in the USSR and in the Comintern, and bring them to a level of theoretical elaboration impossible within the USSR itself. He was also able to apply the very same considerations to Italy, and to bring out some of the general theoretical features required in order to isolate the common and different features of the Soviet and Italian situations. In this, Gramsci's training in Italian linguistics proved to be a valuable resource, especially in his last notebook, number 29, written in 1935.

Here, Gramsci reflected on current debates in Italy about the standard Italian language:

> Every time the question of [the] language [*la quistione della lingua*] surfaces, in one way or another, it means that a series of other problems are coming to the fore: the formation and enlargement of the governing class, the need to establish more intimate and secure relationships between the governing groups and the national-popular mass, in other words to reorganise the cultural hegemony.[33]

It appears that the object of this sentence was not meant to be limited to 'the (Italian) language' (as the available English translation suggests) but, rather, the Italian case as illustrative of a general principle, the 'question of (national) language' (as recently pointed out by Tullio De Mauro).[34] This is important, since in the immediate aftermath of the Revolution of October 1917 the 'series of problems' Gramsci identifies were extremely pressing for a new state based on a minority Russian proletariat amidst a sea of Russian peasants and a myriad of national groups at various levels of economic development and with a

---

33   Gramsci 1975, vol. 3, p. 2346; Gramsci 1985, p. 183.
34   Mauro 2010, p. 61.

variety of cultural traditions. Members of the Russian proletariat were often only semi-literate, while Russian peasants were largely illiterate and spoke non-standard forms. The non-Russian peoples of the former Tsarist Empire not only did not speak Russian, but often had no standardised language forms at all. There was no way in which the 'question of (the) language' could be regarded as peripheral in these circumstances, even while the internationalisation of the Revolution was regarded as fundamental to the survival of the state itself. Not only was the Soviet experience of the national and peasant questions replete with crucial lessons for those members of foreign Communist parties in Russia in the post-revolutionary period, but they had direct applicability for important dimensions of the struggle for workers' power in large parts of Europe.

The economic, political, cultural and social differences between the industrial North and the rural South of Italy were a recurrent problem for Italian Communists, who needed to forge a worker-peasant alliance in order to have any realistic prospect of taking power across the nation. Clearly, the example of the Bolsheviks' success in this area was fundamental for Gramsci when he was in Russia, and it was precisely in this field that Russian Marxists developed their ideas about hegemony. As we will see, for most of the leading Bolsheviks in the pre-revolutionary period, the problematic of hegemony pertained precisely to the need for the proletariat to win political leadership over the peasantry and the oppressed nationalities, and for the towns over the countryside, in the struggle against the autocracy. After the Revolution and Civil War and throughout the period of the New Economic Policy (NEP, 1921–8), the task was to maintain that leadership.

The so-called 'Southern Question', with which the Italian Communists were concerned, was also linked to the question of the language, given the poor levels of literacy in the South and the plethora of regional dialects that persisted. This was an issue that had confronted the Bolsheviks on an even greater scale than in Italy, for not only were there significant regional variations, but there was an extremely complex pattern of nationalities with significant historical grievances against the great Russians. The national question is something that hardly features in Gramsci's published work, though the original typescript of the 1926 *Lyons Theses*, which was drafted shortly before Gramsci was arrested, and which is held in the Moscow archives, includes a brief section on the issue.[35] Behind this passage lay Gramsci's whole experience in Russia and in the debates in the Comintern in which he participated. In March 1925 Gramsci attended the meeting on the Yugoslav Commission of the Fifth Enlarged

---

35   RGASPI 513/1/398/19–41 (l.18).

Plenum of the Executive Committee of the Comintern (IKKI), where he gave a speech that repeatedly stressed the importance of the national question for both the Yugoslavian and Italian Parties and the importance of a coordinated approach towards the issue, not least because Croat and Slovene communities were present in Italy, and because Mussolini was trying to facilitate a Fascist takeover of Yugoslavia.[36] Here Gramsci also raises the importance of the national question for the Party and for the struggle of the proletariat for leadership of the peasantry and oppressed, suggesting (though on this occasion he does not use the term) that he regarded this to be a significant dimension of the struggle for proletarian hegemony.

Marxism and Positivism

The project of hegemony required constant adjustments of policy and an extreme sensitivity to the shifting relations between social groups both at the level of their structural interests and perceptions of those interests. The specificity of individual cases needed to be carefully studied and the implications for policy analysed. As Lenin had argued in the wake of the 1905 Revolution, when the appearance of the soviets had unsettled many Russian Marxists: '[a]bsolutely hostile to all abstract formulas and to all doctrinaire recipes, Marxism demands an attentive attitude to the *mass* struggle in progress', for 'new forms of struggle, unknown to the participants of the given period, inevitably arise as the given social situation changes'.[37] It is a point of principle that 'Marxism *learns*, if we may so express it, from mass practice, and makes no claim whatever to *teach* the masses forms of struggle invented by "systematisers" in the seclusion of their studies'.[38]Adherence to abstract schemata and pre-conceived trajectories were extremely unhelpful in guiding revolutionary practice and this tended to restrain the influence of mechanistic and positivistic conceptions among Russian Marxists. This was particularly the case within cultural and linguistic spheres after the Revolution, where the fluidity of practical politics extended into scholarship. Grants were made available to address a huge array of practical problems dealing with language and culture, ranging from the codification of national languages amid a plethora of regional dialects to the problem of creating a public discourse that would be close to the masses, but at the same time provide a robust structure for educational

---

36   RGASPI 495/163/319/27–9.

37   Lenin 1962a [1905], p. 213.

38   Lenin 1962a [1905], pp. 213–14.

advancement, political engagement and practical mobilisation. Like Gramsci, many Russian linguists had been trained by Humboldtian scholars keen not to separate linguistic from conceptual categories and who were particularly well-suited to the new research programmes that developed. The psychologism of such figures as Aleksandr Potebnia and Jan Baudouin de Courtenay was quickly reworked into sociological approaches that placed the irreducible dimension of discursive interaction at the forefront of attention.

Much of Gramsci's prison writing concerns itself precisely with the need to base theorisation on the detailed analysis of the dynamics of social struggles, and this lies behind his critical remarks about Nikolai Bukharin's 1921 textbook, *Historical Materialism*, and his analyses of the apparent authority of such extravagant positivists as the Italian political economist, Achille Loria.[39] While Gramsci evidently had much respect for Bukharin, especially in the realm of practical politics, he clearly viewed Bukharin's attempt to present Marxism as a systematic sociology as flawed and encouraging an approach that would subordinate the study of particular cases to abstract rules. It is hard to dissent from such an evaluation when we see that Bukharin began his work by arguing that 'the theory of historical materialism has a definite place, it is not political economy, nor is it history; it is a general theory of society and the laws of its evolution, i.e. sociology'.[40] For some time, Bukharin claimed, sociology had been referred to as 'the philosophy of history' or the 'theory of the historical process', but it now stood forth in its Marxist form as a 'method of history'.[41] Bukharin was by no means the most extreme case of this in the USSR in the 1920s, and he often attempted to restrain the numerous groupings who invoked abstract schemas to claim their immediate right to leadership in fields such as art and literature, and to have that leadership recognised by the Party. The arguments put forward by such groups echoed the political terminology of the pre-revolutionary period, claiming that the hegemony of proletarian writers in the cultural sphere needed to be recognised as a direct corollary of the political hegemony of the proletariat. For Gramsci, strategic and tactical flexibility needed to be undergirded by a theoretical perspective free of the mechanistic extrapolations that manifested themselves in such unproductive practical programmes.

The rise of a central bureaucracy throughout the 1920s, with its own institutions aiming at the development of single and coherent administrative principles, nurtured precisely such schemata and conceptions, however.

---

39   See especially Buttigieg 1990.
40   Bukharin 1921, p. 13; Bukhrin 1962 [1926], p. xv.
41   Bukharin 1921, p. 12; Bukharin 1962 [1926], p. xiv.

Moreover, since Marxism was being assimilated by a Russian intelligentsia already steeped in philosophical materialism and positivism, there was a range of scholars willing and able to develop them. Since the time of Nikolai Chernyshevskii, the revolutionary movement in Russia had been associated with philosophical materialism, and the founder of Russian Marxism, Georgii Plekhanov, sought to develop Marxism into a complete philosophical world view by incorporating central aspects of contemporary physiology and anthropological materialism into Marxism. While philosophical idealism increasingly became associated with those intellectuals who broke with the liberation movement and sought to make their peace with the autocracy, especially in the wake of the 1905 Revolution, philosophical materialism was increasingly viewed as a natural ally of Marxism. In this environment, the work of the main positivist anthropologists and philosophers of the day found a ready audience among Marxists, with the works of such central figures as Herbert Spencer, Edward Tylor and John Stuart Mill appearing in Russian translation often within a year of their appearance in English. The same was true of the work of the main figures in French and German materialism and positivism. Plekhanov's work shows generous assimilation of such ideas and the beginning of a blurring of the distinctions between Marxist and positivist categories.

Simultaneously, positivism began to be distinguished from Marxism not by virtue of its fundamentally different philosophical orientation but by the fact that it allegedly shied away from generalisation, concerned itself with facts for their own sake and presented scientific procedures as above socio-political struggles. There was, of course, a significant grain of truth in this characterisation of positivism, but it was a long way from identifying its central aim, which was to seek the rules by which scientific thought liberated itself from myth. Thus, Comte's famous 'law of three stages', according to which human consciousness progresses from theological, through metaphysical, to finally achieve positive stages, came to be correlated with pre-class, class and classless societies and often became confused with the three stages of the dialectic. The grounds for this had undoubtedly been laid by Plekhanov, who presented Marxism as a materialist monism, asserting that 'laws of being are at the same time laws of thought'.[42] This identification of Marxism, materialism and monism proved to be extremely influential in the subsequent period, but it was more oriented on establishing continuity with Enlightenment materialists such as Holbach and Diderot and their Russian heirs, chiefly Chernyshevskii.[43] It was Aleksandr Bogdanov who did most to harmonise Marxist and positivist

---

42   Plekhanov quoted in Steila 1991, p. 79.
43   See Scanlan 1970.

categories in his 'empiriomonism', according to which social being does not determine social consciousness, but is identical with that consciousness. As we shall see, Bogdanov's direct correlation of the forms of labour, relations of production and conceptual structure played a crucial role into the 1930s and beyond, even though the thinker himself had been publicly repudiated. In the 1920s, the above-mentioned distinction between Marxism and positivism was reinforced by the institutional competition between the supposedly 'prole-tarian' science practised in the Socialist, later, Communist, Academy, and the 'bourgeois' science centred on the Academy of Sciences.[44] By the middle of the 1920s, the institutions of the Communist Academy had become centres for working out 'orthodox Marxism', but from 1929 the main function became Party-mindedness [*partiinost'*], increasingly understood as providing theoreti-cal justifications for the concrete policies of the Party. During the first Five-Year Plan, the Communist Academy essentially annexed research institutes that remained outside the Academy of Sciences, chiefly the fifteen institutes under the aegis of the non-Party RANION (Russian Association of Social Science Research Institutes), while the Academy of Sciences was 'Bolshevised'. The final result was, however, that a separate Communist Academy no longer served any purpose for the Party or the State, and so it was effectively absorbed into the restructured Academy of Sciences in 1936.[45]

At the end of the 1920s, when Gramsci was already in prison, a phenomenon distinctly reminiscent of 'Lorianism' was coming to the fore: the rise of the ideas of Nikolai Marr in linguistics. Marr, it should be noted, was, *inter alia*, one of the first academicians from the pre-revolutionary era to collaborate with the revolutionary regime, became deputy head of the Academy of Sciences and played a prominent role in facilitating the ultimate victory of the Academy. He has also been credited with saving the institution itself.[46] It seems unlikely that Gramsci had any significant knowledge of Marrism, but there can be lit-tle doubt that, as a trained linguist, he would have found the authority Marr's ideas gained in the 1930s rather troubling. As we will see, Marrism was in many respects the epitome of positivistic thinking, developed by an unstable per-sonality and indulged by interested powers. Where Comte's 'positive state' generally corresponded to those features European imperial powers saw as distinguishing themselves from more backward states, many Soviet scholars from the 1930s on claimed this mantle for the USSR and presented the capital-ist world as still entangled in metaphysics. Indeed, the general trope was that,

44   See David-Fox 1997, pp. 192–253.

45   Shapiro 1976, pp. 256–331.

46   Vasil'kov 2001, pp. 420–1.

in the heroic age of bourgeois revolutions, the intellectuals of the bourgeoisie made significant strides towards liberating social thought from myth, but withdrew in the face of the rising proletariat, their ideas degenerating into a reactionary metaphysics in all areas of intellectual production – be it modernist art and literature, irrationalist forms of philosophy, or narrow empiricism in disciplines such as linguistics. The Marrist, Vasilii Abaev, made this very point in a 1934 article, arguing that in the work of the 'initiators' of linguistic thought like Humboldt and Bopp we see 'the scholarship of a rising class with the following qualities: courage of thought, breadth of vision, and a highly developed capacity for generalisation', while in the work of figures like the Neo-grammarians, Saussure and Meillet, we find 'the scholarship of a declining class... that is characterised by an unrestrained tendency towards cowardly and wingless hairsplitting'.[47] While such comments gestured towards the comments Marx and Engels had made about their contemporary opponents in comparison with the thinkers of the Enlightenment and early Romanticism, they served, in the 1930s, to present a unitary Soviet scholarship as the progressive force in intellectual life. What mattered now was less the evidence underlying the scientific validity of scholarship, a concern with which was regarded as 'wingless hairsplitting', than the broad thrust of a theory in confirming the progress of the Soviet state towards socialism and the policies of the Communist Party that ensured that progress.

This reversion to a compromise formation between Marxist theory and the interests of the Soviet state had a range of effects that have been dealt with in a number of studies. While 'the unity of theory and practice that had made possible classical Bolshevism' was indeed 'ineluctably destroyed', Anderson was far too categorical in his classic *Considerations on Western Marxism* when he argued that '[a]ll serious theoretical work ceased in the Soviet Union after collectivisation'.[48] It would be more accurate to say that theoretical work of any significance survived only in areas not immediately connected to political and administrative matters, such as work on the origins of literature and the relations between language and early socioeconomic formations. Figures that remain woefully understudied in this perspective include scholars associated with Marr, such as Izrail' Frank-Kamenetskii and Konstantin Megrelidze.[49] Such figures clearly imported significant elements from the positivist and Romantic scholarship that preceded the advent of Russian

---

47   Abaev 2006 [1934], p. 29. For a discussion, see Alpatov 2010, pp. 28–9.

48   Anderson 1979 [1976], p. 19.

49   On Frank-Kamenetskii see Brandist 2011; Tihanov 2012; on Megrelidze see Friedrich 1993, Dzhioev 1973, 1980, 1989; Megrelidze 1989.

Marxism, and their work was often compromised by the one-sided formulations that resulted, but they nevertheless remain significant contributions to Marxist theory.[50] Such works are quite different from Western Marxism of the period after World War II, but they nevertheless constitute 'a priori schemes' for which empirical evidence was secondary to the general pattern of historical development.

Rather than hegemony being 'rendered inoperative' by the advent of the Revolution, the idea was rendered redundant by a bureaucratic system that claimed once and for all to have transcended all social antagonisms within the USSR, and by a shift in theoretical discourse that rendered empirical evidence at best secondary to the exposition of preconceived schemas. It could only now justifiably be applied to international relations or struggles within the capitalist world in the present context, for after the first Five-Year Plan the alliance between the workers and peasants was effectively cancelled. Gramsci effectively kept the idea alive as a critical category for application to contemporary politics in his prison cell, ruminating on some of the dimensions that had been developed in the Soviet sphere and weaving them together into a theoretical fabric that was never completed. Yet Gramsci's engagement with Soviet work was limited, and as such the debates of the time retain a significant surplus which needs to be understood in its own right. These have implications not only for understanding Gramsci's categories, but also for a critique of such disciplines as cultural and post-colonial studies, where stereotypes and misconceptions have rendered the category of hegemony increasingly diffuse and politically ineffective.

The Study

The current study traces the rise of the idea of hegemony in the political and intellectual debates in the last years of the Russian Empire, the various dimensions that were developed throughout the first decade following the Revolution and the way in which the idea disappeared from Soviet-theoretical discourse in the 1930s. It is an *intellectual* history that traces the relationship between ideas about hegemony and about language and how they bore upon each other in both directly political discourse and in more general theoretical approaches to language. As such, it does not provide a comprehensive historical discussion of political and economic practice, except to the extent that it directly bears

---

50   Examples would include Megrelidze 1935a, 2007 [1938]; Frank-Kamenetskii 1929, 1934, 1935a, 1938; Vygotskii 2004 [1931].

upon the formulations themselves. More general histories of language policy and of the development of the Party and state during the 1920s are abundant. At each stage we will see that the idea of hegemony was closely bound up with linguistic and cultural questions, but in ways that flatly contradicted the 'neo-Gramscian' trend of more recent times. As such, the study aims to reveal latent capacities within the notion of hegemony and in the work on the relationship between language and the dynamics of socio-political life that developed in the USSR in the 1920s. We will trace how political considerations of language and culture developed in the course of an ongoing and highly contested dialogical process driven by the need for the predominantly Russian proletariat to exert a progressive hegemony over the Russian peasantry and the formerly oppressed peoples of what became the USSR. The use of the term 'dialogical' here derives from the ideas of Voloshinov and Bakhtin, but since I and others have written a significant amount on these figures elsewhere, they will remain minor characters in the plot that will unfold. Instead, we will see how the various dimensions of hegemony came into focus as ideas became mutually implicated in the process of an intense revolutionary struggle.

Perhaps the biggest obstacle to a sustained consideration of the role of hegemony in post-revolutionary Russian Marxism is that there was no explicit theory of hegemony set out in defined texts, just as one searches in vain for any theoretical elaboration of democracy among its proponents in Ancient Greece.[51] Rather, hegemonic considerations permeated political debate. If one is to speak about a conception of hegemony in Russian Marxism, then it is one that is embedded, often as a background assumption, in a range of political debates and interventions. It was a notion that was sometimes invoked in a principled attempt to bring Marxist theory and objectives to bear in a variety of socio-political engagements, and sometimes, especially at the end of the 1920s and into the 1930s, to provide rhetorical cover for policies that broke fundamentally with Marxist principles. A consideration of these phenomena inevitably results in a rather impressionistic survey in which the main features of a fabric of dialogue can be viewed only at a distance. Linguistic and cultural threads run throughout this fabric, and while they are seldom present as autonomous discussions, they are interwoven with key aspects of social policy. However, the prominence and urgency of such issues were such that the Soviet state specifically funded and framed research projects that dealt with the linguistic dimensions of hegemony. Such considerations were already implicit in the work of some pre-revolutionary linguists and philologists, but now the social structures, functions and dynamics of language came to the forefront of

---

51   Ober 1998, pp. 32–3.

consideration. This resulted in some path-breaking developments in linguistic thought that need careful consideration. This shifts our focus to a much more detailed consideration of the development of linguistic ideas in an institutional context, but one that is necessitated by the relative unfamiliarity of the material to the contemporary audience and the fact that it is here that we find some important, and historically grounded, alternatives to the poststructuralist conception of language that has been grafted onto the notion of hegemony in contemporary scholarship.

The story begins with the development of the idea of hegemony in Russian Marxism at the turn of the century, with political and cultural aspects emerging in the struggles over strategy following the 1905 Revolution. We will see how the notorious conflicts between Lenin and Bogdanov were actually focused more on understandings of how to pursue a hegemonic project in present circumstances than on the philosophical polemics over Bogdanov's 'Empiriomonism'. While Lenin focused on the directly political dimensions of hegemony, Bogdanov foregrounded the need to develop an elaborated proletarian culture in advance of the seizure of state power.[52] It was precisely because Bogdanov's philosophical ideas related to the strategic questions of the time that Lenin felt the need to engage with them. While Bogdanov was defeated in the inner-Party struggle, we will see that his ideas persisted well into the post-revolutionary period and exerted a crucial influence on the policies that were adopted. We will also see that the cultural and linguistic aspects of the struggle for hegemony were crucial dimensions of Lenin's own project of winning political hegemony, not least because of the multi-lingual and multi-ethnic nature of the Russian Empire itself. In Chapter Three the linguistic dimensions of political intervention through agitation and propaganda supplement this discussion. Thus, from the very outset, the project of proletarian hegemony assumed political, linguistic and cultural dimensions, and an appreciation of these dimensions was to deepen in the period leading up to the Stalinist consolidation of power.

In Chapter Two we will explore some of the scholarship and political discourse outside of the Marxist paradigm in Russia, as developed in two crucial

---

52   Gramsci's relationship to Bogdanov's ideas has been discussed by Sochor 1981b and again in Brandist 2012a, where Gramsci's wider relationship to the notion of proletarian culture is also discussed. See also Gramshi *et al.* 1922 and Gramsci *et al.* 2012 [1922]. It is possible that Gramsci actually met Bogdanov, either at a roundtable discussion of Soviet foreign trade at which both Bogdanov and Gramsci spoke in June 1922 (*Pravda* 25 June 1922), or at a meeting with the Central Committee of *Proletkul't* in December 1922 (*Izvestiia* 14 December 1922).

and interrelated spheres: Oriental Studies and philology. The relationship between the Russian language and culture and those of other nationalities within the Empire was a concern for a number of intellectuals who were sharply critical of tsarist nationality policy, even while they supported the Empire as such. We will see that late Imperial Orientalists essentially argued for a hegemonic relationship between the Russian nation and the colonies, proposing policies that would only be implemented on a significant scale in the post-revolutionary period. They also developed a penetrating critique of the Oriental scholarship practised in the West, in particular in France and Britain, and this was to have a considerable, but seldom recognised, influence later. Simultaneously, linguists began to raise the question of the position of minority languages and the stratification of national languages according to social class and other factors, among them ideological. With particular attention to the work of Jan Baudouin de Courtenay and Aleksandr Veselovskii, we will see that although significant advances towards accounting for sociological features in language were made, theoretical elaboration was generally compromised by the dominance of psychologism in certain areas of linguistics and positivism in other areas. Indeed, we will see how the field of philology oscillated between these poles, tracing the teleological and rule-governed dimensions of language use, but was never able fully to account for the irreducible aspects of social interaction. We will also see how, with the development of studies of verbal art, the modalities of borrowing and assimilation of semantic material were discussed with a high level of sophistication, challenging many of the dominant paradigms in philology and laying the foundations of significant theoretical advances in the early Soviet period.

Chapter Three addresses the way in which the cultural and political approaches toward the question of language, hegemony and democracy converged with certain aesthetic and ideological trends that had developed among modernist and avant-garde thinkers quite alien to the Marxist tradition in the immediate post-revolutionary situation. Focus particularly falls on the Theatrical Section of the Commissariat of Enlightenment (TEO Narkompros), which provided a number of arenas in which intellectuals of the so-called Silver Age, symbolist and futurist currents, encountered and collaborated with representatives of the movement for the development of a specifically proletarian culture and Leninist ideas. This involved both practical projects designing the early festivals of the revolution and more sustained and systematic encounters in the forging of certain institutes and research projects. In these encounters, the implicit socio-political aspects of theories that had been mired in mysticism came to the fore, while the institutes that were founded pursued innovative programmes that would have a lasting influence on subsequent work in linguistics and cultural theory. Particularly important in this was the idea of 'living word' [*zhivoe slovo*], which gained a particular resonance as the different senses were layered one on top of another. These included the use of oral speech in deliberation, the emergence of language and logic in labour activity, the archetypal structures of social consciousness and the specific capacities of verbal art. This syncretic formulation expressed both the eclecticism of early revolutionary ideas about verbal culture, but it also stimulated radically new ways to consider the relationship between language and social relations. In this chapter we also see how the notion of hegemony was used extensively in early Soviet discussions about proletarian culture, continuing and developing certain trends from the pre-revolutionary period, but in similarly syncretic forms, so that the official doctrine that emerged incorporated both Leninist and Bogdanovite features.

Chapter Four discusses the way in which the project of hegemony became intrinsically bound up with the need to maintain the *smychka* (alliance) or union between the proletariat and peasantry in the period of the New Economic Policy (NEP). We trace the use of the term in the work of some of the most influential Party leaders and theorists after the death of Lenin. We find the term was used extensively by both Bukharin and Zinov'ev, both of whom Gramsci knew personally while working in the Comintern. It was also at this time that Zinov'ev presented and published his *Lectures on the History of the Russian Communist Party (Bolsheviks)*,[53] the second chapter of which was largely dedicated to the importance and history of the idea of the hegemony of the proletariat. The chapter also discusses the linguistic dimensions of the *smychka* in debates about the role of the press and education. We will see that the need for a public discourse that could facilitate the leadership of the proletariat over the peasantry and provide a means by which the allied classes could articulate their interests and perspectives was the focus of a number of studies and publications. The issue of the relationship between what Gramsci was to call spontaneous and normative grammars was a live issue while he was in Moscow, and these concerns determined some important aspects of social and cultural policy. The chapter also discusses the crucial issue of the role of Taylorism, and the so-called 'scientific organisation of labour' in the USSR in the NEP period, showing how a contest between groups oriented on the old *Proletkul't* agenda clashed with, and ultimately lost ground to, the bureaucratic conception exemplified by the work of Aleksei Gastev. Here we see how the production paradigm and a philosophy of technology or of technique

---

53   Zinov'ev 1924 [1923]; Zinov'ev 1973 [1923].

[*tekhnika*] came to dominate discussion of factory production and gradually came to be extended to other areas of social life.

Chapter Five examines how the new research projects dealing with language and society developed in the USSR in the 1920s, with the development of existing paradigms according to the agenda of social science rather than psychology and positivism. In Leningrad the students of Baudouin de Courtenay and Veselovskii made particularly important contributions in isolating features of discursive interaction, the social stratification of language and the relationship between national-linguistic standards and 'social dialects'. We will see how the Leningrad School never fully accepted the Saussurean paradigm or the clear distinction between linguistics and wider philological issues that it involved, and indeed that the Saussurean paradigm was misunderstood in ways characteristic of the time. While it becomes clear that many linguists did not have a very sophisticated understanding of Marxism, they nevertheless absorbed enough to enable them largely to overcome the dichotomies of their predecessors and to produce work of lasting value. In Moscow the Saussurean paradigm was received in a much more positive fashion and combined with the phenomenological notion of intentionality. Saussure's *langue* was now understood as a social norm and *parole* as a social fact. This was an attempt to provide an account of discursive agency through a sociological reading of the Swiss philosopher Anton Marty's notion of the 'inner-form of the word', according to which speakers employ available semantic means to invoke a sense in the mind of the interlocutor even though the semantic norms available may not be fully suited to the intentional sense. In these works, the speaker's search for available semantic means to render a sense has a sociological significance since it generally means the employment of non-standard forms and ideologically motivated appropriations. Such research provided some extremely promising, if partially elaborated, ways of discussing the semiotics of hegemony, but these were often curtailed at the end of the decade as the bureaucracy sought to establish a semantic uniformity regulated by official mechanisms.

Chapter Six broadens the discussion begun in Chapter Four to the question of the non-Russian parts of the USSR, showing how the idea of the *smychka* and thus the project of proletarian hegemony applied to these areas. Relations between Russian and other languages in such regions constituted a particularly sensitive issue, and the need to codify standard forms of national languages to facilitate education and political participation proved particularly important. The very diversity of the USSR set a massive challenge for linguists and policy makers alike, and this is approached through two test cases: the linguistic situation in Ukraine and the question of the New Turkic Alphabet (NTA), although these in no way cover all the dimensions of the interrelationship of language and hegemony in the non-Russian areas of the Union. In Ukraine the split between a predominantly Russian-speaking working class and a Ukrainian-speaking peasantry brought the linguistic dimensions of the *smychka* into sharp focus and the policy discussions over this issue provide a valuable window onto the way in which the issue was addressed at key points throughout the 1920s. In the Turkic-speaking areas of the USSR, the need to delimit national republics and decide on procedures for standardising languages involved a large number of sensitivities between different strata of the population and between the indigenous intelligentsias of neighbouring areas. Together these cases alert us to some of the important features of relations between the centre and periphery of the USSR and how the process of bureaucratisation and centralisation impinged on certain communities. Crucial in this was the policy of *korenizatsiia* [indiginisation or nativisation], which was introduced by Stalin as Commissar of Nationalities in 1923. As we shall see, the pre-revolutionary Orientalists discussed in Chapter Two were enthusiastic participants in the practice of the policy, since it involved the implementation on a grand scale of the measures they had regarded as necessary to foster a pan-Russian identity and save the Empire. While emerging out of debates in which Stalin had retreated from his highly centralising proposals and conceded legal guarantees for the autonomy of national republics, as Sultan-Galiev feared, the policy of *korenizatsiia* proved to be adaptable to the very cause of establishing the hegemony of the great Russians, as the imperial Orientalists had hoped.

Chapter Seven examines the factors behind the decline of the paradigm of hegemony as it pertained to the USSR, linking it to the fundamental transformations of the period of the first Five-Year Plan and after. We see how the concept largely disappeared from internal Party discussion, with the simultaneous launch of a state offensive against the peasantry and against the vestiges of workers' power in industry. The effects of the offensive in research institutions and among young and more radical linguists are also traced. The one area where the paradigm persisted for a brief period was in the realm of culture, where a renewed struggle for the hegemony of proletarian culture was launched by the groups who were no longer constrained by Bukharin's resolution of 1925. Finally, we see how the new hegemonic arrangement was not subject to direct analysis and criticism, but made its way into the work of probably the most significant proletarian writer of all, Andrei Platonov, who became the target of criticism by the self-appointed guardians of proletarian culture.

The life and career of one of the imperial Orientalists forms the focus of Chapter Eight. Nikolai Marr was to become the officially recognised leader in Soviet linguistics from the beginning of the 1930s until 1950, and his eccentric 'new theory of language' was regarded as the prime example of 'Marxism in linguistics'. It is, however, difficult to regard Marr's work as in any substantial sense Marxist, and we will see how his ideas developed as an eclectic combination of late nineteenth-century psychologism and positivism, which were subsequently hitched up to a superficially Marxist lexicon. While Marr is often treated as an example of the ideological distortion of linguistic science, and his personal eccentricity highlighted, we will see that he was actually a philologist and archaeologist of some significance and was responsible for the first ideology critique of the entwinement of indo-European philology with the interests of European colonialism. However, we will also see how the value of this critique was compromised by a lack of technical competence in linguistics and the fact that it became wedded to a legitimisation of the policies of the Stalin regime. We will see that Marr was not an isolated phenomenon, but perhaps the most characteristic example of the way in which the detailed, evidence-driven scholarship of the 1920s was subordinated to abstract schemata and narratives inherited from the pre-revolutionary period and forced to serve different ends. All of this was made possible by institutional factors and the promotion of positivist thinkers who had imbibed just enough Marxism to allow them to recast their pre-formed ideas in the parlance of the day. The dynamics of hegemony were now either projected back into the distant past, when linguistic 'crossing' was held to have taken place, or was transferred to an international scale where 'progressive' Soviet ideology, including Marr's own theories, competed for dominance with the unitarily reactionary ideologies of the bourgeois world, including all comparative linguistics.

In the Conclusion, we briefly return to Gramsci's relationship to the debates about hegemony, delineating his contribution to political thought and the incomplete nature of his prison writings. It now becomes clear that reading hegemony solely through a Gramscian lens has distorted a significant episode in intellectual history and deprived contemporary theory of important conceptual tools. Appreciating the dimensions of hegemony in revolutionary Russia is necessary for realising the concept's potential in contemporary engagements.

CHAPTER 1

Hegemony in Russian Social Democracy Before 1917

In 1911 Lenin was arguing that 'the idea of the hegemony of the proletariat constitutes one of the fundamental tenets of Marxism'.[1] This may appear a rather
strange claim, given that the term had not acquired a particularly prominent
position in the works of Marx and Engels, who used the term largely as it had
been passed down to political theory from Ancient Greece in the works available at the time. The term originally denoted the leadership or predominant
authority of one state of a confederacy or union over others, and this is precisely how Engels used the term in his discussions of Prussia's hegemony in
Germany or Marx to refer to the hegemony of certain states in the Civil War in
the United States.[2] The term was, by this time, also commonly applied to the
preponderance of certain states in a region – for instance, Britain in Turkey
and Persia or France in Central Europe, and we find this in their writings too.[3]
There were occasional instances of the use of the term 'hegemony' to mean
intellectual dominance or leadership in the works of Marx and Engels, but
these appeared in places that were unlikely to have exerted any significant
influence on Russian Marxists in the period before the revolution.[4] However,
the complex of ideas that came to be denoted by the term 'hegemony' was very
much present in Marxist thought.

---

1   Lenin 1974a [1911], p. 215.
2   See, for instance, Engels 1977 [1848], p. 235; Marx 1984 [1861] p. 40.
3   See, for instance, Engels 1975b [1842], p. 56; Engels 1990 [1887–8], p. 466.
4   In Engels's early newspaper articles, we can find a reference to 'Germanizers' seeking to free
    Germany from 'foreign intellectual hegemony' (Engels 1975a [1841], p. 140) and in a pamphlet
    on *The Prussian Military Question and the German Workers' Party*, written in 1865 but first
    published in 1913, Engels speaks of attempts to 'reap the ripe harvest of bourgeois hegemony'
    (Engels 1985 [1865], p. 58). More substantially, in the first chapter of the text now known
    as *The German Ideology*, Marx and Engels refer to the fact that 'German philosophical crit-
    ics ... agree in their belief in the hegemony of ideas' (Marx and Engels 1976 [1845–7], p. 62)
    and the 'hegemony of spirit in history' (Ibid.), but sections of this text appeared in print
    only in 1920, and the chapter in its entirety was published only in 1924, along with the uned-
    ited version of the 'Theses on Feuerbach'. On the publication history, see Kandel *et al.* 1988,
    pp. 104, 127, 150. *The German Ideology* was assembled and published as a unified text in 1932.

'Political Hegemony' Before 1917

In his seminal work, *Lenin Rediscovered: What Is To Be Done? in Context*, Lars Lih has shown convincingly how the emergence of the Russian Social-Democratic programme of hegemony, if not the specific use of the term, derived from the 1891 *Erfurt Programme* of German Social Democracy, formulated by Karl Kautsky. Lenin held Kautsky in the highest esteem until the outbreak of World War I, when the latter was held to have defected from the revolutionary cause. Marx and Engels had contended that the bourgeoisie had fulfilled its historic role, that it 'was no longer capable of the leadership of society and has even become a hindrance to the development of production'. Historical leadership had now passed to the proletariat, 'a class which, owing to its whole position in society, can only free itself by abolishing altogether all class rule, all servitude and all exploitation'.[5] Kautsky had argued that, to the east of the Rhine, the European bourgeoisie had become especially 'weak and cowardly' and that there 'the regime of the sabre and of the bureaucracy cannot be broken until the proletariat is in a position to conquer political power, so that the fall of absolutist militarism will lead directly to the seizure of political power by the proletariat'.[6] Social Democracy needed political freedom to operate and organise, while the people had a direct interest in this freedom to protect them from the abuse of power. However, as the proletariat's interest in political freedom rose, so the interest of the bourgeoisie in that freedom declined, leaving the proletariat as the only consistent and reliable supporters of political freedom. Social Democracy, the fusion of socialism and the labour movement, must therefore assume leadership of the whole people [*Volk, narod*]. Lih concludes that this proletarian leadership of the bourgeois revolution was what the Russian Marxists called 'hegemony'.[7]

The term 'hegemony' [*gegemoniia*] was already being used by Georgii Plekhanov to denote the leadership of a 'group or party ... in a particular period of the revolutionary movement' in his polemics with the Russian Populists

---

5   Engels 1989 [1877], p. 193.

6   Quoted in Lih 2005, p. 100. For a recent reassessment of Kautsky's views on history, see Blackledge 2006.

7   Lih 2005, pp. 96–101. Lih's study shows that the notion of Social Democracy as a fusion of socialism and the labour movement was the origin of Lenin's contention that the party brings political consciousness to the workers' movement 'from without' in *What Is To Be Done?* (1902). Lih also shows that, when examined in the context of the texts with which Lenin engages in that work, the most striking feature stressed by Lenin is not the vanguard party, but the self-activity of the proletariat. For a multi-faceted discussion of Lih's argument, see the special symposium on the book in Blackledge (ed.) 2010.

as early as 1884, but this did not come to denote a coherent strategy, in the spirit of the *Erfurt Programme*, until a decade later.[8] In an article of 1976 that is valuable to this day, Anderson discussed the way in which the term became a central slogan for the Russian Social-Democratic movement between the late 1890s and 1917 to describe the leading role the proletariat must play in the struggle against absolutism and for political freedom.[9] The Russian proletariat would thereby acquire, in the words of Pavel Axelrod in 1898, an 'all-national revolutionary significance'. In 1901 he argued that 'by virtue of the historical position of our proletariat, Russian Social Democracy can acquire hegemony in the struggle against absolutism'.[10] Plekhanov's use of the term 'hegemony' also acquired this sense at this time and he began to argue that the proletariat is the fundamental class to lead the revolutionary movement. From his earliest Marxist writings, however, Plekhanov tended to argue that the proletariat must be especially careful not to frighten the liberal bourgeoisie and to limit its own immediate aspirations. This was a position adopted by many Mensheviks, such as Aleksandr Martynov, writing in 1905: 'The struggle for influence on the course and outcome of the bourgeois revolution can only be expressed in the proletariat exerting revolutionary pressure on the will of the liberal and radical bourgeoisie, so the more democratic "lower orders" of society makes its "higher orders" agree to carry the Revolution through to its logical conclusion'.[11]

For Lenin, the peasantry had fragmented into a number of strata, some of which were semi-proletarian and some of which approached petty-bourgeois status. Thus, the class struggle in the countryside has a dual character: between the peasantry and all landowning classes on the one hand and between agricultural workers and the bourgeoisie on the other. In order to win hegemony over the peasantry, the proletariat must stand 'with the bourgeois peasantry against the remnants of serfdom, against absolutism, clergy, landowners, together with the urban proletariat against the bourgeoisie in general and the bourgeois peasantry in particular'.[12] This led to serious disagreements with Plekhanov, Axelrod and Martov. Lenin argued that Russian Social Democracy must put forward a demand for the nationalisation of the land and a range of other demands designed to free the peasants from restrictions carried over

---

8   Plekhanov, 1961 [1885], p. 127. On Plekhanov's development of the term, see Kamenev 2003 [1906] and Zinov'ev 1924 [1923], pp. 81–3, 302–4; Zinoviev, 1973 [1923], pp. 36–7, 216–18. On Lenin's development of the idea before 1905, see Ushakov 1974.

9   Anderson, 1976, pp. 15–17.

10   Anderson, 1976, pp. 15–16. Axelrod's argument is in Axelrod 1898.

11   Martynov 1905, pp. 57–8.

12   Quoted in Ushakov 1974, p. 44.

from serfdom and to free the poor peasants from the hold of parasitic groups who obstruct their movement towards a socialist perspective. Plekhanov and others only considered a radical review of rural relations and offered no concrete measures, tending to view the peasantry as a conservative mass whose backwardness was the main support of absolutism, opposing the idea of the nationalisation of the land on the basis that it was acceptable only under socialism.[13] The Party did engage in uneven but often effective agitation and propaganda in the countryside, often by means of worker recruits who still had connections with certain villages.[14]

The 1905 Revolution proved a watershed in the revolutionary movement and led to the political eclipse of Plekhanov. Leon Trotsky, Chair of the St. Petersburg Soviet, regarded the October 1905 strike – which involved 'liberal professions', students and spread to 'law courts, the chemists' shops, the rural administration offices and the town dumas' – to be 'a demonstration of the proletariat's hegemony in the bourgeois revolution and, at the same time, of the hegemony of the towns in an agricultural country'.[15] As Alan Shandro has argued, the events led Lenin to see the soviet as a non-partisan institutional form in which the social, economic and political struggles of the wider masses could be 'combined with the revolutionary struggle for political power, amplifying and reinforcing each other'.[16] The soviet not only provided a means by which the workers' movement could exert political leadership in the struggles of the masses against the autocracy, but it also paralysed the project of the Duma, through which the bourgeoisie attempted to reach a compromise with the autocracy and act as a pole of attraction for the sections of the peasantry closest to the petty bourgeoisie.

For Plekhanov, the desired overthrow of the autocracy could only result in a liberal bourgeois regime that would give political rights to the proletariat. This could then be used by the proletariat for its subsequent economic liberation. Looking back on the position adopted by Plekhanov, the Mensheviks and some Bolsheviks at the time, Trotsky summed up their argument as follows:

---

13   Ushakov 1974, p. 46.

14   Ushakov 1974, pp. 47–74. Ushakov presents a range of archival evidence for the effectiveness of Bolshevik propaganda in villages, but shows that this was often limited to certain geographical areas and suffered from a paucity of materials specifically directed towards the peasants. This often placed them at a disadvantage in relation to the peasant-oriented propaganda of the SRS.

15   Trotsky 1971 [1907], p. 115.

16   Shandro 2007, p.324. This argument is significantly expanded in Shandro's forthcoming monograph about Lenin and the question of hegemony, which I have had the privilege of reading in advance of its publication.

'the political hegemony of the proletariat must be preceded by the political hegemony of the bourgeoisie; a bourgeois democratic republic must serve as a long historical school for the proletariat; any attempt to skip this phase is adventurism; if the working class in the West has not seized power, how can the Russian proletariat set itself such a task, etc., etc.'[17] When the liberal Cadet Party spurned an electoral agreement with the Social Democrats for a platform in favour of a constituent assembly and dropped its demand for the assembly entirely, Plekhanov blamed the Bolsheviks for seeking to expose rather than support the bourgeoisie. Lenin retorted:

> Liberalism ... merits support only to the extent that it actually opposes the autocracy. It is this support of all the inconsistent (i.e., bourgeois) democrats by the only really consistent democrats (i.e., the proletariat) that makes the idea of hegemony a reality.... From the proletarian point of view hegemony in a war goes to him who fights most energetically, who never misses a chance to strike a blow at the enemy, who always suits the action to the word, who is therefore the ideological leader of the democratic forces, who criticises half-way policies of every kind.[18]

The inability of the bourgeoisie to achieve a 'decisive victory over Tsarism' meant that 'a decisive victory means nothing else than the revolutionary-democratic dictatorship of the proletariat and the peasantry'.[19] To the consternation of Plekhanov, Kautsky waded in on the side of Lenin, arguing that since the proletariat had to fight, this would make sense only if the leaders of the class would be prepared to take power.[20] Plekhanov, the founder of Russian-Marxist theory and of the first Marxist organisation in Russia, would never again play a pivotal role in the revolutionary movement. In 1911 Lenin gave a more general formulation of the relationship between hegemony and democracy in political dialogue: 'The hegemony of the working class is the political influence which that class (and its representatives) exercises upon other sections of the population by helping them to purge their democracy (where there is democracy) of undemocratic admixtures, by criticising the narrowness and short-sightedness of all bourgeois democracy, by carrying on the struggle against "Cadetism"

---

17   Trotsky 1971a [1922], p. 345.
18   Lenin 1962a [1905], p. 79.
19   Lenin 1962b [1905], p. 86.
20   Kautsky 1983 [1906]; Kautsky 2009a [1906]; Baron 1963, p. 274.

(meaning the corrupting ideological content of the speeches and policy of the liberals), etc., etc.'[21]

One of the important effects of the Russian defeat in its 1904–5 war with Japan, and the revolution it precipitated, was a cognitive shift in geographical perspectives. For the first time, a major European power had been humbled by an Asiatic power, shaking complacent Eurocentric perspectives to their foundations. It also led the intellectuals of the national minorities of the Empire to become much more self-aware and confident in pressing for recognition of national identity and national rights.[22] We will return to some of the more general, intellectual ramifications of this later, but here we will concentrate on its significance for the conceptualisation of the project of proletarian hegemony. As the national question moved up the political agenda, the project's proponents increasingly needed to recognise how it was an important dimension of the revolutionary movement. This was something that the liberals recognised and, in their attempt to head off revolution, they argued that after the achievement of bourgeois democracy there should be national cultural autonomy within a democratically restructured Russian Empire.[23] Despite a general vision of a united, multinational empire that would be renewed through democratic reform and long-term national cultural development, however, none of the various liberal parties – the Constitutional Democrats [*Kadety*], Octoberists or other 'progressives' – were able to develop a coherent programme on central dimensions of the national question, such as language and religion. Moreover, after a brief liberalisation of policies towards national minorities following the promulgation of the October Manifesto of 17 October 1905, the Stolypin coup of June 1907 inaugurated a trend back in the direction of a repressive policy towards the so-called '*inorodtsy*' [national minorities], who many in the bureaucracy blamed for the 1905 Revolution.[24] The liberals were now caught between an inflexible, reactionary autocratic state and, as the workers' movement recovered after the defeat of 1905 and the movement of national minorities challenged state repression, an increasingly assertive popular movement.

Little wonder, then, that many erstwhile liberals shifted to the right in the wake of 1905 when they felt, in the words of the former 'legal Marxist', Sergei

---

21   Lenin 1974b [1911], p. 79.

22   On the rise in importance of categories of nationhood in this period, see Cadiot 2005. See also Khalid 1998.

23   See, especially, Kondratenko 2005.

24   Löwe 1992.

Bulgakov, 'the breath of the antichrist'.[25] The electoral success of the Cadets in 1906, when a selective electoral law and political repression left the Cadet Party as the most left-wing element within the Duma, initially led the former 'Legal Marxist' Peter Struve to celebrate its 'hegemony over the democratic opposition', since its programme and tactics had managed to 'impress the people [narod] and confirm in its consciousness the rights and legality of the liberation movement, that found the secret key to the popular [narodnyi] heart'.[26] When it became clear that popular demands went far beyond what the liberals were willing to concede, Bulgakov joined with other renegades of the liberation movement in the notorious 1909 collection, Vekhi [Signposts]. It is significant that, in order to justify their withdrawal from the liberation movement, the authors of this collection had to speak in patronising terms of the 'spiritual hegemony' of the movement having passed to the youth, creating a 'pedocracy'.[27] Mikhail Gershenzon spoke for many: 'not only can we not dream about fusing with the people, but we must fear them worse than any punishment by the government, and we must bless that authority which alone with its bayonets and prisons manages to protect us from the popular fury'.[28] The liberals who did not turn to the right found themselves beached. As Boris Kagarlitsky notes, 'a Third Estate uniting the bourgeoisie with the ordinary masses did not exist in Russia', for in the countryside what was taking place was 'the destruction of peasant agriculture under the impact of the new market relations' rather than 'the successful bourgeois transformation of the countryside'.[29] While the left liberals in the Cadet Party could make progressive statements about the rights of nations, they lacked any social base capable of implementing policy: 'large-scale capital in Russia had never shown any particular interest in democratic change, and after October 1905, it began to cool to the idea of constitutional reform as well'.[30]

Already in his 1898 book, The Development of Capitalism in Russia, in which he presented the Russian social formation as one characterised by a rising capitalist mode of production challenging a dominant feudal mode and feudal state, Lenin had argued that tsarist colonial policy exerted a reactionary influence on both oppressed and oppressor nations by retarding the

25　Quoted in Kagarlitsky 2008, p. 243.

26　Struve quoted in Kasarov 1986, p. 7.

27　Bulgakov 1977 [1909], p. 40. Similar sentiments characterise the contributions by Izgoev and Struve.

28　Gershenzon 1977 [1909], pp. 80–1.

29　Kagarlitsky 2008, p. 242.

30　Kagarlitsky, 2008, p. 243.

deepening of capitalist relations, and that this resulted in the survival of aspects of serfdom. However, as he was to point out in 1915, the bourgeoisie remained tied to the tsarist state because its imperial aggression and colonial expansion facilitated the *broadening* of capitalist development. The interests of the autocratic state and of the bourgeoisie thus coincided, social contradictions were eased and so their resolution was deferred.[31] This, along with fear of the workers' movement, was clearly one of the factors preventing the bourgeoisie from leading a revolution against the autocracy, making the national question a crucial dimension of the project of proletarian hegemony. As Elizaveta Drabkina noted, in Lenin's estimation 'the fundamental historical cause determining this connection was that the victory of the democratic revolution could not be achieved without the resolution of the national question, but, in turn, the national question could not be solved without a victorious democratic revolution, the leader of which was the working class'.[32] Lenin saw confirmation of this interdependence in the results of the elections to the Duma in 1907 from the most economically advanced and the most backward non-Russian parts of the Empire, where the party of the proletariat was winning hegemony in the struggle for national liberation:

> A comparison with the non-Russian parts of Russia, with Poland and the Caucasus, provides fresh proof that the real motive force of the bourgeois revolution in Russia is not the bourgeoisie. In Poland there is no revolutionary peasant movement, no urban bourgeois opposition and there are practically no liberals. The revolutionary proletariat is opposed by a reactionary bloc composed of the big and the petty bourgeoisie. There, the National-Democrats were therefore victorious. In the Caucasus the revolutionary peasant movement is very strong, the strength of the liberals is almost equal to that in Russia, but the Lefts are the strongest party there: the percentage of Lefts in the Duma (53.6%) is approximately the same as the percentage of deputies from the peasant curia (49%). Only the workers and the revolutionary democratic peasantry can complete the bourgeois revolution.[33]

In 1911 Lenin argued that '[a]s the only consistently revolutionary class of contemporary society, [the proletariat] must be the leader in the struggle of the whole people for a fully democratic revolution, in the struggle of *all* the

---

31   Lenin 1962e [1915], pp. 303–4.

32   Drabkina 1932, p. 16.

33   Lenin 1962d [1907], p. 206.

working and exploited people against the oppressors and exploiters. The proletariat is revolutionary only insofar as it is conscious of and gives effect to this
idea of the hegemony of the proletariat'.[34]

For Lenin, in contradistinction to the Austro-Marxists and to Stalin, whose
1913 *Marxism and the National Question* is still too often confused with Lenin's
position, the national question is primarily a political question rather than
an economic, psychological or cultural one.[35] National self-determination
would not be an obstacle to proletarian unity and proletarian hegemony but
a precondition of that hegemony, because it 'wholly and exclusively' belongs
to the 'realm of political democracy'.[36] Advocating the unconditional *right*
of oppressed nations to secession did not mean advocating separation itself.
Indeed, this could be combined with agitation and propaganda *against*
separation and the exposure of bourgeois nationalism. The proletariat therefore 'welcomes every kind of assimilation of nations, except that which is
founded on force or privilege'.[37] Policy towards the national question was
therefore part and parcel of the project of attaining proletarian hegemony in
the democratic revolution:

> At a time when bourgeois-democratic revolutions in Eastern Europe and
> Asia have begun, in this period of the awakening and intensification of
> national movements and of the formation of independent proletarian
> parties, the task of these parties with regard to national policy must be
> twofold: recognition of the right of all nations to self-determination,
> since bourgeois-democratic reform is not yet completed and since work-
> ing-class democracy consistently, seriously and sincerely...fights for
> equal rights for nations; then, a close, unbreakable alliance in the class
> struggle of the proletarians of all nations in a given state, throughout all

---

34   Lenin 1974c [1911], pp. 231–2.
35   Lenin commissioned Stalin to write a rebuttal of the Austro-Marxist approach to the
      national question and needed material for a polemic with the Bund and with some
      Caucasian Mensheviks, who were advocating the reorganisation of the RSDRP along
      national lines. However, he subsequently never appears to have endorsed the article and
      there are many discontinuities between the approaches of Lenin and Stalin. These are
      particularly well delineated in Löwy 1976. See also Harris 1990, pp. 71–2. A lack of appreci-
      ation of these fundamental differences still mars Terry Martin's important study of Soviet
      nationality policy from 1923: Martin 2001, pp. 2–12.
36   Lenin 1964a [1916], p. 135.
37   Lenin 1972 [1913], p. 35.

the changes in its history, irrespective of any reshaping of the frontiers of the individual states by the bourgeoisie.[38]

For Lenin it was only by consciously implementing the idea of hegemony in its own activities that the proletariat became a class rather than the 'sum total of various guilds', that is, to move beyond what Gramsci was to call the 'corporatist' phase of proletarian politics.[39] In this sense, the project of hegemony was the recognition that the proletariat as an objective entity [*an sich*] can only act for itself [*für sich*] in connection with the social communities created by the capitalist system itself.[40] Thus was the question of political hegemony posed in the period before 1917.

It only remains to stress two important factors. Firstly, already before the revolution, the question of competing bourgeois and proletarian hegemony was regarded as characteristic of all nations where the bourgeois revolution was incomplete. The Russian case was thus to be seen as a specific instance of a more general situation, particularly in Europe. Secondly, a fundamental aspect of the project of proletarian hegemony in Russia was the expectation that this would result in a 'revolutionary-democratic dictatorship of the proletariat and the peasantry' that would 'carry the revolutionary conflagration into Europe'.[41] It was, however, Trotsky rather than Lenin who first understood the full implications of this:

> The revolutionary authorities will be confronted with the objective problems of socialism, but the solution of these problems will, at a certain stage, be prevented by the country's economic backwardness. There is no way out from this contradiction within the framework of a national revolution.

---

38   Lenin 1972a [1914], p. 434.
39   Anderson 1976, p. 17.
40   Hence Lenin's famous assertion in 1916: 'To imagine that social revolution is *conceivable* without revolts by small nations in the colonies and in Europe, without revolutionary outbursts by a section of the petty bourgeoisie *with all its prejudices*, without a movement of the politically non-conscious proletarian and semi-proletarian masses against oppression by the landowners, the church, and the monarchy, against national oppression, etc. – to imagine all this is to *repudiate social revolution*. So one army lines up in one place and says, "We are for socialism", and another, somewhere else and says, "We are for imperialism", and that will be a social revolution! . . . Whoever expects a "pure" social revolution will *never* live to see it'. Lenin 1964b [1916], p. 355.
41   Lenin 1962b [1905], pp. 56–7.

The workers' government will from the start be faced with the task of uniting its forces with those of the socialist proletariat of Western Europe. Only in this way will its temporary revolutionary hegemony become the prologue to a socialist dictatorship.[42]

Cultural Hegemony

According to the Social-Democratic principle, political organisation must be based on that part of the proletariat that has the greatest insight into its class position, basic interests and historical mission. It must work to expand that awareness into the proletariat as a whole. This awareness was crucial to the achievement of proletarian hegemony in the democratic revolution. In the aftermath of the defeat of the 1905 Revolution, however, direct political activity was severely repressed, Party membership fell and trade unions were forbidden to function as unions. Retrenchment led many activists to focus on building workers' cultural and educational organisations, where direct political conflict could be minimised.[43] Such establishments had been especially important in Germany during the ban on socialist organisations, and the *Sozialdemokratische Partei Deutschlands* [Social-Democratic Party of Germany (SPD)] was actively involved in an impressive range of workers' educational organisations, libraries and theatres.[44] Among one group of Bolsheviks, the cultural turn was regarded as a virtue rather than a necessity and as signifying an organic generalisation of the programme of proletarian hegemony. The most prominent members of this group were Aleksandr Bogdanov and Anatolii Lunacharskii, who became associated with the *Vpered* [*Forward*] faction within the Party from 1909. Bogdanov had distinguished himself by a particularly strong distrust of spontaneous worker self-activity, which he voiced at the Third Party Congress in 1905, and which resulted in a particularly suspicious attitude towards the appearance of the soviets later in the year.[45] After the crushing of the revolution and the tsar's

---

42   Trotsky 1971 [1907], pp. 332–3.

43   See, for instance, the second volume of Kleinbort 1923; Swift 1999.

44   See, for instance, Roth 1963. In 1891, Kautsky argued that workers' organisations only met in public houses, where the lower classes 'can come together freely and discuss their common affairs ... Without public-houses the German proletariat not only has no social life, it has no political life either'. Quoted in Ritter 1978, p. 172.

45   *Tretii S"ezd RSDRP* 1959 [1905], pp. 106–14. As the foremost Bolshevik leader in Russia at the time, Bogdanov was instrumental in formulating the initial negative response of the Party to the soviets in October 1905. On Lenin's attitude toward the soviets, see his unpublished letter to the editorial board of *Novaia zhizn'*, written early in November 1905 in

concession to convene a Duma, Bogdanov tended towards non-participation and entered into a series of disputes with Lenin about the tactical merits of participation. As John Marot argues, however, the matter was secondary since Bogdanov was actually more concerned with shifting Party strategy away from a focus on narrow political issues and towards a much broader, what we might call 'culturalist' reconcepualisation of the project for proletarian hegemony.[46] For Bogdanov, the proletariat had 'assimilated the socialist fundamentals of class consciousness in a superficial and weak way, socialism as a *worldview* is not very widespread'. Topical propaganda had educated the proletariat in a revolutionary-democratic way in connection with the immediate political struggle, rather than fostering an 'integral class worldview'.[47] Participation in the Duma had been symptomatic of this. To rectify this, propaganda must have a 'much more complete and encyclopaedic content'. This required a 'new type of *Party school*' that would aim to systematise the world view of the workers and lessen their reliance on the intelligentsia.[48]

Interestingly, Bogdanov's interpretation of the events of 1905 had something important in common with that of the leading ideologist of the Socialist Revolutionary Party, Viktor Chernov, for whom the events of 1905 and 1906 were not so much a political revolution as a 'colossal *spiritual* overturn': 'The atmosphere of confusion among the authorities and an exaggerated faith in "revolution" were particularly appropriate conditions for the transformation of Russia into a huge political popular [*narodnyi*] university with numerous wandering lecturers, with universally accessible courses of politics and socialism. What could only have been whispered about in narrow circles and passed by ear from one person to the next just recently was carried out onto the square, in the streets; factory workshops and village gatherings were turned into auditoria; in just a few months so much that was new was introduced to the popular consciousness than had been conveyed in many years of hard work'.[49]

While this was going on, Chernov argued, the parties of the Left were engaged in the disputes over the 'hegemony of one fraction over the rest', and,

---

Stockholm, in which he argued that the soviet was 'the embryo of a provisional revolutionary government'. For discussions of this episode, see Cliff 1986, pp. 160–8 and Liebman 1975, pp. 86–90. Bogdanov may well have been the implicit target of Lenin's insistence, in 1906, that 'to attempt to answer yes or no to the question whether any particular means of struggle should be used, without making a detailed examination of the concrete situation of the given moment, means completely to abandon the Marxist position' (Lenin 1962c [1906], p. 214).

46   Marot 1990, pp. 241–61.
47   Bogdanov and Krasin 1934 [1909].
48   Bogdanov and Krasin 1934 [1909].
49   Chernov 1911, p. 188.

because of this 'struggle for hegemony among various socialist fractions, the hegemony of socialism over labouring [*trudovoi*] democracy and the hegemony of labouring democracy over democracy in general was undermined'.[50] The main difference with Bogdanov was that, as a Populist, Chernov did not accept the principle of the hegemony of the proletariat over the peasantry. The Socialist Revolutionaries generally thought the intelligentsia would lead the revolution.[51]

In December 1909 Bogdanov's faction became formalised and the journal *Vpered* became its organ. Underlying Bogdanov's strategic orientation was a philosophical standpoint, over which much ink was to be spilled. This was a monistic positivism that presented the world as pure experience, with the experience of the proletariat, organised collectively in its labour activity and developing comradely relations, seen as providing the decisive force for revolutionary change.

> Bolshevism is not just a political, but is also a *socio-cultural phenomenon*. It was the first to dare to pose the task of the political hegemony of the proletariat over the bourgeois classes in the bourgeois-democratic revolution, in the liberation of bourgeois society. But for those of us who understand the organic inseparability of politics from the other aspects of the ideological life of society, which arise on one and the same social basis, it would be unnatural and strange to consider the proletariat able to achieve political hegemony, not acknowledging its *general-cultural hegemony* [*gegemoniia obshche-kul'turnaia*]. This is the hidden premise of Bolshevism: the idea to create now, within the limits of the present society, a great proletarian culture, more powerful and harmonious than the culture of the declining bourgeois classes, immeasurably freer and more creative.[52]

The hegemony of bourgeois ideology beyond the immediate workplace rendered workers unable to act as a revolutionary collective because it prevented them from perceiving their actual position and role in society. The Party must therefore establish proletarian universities, schools and ideological clubs in advance of the seizure of power to counter this influence and systematise the lived experience of the proletariat.[53] Proletarian culture would organise

---

50   Chernov 1911, p. 206.

51   See, for instance, Shishko 2007 [1910] and Rakitnikov 2007 [1910].

52   Maksimov 1909, p. 5.

53   Voitinskii 1929, p. 78.

human perception and action, overcome mere spontaneity and so move society towards the classless culture of the future. The Party should thus foster a collectivist psychology among the proletariat and recognise that the 'general cultural hegemony' of the proletariat precedes and determines the success of the political and economic revolution.[54] For Bogdanov, writing in 1909:

> There is only one solution: to use the past, bourgeois culture to create a new proletarian culture that can be counterposed to bourgeois culture, and to spread it among the masses: to develop proletarian science, strengthen genuine comradely relations among the proletarian milieu, work out a proletarian philosophy, to direct art to the side of proletarian strivings and experience.[55]

This became the focus of the school for socialist workers that Bogdanov, Lunacharskii and Maksim Gorky established on the Italian island of Capri in 1909 and then in Bologna in 1911. Drawing on German Romanticism, the French syndicalist Georges Sorel and the ideas of the German monist 'worker-philosopher', Joseph Dietzgen, Lunacharskii and Gorky accentuated the mythical dimension of proletarian culture, arguing that such culture would appeal to the religious needs of the proletariat, since the individual proletarian would achieve immortality through the body of the collective.[56] Lunacharskii argued that the semi-proletarian and petty-bourgeois masses, who would participate in the revolution under the hegemony of the proletariat, would not accept 'proletarian truth' in its full form, but would accept socialism in the religious formulations to which they were accustomed.[57]

---

54   Sochor 1981b, p. 72; Scherrer 1989, p. 201. Bogdanov's most important ideas about proletarian culture can be found in Bogdanov 1910 and Bogdanov 1999 [1911]. For general discussions of Bogdanov's ideas about proletarian culture see, Dement'eva 1971; Scherrer 1989; Mally 1990, pp. 3–16; Marot 1991; Karpov 2009, pp. 52–66.

55   Bordiugov (ed.) 1995, pp. 36–76.

56   See, especially, Lunacharskii 1908 and 1911. Even in 1925 after the religious aspects had disappeared from his works, Lunacharskii celebrated the work of Dietzgen as a link between Spinoza's monism and Marxism in Lunacharskii 1925, pp. 124–33. The notion of the proletariat making up a 'collective body' later runs throughout Gor'kii's speech to the 1934 Soviet Writers' Congress at which the principles of socialist realism were encoded: 'Soviet Literature' in Gorky et al. 1977 [1934], pp. 27–69. On the roots of the conception, see Beiser 2003, pp. 43–55, and Dietzgen 1906a [1870–5].

57   Voitinskii 1929, pp. 68–9. It is worth noting that Bogdanov did not endorse these 'god-building' ideas, though he was often associated with them by his opponents.

For Bogdanov, socialism was not just a political system but a whole philosophy in which the individual man, characteristic of the bourgeois world view, would be replaced by the collective 'comrade'. Each fundamental class must work out its own philosophy if it is to be able to conduct a coherent struggle, and this means capturing the essence of the class-differentiated experience of the productive process, for different practical relations give rise to different logics.

He called the 'necessary and universal law of the organisation of experience' 'sociomorphism', which he defined as follows:

> *Thinking takes its form, in the final instance, from social practice*; or, to put it differently:

> *the connection between the elements of experience in cognition is based on the correlation of elements of social activity in the labour process.*[58]

To move beyond a mere collection of elements of collective experience (what he in one place calls 'crystals of labour')[59] within the confines of a single consciousness, requires the generalisation and organisation of the class-differentiated experience of the productive process into a systematic world view through collectively produced methods or science. The intellectuals of the bourgeoisie developed a coherent conception of the world based on commodity fetishism, since social relations are mediated by the quasi-objectivity of the market. The bourgeois pursuit of self-interest in the market gave rise to a fetishised product that exists apart from and outside the producers. The proletariat must similarly systematise its own world view based on the 'new, practical relations that differ from anything that went before' that constitute its class experience.[60] This was linked to the monistic and holistic energetics that Bogdanov had imbibed from Wilhelm Otswald and which had become part of his general philosophical monism.[61] For Bogdanov, labour had become a transhistorical energetic

---

58   Bogdanov 1923a, p. 293. Original italicisation.

59   Jensen 1978, p. 125.

60   Bogdanov 1923a, pp. 267–8. Jensen 1978, pp. 119–23 provides perhaps the best outline of the importance of the 'labour point of view' and 'labour causality' in Bogdanov's philosophy.

61   Otswald granted the status of reality only to energy, the various forms of which are united through systematisation. For a recent overview of Otswald's ideas, see Kim 2008. On Otswald's links to general monism see Sobczinska and Czerwiska 2005, pp. 59–68. Among the discussions of the relationship between Otswald and Bogdanov, see Douglas 2002, pp. 76–94. It is worth noting that Bogdanov's reliance on energy theory wanes in his later work.

and labour power a transcendental principle that takes certain forms (modes of production) at certain stages in the linear development of society. Machine production merely made this principle apparent to workers by systematically transforming one form of energy (physical, chemical and so on) into another and, in so doing, changing the world fundamentally. Embedded in this productive process, workers have a collective experience that allows them to break through the fetishistic appearance and see that 'every process in the world is the possible source of every other process'.[62] Once in possession of this philosophy, the proletariat would be able to extend its world view beyond its ranks, counter the hegemony of the bourgeoisie and capture hegemony for itself.

The Linguistic Dimension of Political Hegemony

The divisions between Lenin and Bogdanov over the relative importance of political and cultural hegemony in the pre-revolutionary period have been subject to a considerable number of studies and so do not need to be discussed here at any length.[63] To some extent, the two trends continued in parallel until the Russian Revolution of 1917 when, as we shall see, there was a conditional, and rather fraught, merging of the two projects at various levels. If we remain in the pre-revolutionary period for now, what has attracted less attention is that although neither Lenin nor Bogdanov theorised language and hegemony together, language played a crucial role in the hegemonic projects envisaged by both.

While, as we will see, Lenin was interested in the *performative* dimension of language and had interesting things to say about the relationship between language and democracy, more significant for our current purposes was the place that the language issue occupied in Lenin's writings on the national question. Some researchers have attempted to present Lenin's awareness of the linguistic dimension of nationality policy as having its origins in non-Marxist thinking. Isabelle Kreindler, for instance, finds Lenin's commitment to the full equality of languages is the only positive aspect of his thinking on the national question and argues that it most likely derives from the ideas of the lay mission-

---

62   Quoted in Jensen 1978, p. 120.

63   In addition to the sources noted above, see, for instance, Biggart 1981, pp. 134–53; Sochor 1988b; Rubinstein 1995. It is, however, worth noting that at the very time the *Vperedists* were developing their perspectives, Lenin was also making a foray into cultural criticism with a series of four short articles on Tolstoy, in which the great novelist was credited with portraying the social and ideological contradictions of pre-revolutionary Russia.

ary and colleague of Lenin's father, N.I. Il'minskii, who saw native languages as no obstacle to the spread of Orthodox Christianity.[64] Vera Tolz argues, more convincingly in my view, that one likely source was the work of pre-revolutionary Orientalists, among them Sergei Ol'denburg, who Lenin had met in 1891.[65] While the reception of Il'minskii's ideas in the Iul'ianov household may have sensitised the young Vladimir Il'ich to linguistic questions, and while he may have known something of the work of Russian Orientalists before the Russian Revolution (he certainly knew more about it afterwards), these are unlikely to have been major influences on Lenin's thought at this point, except to the extent that they influenced the programme of the Cadet Party, to which the Bolsheviks had to respond. A much more likely source is Kautsky's work on the national question.

In a 1908 pamphlet, Kautsky had presented the formation of the nation state and of the national language as two moments of a single process.[66] The bourgeoisie's need for a market unobstructed by feudal territorial and political divisions was accompanied by the need for a linguistic unification, as commerce required increased intercourse across old boundaries. The same developments led to the rise of bureaucracy, which itself required a unified language. Reflecting on the experiences of certain absolutist states, Kautsky observed that where the 'interaction within the state was not powerful enough to prompt the citizens of foreign language communities to use the ruling language, the efforts of the bureaucracy to standardise the language actually created the opposite effect. The foreign nations now felt oppressed and violated'.[67] The result was hostility among the national minorities towards the state in which they live, and this can be boosted by the rise of the democratic movement, especially where the bureaucracy and the people are of different nationalities.[68] Examining the various types of multi-national states, Kautsky argued that as a large centralised state with numerous nationalities that primarily live on the periphery of the Empire, Russia could grant these nations autonomy without any problems.[69] However, he held that economic development would lead to the swallowing up of smaller languages by larger, more unified languages, as more people chose to adopt the dominant language. Ultimately, merchants and educated people would adopt universal languages, national antagonisms

---

64   Kreindler 1977, pp. 86–100.
65   Tolz 2009; On Lenin's meetings with Ol'denburg, see Baziiantz 1986.
66   Kautsky 2009 [1908] and Kautsky 2010 [1908].
67   Kautsky 2010 [1908], pp. 146–7.
68   Kautsky 2010 [1908], p. 147.
69   Kautsky 2010 [1908], pp. 150–1.

would decrease and, with the transition to socialism, a multi-lingual community, or a community that spoke a universal language, would arise.

Lenin's analysis of imperialism and the realities of the imperialist war made him far less sanguine than Kautsky about the evolutionary decline in national antagonisms, but he fully took on board the latter's assessment of the result of state attempts to force subject populations to speak an official language whether through education or public and legal affairs. The main point of Lenin's discussion of the language issue in relation to the national question was that 'to throw off the feudal yoke, all national oppression and all privileges enjoyed by any particular nation or language, is the imperative duty of the proletariat as a democratic force'.[70] The equality of languages will not encourage a fragmentation of the language community, but its unification:

> If all privileges disappear, if the imposition of any one language ceases, all Slavs will easily and rapidly learn to understand each other and will not be frightened by the 'horrible' thought that speeches in different languages will be heard in the common parliament. The requirements of economic exchange will themselves *decide* which language of the given country it is to the *advantage* of the majority to know in the interests of commercial relations. This decision will be all the firmer because it is adopted voluntarily by a population of various nationalities, and its adoption will be the more rapid and extensive the more consistent the democracy and, as a consequence of it, the more rapid the development of capitalism.[71]

Thus proletarian hegemony means raising the languages of the national minorities to formal equality with Russian, providing the population 'with schools where teaching will be carried on in all the local languages' and providing the institutional bases for a democracy based not only on a freedom of speech, but an *equality* of speech, what the ancient Greeks called *Isegoria*.[72]

> Working-class democracy counterposes to the nationalist wrangling of the various bourgeois parties over questions of language, etc., the demand for the unconditional unity and complete amalgamation of workers of *all* nationalities in *all* working-class organisations – trade union, co-operative, consumers', educational and all others – in contra-

---

70   Lenin 1972 [1913], p. 35.

71   Lenin 1972 [1913], p. 21.

72   Lenin 1972b [1914], p. 73.

distinction to any kind of bourgeois nationalism. Only this type of unity and amalgamation can uphold democracy and defend the interests of the workers against capital – which is already international and is becoming more so – and promote the development of mankind towards a new way of life that is alien to all privileges and all exploitation.[73]

Language and Labour

If Lenin's approach to language was primarily related to the way in which it impinged on practical politics, this was not the case throughout the whole Social-Democratic movement. Along with Antonio Labriola, Franz Mehring and Kautsky, it was Plekhanov who attempted, in the words of Perry Anderson, to 'systematise historical materialism in a comprehensive theory of man and nature, capable of replacing rival bourgeois disciplines and providing the workers' movement with a broad and coherent vision of the world that could easily be grasped by its militants'.[74] This involved, for Plekhanov, drawing on physiology and the anthropological materialism of the late nineteenth century and then undergirding it with a philosophical monism that owed much to a materialist reading of Spinoza: 'laws of being are at the same time laws of thought'.[75] Labour power became a force alongside other forces, but one which could ultimately be transformed into consciousness, so that the characteristics of labour power in a given society (*technique*) corresponded to the form of consciousness of the worker. Rather than, as in Marx's dialectical conception, viewing man and nature as mutually constructed, Plekhanov argued that man was able to comprehend other given objects of nature because, through labour, the sensations gained correspond accurately to the properties of the object. The labour process itself now became the precondition of all thought, and relations to the means of production the determining factor in the structure of ideology. Space and time were now not *a priori* in the Kantian sense, but an objective property of nature, with historical materialism studying the 'historical fate' of the human species.

As Plekhanov extended his ideas into discussions of society and culture, his sources for this conception were fundamentally non-Marxist. As well as biological Darwinism and the social evolutionism of Spencer, Plekhanov drew upon the work of the influential German economist and anthropologist,

---

73   Lenin 1972 [1913], p. 22.
74   Anderson 1979 [1976], p. 5.
75   Steila 1991, p. 79.

Karl Bücher, in whose 1896 book, *Arbeit und Rhythmus* [*Work and Rhythm*], physiological time and social time were united through the labour process.[76] Analysing a wide array of work songs, Bücher argued that in traditional societies the duration and tempo of work corresponded to the organic rhythms of the body, and that this was expressed in the chants, hand-clapping and songs through which the group is coordinated in carrying out its collective task. However, these rhythms change along with the technological character of production, which also determines the rise of solos and choruses 'according to the manner in which the work is done, either by one producer or the whole group, the latter subdividing into several sections'.[77] The technical character of work further affects the content of songs, and thus of language and poetry, so that work may be regarded as the 'basic element' of both. Plekhanov concludes: 'If Bücher's remarkable conclusions are correct we have a right to say that human nature (the physiological nature of man's nervous system) has provided him with the faculty of recognising the musical nature of rhythm and of enjoying it, whilst the technique of his production has been the determining factor in the further development of this faculty'.[78]

Bücher's book was published in Russian translation in 1899 and republished in 1923. It exerted a considerable influence, not least because it was cited as a recommended text on the origin of culture in *Proletkul't* bibliographies.[79]

Bogdanov's alternative development of Marxism into a comprehensive monist outlook also involved some similar ways of thinking. His insistence on the class determination of reason and perception and his 'empiriomonist' insistence on the *identity* of social being and social consciousness made language an important issue for him. Rather than focusing on the political manifestation of the language question, Bogdanov sought the foundations of language and ideology in the experience of the productive process and then linked this to the question of hegemony. Bogdanov's chief source here was the German monist philosopher and philologist, Ludwig Noiré, who displays no knowledge of Marxism.[80] For Noiré, it is Schopenhauer's *will* rather than Spinoza's *substance* that is the source of our world and cognition. Yet Noiré strips will of much, though not all, of its metaphysical baggage by presenting it as a Kantian

---

76   For a recent discussion of the influence of Bücher's book in Germany, see Cowan 2008.

77   Plekhanov 1958 [1899], p. 46.

78   Plekhanov 1958 [1899], p. 47.

79   Biggart 1982, p. 89.

80   Bogdanov's references to Noiré are numerous and never less than complimentary, and large sections of some of the former's works are dedicated to an exposition of the ideas of the latter. For a general overview see Grille 1966, pp. 79–91. On the importance of Noiré's ideas for Bogdanov's organisational theory see White 1998.

precondition rather than as a metaphysical entity. Language and reason now form a 'monon' denoted by the Greek term, *logos* [λόγος], which have a common root in will, 'the root of actuality', and the ultimate dynamic principle, for it is a precondition of all experience.[81] In an 1880 book that was translated into Russian in 1925 and, as we shall see, widely received, Noiré stressed the instrumental character of the products of our actions and concluded that language, reason and labour all emerge together:

> Speech and labour are found ... in an inseparable connection, uninterrupted in any single moment of their interaction.
>
> The modifications of the outer world that labour achieves are born along with those sounds that accompany work, and in this way these sounds acquire a definite meaning. This is how the roots of language arose, those elements or primordial cells from which grew all the languages we know.[82]

Thus, 'thought is born with labour, the percept with the result of labour'.[83] It was not difficult to find some common ground between Noiré's ideas and Engels's unfinished 1876 work (published in 1895–6), 'The Part Played by Labour in the Transition from Ape to Man', in which there are some general comments about the way 'the development of labour necessarily helped to bring the members of society closer together by increasing cases of mutual support and joint activity, and by making clear the advantage of this joint activity to each individual. In short, men in the making arrived at the point where *they had something to say* to each other'. Engels concludes: 'first comes labour, after it, and then side by side with it, articulate speech'.[84] In his last major work, *Fundamental Problems of Marxism* (1908), Plekhanov had, on this basis, endorsed Noiré's theory of the origin of language as lying in 'joint activity directed toward the achievement of a common aim, it was the primordial labor of our ancestors that produced language and reasoning'.[85] However, Noiré's work contained a significant amount that was not even implicit in Engels's work, particularly a pervasive anti-realism which, while unpalatable to Plekhanov, was readily imbibed by Bogdanov.

---

81   Cloeren 1988, pp. 186–8. Further on the philosophical background of Noiré's ideas see the discussion by his friend F. Max Müller 1878.

82   Nuare 1925 [1880], p. 41.

83   Ibid.

84   Engels 1940a [1876], pp. 282–5.

85   Plekhanov 1969 [1908], p. 57. It should be noted that Plekhanov's engagement with Noiré is quite cursory.

From here, Bogdanov followed Noiré and Max Müller to argue that all the elaborated forms of language and thought derived from the accretion and synthesis of primordial semantic elements. Bogdanov was, however, less interested in the identification of families of languages than in the way in which the proliferation and combination of 'word-ideas', or 'crystals of labour', organise labour and experience.[86] Collective activity gives rise to the first elements of language (the historical primacy of verbs) and things acquire their names from being passive objects of that activity. Qualities and properties follow as the need for more precision is conditioned by the increasing sophistication of production. What Bogdanov calls the 'primordial dialectic' of the world of actions and the world of things becomes systematised into a notion of causality. Specialised mental labourers or organisers arise as the productive process becomes more sophisticated, concentrating the experience of labour. This requires language and ideology to become more systematised in order for the organisers to communicate complex information, and their authority allows them to organise others to implement actions and to divide the fruits of those actions. Thus arises a systematically authoritarian form of cooperation, and since, for Bogdanov, social being and social consciousness are identical, there is a corresponding generalisation of authoritarian causality. As the organisers become more differentiated from the implementers [ispolniteli], language and ideology become more differentiated from the process of production as a world view [mirovozzrenie]. Bogdanov models fetishism on Max Müller's notion of the 'fundamental metaphor which makes us conceive and speak of ... objects as if they were subjects like ourselves':[87]

> We can see that, in this phase, 'causality' is fully fetishistic, the relationship between things is presented as the relationship between people. It is precisely this authoritarian fetishism that is usually called 'natural fetishism'. It is already born in the fundamental metaphor in which the movement [deistvie] of things is thought in symbols pertaining to the activity of people.[88]

Thus, where an identifiable agent was absent, it was assumed that a human-like agent must be present. This 'authoritarian fetishism', according to which

---

86   The narrative that forms the remainder of this paragraph appears in a number of Bogdanov's works, but may be found in a concise form in Bogdanov and Skvortsov-Stepanov 2011 [1925], pp. 52–60.

87   Müller 1887 pp. 327 ff.

88   Bogdanov and Skvortsov-Stepanov 2011 [1925], p. 56.

the relationship between people is transferred to that between things, was the origin of religion, the first form of which was a 'cult of ancestor-organisers'.[89]

Müller saw mythology arising from a use of language in which a word is used metaphorically but the stages of transfer from the original to a metaphorical meaning have been forgotten. This 'disease of language' was a developmental stage through which humanity must pass on the way to scientific thought, but it was particularly characteristic of Indo-European languages, in which the roots of words were obscured by the accretion of prefixes, suffixes and derivatives.[90] Bogdanov follows the same path, but rather than focusing on a family of languages, he presents the relations of production as a precondition of a conceptual schema. Take the notion of the soul [*dusha*], for instance:

> It is often used in the sense of 'organiser' or 'organising origin', for instance some person is the 'soul' of some action or society, i.e. active organiser of the flow of work or the life of organisation; 'love is the soul of Christianity', i.e. its organising origin etc. From this it is clear that the 'soul' is opposed to the body as its organiser or organising origin, i.e. that here there is a simple transfer to a person or other objects of the notion of a definite form of collaboration, that divides the organiser and the implementer, or the authoritarian labour bond.[91]

Such a critique of language was, for Bogdanov, as for Müller and Noiré before him, an important aspect of the demystification of forms of social consciousness.

Bogdanov developed a fairly detailed narrative of the development of forms of social consciousness, which he elaborated in a number of his works, and on one occasion in a popular course taking the form of questions and answers.[92] He argued that it was in the feudal era that authoritarian causality achieved its zenith, and that speech achieved full breadth and flexibility. At the same time, families of languages achieved their characteristic forms and a complex mythology and epic literature encapsulated popular knowledge.[93] As techniques of production developed, however, burgeoning exchange began to dominate production, with the result that 'ancestor-organisers' (the church)

89   Bogdanov and Skvortsov-Stepanov 2011 [1925], p. 58.
90   See especially Müller 1885. For discussions on this see, *inter alia*, Olender 1992, pp. 82–92 and Cloeren 1988, pp. 163–79.
91   Bogdanov 1989 [1922], p. 47.
92   Bogdanov 1914.
93   Bogdanov and Skvortsov-Stepanov 2011 [1925], p. 147.

became separated from production. The new class of organisers was the bourgeoisie, under whose influence a new form of fetishised 'abstract causality' began to take hold. The organisers of production were no longer based on descendents from ancestors whose authority was based on tradition, but a new class of organisers who pursue their own interests in competition with others subject to the abstract force of the market. In the eyes of the individual in bourgeois society, exchange value systematically overshadows the real source of value in collective labour. Abstract economic necessity consequently becomes the dominant causal paradigm. The 'fundamental metaphor', according to which the social relationship between people was transferred to that between things, now took the form of commodity fetishism [*menovoi fetishism*] with the stages of the transfer of the metaphor obscured. Thus, while the form of fetishism had changed, the basic characteristic remained the same. Where in the religious myth man was subject to the will of deities, so in the bourgeois myth commodities entered into relations with one another on the market. As John Marot points out, Bogdanov, unlike Marx, did not acknowledge a fundamental difference between deities which owed their existence to humans and commodities which, although produced by human labour, were nevertheless required to maintain the existence of humans themselves.[94] For Bogdanov, the granting of a semblance of objectivity to the commodity was itself a clear manifestation of fetishism.

Where Müller saw the science of language as crucial in treating the 'disease of language' by revealing the stages of metaphorical transfer, Bogdanov argued that what was required was a universal organisational science, which he called tectology. Language constituted a kind of tectological instrument, and it was the task of tectology to build upon this a second-order body of language to further systematise organisational experience.[95] Along with this, it was necessary to develop a culture which distilled and systematised the unique perception of the industrial working class in the productive process. Together these would hold the key to bringing about the 'fall of the great fetishism', but only if they were instilled in the consciousness of the masses. By virtue of its position in production, industrial workers could perceive directly that behind the fetishised appearance of the market lay socialised, cooperative labour, and that this was expressed not in individual competition but in conscious and comradely cooperation. However, while the bourgeoisie monopolised schools, universities and media beyond the factory gates, the class experience of the proletariat could not be totalised but remained fragmentary. A totalised, supra-disciplinary, Party-run educational programme would thus be needed.

---

94   Marot 1991, pp. 267–9.

95   See Susiluoto 1982, pp. 49–51.

Meanwhile, proletarian writers and artists would transform the general ideological sphere by infusing it with its own labour world view. In this way, the proletariat could challenge the hegemony of bourgeois ideology and bring about the transformation of the whole social edifice. It was to this end that, one week before the October Revolution, *Proletarskie kul'turno-prosvetitel'nye organizatsii* [*Proletarian Cultural and Enlightenment Organisations*], otherwise known as *Proletkul't*, came into being.

Conclusion

The different trends in thought about hegemony that have been discussed in this chapter pertain to two very different understandings of the place of the proletariat in history. For Lenin, Trotsky and others developing what I have called the notion of political hegemony, the crucial factor is the place the proletariat occupies in the structure of society, which gives it the capacity to lead a revolutionary movement against the autocracy. The collective nature of the productive process, the concentration of the workers in factories and the specific interests they share by virtue of their relationship to the means of production allow for the development of a class that can become conscious of its own interests and develop an awareness of its historical capacities to transform society. As Arkadi Kremer and Julius Martov put it in a remarkable pamphlet of 1896, '[i]t is only when the aspirations of the proletariat collide head on with current political forms, only when the torrent of the workers' movement meets political force, that the moment of transition in the class struggle to the phase of consciously political struggle occurs'.[96] The proletariat *an sich* thus has the capacity to become a class *für sich* and it is the responsibility of the Party to facilitate this transformation through political interventions, especially through, as we will see, a dialectic of agitation and propaganda. This illuminates the relationship between economic interests and political interests, between class-based organisation and the pursuit of political democracy.

After the toppling of the autocracy in February 1917, there was a fundamental reconsideration of the hegemonic relationship that had been necessary for the achievement of political democracy. Where almost all Marxists had expected the bourgeois-democratic stage of the revolution to be relatively protracted, the objective circumstances brought about by the war undermined any realistic prospect of this. When Lenin returned to Russia and stunned the Bolshevik leadership with his April Theses advocating 'all power to the soviets' the strategy of hegemony had converged with the logic of Trotsky's theory of

---

96   Kremer and Martov 1986 [1896], p. 194.

permanent revolution.[97] However, while Russia might be the 'weakest link in the capitalist chain', it was not realistic to expect the entire proletariat of Europe to move in unison.[98] As working-class militancy rose throughout 1917, the threat of a reactionary coup materialised and a seizure of power by Bolshevik-led soviets became a realistic prospect, it became increasingly apparent that decisive action was needed. The Russian proletariat could only pursue its interests beyond the bourgeois-democratic stage in alliance with the numerically preponderant peasantry and the oppressed nationalities of the Empire. Political hegemony now meant that the Bolsheviks, as the political leadership of the proletariat, would need to play a leading role in a revolutionary government that involved representatives of the poor peasantry (the Left Socialist Revolutionaries, SRs). This governmental arrangement would be the expression of a more fundamental class alliance, what was to be called the *smychka*. It was this that could make of the bourgeois and socialist revolutions a single process which culminates in, and is ultimately dependent on, carrying the revolutionary conflagration into Europe.

There is nothing in this model that suggests that shared class experience of the productive process itself fosters a proletarian mentality that makes the class uniquely placed to lead the society in a progressive direction. In other words, there is no suggestion that a shared factory culture is the embryo of a potentially hegemonic culture that can consolidate the movement towards a socialist society. This is, however, the crux of the *Vperedist* conception of cultural hegemony. One could draw a link from this conception through to the cultural conception of class in the work of E.P. Thompson and then to 1970s Cultural Studies, led by figures such as Stuart Hall. One might also find a link to Pierre Bourdieu's idea of the working class habitus as a set of material dispositions that arise from the workers' class experience. These have all been legitimate research programmes that have yielded some valuable and many interesting results. However, this has been consistently mixed up with the political conception discussed above, which ultimately contributed to the degeneration of the conception of hegemony and the impression that the nature of the proletariat as a potentially hegemonic class in the political arena is based on its shared cultural experience. As we shall see, this process began immediately after October 1917.

---

97   Lih 2011a argues that the April Theses did not constitute the dramatic break with the strategy of hegemony that is often claimed.

98   James White 2001, pp. 120–1, has, however, claimed that the 'weakest link' conception originated with Bukharin and was not actually shared by Lenin.

CHAPTER 2

Orientology, Philology and the Politics of Empire: Traditional Intellectuals in Late Imperial Russia[1]

The relationship of Russia to its colonies and, by extension, Russians to the other peoples of the Empire, was a significant concern for liberal intellectuals and could not but colour their reflections on language and culture. We have seen that the liberal project involved an aspiration for a united, multinational empire that would be renewed through democratic reform and long-term national cultural development, but this never crystallised into a coherent party programme. The problematic of hegemony, if not the term itself, was raised continually as reform-minded intellectuals ruminated on the increasingly restive relationship between the imperial state and its colonies. Such scholars often made important attempts to influence imperial policy through research and sometimes more directly, by intervening in political debate. As they focused on the relationship between the official language and dialectal forms within Russian-speaking areas, or between Russian and the myriad other languages spoken by the peoples of the Empire, philologists could not but raise issues central to the linguistic and cultural dimensions of hegemony. The extremely significant and subtle research that emerged consistently problematised the relationship between standard and non-standard forms, as well as the way in which relations of authority and intellectual subordination were exercised, without these analyses ever quite achieving a fully elaborated form. This resulted from an intellectual field sandwiched between positivism and psychologism, which ultimately rendered these traditional intellectuals unable to grasp the specificity of the social, ensuring that it tended to be assimilated either to the realm of natural laws or to the realm of psychology.

Oriental Studies and Empire

One particularly clear example was the new school of orientology that emerged at St. Petersburg University in the 1890s under the leadership of Baron

---

1 I use the term 'traditional intellectual' in the Gramscian sense of a professional intellectual not having arisen from a popular movement and in contradistinction to the idea of the 'organic intellectual'.

Viktor Rozen, which included such notable figures as the Indiologist, Sergei Ol'denburg, the historian of Central Asia, Vasilii Bartol'd, and the philologist and archaeologist, Nikolai Marr.[2] As Vera Tolz has shown in an important recent study, Rozen reoriented Oriental studies towards 'Russia's own orient' and presented Russia not as the property of one ethnicity, but as a space of communication for all peoples of the Empire, whether from the west or east.[3] This was part of a general reorientation within the humanities at St. Petersburg University, in which specialists in European and Asian languages and cultures converged and centred their scholarship on the territory of the Russian Empire. They viewed the space occupied by the Empire not as, in the words of the German linguist, August Friedrich Pott, a '*Völkerbrücke aus Asien nach Europa*', that is, a bridge of peoples from Asia to Europe,[4] but as an arena for the inter- action of national cultures including, but not limited to, the Indo-European or 'Indo-Aryan' family. Representative of the impressive range of scholars who may be included are one of the founders of comparative literature, Aleksandr Veselovskii, the linguists, Jan Baudouin de Courtenay and Aleksei Shakhmatov, and the historian of art, Nikodim Kondakov. The scholars who will be dis- cussed in this chapter were often in close contact with each other. Veselovskii, Baudouin and Marr attended meetings of the Neo-Philological Society at St. Petersburg University from 1885.[5] Veselovskii maintained regular correspon- dence with a number of Orientalists, including Rozen, Marr and Ol'denburg.[6]

Drawing on the recent innovations of German orientology, Rozen's new approach questioned the simple hierarchical dichotomies of the rational West, Russia and Orthodox Christianity versus irrational Asia and the non-Christian East. Orientalism was becoming professionalised and, in so doing, it defined itself in opposition to the dilettantism of missionaries. As Mark Batunsky has argued, Rozen generated a new research agenda, organised concrete pro- grammes, facilitated a critique of existing approaches, brought expert knowl- edge to bear on all stages of research, inaugurated effective communication of new knowledge among researchers and brought about the practical realisation

---

2 On Rozen, see, *inter alia*, Krachkovskii 1947; Batunskii 2003, pp. 7–60. See also the collection of articles by his students, Rozen 1897. I will limit my discussion of Marr here and take up the main aspects of his work in a later chapter.

3 Tolz 2011.

4 Quoted in Benes 1984, p. 117.

5 Anon. 1914; PFA ARAN R-IV/24/4. The Neo-Philological Society began as the Romano- Germanic section of the Neo-Philological Society at the imperial St. Petersburg University. For a short history of the Society's activity, see Petrov 1910.

6 Kulikova 2001, pp. 142–59. For more on Marr and Veselovskii, see Shishmarev 1937.

of projects.[7] In place of the previously assumed chaos and arbitrariness in the Moslem world, as opposed to the order of Christian Europe, the new orientology applied formal explanatory schemes, which revealed the interconnections between different elements, brought order to constantly changing problems and formulated scientific (as opposed to unscientific) and rigorous (as opposed to non-rigorous) scholarly criteria of value.[8] Thus one of Rozen's 'disciples', the most significant pre-revolutionary historian of Central Asia, Vasilii Bartol'd, argued that all pursuit of genuine knowledge requires '1) the recognition of causal laws and the establishment of causal connections between separate facts; 2) the systematic exposition of facts on the basis of the causal relations between the facts that have been revealed; 3) the establishment of objective criteria for ascertaining the reliability of facts that have entered the system'.[9] For Bartol'd, Auguste Comte's attempts to establish universal laws of social development were hampered by the fact that the majority of facts gathered by historians, on which 'sociology' was reliant, were based on European societies, which constitute but a small minority of the societies which enter into 'world-historical intercourse'. The relative vacuum was filled by a speculative philosophy of history that gave rise to an unscientific notion of 'progress' and a series of stereotypes.[10] While 'progress' became an established characteristic of the West, 'stagnation' became a perceived characteristic of the 'East' among educated Europeans.[11] In place of this, historical research needs to be underlain by a more neutral 'law of "evolution", i.e. the gradual and consequential change in all the conditions of life of human societies'.[12] However neutral such laws might be, Bartol'd did not doubt the direction of the process: 'the gradual convergence of an ever greater number of separate societies'.[13]

Bartol'd's evolutionism was based on a positivist universalism that was quite in line with that of figures like Edward Tylor, Herbert Spencer, Andrew Lang and others, all of whom rejected the racial exclusivity of social development and posited universal laws. Bartol'd complained that most historians of the East had presented the cultures of each nation as a 'self-contained process' defined by racial origin. However, recent German historians, specifically the Assyriologist

---

7   Batunskii 2003, p. 20.

8   Batunskii 2003, p. 180. It is worth noting here that a penchant for such historical schemas stayed with Marr throughout his career. On this, see Khudiakov 1935.

9   Bartol'd 1977a [1911], p. 207.

10   Bartol'd 1977a [1911], pp. 220–2.

11   Bartol'd 1966b [1903], p. 303.

12   Bartol'd 1977a [1911], p. 222.

13   Bartol'd 1977a [1911], p. 208.

Hugo Winckler, had shown that 'the history of the ancient East, just as much as that of Europe, was determined by the influence of one nation on another and the distribution of the culture of one or several advanced nations over an ever wider geographical region'.[14] Bartol'd's explicit opposition to what we would now call Eurocentrism allowed him to present his approach as free of ideology and thereby rigorously scientific. The approach was in reality, however, deeply ideological, for Bartol'd's valorisation of 'cultural exchange', 'mutual influence' and so on served to provide scholarly justification for imperial expansion. The ethnographic particularities of a nation were held to be secondary in importance to the consolidation of access to trade routes which, in turn, provide the means for the transfer of a more advanced culture from one society to another. The Russian Empire's military expansion into Turkestan was justified thus:

> The measures taken by specific governments to close down and open up markets, including the aggressive campaigns, were merely unconscious steps on the road to the establishment of the ever more apparent historical mission of Russia – to be the intermediary in the overland trade and cultural intercourse between Europe and Asia.[15]

The Mongol Empire could also be rehabilitated for, again unconsciously, laying earlier foundations for this historic mission. Despite the 'elemental savagery' of the Mongols and their 'lack of understanding of culture', they created 'better conditions for international intercourse' and greater 'political stability'.[16] As Batunskii notes, under the idea of the progress of some universal culture, Bartol'd posed a 'generalised invariant formula of those material and spiritual advantages' that would accrue to all socio-cultural localities by being incorporated into a 'large-scale centralised statehood'. This culture is a 'normative value structure that appears sooner or later due to the compulsion to participate' in the forward movement of human history.[17] The sooner those with a 'lower' culture are assimilated into a state with a 'higher' culture, the better placed they will be actively to participate in the universal process of cultural exchange. It is quite logical that such an approach precluded the right of self-determination up to and including secession, and once separatist tendencies

14   Bartol'd 1977a [1911], pp. 233–4.
15   Bartol'd 1963b [1927], p. 432.
16   Bartol'd 1964 [1918], p. 28.
17   Batunskii 2003, pp. 142–3.

were identified in Ukrainian nationalism during World War I, the Orientalists became much more critical of them.[18]

Rozen's orientalist 'disciples' viewed the new orientology as providing a knowledge base that could engender reform of what they saw as the state's unenlightened policy towards the non-Russian nationalities of the Empire. As Heinz-Dietrich Lowe has argued, from the time of Catherine the Great, Russian policy towards non-Russian minorities was 'geared towards eliminating any historical, political and social structures which had developed independently from those of the Great Russians and which were different from them, and to replace them with the general structures of the Empire'.[19] This, the Orientalists argued, was not only oppressive, but ultimately counterproductive, since it only exacerbated separatist feelings among minorities. Instead, they argued for a liberal policy in which the imperial state would achieve hegemony by promoting the national cultures of the various people of the Empire. As Tolz puts it:

> [T]he concept was based on the assumption that to promote a sense of regional loyalty to the entire state-framed community, one should first develop a thorough knowledge of and love for the history and cultural tradition of one's place of birth and permanent residence. Russia was so large that it was impossible to know it all well and to love it as a whole, equally, in abstract terms. There was no conflict between a strong local identity and an overarching pan-Russian one. Instead people would achieve a complementary fusion of the two identities.[20]

The Orientalists thus envisioned a multi-cultural and multi-lingual state in which living cultural diversity would be promoted and celebrated and the interaction of various groups would be studied along with their archaeological remains. In practical terms, the activity of the Orientalists was undoubtedly progressive. Even where a sense of national identity was weak, they argued that one should be actively promoted through museums, national theatres, the codification of national languages and education. Such promotion of national languages and cultures would contribute to a pan-Russian identity based on normative civic values [*grazhdanstvennost'*].

The Orientalists worked tirelessly to undermine the stereotypes of the history of the Moslem regions of the Russian Empire, countering the distortions

---

18   Tolz 2011, p. 43.

19   Lowe 1992.

20   Tolz 2011, p. 37.

of missionary discourses and imperial propaganda aimed at presenting the regimes that preceded imperial expansion in as poor a light as possible. The Eurocentric myth which, in the words of Ol'denburg in 1915, presented 'material culture' and 'culture in general' as synonymous, led to the assumption that 'where there were no visible features of the former... there are only savages or people who have lost their culture'. The East came to be seen as 'a strange, fairytale wonderland, alien, wild and strange', which only the 'scientific movement of the 19th Century' was able to erode by showing that the East is 'one of the necessary links of world, all-human culture'.[21] However, the legacy of this scholarship was ambiguous since, as Bartol'd noted in his speech before the defence of his dissertation in 1900, Russian scholarship was an index of its higher position in the cultural hierarchy: 'the peoples of the east will believe in the superiority of our culture all the more when they are convinced we know them better than they know themselves. In this way, Russian Orientalists could contribute to the 'peaceful convergence of the peoples of the east with Russia'.[22] The state must therefore recognise its historic duty: 'The duty of a great country is to carry its population forwards and not backwards, regardless of their nationality; but a thorough study of the culture of the past and the careful preservation of the monuments of the culture remains one of the fundamental features of a civilised state'.[23]

The Limitations of Liberalism

While there were certainly differences of opinion among the Rozen-school Orientalists, their ideas about empire tended to coalesce around a liberal-imperial perspective. Ol'denburg was actually one of the founders of the liberal Constitutional Democratic (Cadet) Party while, according to Tolz, the other Rozenites were also close to the Cadets.[24] Ultimately, the belief that Oriental scholarship could lead the government to adopt a more enlightened nationality policy was chimerical. The economic and military power of Russia, along with its institutions of scholarship, which in many respects equalled those of European powers, had been the achievements of serfdom and autocracy under pressure of military competition from more advanced imperial states.

---

21   Ol'denburg 1915, p. 2. Anikeev 1969, pp. 38–40, traces the opposition to Eurocentrism among Russian scholars back to the 'civic critics' Belinskii and Chernyshevskii.

22   Bartol'd 1963a [1900], p. 610.

23   Bartol'd 1977b [1914], p. 533.

24   Tolz 2011, p. 44.

Despotic central authority was a constitutive feature of the Empire and could not simply be replaced by the rational state administration envisaged by the liberals. The reforms that were being adopted at the beginning of the twentieth century in no way altered the position of the Russian state *vis-à-vis* other imperial powers or the relatively disadvantageous position of the Russian economy within the emerging international order. The hegemonic project envisaged by the Orientalists thus had no institutional foundations, and appeals to some transcendental process of historical evolution could not compensate for that absence.

It is difficult not to agree with Batunskii when he argues that 'by perpetually stressing the equalising function of trans-ethnic, trans-racial and trans-religious processes like "international cultural exchange", "international cultural interaction", "common human ideals" etc.', they became 'a world view-axiological filter' that did not permit any 'radical conceptual restructuring'.[25] Research into Islam (and we could add other objects of study) became oriented toward 'a monotonously cumulative, continuous development' accompanied by the 'standardisation . . . of conceptual systems'.[26] While a belief in a preset direction of linear development, abstract common ideals and the presumption of the general virtues of empire dominated analysis, they allowed little understanding of the socioeconomic realities underlying the particularities of the Russian Empire as such. The liberals were attempting to graft what they understood to be a bourgeois democratic political structure onto a system of socioeconomic relations that were fundamentally different from those that could sustain such a structure. While there had certainly been times during which liberalism had progressed, as during the reign of Alexander II and immediately after the 1905 Revolution, such movements ran aground in the face of the intractability of institutional interests and international pressures. The development of 'normal' bourgeois economic relations was stifled by the close ties the largest capitalists had with the central bureaucracy, which was its main customer, while the looming threat of the working class inclined even the most reform-minded of the commercial bourgeoisie to seek the protection of the state. As Kagarlitsky puts it, '[t]he petty and middle bourgeoisie, living on their sales to the domestic market, were weak, provincial and ill-educated, while the upper bourgeoisie were dependent on foreign capital and were "tied hand and foot to the landowners" '.[27] Money generated from semi-serf exploitation in the countryside was used to finance private industry, alienating the peasantry and

---

25   Batunskii 2003, p. 144.
26   Ibid.
27   Kagarlitsky 2008, pp. 240–1.

making the bourgeoisie ever more dependent on the very autocratic state that hampered the development of the capitalist economy and subjugated national minorities to the needs of the Empire. On the one hand, the bourgeoisie complained about the state, but could not consistently struggle against it, and was certainly unable to carry through the revolutionary transformation needed to free itself from the restrictions of the autocracy.

Ol'denburg in particular attempted to bring the new approach to nationality policy to practical realisation as a founding member of the Cadet Party and, very briefly, as a minister in the provisional government for five weeks in the summer of 1917. While the loosening of policy immediately after 1905, as well as the simultaneous appearance of movements for national self-consciousness among a number of national groups, gave the liberals some grounds for optimism that they would be able to reorient policy, such hopes were seriously deflated after 1907. The clearest example of the clash of liberal ideals and political realities came from outside the field of oriental studies. The linguist, Jan Baudouin de Courtenay, was also engaged in political organisation as a member of the Cadet Party when he worked at St. Petersburg University. Born in Poland, Baudouin was to return to Warsaw in 1918, where he was proposed as a candidate to be the first president of independent Poland. However, Baudouin was no Polish separatist and supported the Cadet policy of advocating autonomy within a democratised Empire. In a pamphlet of 1906 proposing a solution to the 'Polish question', Baudouin argued that while the language of the central government has to be that of the most numerous nationality, the use of other languages should not be prohibited: 'every citizen has the right to communicate with central state institutions in his own native language'. Education must also be available in the languages of the national minorities, for 'completely free choice of language' is the best means of ensuring a harmonious multi-national state'.[28] In 1913 he published another pamphlet, which he had written in 1906, about the relationship between nationality and the concept of territorial autonomy. Here he argued that nationality was not necessarily the best basis for delimiting autonomous regions, since the former is a matter of conscious commitment and one may belong to a number of nations within a single state. Instead, autonomous territories should be decided purely on the

---

28   Boduen de Kurtene 1906, pp. 12–16. Baudouin was to criticise the language policy of the Polish state after its reconstitution in 1918 for a policy towards minority languages that in some respects compared unfavourably with that of Tsarist Russia. Olmsted and Timm 1983, p. 434.

basis of landed, economic and political interests.[29] The state should be neutral towards religion, nationality and language and concern itself solely with common economic and political matters.[30] Such a stance was crucial if the Russian Empire was to survive, and repressive tsarist policies towards national minorities, he predicted, could only lead to the collapse of the Empire, and deservedly so.[31] The delay in publication had serious consequences, for with increasingly restive national minorities, the pamphlet was viewed as evidence of anti-state activity, and Baudouin spent several months of 1914 in prison.

Even when liberal scholars encountered Marx's works, they tended to assimilate the ideas into a unilinear narrative of social evolution. The so-called 'legal Marxists' (Petr Struve and others) were particularly quick to interpret Marx's works as showing the law-governed inevitability of the triumph of capitalism over the semi-feudal structures of the Russian state and countryside and the consequent inevitability of a bourgeois-democratic political system. The chimera of some pure form of capitalism with its associated bourgeois-democratic superstructure replaced an analysis of the variety of ways in which the capitalist mode of production could be historically configured.[32] These intellectuals were thus unable to appreciate the structured variety of capitalism and the way in which the internationalisation of the system led to the compromise formations between the autocratic state and capital typical of Eastern Europe and of Russia in particular. The idea that if the political structure of

---

29   Boduen de Kurtene 1913, pp. 20–4. Baudouin was here clearly following the *völker-psychologische* understanding of the nation, which Benes (Benes 2008, p. 247) characterises as 'a voluntary discursive community whose members inhabited a shared spiritual realm'. Benes continues, quoting Lazarus, 'only "a mass of people who regard themselves as a *Volk*" constituted a nation'; the nation existed ' "merely in the subjective view of [its] members". "The individual himself determines his nationality in a subjective manner" ... "he reckons himself part of a nation" '.

30   Boduen de Kurtene 1913, pp. 57–8.

31   Boduen de Kurtene 1913, pp. 84–6. Viktor Shklovskii recalls Baudouin repeating this claim in a public appearance in Easter 1914, while waiting for his imprisonment to begin. When in prison, he wrote to Shakhmatov that: '... here everything is the same as in the large prison called the contemporary state. The difference is only quantitative, and not qualitative. And most likely it is somewhat better in some respects: it is clear, in plain terms, without the hypocrisy'. Shklovskii 1966, p. 101.

32   For a particularly detailed methodological discussion of this question, see Banaji 2010, pp. 1–44. This problem persists up to the present time in postcolonial theory and in subaltern studies, where the socioeconomic formations of the contemporary 'East' are presented as apparent deviations from some putative norm of capitalist development, exemplified by twentieth-century liberal culture in European societies. On this, see Chibber 2013.

the Empire could remain in step with, and even promote, the formation of nationhood among its subject peoples then it would also remain in step with the laws of historical development was typical of a rather simplistic progressivism. Even if, as in the case of Bartol'd, Asia was incorporated into international processes, the progressivism remained no less ideological. Unsurprisingly, the 'Legal Marxists' soon abandoned Marxism of any kind for a general liberalism, but then found themselves in an increasingly painful position, quietly railing against bureaucratic intransigence and ineptitude in nationality policy but lacking any capacity to implement an alternative.

An alternative perspective was gestating, however, in which the multi-linear aspects of Marx's works would achieve fuller development. While in the 1848 *Communist Manifesto* Marx and Engels had presented an implicit narrative of social development that might be regarded as generally unilinear, this had changed considerably from the 1850s, especially in the *Grundrisse* and the French edition of *Capital*. While some of these texts were not available until the post-revolutionary period, a significant amount of relevant material was indeed available, not least *Capital*, the Preface to the 1882 Russian edition of the *Communist Manifesto* and the 1877 letter to the editor of the journal *Otechestvennye zapiski* (published 1882 and 1886 respectively), in which a multi-linear perspective was affirmed.[33] It was the Populists who drew a fully multi-linear conclusion from Marx's last works, arguing that Russia could proceed to socialism on the basis of the peasant commune. Among Russian Marxists there was a variety of positions. Plekhanov was particularly wedded to a unilinear perspective, while a certain multi-linear perspective was implicit in Lenin's polemics with him about the question of the nationalisation of land in *The Agrarian Programme of Social Democracy in the First Russian Revolution, 1905–7*.[34] An awareness of the variations in paths of social development was very clear in David Riazanov's 1903 commentary on 'The Draft Programme of "Iskra" and the Tasks of Russian Social Democrats', Parvus's comments in January 1905 on 'What was Achieved on the Ninth of July' and in some of the contemporary writings of Trotsky.[35] One can also see a serious attempt to grapple with these issues in Kautsky's 1906 writings on Russia.[36] It is, however, only in Trotsky's remarkable 1930 comments on 'the peculiarities of Russia's

---

33   Marx and Engels 1989 [1882]; Marx 1989 [1886].
34   Lenin 1972 [1907].
35   Ryazanov 2009 [1903]; Parvus 2009 [1905].
36   Kautsky 2009 [1906a]; Kautsky 2009 [1906b].

development' in his *History of the Russian Revolution* that this finds full expression in Russian Marxism.[37]

Late Imperial Philology

The example of Baudouin alerts us to some of the particularities of late imperial philology, especially amongst those of a generally liberal disposition. Just as the Orientalists had found the meta-narratives of Western-imperial Orientalism unacceptable, so philologists more generally found it difficult to accept the dominant framework of Indo-European linguistics in its entirety. Rather than joining the predominant trend among German philologists to combine reflections on linguistic and ethnic descent to view cultural origin as the source of national identity, many Russian philologists and Orientalists drew closer to the notion of a 'consensual conception of linguistic community' that Douglas Kibbee argues was predominant among French philologists after the Russian Revolution.[38] The research programme that developed among scholars in France throughout the nineteenth century was fundamentally affected by the idea that the 'language of the people is a common repository of the language, and the literary language is an artificial extension of that language'.[39] We will see that this perspective also permeated Russian linguistic scholarship in the 1920s, but it was already influential before this time. The most obvious bridge between the Orientalists and the philologists is Nikolai Marr, who combined work in both disciplines with an extremely critical approach to Indo-European philology. Due to Marr's central role in the development of the disciplines in the Soviet period, his paradoxical legacy will be dealt with later. Yet even if we bracket out Marr for now, we can see that late imperial philologists often had a somewhat sceptical attitude towards the dominant trends in Indo-European scholarship and maintained a particular sensitivity towards the social stratification of language. Although a student of Indo-European languages, Baudouin was a particularly trenchant critic of the class and Eurocentric biases of contemporary philology. 'Western European Scholars have no monopoly on scientific discoveries and generalisations', he declared in a 1901 article, 'On the Mixed Character of All Languages',[40] and three years later he celebrated the decline of the 'old aristocratic attitude which was inspired by admiration for the erudition

---

37   Trotsky 1967 [1932], 21–32.
38   Kibbee 1999, p. 114.
39   Ibid.
40   Baudouin de Courtenay 1972b [1901], p. 217.

of philology and which considered worthy of investigation only noble, literary languages conferred with divine or regal power' in the face of 'the ever growing democratisation of linguistic thought'.[41] The work of Steinthal was particularly singled out for praise in this regard, for such research undermined the idea that dead languages were the appropriate starting point for the study of language.[42] The 'overestimation of Sanskrit's importance *vis-à-vis* the study of less ancient languages; the overestimation of Latin and ancient Greek, of Gothic and Old Church Slavonic *vis-à-vis* the later representatives of the same linguistic family' was symptomatic of a general 'scorn for the surrounding world, for the *linguae vulgaris*'.[43] Such observations were remarkable for the time, but as with his thoughts on the national question, such insights were limited by an inability among philologists to link their findings to a developed social science. Instead, a positivist approach to economic and political formations was accompanied by a neo-Romantic and psychologistic approach to national cultures. These entered into complex and often fascinating combinations, but the irreducible structures of social interaction were never adequately accounted for. It was not without reason that the Moscow Linguistic Circle linguist, Mikhail Peterson, could write in 1927 that linguists had hitherto recognised the social nature of language mainly by accident.[44] But recognise it they had.

Sharp debates over the formation of the Russian national, 'literary' language from Church Slavonic, common parlance and foreign borrowings dominated much intellectual life from the mid-eighteenth to the mid-nineteenth centuries.[45] As linguistic science arose in nineteenth-century Russia, the social origin of the elements of the 'literary' language was at the forefront of scholars' attention, and this question was given a particular ideological sharpness in the articles of the 'civic critics' in the middle of the century. Thus, Vissarion Belinskii could write in the 1840s that each social estate possesses specific linguistic traits and that the spirit of disunity in Russia is such that, if one found oneself in the 'chance company' of various social groups, 'you might think you were present at the distribution of tongues'.[46] The Russian novel also focused attention on the stylistic and ideological variety of extra-literary language, linking this variety to that of particular social groups, with the writer's own

---

41   Baudouin de Courtenay 1972c [1904], p. 241; Smith 1998, pp. 28–9.

42   Ibid.

43   Baudouin de Courtenay 1972 [1889], p. 127.

44   Peterson 1927.

45   Desnitskaia 1981.

46   Belinsky 1963, p. 3.

ideological position often emerging in relation to those styles. With academic linguistic and literary studies still fused into a unitary discipline of philology, it was impossible for linguists not to be acutely aware of the social dimensions of language, but how systematically to account for relations between language and society was another matter. In the 1870s and 1880s, the main thrust of philological studies in Russian academic institutions was within ethnographic and cultural history, with linguistic research often arising as a by-product or 'auxiliary tool', while the first systematic course in sociology was taught at a Russian higher-education institute only after the 1905 Revolution, and even this was at the private Psycho-Neurological Institute in St. Petersburg.[47]

Linguists who came through the pre-Revolutionary university system generally encountered social theory only tangentially, through studies in law, philosophy, psychology or philology, and even those who studied abroad had to contend with the fact that social science was only then becoming established as a distinct discipline. However, it is also important to recognise that the discipline of linguistics itself was also only becoming firmly established at the time of the Russian Revolution. For instance, the young Nikolai Trubetskoi, who shared some of the same ideas as the Orientalists and would later write the influential and posthumously-published *Grundzüge der Phonologie* [*Principles of Phonology*],[48] still did not see linguistics as an autonomous discipline. Rather, as Matejka notes, for him it was:

> ... an auxiliary tool for dealing with non-Russian cultural material from the vast area of the Russian Empire, which at that time included Finno-Ugric languages in the West and North, Siberian languages in the East, and Caucasian languages in the South. The primary target of Trubetzkoy's interest was the spiritual link between Slavs and non-Slavs within the Russian Empire. An ardent patriot, he wanted to illuminate the Eurasian roots of Russian culture and to define his intellectual position vis-à-vis Europe on the one hand and Asia on the other. He was more a culturologist than a linguist in this endeavour, although knowledge of non-Indo-European languages was essential for his quest.[49]

---

47   Vucinich 1976, p. 157.
48   Trubetzkoy, 1969 [1939].
49   Matejka 1987, pp. 307–8. On the convergence of the ideas of the Orientalists and the Eurasians, see Tolz 2011, pp. 62–7.

A sharp distinction between philology and linguistics had been proposed by probably the most influential theorist of language of the mid- nineteenth century, August Schleicher, who presented the former as a historical discipline which treats language as a 'medium for investigating the thought and cultural life of a people' and the latter as a natural science based on the 'direct observation' of a phenomenon 'outside the realm of the free will of the individual'.[50] With the development of the neo-grammarian school, professorships in individual branches of the Indo-European language family soon sprang up throughout Europe, but it proved difficult to draw a sharp conceptual line between the disciplines in practice and they generally appeared to be complementary disciplines. As linguistics emerged from general philology in Russia, however, the status of linguistics as a natural science was coming into serious question.

Particularly important on the eve of the revolution were the Moscow School of Filipp Fortunatov and Aleksei Shakhmatov and the Kazan School of Baudouin de Courtenay (a former student of Schleicher) and Mikołaj Kruszewski. The Moscow School gradually morphed into the Moscow Linguistic Circle, while, following the early death of Kruszewski, Baudouin founded the St. Petersburg School. The younger generation of these groups will feature in subsequent sections of this book. The Moscow School strove to bring mathematical rigour to linguistics, with close attention paid to formal questions; however, in the latter part of his career, Shakhmatov became increasingly concerned with psychological and social factors and turned his attention to syntax. The younger generation of the Moscow School became ever more concerned with sociological factors through their folklore studies and dialectology, but it was not until after the revolution that the Moscow Linguistic Circle specifically incorporated aspects of social theory. The Kazan-Petersburg School anticipated many aspects of Saussure's structural linguistics and made many important advances in dialectology.[51] In each case, dialectological research continually raised the need for a fully sociological approach to the study of language, but despite significant advances towards accounting for

---

50   Koerner 1997, p. 170. As Koerner shows, the terminology becomes quite slippery at the
       end of the nineteenth century. Schleicher seems initially to have used the term *Glottik*
       to mean *Sprachwissenschaft*, or 'linguistic science' (a term later popularised by Max
       Müller). This was later picked up by Marr, who wrote of a 'unified Glottogonic process'.
       Sprachwissenschaft becomes rendered in Russian as *iazykoznanie*, with *lingvistika* emerg-
       ing in Russia in the twentieth century and tending to refer to post-Saussurean linguistics.
51   On the place of Baudouin in the formation of the discipline of linguistics see, *inter alia*,
       Sharadzenidze 1980 and Amsterdamska 1987.

the social dimensions of language, progress was hampered by the absence of an elaborated social theory. Academic work on language and other social phenomena tended to find itself somewhere on a continuum between positivism and psychologism, or eclectically combined aspects of the two.

Most Russian social theory was developed through the revolutionary movement, with neo-Kantian, positivist and Marxist trends making their way through the writings of populist and Marxist thinkers and achieving published status after 1905. While, as we have seen, this did often achieve a significant degree of sophistication, the main trends of linguistic study remained isolated institutionally and intellectually from the influence of systematic thinking about social structure. Even when a linguist consciously adhered to Marxism in socio-political matters, this did not necessarily have direct effects on linguistic ideas. Dmitri Kudriavskii, for instance, participated in the revolutionary movement and wrote Marxist pamphlets, but as the author of an introduction to linguistics (1912), there was little to reflect these concerns.[52] In place of social science it was psychology that tended to mediate between linguistic and social concerns and it was the achievements of German Romantic researchers in folklore and the works of philosophers like Johann Herder and Wilhelm von Humboldt that proved particularly influential. Humboldt's contention that 'there resides in every language a characteristic *world-view*', that 'every language contains the whole conceptual fabric and mode of presentation of a portion of mankind', was to prove particularly enduring and productive.[53] These ideas were systematised and developed into a form of collective, or cultural, psychology, *Völkerpsychologie* (in Russian, *psikhologiia narodov*, meaning the psychology of nations, or of peoples).

The version of *Völkerpsychologie* developed by Moritz Lazarus and Haymann Steinthal proved the most significant, but that of their successor, Wilhelm Wundt, was also widely received. Russian philologists were especially receptive to the central principle, that the common activity of individuals gives rise to objective cultural forms that in turn produce the individual psychological subjects who engage in common activity.[54] Accepting the *völkerpsychologische* notion that language is primarily a ' "psycho-physical activity", a "linguistic continuum" unfolding in time and space through the linguistic activity of the totality of individuals that make up society',[55] the prominent Russian philologist

---

52   Alpatov 2000a, p. 173. Kudriavskii's most famous work is Kudriavskii 1912. On Kudriavskii
      see, especially, Smirnov 1970.
53   Humboldt 1999 [1836], p. 60.
54   Lazarus 1851; Shteintal' and Latsarus 1851.
55   Amirova *et al.* 1975, p. 373.

Aleksandr Potebnia referred enthusiastically to Steinthal's 1858 book on the origin of language, in which the laws of both individual psychology and *Völkerpsychologie* are shown to govern the relationship between thought and language. The influence of this book was clear as early as 1862, in Potebnia's book *Thought and Language*.[56] Potebnia, and the person who would arguably become the other most important pre-revolutionary Russian philologist, Veselovskii, attended Steinthal's lectures in Berlin in 1862–3. A year later, a Russian translation of Steinthal and Lazarus (1860) appeared in the prominent journal *Philological Notes* [*Filologicheskie zapiski*].[57] Potebnia and Veselovskii went on to publish in the organ of the *Völkerpsychologie* movement, the *Journal for Völkerpsychologie and Linguistics* [*Zeitschrift für Völkerpsychologie und Sprachwissenschaft*],[58] and to apply the principles of the new discipline in their works.[59]

This trend still dominated linguistic thought at the turn of the century. For Shakhmatov, psychology studies the laws of individual thought, while syntax studies the norms of the verbal expression of thought; where psychology deals with individual thinking and generalises from observations of the spiritual life of individuals, syntax deals with the norms worked out in a particular medium that are obligatory for all speakers who want to be listened to and understood. The functioning of language in society is now determined by the interplay between psychological and linguistic laws, with the 'social' limited to the factors that are common to all individuals involved.[60] As Grigorii Vinokur noted, when Shakhmatov speaks about the language of a society, a people and the like, it is 'only as a combination of languages of individuals who engage in certain relations thanks to the unity of their common origin'.[61] This is a typical *völkerpsychologische* position. Like Potebnia before him, then, Shakhmatov insisted that the study of linguistic form is more than a technical support for psychology, but nevertheless accepted the idea that linguistic structures are, and should be studied as, the products of general psychological laws, the realm of *Völkerpsychologie*. Shakhmatov thus praised Wilhelm Wundt for revealing 'the psychological processes that gave rise to language and its further development', but reproached him for paying too little attention to the concrete history

---

56   Potebnia 1993 [1892].
57   Shteintal' and Lazarus 1864.
58   Toporkov 1997, pp. 338–9.
59   See, especially, Berezin 1976, pp. 9–39 and Zhirmunskii 1939.
60   Bezlepkin 2002, p. 125.
61   Vinokur 1925, p. 14.

of the languages of ' "cultured peoples" as found in their cultural monuments', and for basing his observations on the languages of 'primitive' peoples.[62]

The Kazan' (later Petersburg) School was even more closely integrated into the tradition of *Völkerpsychologie*. In a survey of linguistics written at the beginning of the twentieth century, Baudouin noted that there was a movement away from the philological approach to language and that linguistics was moving nearer to 'other sciences that are more closely related'.[63] Psychology was one of the most significant of these sciences, and Baudouin's pupil, Stanislaw Szober, noted immediately after his teacher's death that Steinthal had exerted a strong influence on Baudouin. Several other commentators have since commented upon Baudouin's debt to Steinthal. Amirova *et al.* convincingly argue that Baudouin adopted Steinthal's notion of language as a 'linguistic continuum' in opposition to Schleicher's notion of language as organism.[64] For Baudouin, as for Steinthal,[65] 'Language exists only in individual brains, only in souls, only in the psyche of individuals or individual persons who comprise a given language community'.[66] Sharadzenidze goes as far as to argue that Baudouin remained a follower of Steinthal to the end of his life, adopting his 'general linguistic conceptions together with Herbartian associative psychology and *Völkerpsychologie*'.[67] There is certainly evidence for this. Baudouin's 1903 encyclopedia article on linguistics argues that: 'The originally metaphysical character of this branch of science has receded more and more behind the psychological treatment of language (Steinthal, Lazarus, & others), which today receives more and more adherents and which will gradually, in agreement with the psychic basis of the human language, become the sole trend in linguistics'.[68]

Völkerpsychologie both stimulated and limited a sociological perspective on linguistic phenomena. On the positive side, it looked at language as a crucial and inseparable part of social life, specifically of culture, the *Volksgeist*. This *Volksgeist* is the 'law-governed behavior and development of inner activity' of a *Volk*, and this is itself but a variety of 'group spirit' [*Gestamtheitgeist*], or 'objective spirit' [*objektiver Geist*]. There may be such *Geister* of 'religious communities, of social estates, of scientific and artistic schools and

---

62   Quoted in Berezin 1976, p. 166.
63   Boduen de Kurtene 1963a [1904], p. 110.
64   Amirova *et al.* 1975, p. 373.
65   Shteinthal 1864, pp. 68–9.
66   Boduen de Kurtene 1963b [1904], p. 71.
67   Sharadzenidze 1980, p. 30.
68   Quoted in Koerner 1973, p. 145, n. 8.

others indeed'.[69] This approach clearly promised to facilitate the investigation of the principle of unity behind specific social dialects and, at the very least, raised the problem of the relationship between these dialects and the national language. On the negative side, however, this potential was undermined by the inability of theorists to investigate social interaction and a related inclination to view the *Geist* of the national group as a prototype for all the others.[70] Thus *Völkerpsychologie* involved a fundamental incapacity to distinguish between social communities based on some sort of constructed identity (whether as 'genetically continuous groups (races), historical socio-political groups (nations) or cultural groups (ethnic groups)') on the one hand, and 'analytic categories, statements about contradictions in an historical system' on the other.[71] Thus, the Marxist distinction between a class *in itself*, which belongs to the second category, could not, according to such a theoretical construction, be distinguished from the class *for itself*, which belongs to the first category.[72] This was particularly important, since the project of hegemony was a self-conscious attempt to construct a socio-political community on the basis of social categories identified in socio-political analysis.

Baudouin maintained a personal friendship and long-standing correspondence with Antoine Meillet, as well as with Saussure, and he occupied a position somewhere between *Völkerpsychologie* and the positions of his two French interlocutors: sociological and structural linguistics, respectively. His closeness to Meillet was visible in the significant amount of attention he paid to the social stratification of language according to regional, socioeconomic, religious and other factors.[73] On the one hand, he saw languages as stratified 'horizontally' according to national [*narodnye*], territorial and ethnographic features, marked by differences of pronunciation. On the other hand, languages were stratified 'vertically' according to education, profession and social class, with language used in different ways as expressions of varying world views.[74] Baudouin was here clearly adapting Humboldtian principles of language as world view to sociological investigation in a way that had not previously been attempted. Baudouin also argued that, looking at a given language over time,

69   Kalmar 1987, p. 675.

70   Danziger 1983, pp. 310–11.

71   Wallerstein 1991, pp. 78, 84.

72   Edward Andrew argues, however, that the main distinction in Marx's own work is that between a class against capital and a class for itself, and that the in/for itself distinction is a 'Leninist constriction of Marxist politics' (Andrew 1983, p. 584).

73   Leont'ev 1966, pp. 329–32.

74   Boduen de Kurtene 1963c [1908].

one can discern centripetal and centrifugal forces at work and social regulari-
ties in language change. Because he theorised language in this way, Baudouin
was the most significant pre-revolutionary sociological thinker on language;
nevertheless, like Shakhmatov's, his sociological reflections were always subordinated to psychology. As he notes toward the end of his 1904 article: 'Language
does not exist and change arbitrarily, according to some caprice, but according to permanent laws – not according to [neo-grammarian] "sound-laws", for
such laws do not and could not exist in language, but according to psychological and sociological laws, which is why we identify sociology with what is
known as the psychology of nations (*Völkerpsychologie*)'.[75] This preponderance
of *Völkerpsychologie* in Baudouin de Courtenay's thought led Meillet, a rather
more orthodox sociologist, to note in a letter to Baudouin: 'I am inclined to
reproach you for paying too much attention to the *psychological* side, to the
detriment of the *physiological* side and the *sociological* side, which, in my opinion, are at least as important'.[76]

Baudouin's psychologism did not, however, prevent him from making some
remarkable observations about the way in which a language is a phenomenon
that is socially and functionally stratified:

> One and the same tribal or national language can play the roles of a state,
> administrative, clerical, school, scholarly language etc. Everyday language
> is distinguished from 'noble' and elevated language, the popular language
> is distinguished from that of the 'educated class' and so on ... languages
> of certain artisans, professions (the language of actors, for instance) may
> arise, along with those of particular social classes, languages of women
> and of men, of different age groups.[77]

Moreover, Baudouin's immersion in *Völkerpsychologie* inclined him to conceive of the particularities of language in use as having an ideological significance: 'Human language, or speech, reflects various worldviews and moods of

---

75 Boduen de Kurtene 1963b [1904], p. 94. This notion of sociology as the child of
    Völkerpsychologie was also common in Germany at this time. Lazarus Schweiger won the
    1899 Moritz Lazarus Prize for a study of *Völkerpsychologie* and sociology, in which the for-
    mer was said to constitute an 'initial stage' of the latter. On this, and the debt of the early
    sociologist Georg Simmel to Steinthal and Lazarus, see Frisby 1984, p. 122.

76 Leont'ev 1966, p. 331.

77 Boduen de Kurtene 1963b [1904], p. 74. For an overview of Baudouin's sociolinguistic
    thought, see Olmsted and Timm 1983.

both individuals and whole groups of people'.[78] The problem was that while psychologism reigned, sociolinguistic phenomena could only be conceived of as manifestations of collective subjectivity rather than registering structures of social relations.

A.N. Veselovskii's History of Discursive Art

For our purposes, the other most significant philologist is undoubtedly Veselovskii, who combined positivist laws of development and reverence for facts with a *völkerpsychologische* commitment to linguistic and literary forms as the embodiment of the collective consciousness. Veselovskii was also perhaps the most important pre-revolutionary conduit for the ideas of British social anthropology in the humanities in Russia. His lasting influence derived from the way he employed the comparative method in the study of world literature with an unrivalled thoroughness and breadth, employing great erudition and subtlety. 'The history of literature, in the broad sense of the word', he argued, 'is the history of social thought' in 'image-poetic experience and expressed in its forms'.[79] By literature, Veselovskii here had in mind all forms of verbal art [*slovesnoe tvorchestvo*]. This history is, by definition, a universal history, since the 'literary process' is a universal process, but one that is built up through the history of relations between nations [*narodnosti*].[80] In a positivist vein, he aimed to study a series of literary facts, establish consecutive relations between those facts, deduce conformities to regular principles, consider whether such principles are causal and, through accumulated verifications, lead the 'generalisations formulated' to 'approach the exactitude of a law'.[81] Following Andrew Lang, Veselovskii viewed E.B. Tylor's 'doctrine of survivals' as the basis for a kind of evolutionary sequence of genres from mythology through folklore to developed literary formations.[82]

In this way, Veselovskii diverged from the Indo-Europeanists who limited the comparative method to the study of peoples whose common descent was

---

78 Boduen de Kurtene 1963b [1904], p. 79.

79 Veselovskii 2004a [1870], pp. 47, 52. See also Engel'gardt 1924, pp. 52–64; Zhirmunskii 1938; Zhirmunskii 1939; Eremina 2011.

80 Eremina 2011, part 1, pp. 17–18.

81 Veselovskii 2004a [1870], p. 47.

82 Stocking 1995, p. 52. See also Montenyohl 1988. Veselovskii was particularly influenced by the chapter on 'The Method of Folklore' in Lang 1904 [1884], pp. 10–28, and Lang 1899. On this see Zhirmunskii 1938, pp. 52–3.

suspected, to uncover common ancestors who spoke a proto-language and partook of a shared mythology. Instead, he adopted Lang's dictum that 'similar conditions of mind produce similar practices, apart from identity of race, or borrowing of ideas and manners'.[83] For Veselovskii, as for Lang, '[h]olding that myth is a product of the early human fancy, working on the most rudimentary knowledge of the outer world, the student of folklore thinks that differences of race do not much affect the early mythopoeic faculty'.[84] If Lang represented the most powerful and dogged opposition to the ethnically exclusive work of Indo-Europeanist philology in Britain, especially directed against the work of Max Müller, Veselovskii took that mantle in Russia, polemicising against the work of the so-called 'Mythological School' as a whole, including that of his teacher, Fedor Buslaev.[85]

To the work of the British anthropologists, Veselovskii added, *inter alia*, the idea that literary and linguistic forms arose together in ancient syncretism, which he defined as 'the combination of rhythmical, orchestrated movement with song-music and elements of the word'. Veselovskii developed this idea from German Romanticism and *Völkerpsychologie*, especially from the work of Ludwig Uhland, but he also drew upon ideas of communal living that he found in sources such as Lewis Morgan, the sociologist, Maksim Kovalevskii, and the Swiss Jurist and anthropologist, Johann Bachofen. Veselovskii drew selectively on Bücher to argue that the appearance of 'song-games' answered the need for the release of 'accumulated physical and psychical energy by means of rhythmically organised sounds and movements'.[86] This rhythmic organisation of choral singing arose in the play and dancing that embodied 'psychophysical catharsis'. At this time, the verbal element was incidental and almost without content, since emotional factors predominated. There followed a gradual disintegration of the choral mass, with the emergence of a soloist and the development of a dialogue between soloist and chorus. Thus arose poetry and, simultaneously, a more elaborate language, since the differentiation of social relations and material interests, which raised the importance of the

---

83   Lang 1904 [1884], p. 22.

84   Lang 1904 [1884], p. 23.

85   On Lang's debate with Müller, see Dorson 1955 and Montenyohl 1988. For Veselovskii's critique of the mythological school, including Müller, see Veselovskii 2004b [1897–1906], pp. 501–4. It was, however, Friedrich von Schlegel who had developed the theory of Indo-European roots into a full-blown ideology of cultural superiority. This was subsequently developed by figures like Renan and Müller. On this, see Krishnaswamy 2005, pp. 66–7.

86   Veselovskii 2004c [1899], p. 201.

content of words, demanded clearly defined word meanings and a sophisticated form of syntax.[87]

Veselovskii thus supported the 'theory of common psychological autogeny', according to which 'the unity of common conditions and psychological acts lead to a unity or convergence of symbolic expression'.[88] This, for Veselovskii, explains the convergence of narrative motifs (in tales), the identity of everyday forms and religious notions that are distanced from practical life but retained in the experiences of poetic schemes.[89] However, while such a theory explains the repetition of particular motifs, it cannot explain the repetition of its combinations. Such an approach does not, therefore, exclude the possibility of borrowing, but any such phenomena cannot be understood mechanically. The efforts of Theodor Benfey to trace the migration of narrative literature along four routes from the original Indo-European homeland [*Urheimat*] to India and Europe, or Julius and then Kaarle Krohn's efforts to trace Finnish folktales back to specific locations were viewed as replacing historical scholarship with hypotheses of a mechanical movement through space.[90]

It is in his discussion of borrowing that Veselovskii's work has significant implications for the project of hegemony, because he contended that what is borrowed by one culture from another is a form of social thinking, meaning that there must be a historical convergence of the thinking of the lending and borrowing cultures. The merging of trends of thought, of directions of thinking, of analogous images, presupposes some shared foundation in the forms of life of a given epoch that give rise to corresponding psychological processes.[91] Patterns of borrowing in literature cannot be traced simply by pointing out analogous motifs that may in actual fact be 'universal, an autogenous expression of common forms and notions that existed among all peoples at a certain stage of development'.[92] Rather, an investigation of borrowing must be based on *plots*, 'that is combinations of motifs, complex tales, with a chain of moments, the consistency of which cannot be accidental'.[93] Moreover, once a borrowed plot formation is introduced into a new milieu, its meaning is necessarily transformed as it is assimilated into the popular consciousness. In this

87   Veselovskii 2004c [1899], pp. 203–13. See also Engel'gardt 1924, pp. 130–53.

88   Veselovskii 2004b [1897–1906], p. 513.

89   Ibid.

90   On Veselovskii and Benfey, see Gorskii 1975, pp. 156–60. On the relationship of Veselovskii and his followers to Krohn, see Jason 1970.

91   See the discussion in Gorskii 1975, pp. 173–81.

92   Veselovskii 2004b [1897–1906], p. 504.

93   Ibid.

sense, it is no different from the stock of traditional plots and motifs that one generation inherits from another. The traditional material is difficult to transform, but is constantly enriched by the 'growth of social consciousness' that occurs along with changing conditions of life.[94] Thus, it makes little sense to speak about a one-way flow from East to West in language, myth, folklore and literature since, at each stage, there is an interaction between cultures and the formation of something new. Moreover, there is not simply a flow of written texts so much as constant interaction between written and oral forms of verbal art that is constitutive of literature as such. Where a written literary culture lends forms of plot to a predominantly oral culture, the original form does not survive unscathed but is transformed through its convergence with the social psychology embodied in pre-existing narrative forms.

One particularly interesting consequence of Veselovskii's method was a reconsideration of the period of *'dvoeverie'* ['dual belief'] at the beginning of the eleventh century, when Christianity was imposed on a pagan population. As Eremina explains, the received idea was of a primordial pagan belief structure surviving intact beneath a Christian veneer of names and rituals. For Veselovskii, however:

> Even if dual belief was originally a superficial combination of two different forms of thought, then at a certain stage it began to reverberate among ancient scribes, then after some time popular beliefs could not but experience a certain metamorphosis. Pagan and Christian elements had to undergo mutual influence and it seems that the ones that prevailed were, on the one hand, those that ran through the memory of the old paganism and undermined the source of its development and, on the other hand, broadened the influx of concepts, legends, beliefs and superstitions of the Christian store. Research into popular beliefs must certainly take account of the gradual increase of these Christian influences, and especially in their popular, 'semi-poetic', 'semi-superstition' forms.[95]

Here we see that the character of the collective belief that emerges from the imposition of a written culture of power onto an oral indigenous culture depended upon the ways in which the former provided an 'outer form', or semantic means for the 'inner' world view of the latter. Over time, the former was enriched by the latter, while gradually replacing the latter's original forms.

---

94   Gorskii 1975, pp. 175–6.

95   Eremina 2011, part 1, p. 44.

Structures of Social Thought and Relations Between Them

All of the thinkers discussed in this chapter contributed to an understanding of languages, literatures and religions as structures of social thought, with relations of mutual dependence between their constitutive elements that are in contact with other structures of social thought. The Orientalists viewed the Islam of Central Asia (Rozen, Barthol'd), as well as the Buddhism of the Russian Far East (Ol'denburg and Fedor Shcherbatskoi) and Japan (Otton Rozenberg), as structures of a living culture rather than a disorganised collection of elements that could only be illuminated by the light of European systems of thought.[96] The Orientalists thus spoke about the 'Muslim world', 'Muslim civilisation', the 'Muslim East' and so on as constituted by relations of mutual dependence which developed in a unified whole. The Ol'denburg-Shcherbatskoi school established the integral study of the problem of Buddhist culture, worked out new scholarly principles for the study and translation of original Buddhist texts and questioned the 'philological', literal translations that dominated scholarship at the time.[97] To achieve this, they began to utilise the oral Buddhist tradition, insisting that 'an understanding of the monuments of ancient Buddhist writings that are preserved in difficult, little-studied languages is for the most part impossible without reference to the oral tradition of Buddhist learning, and attempts to proceed in its absence can lead only to extremely limited results'.[98] In his book *The Problems of Buddhist Philosophy* (published in 1918), Rozenberg continued this orientation, presenting philosophy as an 'organic component of Buddhism', which could be identified only if the categories of the doctrine are examined 'from within'. This meant, first of all, an acquaintance with the works of contemporary Buddhists and an examination of the ' "philosophical" sutras'. It was crucial that boundaries between popular and scholastic forms of Buddhism be clearly defined, since failure to do so could only lead to confused interpretations.[99]

What we have here is an argument for a synchronic study of the religion, which identifies its structural and inner coherence in a manner that is

---

96   On Russian studies of Buddhism prior to the work of the new school, see Ermakova 1995, pp. 139–47. Shcherbatskoi published a work on Buddhist logic as early as 1904, and continued to work on this until the 1930s, especially at the short-lived Institute of Buddhist Culture in Leningrad (1927–30). In English, see Stcherbatsky 2008 [1930].

97   Khamaganova, 1998, p. 113. For a detailed overview of Russian Buddhology, see Ermakova 1998.

98   Cited in Khamaganova, 1998, p. 113.

99   Ignatovich 1991, pp. 6–17, 13.

analogous to Saussure's *langue* and which needs, methodologically, to be separated from the *parole* of popular belief. This synchronic analysis was also seen as fundamental for understanding how these cultures related to others in the process of the evolution of the putative universal culture of humanity – the centre of their concerns. We find a similar argument in Veselovskii, where 'enduring poetic formulae' are bequeathed from one generation to another, which are then enriched by the progress of social thought that occurs within these boundaries.[100]

Baudouin is internationally recognised as a pioneer in viewing language as an interrelated set of elements, a trend that was perhaps developed most fully by his colleague, the mathematically-trained Kruszewski. As early as 1870, Baudouin distinguished between language *'in potentia'* [*iazyk*] and language *'in actu'* [*rech'*] in the same way as Saussure was to distinguish between *langue* and *parole*, explicitly assigning the phoneme to *langue*. Baudouin and Kruszewski were soon presenting path-breaking work on the phoneme as a functional concept, with a firm focus on the relations between sound and meaning. However, following Kruszewski's early death, Baudouin abandoned this autonomous study of phonetics and sought a bridge between phonetics and psychology that he called 'psychophonetics'. The *völkerpsychologische* idea that language is a 'psycho-physical activity', an idea that underlies the perspective on language developed by the neo-grammarians, reasserted itself in his later works, and ' "individual psychic processes" are considered as the only reality of language, while its social aspect is branded a pure fiction, devoid of objective existence, or an artificial product'.[101]

While this move provoked criticism from structuralists and beyond, it should probably be viewed as an attempt to avoid, *avant la lettre*, the reification of *langue* that was to plague the structuralists in the years to come. He was also attempting to explain the social bases of language change in the absence of any adequate social theory. We have seen how Baudouin was acutely aware of the power-differentiated relations between linguistic structures within the Russian Empire, and this was undoubtedly reinforced by his extensive fieldwork into Slavonic dialects and minority languages in Italy and Austria-Hungary.[102] Baudouin continued to regard languages as structured wholes, but stressed that these structures are open and constantly interacting with each other. All languages, Baudouin held, are mixed, and the particularities of

---

100   Veselovskii 2004 [1870], p. 51. On this aspect of Veselovskii's work, see Byford 2005.
101   Jakobson 1971, p. 419. See also Amsterdamska 1987, pp. 258–9 and Loia 1929, pp. 131–214, pp. 133–8, Olmsted and Timm 1983, pp. 439–41.
102   See, for instance, Lenček 1977.

certain forms in languages could be traced to the influence of the substratum of the prior structure beneath the assimilated elements or structures, rather than to the mechanics of neo-grammarian sound laws.[103] Such matters are not, for Baudouin, merely technical changes of material and formal structuring, but involve changes in the collective-psychological or conceptual structure embodied by the language. Baudouin thus shared Graziado Ascoli's idea of linguistic substratum, according to which the convergence and ultimate fusion of two languages that find themselves in contact over a protracted period of time necessarily involves one being placed in a subordinate position.

Veselovskii's account of narratives as structures of social thought that arise in disparate forms, but merge as a result of contact between peoples and the convergence of their way of thinking, is also a theory of cultural substratum. The mode of assimilation of a borrowed element may vary, but in each case it has structural ramifications that require formal and ideological adjustments. The relationship between written literature and oral folklore is by nature unequal, but it always involves some degree of formal and ideological negotiation and restructuring. The inherited or acquired stock of narratives and motifs are again analogous to Saussure's 'langue', but, like Baudouin, who shared the same *völkerpsychologische* understanding of semantic material, there is an inseparable connection between inner and outer forms. Without social theory as such, Veselovskii's own various theoretical developments remained, as Zhirmunskii put it, working hypotheses to explain various historical phenomena, rather than being integrated into a fully developed theoretical perspective.[104]

Veselovskii represents an exemplary point at which the *völkerpsychologische* and evolutionary-positivist trends converge, along with general philology, ethnography and Oriental studies. The convergence mitigated some of the worst forms of ethnocentrism that plagued evolutionism in other imperial countries, along with the reifications of German idealism. Yet, as Zhirmunskii's judgement suggests, it was more a matter of negotiating the various dangers of each trend while adopting what was conducive to a particular analysis, rather than establishing a systematic approach to social phenomena. Lacking an appreciation of the *differentia specifica* of the social sciences, the thinkers we have considered in this chapter oscillated between attempts either to collapse the social into the natural sciences (the search for 'laws') or erect a Chinese wall between

103   Boduen de Kurtene 1963 [1901], pp. 362–72.
104   Zhirmunskii 1938, p. 57.

them (psychologism).[105] It was this that prevented these thinkers from advancing theories of hegemony, even if they were clearly groping in this direction.

While the philologists undoubtedly developed sophisticated models of the relations between structures of thought, neither Baudouin nor Veselovskii fully accounted for the role of socioeconomic relations or the resulting relations of power within their frameworks. Thus the constant inclination to reduce objective social structures to shared understandings of those structures and a consequent inability to theorise the relationship between them. Meanwhile, the historian, Bartol'd, correlated the exercise of socioeconomic power with socio-cultural progress as if it was governed by natural laws. All empirical tendencies in this area were considered only to the extent that they conformed to, and could be explained by, the operations of this law – hence the aforementioned justification of the Mongol invasion and Russian military aggression. Thus Bartol'd discussed, with great intelligence and insight, the economic and political determination of the rise and consolidation of the ideological opposition of East and West, which still structured British and French Orientalism.[106] Yet he clearly viewed his own critique of the opposition and attempts to undermine this stereotype as a conscious expression of the rise of the Russian Empire fulfilling its historical destiny.[107] The struggle against Eurocentric conceptions of the East was therefore the ideological accompaniment of the economic and military struggle of the Russian state to overcome its subordination in the international order. Inasmuch as this constituted a theory of hegemony, it remained within the traditional understanding of the term.[108] The national minorities of the Russian Empire were treated as collective subjects, or national psychologies, which needed to be reconciled to the socioeconomic subordination demanded of them by the laws of social evolution.

---

105   On this trend within positivism, see Bhaskar 1998, p. 126. Bhaskar finds this dichotomy to be based on 'a confusion of generalisation with abstraction and of empirical invariances with laws'.

106   See, especially, his preface to Bartol'd 1966a [1918], pp. 143–6, and Tolz 2011, *passim*.

107   This is clear in his speech before the defence of his dissertation quoted above, and elsewhere.

108   The only use of the term 'hegemony' I have been able to trace in Bartol'd's works is in his review of Léon Cahun's 1896 book, *Introduction à la historoire de l'Asie. Turcs et Mongols des origins à 1405*, Bartol'd 1968 [1896]. In this case, the term appears to be used only because Cahun uses the term in the traditional sense.

Verbal Art and Revolution: The Living Word

It is clear that the pursuit of proletarian hegemony was closely bound up with the pursuit of political freedom. However, the nature of that freedom was inevitably problematic, since the achievement of bourgeois representative democracy was not conceived as the ideal towards which revolutionaries were striving. Pre-revolutionary Marxists viewed bourgeois democracy as a stage on the way to a higher form of democracy that would only be possible by transcending capitalism. In a society still subject to autocratic rule, basic freedoms of expression and of assembly were important interim goals, and a constitutional regime was undoubtedly perceived as a significant step forward. In one of his polemics from 1911, Lenin argued that if one compares the political systems in Britain and France, on the one hand, and Prussia on the other, the former were undoubtedly more democratic than the latter and 'much more favourable for the struggle of the working class, and have to a much greater degree eliminated the medieval institutions which distract the attention of the working class from its principal and real adversary'.[1] This meant that the Party must support attempts to remodel the political system in Russia along the lines of the former, rather than the latter. However, the reason why the former developed more democratic systems than the latter was that, as the two former systems were being formed, the urban lower classes constituted a powerful pole of attraction for the peasantry and so were in a position to prevent the bourgeoisie making compromises in its struggle with absolutism. The political rights associated with bourgeois democracy were not, therefore, the result of the bourgeoisie achieving hegemony by articulating the interests of the 'subaltern classes' as part of a general struggle against feudalism, but were concessions to those classes in the face of their mass mobilisation. Where that mobilisation was weakest, so the political freedoms were more restricted. A general lesson could be drawn from this:

> Every capitalist country passes through an era of bourgeois revolutions which produces a definite degree of democracy, a definite constitutional or parliamentary regime, a definite degree of independence, love of liberty, and initiative among the 'lower classes' in general and the proletariat in particular, a definite tradition permeating the entire political and

---

1 Lenin 1974a [1911], p. 212.

social life of the country. The particular degree of democracy, or the particular tradition, depends on whether, in the decisive moments, the hegemony belongs to the bourgeoisie or to those at the other end of the scale; it depends on whether it is the former or the latter which (again in those decisive moments) constitutes the 'centre of attraction for the democratic peasantry' and, in general, for all intermediary democratic groups and sections.[2]

Thus, for Lenin, the European capitalist class embraced no 'universalising tendency' expressed in it striving for the liberalisation of politics and culture of the type supposed by legal Marxists or, indeed, by the proponents of 'subaltern studies' today. The portrait of the progressive bourgeoisie drawn in works such as Ranajit Guha's landmark 1997 book, *Dominance without Hegemony*, from which the post-colonial bourgeoisie allegedly diverged, bears a striking resemblance to that held by the Russian liberals.[3] As we have seen, capitalist support for Russian liberalism was very limited, and the entire project of proletarian hegemony had been forged precisely because the bourgeoisie was increasingly incapable of challenging European absolutisms in any fundamental sense. In all cases, political rights needed to be wrested from the bourgeoisie through mass struggle, which could only be successful through the achievement of proletarian hegemony over the peasantry.

In winning such hegemony, leadership was understood as a process by which the relationship between economic interests and political forms is to be revealed. This was the dialectic of agitation and propaganda first delineated by Plekhanov in *On the Tasks of Socialists in the Struggle with Hunger in Russia* (*Letters to young Comrades*) of 1892, but subsequently developed by Arkadi Kremer and Julius Martov in the 1896 pamphlet *On Agitation* [*ob agitatsii*], and by Lenin in *What is to be Done?* (1902).[4] For Plekhanov, the shift to agitation marks a revolutionary organisation's shift from a sect to a party.[5] The classic distinction Plekhanov draws between propaganda and agitation is that 'the propagandist conveys *many* ideas to one person or to a few people, whereas the agitator conveys *only one* or *only a few* ideas, but he conveys them to

---

2 Lenin 1974a [1911], p. 215.
3 Guha 1997, which developed an argument initially put forward in articles published in 1989 and 1992. A sustained and convincing critique of Guha's argument is offered in Chibber 2013, but without reference to how the issue had been discussed by Russian Marxists.
4 Plekhanov 1923 [1892]; Kremer and Martov 1983 [1896], pp. 192–205. For a discussion, see Cliff 1986, pp. 42–68, 79–98.
5 Plekhanov 1923 [1892], p. 396.

a whole mass of people, sometimes to almost the entire population of a particular locality'.[6] The task 'involves putting into circulation in each particular case the maximum possible number of revolutionary ideas that are accessible to the mass', which requires a careful assessment of the specific conditions of the intervention.[7] This means to give to the audience 'fully conscious expression to the mood that it already holds, which it is not itself aware of'.[8] The agitator must give 'object lessons' to illuminate the relationship between demands for political freedom and the 'irreconcilable contradiction' that exists between the workers' and poor peasants' economic interests on the one hand, and the interests of the capitalist, landowner and kulak on the other.[9]

Language was necessarily of interest to the Party from a *performative* perspective. What was significant was the place and employment of language in political life, whether written or spoken. To quote, in abridged form, Lenin's famous elaboration:

> [T]he propagandist ... must present 'many ideas', so many, indeed, that they will be understood as an integral whole only by a (comparatively) few persons. The agitator, however, speaking on the same subject, will take as an illustration a fact that is most glaring and most widely known to his audience ... will direct his efforts to presenting a *single idea* to the 'masses' ...; he will strive *to rouse* discontent and indignation among the masses against this crying injustice, leaving a more complete explanation of this contradiction to the propagandist. Consequently, the propagandist operates chiefly by means of the *printed* word; the agitator by means of the *spoken* word [*zhivoe slovo*].[10]

It is hardly surprising that we can find a significant amount of attention to the precise usage of terminology in Bolshevik propaganda and some general philosophical asides on the relationship between language and the extra-discursive world scattered throughout Lenin's pre-revolutionary works.

A historical analysis of these debates, which refuses to view the ideas through the distorting lens of later developments, shows that revolutionaries recognised that the transformation of political organisation from a small sect to a mass party required that attention be turned to what Aristotle had shown

---

6   Plekhanov 1923 [1892], p. 397.
7   Plekhanov 1923 [1892], p. 414.
8   Plekhanov 1923 [1892], p. 415.
9   Plekhanov 1923 [1892], p. 417.
10   Lenin 1961 [1902], pp. 409–10.

to be the interdependent triad of rhetoric: speaker, subject and audience, with the latter determining the end and object of speech. While reference to the classical tradition is absent from these political works, analysing agitation leads inexorably to the resurrection of the same questions as classical rhetoric.[11] Agitation and propaganda represent the poles between which an argument can be constructed, with *ethos* [establishing confidence in the speaker], *pathos* [arousing the feelings of the audience] and *pistis* [proof] appropriately balanced to establish the expediency or harmfulness of a proposed course of action.[12] It is important to stress the inclusion of evidence here, for Lenin and Plekhanov, like Aristotle, regard the example [*paradeigma*], articulated for reception by a specific community, to be the core of deliberative rhetoric. To determine the *prepon* [appropriateness] of a specific piece of evidence required the assessment of the specific sociological characteristics of an audience and an orientation on its values.[13] Agitation and propaganda were thus aspects of *symbouleutikon* [deliberative rhetoric] in specific circumstances: the strategic and tactical discursive intervention in free assemblies (such as trade-union meetings, campaign meetings, soviets, etc) where various perspectives competed to win leadership in specific (generally limited) struggles, highlighting the nature of that specific struggle as part of a wider socio-political struggle. This had profound implications for notions of democracy, because those being persuaded, whose minds the speaker had to engage, were to vote and take the decisions having listened to all sides and made up their minds.

Not only did the question of deliberative rhetoric lead to considerations of the classics, but the search for alternative models of democracy to the limited form compatible with bourgeois control of the economy necessarily invited comparison with Athenian *dēmokratia*. As Ellen Meiksins Wood reminds us, Aristotle defined *dēmokratia* as a constitution in which 'the free-born and poor control the government – being at the same time a majority' as distinct from an oligarchy, in which 'the rich and better-born control the government – being at the same time a minority'.[14] Paul Cartledge notes that the very term

---

11   Karl Bühler, whose work was extremely influential in Russia in the 1920s, argued the same point with reference to 'the analysis of representational language'. See Bühler 1990, p. 65.

12   For excellent discussions, see Vickers 1988.

13   Compare Aristotle's discussion of the need to assess the audience in Aristotle 1991, pp. 235–7, and the discussion in Vickers 1988, pp. 296–7. This aspect of revolutionary strategy is missed by some important commentators on the period, who fail to see the significance of the division between agitation and propaganda. See, for instance, Kenez 1985, p. 8, where the distinction is completely effaced.

14   Wood 1996, p. 126.

dēmokratia may have been coined by its opponents and that 'by its very ety-mology (*dēmos* in the sense of the poor masses, *kratos* in the sense of a forcible grip on the disempowered wealthy few) *dēmokratia* could be construed nega-tively to mean something approaching the "dictatorship of the proletariat" '.[15] While those involved in formulating the principles for revolutionary activity did not develop their arguments in relation to the classical world, as we shall see, there were others who did make this connection.

After the October Revolution, when the Constituent Assembly had been dis-solved, causing a chorus of disapproval from abroad in defence of 'pure democ-racy' and 'democracy in general', Lenin developed his argument by insisting that, for Marxists, the political form cannot be separated from the economic structure, since there is no such thing as 'non-class democracy'.[16] Bourgeois democracy is a historically limited form that can be exploited by the prole-tariat in its struggle for power, but must be superseded. It is characterised by the limitation of democracy to a sphere of abstract citizenship and denies any democratic control of the economy, with the effect that political rights for the proletariat are *in practice* limited. In a bourgeois society, 'freedom of the press', for instance, is actually '*freedom for the rich* to buy and bribe the press' and to put forward its perspectives, because beneath the forms of bourgeois democ-racy resides an actual dictatorship of the bourgeoisie.[17] Proletarian democracy means the extension of these democratic rights to the proletariat *in fact* and not only in principle. Thus the dictatorship of the bourgeoisie is replaced by that of the proletariat:

> This means a gigantic, world historic *extension* of democracy, its trans-formation from falsehood into truth, the liberation of humanity from the shackles of capital, which *distorts* and truncates any, even the most 'democratic' and republican, *bourgeois* democracy. This means replacing the bourgeois state with the *proletarian* state, a replacement that is the sole way the state can eventually wither away altogether.[18]

This is an excellent example of the rhetorical strategies that were subject to a considerable amount of attention by linguists and literary scholars after the October Revolution. Here we can see Lenin's tendency to 'decanonise'

---

15   Cartledge 1996, p. 183.
16   On the dissolution of the Constituent Assembly see, *inter alia*, Serge 1992 [1930] and Rabinowitch 2007.
17   Lenin 1974d [1919], pp. 370–1.
18   Lenin 1974d [1919], p. 371.

[*dekanonizovat'*] and to lower or deflate [*snizhat'*] the misleading use of abstractions, such as 'freedom' and 'democracy', in the rhetoric of his opponents, revealing the actual social content of terms in particular uses.[19]

The Aesthetics of the 'Living Word'

While Russian revolutionaries were working out their strategies and tactics following the 1905 'dress rehearsal', many traditional intellectuals were partaking of the 'effervescence of mysticism' that swept Russia.[20] What is interesting about this phenomenon from the point of view of our current concerns is that, as intellectuals withdrew from direct political engagement into a specific brand of aestheticism, ideas about the relationship between hegemony and democracy were recast in mystical terms. Writing about the rise of philosophical aesthetics in eighteenth-century Germany, Terry Eagleton rather shrewdly remarks that aesthetics emerged among intellectuals trying to exert 'cultural and spiritual leadership beyond the reach of the self-serving aristocracy' in the context of a feeble bourgeoisie unable to challenge the absolutist state.[21] While not directly challenging the state, these intellectuals provided an aestheticised vision of power and of a social life, as yet unachievable, bound by 'habits, pieties, sentiments and affections':[22]

> If the aesthetic comes in the eighteenth century to assume the significance it does, it is because the word is shorthand for a whole project of hegemony, the massive introjection of abstract reason by the life of the senses. What matters is not in the first place art, but this process of refashioning the human subject from the inside, informing its subtlest affections and bodily responses with this law which is not a law.[23]

The aesthetic ideal is of individuals woven together into a unity with no detriment to their particularity. Reeling from the 1905 defeat and many of them terrified by the appearance of the proletariat as a political force, the aesthetic took on a particularly mystical form among the intellectuals of Russia's so-called 'silver age'. While the Russian symbolists rejected the instrumental life-praxis

---

19   Shklovskii 1924; Iakubinskii 1924.
20   Bachtin 1963a, p. 47.
21   Eagleton 1990, p. 14.
22   Eagleton 1990, p. 20.
23   Eagleton 1990, pp. 42–4.

that dominated the emerging bourgeois society, their art could not quite become a compensatory realm into which they could withdraw, but neither could it organise a new life-praxis as was the aim of the avant-garde.[24] Instead, art was viewed as a religious force that could achieve cultural hegemony.

Perhaps the clearest example of a mystical rendering of the project of hegemony is to be found in the work of the symbolist poet and ideologist, Viacheslav Ivanov, who argued that implicit in the new forms of class struggle was a demand for 'cultural integration'.[25] This, he claimed, opened 'vast horizons of mysticism', understood as the 'free self-affirmation of faith in the suprapersonal will in the individual'.[26] Ivanov thus advocated a 'mystical anarchism' that, in its pure form, is a 'synthesis of unconditional individual freedom with the beginning of communal [*sobornyi*] unity'.[27] According to this doctrine, the development of individuality would not be compromised by external ties and institutions, but members of the society would freely participate in communal life, for which he used the religious term *sobornost'*.[28] The model for this was the ancient-Greek theatre, and especially the chorus in Greek tragedy, which he adopted from Nietzsche's *Birth of Tragedy* and revised in accordance with his own predilections.[29] Audience participation in choral theatre would, he hoped, result in a 'process of collective myth-making [*mifotvorchestvo*]', as individuals regained contact with the 'collective consciousness'.[30] Although some proponents of mystical anarchism were clearly anti-Marxists and sought freedom *from* economics, Lunacharskii contributed to symbolist collections and he was also among the visitors to Ivanov's literary salon, 'the tower', where these ideas were developed and discussed. Gorky was a supporter of the idea

---

24   Bürger 1984, pp. 32, 45–50.

25   Ivanov 1974 [1906], p. 89.

26   Ibid.

27   Ibid.

28   As Rosenthal 1977, p. 609 notes, *sobornost'* was originally used to denote a 'collective body within which the elements retain their individuality', and here has the sense of a 'spiritual commune'. It is worth noting that the Slavophiles had long regarded *sobornost'* to be a distinguishing feature of Russian Orthodox Christianity. See Esaulov 1995.

29   Neitzsche 1967 [1878]. Symptomatically, Nikolai Berdiaev complained that: 'This solitary despiser of all democracies [Nietzsche] underwent the most shameless democratisation in our hands.... the hungry Russian intelligentsia... feeds on everything, in the hope of vanquishing the evil of autocracy and freeing the people'. 'Philosophic Truth and Moral Truth': Berdiaev 1977 [1909], pp. 16–17. On Ivanov and Nietzsche, see Biebuyck and Grillaert 2003.

30   Biebuyck and Grillaert 2003, p. 67.

of myth-making theatre in 1905.[31] These 'god-builder' enthusiasts for proletarian culture found a clear point of continuity between the collectivism of
Bogdanov's view of proletarian culture, the syndicalist idea that workers have
the potential to be morally pure bearers of the ideal of a new society and the
symbolist vision of a theurgic, collective and socially transformative art. In his
work on poetry, Ivanov (and to some extent other Symbolists), believed that
the Russian poetic language had, through the liturgy, inherited the capacities
of ancient poetry and, as such, could awaken the mind of the masses to the
mythical archetypes that resided in the collective consciousness of the people.
The poetic word, as a symbol that may at once be polyvalent and incantatory,
is able to affect the subject as no other language can, for its prototype is the
divine *logos*.[32] The language of poetry and the collective experience of theatre
structures the subject from within, brings what was only implicit and subcon-
scious to full awareness, through a mystical-aesthetic process that is at once
erotic and theurgic, i.e. Dionysian.

In the 1910s the frenetic mystical anarchism was replaced by the more
sedate but portentous idea that Russia would lead a Third Renaissance (following the earlier Romance and Germanic Renaissances) in which the ideals of
the classical world would be resurrected. Ivanov argued that, through reunion
with its Hellenic source, Russia could lead a rebirth of culture, the *logos*, and
so banish the barbarism of the modern age. The Classicists, Faddei Zelinskii
and Innokentii Annenskii (the latter was also a significant poet), developed
the idea further, appealing both to the ideologues of 'slavophilism' and the
'Westernisers' who cherished the classical ideal.[33] Both Athens and Rome now
became examples to emulate, cultures to assimilate in order to bring about a
renovation of civilisation. In a 1922 article, Zelinskii presented an account of
the fall of the living word and the possibility of its resurrection. He argued that
'the word [*slovo*], which lay at the basis both of the civil life of adults and the
upbringing of the young, was the real ruler of the ancient world'.[34] This led to
the identification of the living word with reason and the Greek term, *logos*,

---

31   Rosenthal 1977, pp. 619–20; Geldern 1993, p. 38. On Ivanov's Tower, see Shishkin *et al.* 2006.

32   There is a large body of work about the importance of the notion of *logos* in relation to
      Russian religious philosophy and Russian symbolism. In general, one might say that it
      came to denote a combination of philosophical truth, in the sense used by Plato, and
      divine creativity or the Evangelic message in Christianity. For general considerations, see
      Cassedy 1990, pp. 106–8 and Seifrid 2005. On the passage of the notion of *logos* from clas-
      sical times to Christian theology, see Kelly 2002, pp. 11–38.

33   Khoruzhii 1994; Nikolaev 1997; Bagrinskaia 2004; Senderovich 2010; in English, see Kalb
      2008, pp. 22–4. For a recent overview of Zelinskii's career, see Novikov and Perfilova 2011.

34   Zelinskii 1922b, p. 171.

(like the Russian *slovo*) expressed both concepts. The growth of the conviction that *logos* rules the world led to the mystical and evangelical understanding of the role of *logos*, which was the 'apotheosis' of the rule of the living word. This was inherited by Christianity and institutionalised by the deadening bureaucratic hand of the church, for which the written *logos* of the gospels should rule the world and men's hearts. Thus, the word killed the gesture and writing killed the word.[35] With the rise of political activism, parliamentary speeches and courtroom appearances, especially following 1905, the idea that what was taking place in Russia was a veritable rebirth of the living word, *zhivoe slovo*, was widespread, and a number of studies of the phenomenon arose.[36] Zelinskii had been writing enthusiastically about the Roman orator, Cicero, since the early 1890s, but now more general considerations of oral speech came to the fore, with the publication of handbooks on such questions as courtroom rhetoric and theoretical considerations of oral delivery from the perspective of performance.[37]

Proletarian Culture

The struggle for proletarian hegemony within the cultural field was initially lead by *Proletarskie kul'turno-prosvetitel'nye organizatsii* [Proletarian Cultural and Enlightenment Organisations] known in contracted form as *Proletkul't*, which was established one week before the October Revolution, with Lunacharskii as one of its main organisers. Bogdanov became involved the following year. While Bogdanov's ideas about the culture arising from the collective experience of the proletariat permeated the movement, *Proletkul't* was not a simple expression of the *Vpered* programme. Between the February and October revolutions in 1917, Lunacharskii returned to Russia, was reconciled with

35   Zelinskii 1922b, p. 172. Here we can see how Zelinskii recapitulated Wundt's argument that all language arose from gestures, taking on the expressive functions associated with those gestures. Zelinskii appears to share Wundt's Romantic celebration of the earliest forms of expression as being closer to the living consciousness.

36   See Ivanova 2003.

37   On Zelinskii's studies of Cicero, see Belkin 2002; the most renowned handbook was the handbook of rhetoric in court, Porokhovshchikov 1988 [1910]. Perhaps most significant was the appearance of a regular section of the St. Petersburg journal, *Biblioteka teatra i iskusstva*, called '*Golos i rech*'' ['Voice and Speech'] between December 1912 and December 1913, which explored psychological, historical and theatrical aspects of oral speech. From 1913 to 1919, Vasilii Serezhnikov ran courses of diction and declamation in Moscow, which formed the basis of an institution founded in 1919.

Lenin and, following the October Revolution, became the first Commissar of Enlightenment, working alongside Lenin's wife, Nadezhda Krupskaia. However, Lunacharskii retained central conceptions from the *Vpered* programme that he had actively supported for many years, and at least some of these were to become guiding principles for early Soviet cultural policy. As Maria Levchenko argues, the *Proletkul't* programme that emerged was a fusion of the Vperedist conception of culture and the Bolshevik political programme in the context of a 'victorious proletarian revolution', and the main pronouncements of the *Proletkul't* theorists at the inception of the organisation constituted a 'palimpsest' of the two trends.[38] Lunacharskii's theses from the conference, which were published in *Pravda* less than a week after the seizure of power, noted:

> the cultural-enlightenment movement must occupy a place within the general workers' movement alongside the political, economic and cooperative forms of the movement. The proletariat's cultural-enlightenment movement must be permeated by a combative socialist spirit, and its aim is to arm the working class with knowledge, *to organise its feelings with art*, for success in its titanic struggle for a new social order, because it believes that, in both science and art, the proletariat will manifest its own independent creativity. But for this, it must take possession of all the cultural heritage of the past and present. The proletariat is willing to accept collaboration with the socialist and even non-Party intelligentsia in this cultural-enlightenment work, but it *considers it necessary to maintain a critical attitude toward the fruits of the old culture*, which it looks on not as a student, but as a builder, called upon to erect new buildings of light with old stones.[39]

Proletkul't developed into a large organisation with a significant number of publications during the Russian Civil War of 1918–21. This was less a result of the Vperedist programme, however, than it was the success of the October Revolution, even though the Vperedist conception of proletarian culture still predominated, as can be seen in the italicised portions of the passage quoted above, and Bogdanov played an important role. When Lenin and Bogdanov clashed over the latter's demands for the independence of *Proletkul't* from the new proletarian state, Lunacharskii sided with Lenin, and *Proletkul't* was subsequently subordinated to the Commissariat of Enlightenment, headed by Lunacharskii.

---

38   Levchenko 2007, pp. 38–40.
39   Quoted in Levchenko 2007, p. 40. Levchenko's emphasis.

It should also be noted that, in the summer of 1920, Lunacharskii established an International Bureau of *Proletkul't* at a meeting immediately after the Second Congress of the Comintern.[40] The bureau identified its first tasks as 'spreading the principles of proletarian culture, the creation of *Proletkul't* organisations in all countries and to prepare for a world congress of *Proletkul't*'.[41] This led, among other things, to the establishment of an Institute of Proletarian Culture in Turin, in which Gramsci played a leading role.[42] An attempt to renew the initiative was made in October 1922, when a meeting between the Proletkul't Central Committee and Comintern representatives took place. Gramsci was present at this meeting, but in the new conditions of the time, nothing appears to have come of the initiative.[43]

The Theatre Section of the Commissariat of Enlightenment: *TEO Narkomprosa*

In the confused but vibrant atmosphere following the October Revolution, these trends all came together, especially concentrated in the theatre section of the Commissariat of Enlightenment (hereafter TEO), which was formed in January 1918 and was directed by Lunacharskii and the theatre director, Vsevolod Meierkhol'd. TEO originally comprised historical-theoretical, peda-gogical, repertoire and director sections and played an important role not only in the administration of theatres, but also in the organisation of the public spectacles to mark important dates in the new calendar.[44] TEO also led the formation of a range of innovative institutions, within which new directions of teaching and research about the performative dimensions of language were pioneered. In 1920, TEO was split into two halves while remaining within the Commissariat of Enlightenment, with part of its responsibilities now fall-ing under the authority of the administration of Academic Theatres and the other becoming part of *Glavpolitprosvet*, the Main Committee for Political Enlightenment, which was also responsible for clubs, libraries, village reading-huts [*izby-chital'ni*], adult education and Party schools. *Glavpolitprosvet* was

---

40   Anon. 1920, p. 5.

41   Ibid.

42   Gramshi *et al.* 1922; Gramsci *et al.* 2012.

43   'Protokol soveshchaniia prezidiuma TSK Proletkul'ta s predstaviteliami kominterna, 22/10/1922', RGALI 1230/1/9/1.

44   On the festivals, see Tolstoy *et al.* (eds.) 1990 and Geldern 1993.

led by Krupskaia from its formation in 1920 until it was absorbed into the general structures of the Commissariat in 1930.[45]

One of the most significant intellectual convergences facilitated by TEO was between the ideas of the symbolists and advocates of proletarian culture. Writing in 1920, Lunacharskii celebrated how the most prominent symbolists had come over to the side of the revolution and found 'consonance' with the vague *sobornost'* of the present day.[46] Ivanov had immediately become involved with TEO and hoped to lead a movement towards the collective theatre of which he had long dreamed.[47] In 1919 he was to write the following:

> We have now been set one task: as in the ancient times when farmers awoke the universal spirit of fertility with their magic rites, so we must summon the hidden energy of the people's [*narodnyi*] creativity, so they behold themselves in the depths of the soul of the people [*dusha narodnaia*] and dare to express themselves in a new festival, in a new activity, in a new game, in a new spectacle.[48]

These ideas became combined with the *Proletkul't* agenda from the outset. In some ways, this combination reflected Lunacharskii's particular brand of eclecticism, which combined silver-age mysticism with the epistemological collectivism of Bogdanov and the political ideas of Lenin. We have already seen how Bogdanov had adopted from Noiré a conception which combined language and reason as *logos*, which arose in the productive process and led to the contention that different classes are the bearers of different logics and world views. This was easily linked to the notion of the living word and *logos* as discussed by the symbolists, as well as to their ideas about collective theatre. However, Lunacharskii was but one point at which these currents converged and began to find institutional forms. In his influential 1918 book, *Creative Theatre* [*Tvorcheskii teatr*], the *Proletkul't* theorist Platon Kerzhentsev, for instance, combined Ivanov's ideas on theatre with the collectivist ideas of Bogdanov, Richard Wagner's writings on art and revolution and Roman Rolland's ideas of popular theatre to argue that theatre should become a mass participatory arena with no division between performers and audience. The posited unity of ritual theatre had, according to Kerzhentsev, become a reality, as the

---

45   For an overview, see Andreeva 1968.
46   Lunacharskii 1965 [1920], p. 390.
47   Zubarev 1997, pp. 128–9. On Ivanov's work with TEO, see also Zubarev 1998 and Berd 2006.
48   Ivanov from 1919, quoted in Ivanova 2010, p. 66.

proletariat had replaced Ivanov's utopian 'people' [*narod*] as its social base.[49] In 1919 Ivanov joined with Kerzhentsev and the actor and theatre historian, Vsevolod Vsevolodskii-Gerngross, to establish principles for a worker-peasant theatre that would bridge actor and spectator.[50] Like Ivanov, the symbolists, Aleksandr Blok and Andrei Belyi, collaborated with *Proletkul't* on a number of occasions in 1918–19,[51] while Bely, the poet Aleksandr Blok, the symbolist philosopher Konstantin Erberg (pseudonym of Siunnerberg), the theatre director Meierkhol'd and the literary scholar R.V. Ivanov-Razumnik attempted to set up a Free Philosophical Academy (*Vol'fila*) within TEO.[52] Although this institute was not realised, the group continued as the Free Philosophical *Association* until 1924 and presented an area for working out 'questions of cultural creativity in the spirit of philosophy and socialism'.[53] The range of discussion was defined as lying between anthroposophy (of which Bely was a particular enthusiast) and Marxism, which explains the involvement of the future Left Oppositionist, Victor Serge.[54] Erberg led a circle within the association to study the philosophy of art, one product of which was the collection that included Zelinskii's 1922 article discussed above.

Lunacharskii, Vsevolodskii-Gerngross, Erberg, the linguists and Baudouin's students, Lev Iakubinskii and Lev Shcherba, as well as the Acmeist poet, Nikolai Gumilev, met to establish an Institute of the Living Word [*Institut zhivogo slova*, hereafter IZhS] in Petrograd.[55] This institute opened in October 1918 with Vsevolodskii-Gerngross as director.[56] The institute had the following

49   Kerzhentsev 1920; Kleberg 1993, pp. 44–64; Leach 1994, pp. 22–5.

50   Geldern 1993, pp. 136–7.

51   See Ivanova 1993a and Ivanova 2010, pp. 64–71.

52   TsGA (SPb) 2551/1/129/11–12. On Blok's involvement with TEO, see Ivanova 1993b; on Erberg's involvement, see Zabolotskaia 1996.

53   'Proekt ustava Vol'noi filosofskoi assotsiatsii', TsGA (SPb) 2551/1/129/11. For different perspectives on the association, see Belous 2007 and Ivanova 2010. The proceedings of the meetings have been published as Belous (ed.) 2005.

54   See Serge 2002, pp. 151–2.

55   In his memoirs, Viktor Shklovskii (Shklovskii 1966, p. 101) recalls that Baudouin spoke at a session organised by Futurists on the idea of the living word shortly before his imprisonment in 1914. Here he sharply criticised tsarist nationality policy as well as attempts by certain Futurists to separate the word [*slovo*] and its sense [*smysl*]. On Baudouin's critique of the *zaumniki*, see Janaček 1981. Shklovskii (Shklovskii 1966, pp. 127–8) also notes that Iakubinskii 'was not only Baudouin's favourite student, but also the person who wanted to overcome the empiricism of the old scholar. Iakubinskii strove to understand speech as part of life, he moved towards generalisations and approached Marxism with some difficulty'.

56   Chown and Brandist 2007 and Vasena 2007.

aims: 1) scientific-practical working out of questions relating to the realm of the living word and associated disciplines; 2) the preparation of specialists of the living word in pedagogical, socio-political and artistic fields; and 3) the distribution and popularisation of knowledge and mastery of the field of the living word.[57]

Archival documents show that the institute was of a considerable size and had five sections: general, oratory, verbal [*slovesnyi*], theatrical and pedagogical. In the first year, the institute had 62 teaching staff, while up to eight hundred people studied, with up to five hundred attending lectures and up to four hundred taking part in practical courses. The aims of students varied, with 29.5 percent claiming to attend for general education; 24 percent specifically aiming to study the 'living word'; 23.4 percent showing an interest in working on the stage and 11.4 percent aiming to train as teachers.[58]

The speeches at the opening of the institute highlighted the connection between these aims and the process of democratisation. Lunacharskii affirmed that the revolution had made democracy possible and that it was now necessary to 'teach the whole nation [*narod*] to speak [publicly], from the great to the small'.[59] Democracy was here linked to the notion of *isegoria*, or the equality of speech, practised in ancient Athens. In his speech, Zelinskii similarly stressed that 'Athenian democracy was that cell that nourished the living word', and that the subsequent history of the ancient world proved that the two concepts, 'democracy and the living word', are inseparable.[60] All this fitted well with Nadezhda Krupskaia's February 1921 argument that Soviet Russia was the 'new Athens'.[61] Zelinskii argued that the Russian resurrection of the living word predated the revolution and began with the juridical reforms of the 1860s, subsequently intensified by the political reforms that followed 1905.[62] The presence at IZhS of the veteran jurist, Anatolii Koni, who had defended the revolutionary, Vera Zasulich, in a *cause célèbre* trial of 1877, served to confirm this contention.[63] For Zelinskii in 1922, this represented a stage on the incomplete path towards the resurrection of forms of antiquity in

---

57   *Zapiski* 1919, p. 25.

58   GARF A-2307/4/54/23.

59   *Zapiski* 1919, p. 23.

60   *Zapiski* 1919, p. 8.

61   Krupskaia 1921.

62   Zelinskii 1922, p. 172.

63   A detailed account of the trial has recently appeared as Pipes 2010. Koni's memoirs of the case were written up in 1904 and published only in 1930: Koni 1933 [1904]. They are available online at a number of websites.

Russia, which would only be complete when the 'Russian language regains all the powers with which nature had invested it and knows itself as the powerful weapon of the oratorical word'.[64] The implication was, of course, that the revolution had provided the conditions for this to be achieved. These ideas also resounded among thinkers not immersed in the mysticism of the 'Third Renaissance', so that in Moscow the most prominent champion of the study of the 'living word', Aleksandr Shneider, claimed that the 'living word almost died out in our culture' but that today (1920) we could see 'the tide had now turned' and there was a 'return to the living word'.[65] Futurist poet, Vladimir Mayakovsky, was recorded reading his verse at the IZhS in 1920,[66] and in a 1927 issue of the journal *Novyi Lef* still looked forward to the 'broadening of the verbal basis' through, in particular, the development of radio as a tribune for 'the audible word [*slyshimoe slovo*], audible poetry'.[67] Meanwhile, Koni taught the 'socio-political tasks of the living word, the weapons of speech [*rech'*], the forms of addressing the listener, the necessary conditions for the influence of the living word, the connection between the living word and literature'.[68] Zelinskii proposed a course on the 'psychological foundations of ancient rhetoric', while several others even discussed a course on cultic speech, with materials taken from ancient, Eastern and contemporary-church discourses.[69] Along with Iakubinskii, Erberg began working out the theoretical bases of public discourse [*rech'*], which they were to continue throughout the decade.

A year after the opening of IZhS, an Institute of Declamation opened in Moscow. Among its aims was work on 'artistic reading', individual and 'collective declamation' and associated disciplines such as phonetics, the rhythm of poetry and prose and the 'psychology of speech, feeling and thought'. It sought to train 'readers', 'orators' and 'specialists in reading artistic texts' and to popularise the discipline.[70] Speaking at the institute's opening, Lunacharskii raised an argument that was at once collectivist and Ivanovian, noting that the institute reflects the revolution's 'striving for pan-psychism, broad collective feeling':

---

64   Zelinskii 1922, p. 176.

65   'rech' na torzhestvennom zasedanii khudozhestvennogo soveta Gosudarstvennogo instituta slova (5/12/1920)' RGALI 2238/1/4/3.

66   Recordings of some of these readings are available at http://www.hlebnikov.ru/audio/voices.htm (11 January 2012).

67   Maiakovskii 1959 [1927], p. 162. In such statements one can see precursors to discussions about literacy and orality developed by recent figures such as Eric Havelock and Walter Ong.

68   *Zapiski* 1919, pp. 82–4.

69   RGALI (SPb) 82/1/22/12–120b.

70   'Polozhenie o Gosudarstvennom Institute Deklamatsii', GARF A2306/24/543/42.

The person of our time moves gradually from small everyday individual-ism, from the petty 'I' to a broad collective consciousness and feeling, towards the 'person', and makes a drop, a wave in the human sea, not losing anything of the great value of consciousness, thought and feeling. This organ of universal oneness, of universal coupling, remains the word, which we can understand, in general, as every gesture and phenomenon of art. This feature of the word, this vibrant, creative life of literature, needs to be developed and deepened, which is the mission of the State Institute of Declamation.[71]

Ivanov spoke at the institute on more than one occasion, one of his lectures, characteristically, on the 'Choral Origins of Art'. He also led a group for the study of poetry.[72] Coinciding with the reorganisation of TEO, in 1920 the insti-tute was reorganised as the Institute of the Word [*Institut slova*], which had a broader remit. Declamation was by now but one faculty, with others added that gave it more of the character of a practical institute of verbal art.[73] In Moscow research on the living word was transferred to the Commission of the Living Word in the literary section of GAKhN in 1926. Notable papers included Aleksandr Peshkovskii's work on the relationship between intonation and syntax in oral speech, the classicists Sergei Radtsig and Nikolai Deratini on the 'Cult of the Word in the Ancient World' and 'The Perception of the Orator in Ancient Rome', as well as numerous papers by Shneider about aspects of oratory.[74]

These institutes assembled a remarkable group of scholars. The IZhS included Zelinskii, most of the Petrograd formalists (Boris Eikhenbaum, Viktor Shklovskii, Iurii Tynianov, Boris Tomashevskii), Koni, and the linguists Shcherba, Iakubinskii and Sergei Bernshtein. While perhaps less distin-guished, the Moscow institute involved, among others, the literary critic Petr Kogan and the linguist Dmitrii Ushakov. With the exception of Koni, all of these figures were to pursue significant careers as researchers in Soviet insti-tutions, which they had to some extent piloted at these institutes. However, the theatrical base of the institutes sometimes made more general studies of

71   Lunacharskii 1981 [1920], pp. 228–9.

72   On Ivanov's relationship to collective declamation, see Obatnin 2010.

73   'Otchet o deiatel'nosti Gosudarstvennogo Instituta Slova v sviazi s istoriei ego vozrikno-veniia (23 noiabria 1913 g. pod nazvaniem "Pervykh Moskovskikh Kursov Diktsii i Deklamatsii" svobodn. khudozhnika V.K. Sereznhikova', GARF A2306/24/183/1–8.

74   *GAKhN Biulletini* 4–5 (1926), pp. 35–41; 10 (1927–8), pp. 23–4; 11 (1928), pp. 39–40. A summary of Peshkovskii's paper, which anticipated some of his later pioneering work on Russian syntax, and the discussion that followed, is in the archives: RGALI 941/6/40/13–140b.

the performative dimensions of speech appear a secondary concern. Thus, in the memoirs of one former student we see that the resources of IZhS tended to be focused on the theatrical section, with the development of a new Experimental Theatre at the expense of the verbal [*slovesnoe*] and oratory sections, where most of the theorists of language were concentrated.[75] In spring 1924, IZhS was closed for allegedly duplicating provisions that were available elsewhere and, following a student-led campaign, a new establishment, State Courses of Speech Techniques [*Goskursy tekhniki rechi*], was opened on the basis of the oratory section, with Iakubinskii as director and most of the notable members of staff intact. Here were three sections: 1) literary art and journalism; 2) speech pedagogy; 3) public speech. Courses were directed at worker and peasant correspondents, regional Party workers and various educationalists.[76] The courses were, however, by no means narrow, involving historical courses on philosophy and literary history, as well as practical courses on techniques of agitation and the fundamentals of political science. Many of the innovative research projects that had been established at the IZhS ended up in a number of other institutes such as the Russian (later State) Institute of the History of Arts [*Rossiiskii (Gosudarstvennyi) institut istorii iskusstv*, hereafter GIII] and the Institute for the Comparative History of the Literatures and Languages of the West and East [*Nauchno-issledovatel'skii institut sravnitel'noi istorii literatur i iazykov Zapada i Vostoka*, hereafter ILIaZV].[77] In Moscow the main centres of such research became the State Academy of Artistic Studies [*Gosudarstvennaia akademiia khudozhestvennykh nauk*, GAKhN] and the sister Institute of ILIaZV, The Institute of Language and Literature [*Institut iazyka i literatury*, IIaL].

Proletarian Culture under NEP

The new sobriety that followed the defeat of the German Revolution in 1923 dealt the final blow to the mystical and apocalyptic attitude towards the

---

75   Nina Galanina, 'Vospominaniia byvshei studenta Instituta Zhivogo Slova' (1974) IRLI 474/659/14.

76   TsGAIPD 2720/1/4/1.

77   Like many institutes, it changed its name and form a number of times. It was the Aleksandr Veselovskii Institute of Language Studies and the History of Literature [*Institut iazykovedeniia i istorii literatury im.ak. A.N. Veselovskogo*] 1921–3, ILIaZV 1923–30 and The State Institute for Discursive Culture [*Gosudarstvennyi institut rechevoi kul'tury*, GIRK) 1930–3]. On the history of the institute, see Brandist 2008.

Russian Revolution. The representatives of the silver age had largely departed the scene by this time. Zelinskii emigrated to Poland in 1920, the poet Aleksandr Blok died in 1921 and Ivanov moved to Baku in 1920, where he worked as a professor in Baku University, then as deputy head of the Azerbaijan Commissariat of Enlightenment and then left the USSR in 1924. The mystical elements that had become attached to proletarian culture during the Civil War faded and, in the new circumstances of financial stringency, *Proletkul't* itself withered. However, the agenda of proletarian culture was taken up by certain literary groups and Party leaders. During the NEP period, many of Bogdanov's ideas about proletarian culture found an advocate in Bukharin, who ultimately tried to reconcile certain of Bogdanov's ideas with Lenin's final writings about combating the growth of the bureaucracy to create a general theory of cultural revolution.[78] One of the many differences between Lenin, on the one hand, and Bogdanov and Bukharin on the other, regarding this question, was the latter's contention that it was the technical intelligentsia that represented the greatest danger to the revolution by potentially becoming a new ruling class. Bukharin thus linked the struggle against bureaucratisation with the development of proletarian culture, but this was only to develop fully after Lenin's death, since the latter specifically viewed the intelligentsia as an ally in the fight against bureaucratisation. For Bukharin, the nationalist intelligentsia, exemplified by the 'Changing Landmarks' movement [*smenovekhovstvo*], threatened to become a Trojan horse within Soviet institutions and needed to be countered by the creation of a new 'worker intelligentsia' under Party supervision.[79] The debate about proletarian culture was launched in the Soviet press as a result of rising concerns that a restoration of bourgeois ideology would accompany the restoration of market forces under the NEP. The Politburo launched the debate in *Pravda* at the end of August 1922, a debate that engaged the Party's leading theoreticians for a number of years. As John Biggart notes, the debate concerned whether, in exercising political and economic dominance, the proletariat had a culture specific to itself, and it 'raised the broader issue of redefining socialist revolution in cultural terms'.[80]

The question of cultural hegemony soon became a crucial point of contention in the debate. On 16 September 1923 Trotsky published an article in *Pravda*, which would also appear in his book *Literature and Revolution*, arguing that although the appearance of proletarian writers was 'expressing in writing the molecular process of the cultural rise of the proletariat', the idea

78   Biggart 1992, pp. 131–58.
79   Bukharin 1922.
80   Biggart 1987.

that there could be an elaborated proletarian culture was incoherent since the proletarian dictatorship would only mark a relatively brief period between capitalism and a classless society.[81] He thus maintained that a party that lays claim to 'ideological hegemony' should not presume to judge the work of fellow-traveller writers with the arrogance characteristic of certain 'Marxists in literature'.[82] The point infuriated bellicose advocates of proletarian literature and some avant-gardist thinkers who were vying for leadership in the cultural sphere. Each tended to link Trotsky's position with his lack of confidence in the ability of the Russian proletariat to move towards socialism in conditions when the immediate revolutionary wave in Europe had subsided. The argument was thus connected to Trotsky's move into opposition against the policy that would subsequently become 'socialism in one country'. Writing in one of the periodicals of *Proletkul't*, the avant-gardist *Lef* critic Nikolai Chuzhak objected that Trotsky reduced the exercise of the Party's ideological 'hegemony' in literature to 'attentive monitoring'.[83] At the same time, between 1923 and 1925, the Moscow-based journal *Na Postu* [*On Guard*] constantly demanded the implementation of the hegemony of proletarian literature by giving its advocates a leading role in all Soviet literary publications.[84] These claims became especially bold after the *On Guard*-ists had gained control of the All-Union Association of Proletarian Writers (VAPP). At the First Congress of VAPP in January 1925, a resolution was passed in which it was stated that it was no longer sufficient merely to recognise proletarian literature, for now there must be 'recognition of the principle of the hegemony of this literature ... an unyielding, systematic struggle ... for victory, for the absorption of all types and kinds of bourgeois and petty-bourgeois literature'.[85]

At a meeting of the Central Committee of the Party to discuss the question of the Party's literary policy a month later, Bukharin slapped down the *On guard*-ists for actually demanding the 'principle of the hegemony of VAPP', but he endorsed the principle of the hegemony of proletarian literature:

> When we won power, then in that very struggle, the direct revolutionary overturn, we already won the historical right to hegemony. We have

---

81   Trotsky 1991 [1923], p. 230.

82   Trotsky 1991 [1923], p. 251.

83   Chuzhak 1923, pp. 81–8.

84   It should be noted that, at this time, the Futurists associated with the journals *Lef* and *Novyi Lef* were also putting their own work forward as worthy of Party support.

85   VAPP (1925) 'Ideologicheskii front i literatura', Online at http://www.teencity.ru/projects/ myaeots/bibl_11/manifest/proletcult/proletcult3.htm (accessed 10 April 2011).

that. We earned it by standing out in the struggle on the barricades, a struggle that brought all our previous organisational work, political tempering, political experience – all those features that are necessary for a triumphant revolution, to fruition. But when we turn to the question of art, science and so on, and we ask ourselves whether our hegemony has matured, then I maintain that it has not. If it has still not matured, and if we are entering an epoch when we conquered political power while our cultural hegemony had still not matured, then, comrades, it is quite clear that it is our task to pose the matter in such a way that will enable us to win that hegemony. Or, as I say, we must earn the historical right to social leadership [*rukovodstvo*] through our own prominence in the fields of literature and culture.[86]

This principle was codified in the Party decree of July 1925, in which the possibility of proletarian culture was officially accepted for the first time, and in which it was stated that: 'There is not yet a hegemony of proletarian writers, and the Party must help these writers win for themselves the historic right to this hegemony'.[87]

Herman Ermolaev was undoubtedly correct to note that in placing proletarian culture as 'a practical task of the moment', the 1925 resolution marks the abandonment of the Leninist policy towards literature.[88] It nevertheless codified the merging of the *Vpered* cultural programme with the Leninist political programme that had coexisted since the beginning of the October Revolution. In the meantime, proletarian culture needed to be viewed from 'an all-state [*obshchegosudarstvennyi*] point of view' and this meant, above all, the maintenance of the union between the proletariat and peasantry, the *smychka*.

Conclusion

Language and the 'living word' remained vital cultural and political issues throughout the 1920s, resulting in a series of innovative reformulations of the tasks of linguistic study. In the course of the decade, the word, as *logos*, was stripped of its religious and mystical forms and became the organising principle of social life. Its divine origins were displaced by the Noiré-Bogdanov

---

86 Bukharin 1993 [1925], p. 73.

87 RKP(b) 'On The Policy Of The Party In The Sphere Of Artistic Literature (1 July 1925)'. Online at http://www.sovlit.com/decreejuly1925/ (accessed 10 March 2011).

88 Ermolaev 1963, pp. 44–54.

notion of will as a precondition of the language and logic of social classes. In the post-revolutionary context in which the post-Symbolist and *Proletkul't* conceptions merged, groups presented art as having cast off its divine pretentions and become the organiser of the thoughts and feelings of the masses on the basis of a core proletariat that was the bearer of a privileged form of consciousness. The living word as collective performance and organisational principle could permeate the masses and restructure their inner experience, but at the same time provide a more robust and effective structure for the flourishing of their own personalities. In the TEO institutes, this conception of the living word merged with the notion of agitation, which revealed the relationship between the political structure and the concrete economic situation and anticipated a new form of democracy that would return to the classical equality of speech, but on a new, higher level. The functions of the state would be re-absorbed into civil society. From about 1923, however, the process went into reverse and civil society was gradually absorbed into the state. A Hegelian 'ruse of reason' began to transform categories into their opposites, but this would take some time to complete.

As we will see, the foci of attention in research institutions began to shift. Categorisation of the techniques of agitation and oratory developed in connection with the training of professionals in journalism and pedagogy, while the relationship between 'living' and standard languages came to preoccupy most linguists. Researchers showed that in search of means of communication adequate to their social purpose, speakers actively plunder the resources afforded by the structures of signification which are available to them. Forms closely related to the improvisational boldness of the lower social groups prove particularly fruitful, while the more abstract standard tends to ossify and become the object of an ironic engagement. The standard therefore needs to be continually renewed, reinvigorated through constant engagement with the life praxis of the masses, for alternative sources of innovations are always on hand.

Metamorphoses of Hegemony in the Period of the NEP

Throughout the 1920s, the idea of hegemony not only featured in debates about the international sphere, but was also central to discussions about the domestic political situation following the end of the Civil War. Having taken power as a majority in the soviets at the end of 1917, the Bolsheviks soon found that they had to rule alone, as the Left Socialist Revolutionaries left the government and then a civil war, which had at least been latent since the August 1917 coup attempt by General Kornilov, burst into the open and threatened to destroy the new regime. The experience of the January–May 1918 Civil War in Finland made the Bolsheviks take particularly resolute action when hostilities began in earnest.[1] The leader of the Red Army, Trotsky, argued that the Civil War was simultaneously a military and a political process, a struggle between the aristocracy and proletariat 'for the political reserves, above all the peasantry', and that after a period of vacillation, 'the peasantry ultimately decided for the proletariat'.[2] As the peasant uprisings that followed the end of the Civil War showed, however, the struggle for the peasantry outlived the end of military operations. Lenin argued at the end of the war that the union with the peasantry had been a military union, but *'the military union cannot exist without an economic union* . . . Our union with the peasantry cannot in any way hold for a protracted period of time without an economic foundation'.[3] In this way, the problematic of hegemony began to be reformulated. Key moments in this reformulation came at the eighth and tenth congresses of the Bolshevik Party in 1919 and 1921 respectively, but this reformulation was incremental and carried on for some time.[4] At the latter congress, the Party formulated an approach that combined a retreat to a limited and regulated form of market economy to restore the economy after the Civil War, and so guarantee the survival of the revolutionary state, with a political form that would support and nourish an international struggle, just as the revolutionary wave in Europe was

---

1 The best account of the Finnish Civil War in English is Alapuro 1988, while the link between the Finnish and Russian Civil Wars is well explored in Serge 1992 [1930].

2 Riddell (ed.) 2012, p. 349.

3 Quoted in Zinov'ev 1926, p. 231.

4 Thomas 2009, pp. 232–4.

subsiding. Proletarian hegemony thus needed to be maintained over subaltern classes, coupled with a dictatorship over the bourgeoisie.

Zinov'ev argued that '[t]he New Economic Policy was produced by the necessity...to reinforce "good relations" with the peasantry on the basis of a new economic policy. It required a concession to the peasantry, an immediate and decisive concession'.[5] However, in conditions when the revolutionary wave in Europe had ebbed, this concession soon began to be viewed as 'the largest, most responsible, the most decisive strategic manoeuvre of the proletarian party'.[6] 'In NEP', argued Zinov'ev, 'we found the concrete path towards socialism in a peasant country still under bourgeois encirclement'.[7] The idea of the hegemony of the proletariat over the peasantry and oppressed masses, which had been a political programme to defeat the autocracy and achieve political democracy, now began to 'grow over' into the role that the proletariat would play in the internal development of what became the USSR. This metamorphosis became stronger with the failure of the 1923 uprising in Germany, but throughout the 1920s it was to some extent offset by the declining idea that the USSR was to play a leading role in the international revolution. The various dimensions of hegemony, in this new sense, were things that came to the attention of the leadership only by degrees, and as the new Soviet research institutions grappled with the enormous social and cultural problems that faced the state, whole new fields of study began to open up and to be funded. During the period of the NEP, hegemony became almost synonymous with the task of maintaining proletarian leadership, the so-called *smychka* of the town and countryside, proletariat and peasantry.

Political Hegemony in Party Discussions

The project of hegemony was implicit in much Party discussion, even when the term itself was not used. A good example is to be found in a resolution adopted at the Eighth Congress in 1919, which dealt with the role of schools within the Commissariat of Enlightenment, *Narkompros*:

> During the dictatorship of the proletariat, that is to say, in the period of establishing the conditions that make the full realisation of communism possible, the school should not only be a conduit for the principles of

---

5 Zinov'ev 1926, p. 233.

6 Zinov'ev quoted in Vasetskii 1989b, p. 23.

7 Zinov'ev 1926, p. 245.

communism in general, but also for *the proletariat's ideological, organisational, educational influence on the semi- and non-proletarian strata of the toiling masses*, with the goal of educating a generation that will be able to establish communism once and for all.[8]

The state now appeared as an apparatus of hegemony in relation to 'the semi- and non-proletarian strata of the toiling masses', but an apparatus of force against the bourgeoisie.

An examination of the transcripts of the Party congresses between 1919 and 1923 (from the Eight Congress to the Twelfth Congress) show that it was Zinov'ev who used the term 'hegemony' most frequently in both international and domestic contexts, and his position as a member of the Politburo, head of the Leningrad Party and Soviet and Chair of the Executive Committee of the Communist International made this use particularly influential.[9] As Lars Lih has recently shown, Zinov'ev's post-revolutionary thought was structured around what Lih calls a 'drama of hegemony' in which the proletariat and kulak are struggling for leadership over the peasantry.[10]

Two of Zinov'ev's interventions were especially significant at this time. At the Eleventh Congress in 1922, he argued that the project for winning hegemony in the revolution meant that 'the working class had to regard itself not from the point of view of guild [*tsekhovoi*] interests but from an all-state [*obshchegosudarstvennyi*] point of view'.[11] After the seizure of power, 'the working class as a hegemon, as the leader of the revolution on a national and international scale', must understand that it can only 'improve its conditions of life' by maintaining the union [*soiuz*] with the peasantry.[12] The relation between the working class and the peasantry was therefore the most important question

---

8   KPSS *v rezoliutsiakh, chast'* 1, 1953, p. 419 [my emphasis].

9   See, for instance, *Vos'moi s"ezd RKP(b)* 1959 [1919], pp. 136, 137, 291; *Protokoły odinatsatogo s"ezda* 1936 [1922], pp. 410–11; *Dvenadtsatyi s"ezd RKP(b)* 1968 [1923], pp. 28, 606–7. He dedicated most of a lecture to the history of the idea of hegemony, which he credited solely to Plekhanov and Lenin, in his 1923 course on the history of the Russian Communist Party, the published version of which was an important reference point for everyone in the movement in the mid-1920s. Zinov'ev 1973 [1923], pp. 27–62. Interestingly, while Zinov'ev features prominently in histories of the period, there is no full-length biography. The most complete is a 64-page pamphlet (Vasetskii 1989b) and an article (Vasetskii 1989a).

10   Lih 2011b, p. 51.

11   *Protokoły odinatsatogo s"ezda* 1936 [1922], p. 410. Zinov'ev here presents this in opposition to the position of the Mensheviks, who held a narrow conception of class interests.

12   *Protokoły odinatsatogo s"ezda* 1936 [1922], p. 411.

on every level, and this meant that the proletariat needs to be ready to make economic and political concessions to the peasantry.

At the Twelfth Congress the following year, Zinov'ev broadened the conception considerably:

> One has to know how to understand the hegemony of the proletariat. In 1895 it led to the formation of the 'Union for the Liberation of the Working Class'. In 1903 it led us to create an organisation of professional revolutionaries. In 1912 it led us to maintain the Bolshevik centre at a time of counterrevolution ... In 1917 it led to an uprising. In 1918–19 it led us to organise the Red Army and learn to wage war. In 1920–1 the hegemony of the proletariat consisted in helping to improve the situation of the peasantry and enter into contact with them, to revive the agricultural economy. In 1923 hegemony demands that we organise the export of bread. And in 1930 hegemony may be expressed in Russian communards fighting side-by-side with foreign workers on the streets of European capitals.[13]

It was, however, in the sphere of the national question, which was particularly prominent at the congress, that Zinov'ev made his most significant statement linking the question of hegemony within the USSR to the struggle for hegemony in other countries: 'we must remain the hegemon of the Union of Soviet Republics and be an example to all the peoples of the East and to the whole world', the 'hegemony of the proletariat ... cannot properly exist if we do not solve the national question'.[14] The Russian proletariat had to try to achieve and maintain leadership over a wide variety of ethnic groups and cultures, many of whom had none of the features fundamental to a nation state, such as a specifically national sense of identity, culture or even a standard form of language. Here both Bukharin and Zinov'ev followed Lenin's advice, the former arguing that as members of a 'former great-power nation' the Russian proletariat must 'head-off national strivings and place ourselves in an unequal position in the sense of making even greater concessions to national currents', as only this would allow us to 'purchase the real trust of previously oppressed nations'.[15] Zinov'ev claimed that 'despite our poverty', and the fact that 'our nation's resources are miserly', we must provide 'material help to the peasants, and especially to the peasants of the frontier areas that speak other languages, to all peoples that were previously oppressed'.[16] The Ukrainian Party Central

---

13   *Dvenadtsatyi s"ezd RKP(b)* 1968 [1923], p. 28.
14   *Dvenadtsatyi s"ezd RKP(b)* 1968 [1923], pp. 606–7.
15   *Dvenadtsatyi s"ezd RKP(b)* 1968 [1923], p. 613.
16   *Dvenadtsatyi s"ezd RKP(b)* 1968 [1923], p. 605.

Committee member and future Left Oppositionist, Khristian Rakovskii, argued that the Party must confront the question of 'how to find the *smychka* between our proletarian and Communist internationalism and the national development of wide layers of the peasant masses, with their aspiration for a national life, for their own national culture, for their own national state'.[17] He also argued that the constitutional arrangement of the USSR must ensure a high level of regional autonomy in order to embody the *smychka* of the revolutionary Russian proletariat with 'sixty million non-Russian peasants'.[18]

The policy outcome of the Twelfth Congress was ambiguous. On the one hand, the initial draft of the policy of *korenizatsiia* [indiginisation or nativisation] was adopted. This was the first policy to be based on Stalin's definition of nationality as '*a historically constituted, stable community of people, formed on the basis of a common language, territory, economic life, and psychological make-up manifested in a common culture*'.[19] Each of the practical measures adopted addressed these criteria, such as the idea that 'the organs of the national republics and regions should be staffed mainly with people from among the local inhabitants who know the language, manner of life, habits and customs of the peoples concerned'.[20] However, the theses that were adopted were marked by a series of amendments on the national question, to which Stalin had yielded. As Jeremy Smith notes, while the centralisation of the political and economic structures was being reinforced, the rights and status of the national minorities remained strong for most of the 1920s as a result.[21] Indigenous nationalities were promoted in the Party apparatus and state agencies. The use of national languages in the Party, economic enterprises, education and media was increased in those areas where standard, written forms were already in existence. Where such standard forms were absent, which was on a massive scale, projects to create and codify such languages were launched. On the other hand, Rakovskii's attempt to link the approach to the national question within the USSR to the struggle for national liberation in the colonies of the imperial nations was rejected, and the position of the Stalin-Zinov'ev-Kamenev triumvirate and the central bureaucracy was consolidated against the Left Opposition led by Trotsky.

The economic front was, of course, fundamental. In response to the so-called 'scissors crisis', according to which the cost of industrial goods rose

---

17   Rakovsky 1980 [1923], p. 81.
18   Ibid.
19   Stalin 1953 [1913], p. 307.
20   Stalin 1954a [1923], p. 194. See also Borisenok 2006, pp. 77–81.
21   Smith 1999, pp. 213–28. On the dual pressures on national policy, which was caught between regional autonomy and central economic planning, see Hirsch 2005, pp. 62–98.

disproportionately to that of grain, Evgenii Preobrazhenskii formulated an oppositionist economic policy that proposed an adjustment of the NEP to favour industrialisation funded by increased taxation on the wealthier peasants.[22] As part of the programme of the Left Opposition, this was to be accompanied by increased democracy within the Party (which had been limited as a result of the domestic emergency) and within industrial enterprises, which posed a significant threat to the rising Party (and all-state) bureaucracy. Bukharin tackled Preobrazhenskii's arguments directly, developing Stalin's theory of socialism in one country, according to which maintaining the domestic *smychka* became the overriding aim of *both* domestic *and* foreign policy, due to the 'relative stabilisation of capitalism'.[23] The Opposition's economic policy, was, therefore, presented as a reassertion of 'guild [*tsekhovoi*] ideology', which had nothing whatever to do with the 'worker-peasant bloc and proletarian hegemony within that bloc':[24]

> Comrade Preobrazhenskii's position threatens the bloc of workers and peasants, a bloc on which the whole position of Orthodox Bolshevism was, and is, built. It is not difficult to understand that in a period when the working class is in power, that its political hegemony, its political leadership cannot be durable unless it is underlain by a base of *economic hegemony*. But this economic hegemony cannot be accomplished in any other way than by an adaptation of industry to the peasant market, gradually taking possession of this market, introducing new methods into agricultural production thanks to the help of industry, gradually involving the peasantry in the network of cooperatives and, finally, introducing a new technical foundation (electrification) according to the growth of socialist accumulation.[25]

Zinov'ev presented the policy toward the countryside in a similar vein:

> Our peasant policy of 1925 is an attempt to adapt the task of socialist politics to the conditions of the production of 'the small and petty peasantry'. We are quite confident that by taking this path we will *retard*

---

22   See Carr 1969, pp. 11–158.

23   Bukharin began to stress this from the Thirteenth Party Congress of May 1924. See also Kozlov and Weitz 1989, pp. 387–410.

24   Bukharin 1988 [1925], p. 115. One subsection of this article was tellingly entitled, 'Communism or a "kingdom of the Proletariat"?' (p. 89).

25   Bukharin 1988 [1925], p. 109 [original emphasis].

the capitalist evolution of the village and *swing* it onto other, socialist tracks ... One should not see in the countryside today *only* class struggle. But one should not see *only* growing over into socialism there either. To grasp the whole process, one has to see both things: both the shoots of socialism (nationalisation of the land under a proletarian dictatorship, cooperatives) and class struggle on the basis of the stratification of the village. Victory will be for Socialism.[26]

As Chair of the Executive Committee of the Comintern, Zinov'ev criticised 'hothead' Trotskyists who 'posited the internal development of the country as directly dependent on revolutionary events in other countries'.[27] Trotsky was presented as an advocate of 'frontal assault', despite the fact that it was Trotsky who was the main theorist of the united-front strategy, designed precisely to combat such an approach.[28] After the debacle of the 1923 German uprising and the defeat of the opposition at the Twelfth Party Congress, the Comintern conflated the positions as heresies.[29] This orientation was intensified when Bukharin succeeded Zinov'ev. As Isaac Deutcher noted, these 'heresies' were 'defined as "ultra-left" and negative attitudes toward "alliances with the middle strata", a fundamental unwillingness to make such alliances and an unwilling-ness to recognise that bourgeois revolution, especially in the underdeveloped countries, formed a separate stage of the historical development, in which the bourgeoisie played a progressive and even revolutionary role'.[30] Stalin rein-forced the same argument in his speech 'The Political Tasks of the University of the Peoples of the East', in May 1925, where he argued that in the colonies of the imperial powers, the Communist parties must pursue a policy aimed at winning 'the hegemony of the proletariat ... [b]ut the Communist Party can and must enter into an open bloc with the revolutionary wing of the bourgeoi-sie in order, after isolating the compromising national bourgeoisie, to lead the vast masses of the urban and rural petty bourgeoisie in the struggle against imperialism'.[31] Such alliances were very different to the policy of hegemony the

---

26 Zinov'ev 1926, p. 257 [original emphasis].

27 Vasetskii 1989b, p. 22.

28 Trotsky 1974 [1922]. See also Anderson 1976, pp. 72–5. It is also worth noting that Trotsky did not support important aspects of Preobrazhenskii's economic policies. On this, see Day 1990.

29 The classic account of the failed Sparticist uprising and its relationship to Comintern policy is Broué 2006 [1971]. See also Carr 1969, pp. 209–51; Bayerlein 1999, pp. 251–62.

30 Deutscher 1982, p. 143.

31 Stalin 1954c [1925], p. 151.

Bolsheviks had pursued in Russia before 1917, since in practice the Communist parties were subordinated to the bourgeois parties to which they were allied. Scepticism towards alliances *tout court* was now presented as a hallmark of Trotskyism, while the policy of formal alliances with bourgeois nationalists led to a disaster in China in 1927 that was to set a pattern for decades to come.[32]

An account of the international dimensions of this question is beyond the bounds of the current study, and it has already found many able researchers. Here it is the dimension of the debates within the USSR itself that are the focus of attention, although the two dimensions are by no means completely separable. In his 1926 book *Leninizm*, Zinov'ev cited the resolution to the Third Congress of the Comintern on the peasant question: 'state power in the hands of one class, the proletariat, can and must become an instrument for the attraction of the non-proletarian masses of toilers to the side of the proletariat, a weapon in the reconquest of these masses from the bourgeoisie and from the petty-bourgeois parties'.[33]

Within the Soviet Union, the centre of the discussion about hegemony, as this project of 'attraction', tended to shift away from direct political discussion and toward the cultural aspects necessarily involved in the maintenance of the *smychka*, and in trying to solve the national question by administrative means. In essence, the leaders of the Party had to address the various dimensions of the problematic of hegemony as they arose, each as an unintended consequence of the Party finding itself governing alone in a state where the proletariat was, at best, fragmented and numerically disadvantaged on a massive scale. While this led to some important developments of the notion of hegemony, tendencies that would ultimately undermine the applicability of the programme of hegemony within the USSR were growing.

Apparatuses of Hegemony

It was in the realm of linguistic relations that the question of hegemony became particularly important, since the Russian Empire consisted of a largely illiterate or semi-literate Russian population, most of whom spoke a variety of non-standard forms of the language, and a large variety of speakers of other languages, most of which had no standard written forms. A measured,

---

32   Isaacs 2009 [1938]; Harris 1978.

33   Zinov'ev 1926, p. 204. The resemblance between this formulation and Gramsci's account of '*fascino-prestigio*' [binding-prestige] in the *Notebooks* is striking, even though the term probably derived from Bartoli.

systematic approach to this question was rendered impossible when the revolution immediately descended into a brutal civil war against former tsarist officers, who were supported by a range of foreign powers. The question of maintaining hegemony loomed large and the linguistic dimensions soon forced their way into the consciousness of the leadership. The Bolsheviks had initially not planned on creating a standing army, but the low proportion of worker, as opposed to peasant, recruits and a relatively poor railway system in a huge territory had made the preferred, territorially-based militia-defence system impossible to organise.[34] A centralised military structure arose, and from the beginning of the Civil War the Bolsheviks were compelled to reappoint former tsarist officers and place them under the supervision of political commissars. Marx could have scarcely found a better illustration for his rhetorical question to Engels in a letter of July 1866: 'Is there any sphere in which our theory that the *organisation* of labour is determined *by the means of production* is more dazzlingly vindicated than in the industry for human slaughter?'[35]

Trotsky immediately recognised that the army needed to be governed according to the principles of the hegemony of the proletariat, meaning that a dictatorship over the ex-tsarist officers must be coupled with leadership of the peasantry. For the latter, the 'blind herd instinct' of the tsarist army needed to be replaced by a new 'psychological cement by means of which we can create a new army, a real, conscious Soviet army, bound together by a discipline that has passed through the soldiers' brains, and not just the discipline of the rod'.[36] Trotsky made it clear that the aim was to form a peasant and worker soldier who is 'aware of himself as a human personality, with a right to respect, but also feels that he is part of the working class of republican Russia and will be prepared unquestioningly to lay down his life for this republican Soviet Russia'.[37] Political work among rank-and-file soldiers became as important as the supervision of ex-tsarist officers, and a dedicated system to facilitate this arose. Although the army had special detachments for ethnic minorities, the standing-army principle required a core that was based on a single language of command.[38] From the time of its formation, the Red Army was viewed as a vital instrument in the dissemination of enlightenment throughout a

---

34   Smilga 1921, pp. 16–17.
35   Marx 1987 [1866], p. 289.
36   Trotsky 1979a [1918].
37   Trotsky 1979a [1918].
38   This was something that Kautsky had already recognised to be crucial to all standing armies in his work on the national question. See Kautsky 2010 [1908], p. 146.

backward country, and for this reason the army was immediately committed to the eradication of illiteracy.

The Agitation Department of the Political Administration of the Military Soviet [*Politicheskoe Upravlenie Revoliutsionnogo Voennogo Soveta Respubliki* (PUR)] argued that a soldier who was illiterate when drafted, but literate on demobilisation, 'would never forget that the workers' and peasants' government had provided him with the most powerful weapon for the defence of his interests – enlightenment'.[39] Literacy classes were made mandatory for soldiers, along with classes in the rudiments of political knowledge, the two being united in the notion of 'political literacy' [*politgramota*].[40] Some one hundred thousand recruits were basically literate by 1920.[41] One leader, formulating the principles in a report to the Ukrainian Commissariat of Enlightenment in 1919, argued that in order for the political consciousness of the soldier to be profound, 'it must be based on a general-cultural foundation', and from this it followed that 'both political and cultural-enlightenment work must go hand in hand, reinforcing each other'.[42] Considerable attention was given to formulating materials that were relevant and accessible to recruits, as well as to developing techniques to encourage the active engagement of recruits in lessons. Instructions issued to teachers the same year stressed the need to 'widen the intellectual horizon of the soldier, to raise his curiosity and confidence': 'The teacher should lead discussions on questions of social science [*obshchestvo-vedenie*], natural science, history and literature. Having posed a problem, the teacher should only lead the thread of the discussion and explain the unfamiliar, allowing the soldiers to find the truth by means of the exchange of views, that is, raising their self-confidence'.[43]

This was backed up by instructional theatrical performances and the production of newspapers, to which soldiers often wrote with complaints and questions. This combined the *Proletkul't* agenda with the Leninist focus on the importance of the press and led to the *Rabkor* [worker correspondent] and *Sel'kor* [peasant correspondent] movement, which became the backbone of

---

39   Quoted in Hagen 1990, p. 97.

40   During the Civil War, political education in the Red Army was often aimed at halting atrocities. Success was limited but the very attempt distinguished the Red Army from the White Army. See Brown 1995, pp. 82–99.

41   Kenez 1985, p. 77.

42   TsDAVOVUU 166/2/453/4.

43   TsDAVOVUU 166/2/453/30.

the popular press during the NEP period.[44] It was a testament to the effectiveness of instruction within the army that a significant proportion of the *Sel'kor* was made up of recently demobilised soldiers.[45]

The Press

At the Eleventh Party Congress in 1922, a restructuring of the press was recognised as necessary to combat the growth of bourgeois influence, along with that of capitalist relations under NEP. The Party needed to 'broaden and deepen its agitation and propaganda work', and the press constituted the most important weapon in the struggle for influence over the masses.[46] As well as having propaganda functions, during the time of the NEP the Soviet press had a number of other related functions: 'to disseminate news and information, educate the far-flung and ignorant peasant masses, be a bulwark against corruption and nepotism in the emerging state and Party bureaucracies, and, through the worker-peasant correspondent [*rabsel'kor*] movement, facilitate communication from the masses to the regime'.[47] While there had been amateur correspondents involved with some Populist and labour-movement newspapers before the revolution, a concerted attempt to strengthen the links between workers, peasants and the press was launched only with the NEP. Bukharin, Trotsky, Mikhail Kalinin and Lenin's sister, Mariia Ul'ianova, all saw the importance in establishing correspondents from the masses to facilitate communication between the masses and government in the fraught environment following the Civil War.[48] Bukharin and Ul'ianova presided over the First Congress of *Rabsel'kor* at the end of 1923, at which the *Rabkor* was acknowledged to be an independent workers' voice made up of volunteers. Nevertheless, Bukharin made it clear that *Rabkor* organisations are affiliated to the Party's educational, political and cultural work. Most *Rabkor* articles were sketches of worker life [*rabochii byt*] published in popular newspapers, often wall newspapers [*stengazeta*], associated with different sections of industry, or specific localities in the case of *Sel'kor* sketches.[49] Wall newspapers were

---

44   On the movement, see Alferov 1970; Clibbon 1993; Gorham 1996; Coe 1996. On the significance for the development of proletarian literature, see Dobrenko 2001; Hicks 2007.

45   Coe 1996, p. 1153.

46   *KPSS v rezoliutsiakh i resheniiakh*, 1, 1953, pp. 642–3.

47   Mueller 1998, p. 851.

48   Trotsky 1973a [1924]; Bukharin 1926 [1924].

49   For a general discussion of the *stengazeta*, see Kelley 2002.

displayed in factories or in 'reading huts' in the village. Given the low levels of general literacy, the correspondents often only had a tenuous connection with the communities they served, but as time went on more ordinary workers were trained to write, through study circles and then more formal institutions. The *Rabkor* were also often linked to *Rabkrin*, the Workers' and Peasants' Inspectorate that was set up to combat bureaucratisation and administrative abuses. Thus the movement was viewed by many workers as a means by which their grievances could be aired. As Lenin was to recognise at the end of his life, however, *Rabkrin* was itself increasingly falling under the influence of the Party bureaucracy and gradually losing its independence.[50] These paradoxically bureaucratic measures against bureaucracy were designed to buy time until help came from the revolutionary movement in more central areas of the international capitalist system. The problem was that when the prospect of this help receded, and policy shifted towards the creation of socialism in one country through bureaucratic measures, the official attitude towards the more backward areas of the USSR took on an increasingly paternalistic form.

This process was significantly assisted by the February–April 1924 'Lenin Levy', in which Lenin's longstanding ambition to keep the Party small was abandoned, rules governing admission were relaxed, two hundred and forty thousand new members admitted into the Party and its total membership increased by more than fifty percent.[51] The new recruits were not individual political enthusiasts, but 'workers from the bench' and workers of peasant origin, who had little political experience and owed career advancement to the Party bureaucracy. At the same time that workers were being admitted into the Party, their ranks were being swelled by new arrivals from the countryside, first-generation city dwellers who had no grounding in the traditions of the labour movement. The 'proletarian dictatorship' was now set on a path towards becoming a populist regime in which the 'Soviet people' [*narod*] would become the ideological underpinning of the state. One advantage for the leadership was that the new entrants into the Party provided 'voting fodder' for the centre to overcome the opposition, but this development also necessitated a stronger central authority and a significantly expanded Party-education structure.

This manifested itself in a number of ways. The training of journalists involved a wide range of general-education courses dealing with historical, economic, literary and even psychological themes, but this narrowed considerably to focus on Party history and policy after 1924, when the Moscow Institute

---

50   Lenin 1965c [1923].

51   Hatch 1989; Carr 1970, pp. 193–201.

of Journalism became a Party academy.[52] This also follows the same pattern as when the IZhS was reorganised at the same time. In June 1925 the Party pronounced the *Rabsel'kor* organisations to be 'schools of communism' and correspondents were expected to assist in drives to tighten up production, increase industrial efficiency and cut waste.[53] The struggle against '*biurokratizm*' was increasingly identified with efficiency drives, with the effect that the rapidly growing ranks of the *Rabkory* and *Rabkrin* were gradually transformed into agents of management. However, the process was only completed with the first Five-Year Plan, and so throughout the 1920s the *Rabkor* remained a body that was subject to the pressures of both management and labour in a period when management pressures and labour dissatisfaction ebbed and flowed. The second part of the 1920s saw a moderate management offensive, but this was to take a qualitatively different form at the end of the decade.[54]

The *Sel'kor* was particularly important in the project of maintaining the *smychka*. The village press was meant to establish communication between the Party and the masses in those areas where the Party's organisational presence was still relatively weak. At the end of the Civil War, when the common enemy was no longer a tangible threat and relations between town and country began to come apart, culminating in the Basmachi movement in Central Asia and the Kronstadt rebellion in Russia itself, the need to re-establish hegemonic relations were subject to renewed attention. As the peasant economy began to revive with the consolidation of NEP, even more attention was paid to the rural areas as the maintenance of hegemony was held to depend on the adaptation of industry to the peasant market. At the Twelfth Party Congress, Stalin argued for the need for:

> ...a system of government...which enables us to foresee with accuracy all changes, all the circumstances among the peasants, among the nationals, among the so-called 'aliens' and among the Russians; this system of supreme organs possesses a number of barometers which forecast every change, which register and warn against a Basmach movement, a bandit movement, Kronstadt, and all possible storms and disasters. That is the Soviet system of government. It is called Soviet power, people's power, because, relying on the common people, it is the first to register any

---

52   Clibbon 1993, pp. 134–41.
53   Clibbon 1993, pp. 85–7.
54   See, in particular, Murphy 2005.

change, it takes the appropriate measures and rectifies the line in time, if it has become distorted, criticises itself and rectifies the line.[55]

The *Sel'kor* had a particularly important position as just such a barometer, but this meant displacing and replacing the existing sources of authority in the village, such as the clergy, the old rural administrators and local notables, as well as isolating the kulaks and limiting their influence on village life.[56] Here was precisely the same issue Gramsci was to face when discussing the obstacles to proletarian hegemony in the predominantly rural areas of the south of Italy. In the autumn of 1924, the Party made a concerted attempt to 'revitalise' the village soviets, improve local administration and raise the quality of local officials. Here, the *Sel'kory* were expected to explain the Party's policies in ways accessible to the local population, while articulating local grievances and exposing the corruption of local officials.

The proportion of *Rabsel'kory* who were members of the Party increased significantly with the Lenin Levy, giving them significant opportunities for career development. They were now also subject to central-Party discipline and training. The Party was increasingly viewed as a 'source of higher privilege rather than higher obligation' and the correspondents often looked to the Party as an opportunity for career advancement.[57] However, the fact that a significant number of *Rabkory* were now members of the Party did not necessarily make them members of a political vanguard. As Carr noted, one important result of the Lenin Levy was that, unlike in the preceding period:

> ... the vanguard was formed not of the party as a whole, but by a group within the party which was to lead and instruct the mass party membership and at the same time the masses which still remained outside the party. The distinction between leaders and led, between vanguard and masses no longer corresponded to the distinction between party and non-party. As time went on, the mass of the party and the non-party masses might even seem to have more in common with one another than the mass of the party with the party *élite*.[58]

This was reflected in the language that the correspondents used. Correspondents were encouraged to use the 'fresh', 'living', even 'succulent' 'language of

---

55   Stalin, 1954b [1923], p. 265.

56   Coe 1996, p. 1156.

57   Carr 1969, pp. 362–3, Carr 1970, pp. 212–13.

58   Carr 1970, p. 209.

the people', to exploit its expressive richness and freedom from journalistic cliché. As Clibbon notes, the language was celebrated for being 'free of book-ishness', while expressive and rich in metaphor. It was creative, with intelligent manipulation of language, and redolent with a biting humour. It drew on urban and rural folklore, such as the use of anecdotes, *chastushki* [popular rhyming couplets] and other forms of popular verse.[59] Such features attracted the admiration of literary critics and also the poet Mayakovsky, who, in his 1926 article on the creation of poetry, demanded 'immediately to give full rights of citizenship to the new language'.[60] 'The revolution has thrown the clumsy speech [*govor*] of the millions onto the streets, the jargon of the margins poured through the central avenues, the supine lingo [*iazychisko*] of the intellectuals, with its gelded words "ideal", "principles of justice", "divine origin", "the transcendental face of Christ and the Antichrist", all these discourses [*rechi*], that are murmured in restaurants are overrun. This is the new element of language'.[61] For Mayakovsky, such language can be made into poetry according to 'social command [*sotsial'nyi zakaz*]' with the aim of the 'victory of the proletariat, conveyed in new words, expressive and comprehensible to all, worked out on the table, equipped by NOT [the scientific organisation of labour – CB], and delivered to the editor on an aeroplane'.[62]

Trends were running against Mayakovsky's vision of liberation, however, and, as we shall see, the invocation of NOT as a model for the liberation of workers was to become increasingly problematic as the decade progressed. As they were drawn into the lower ranks of the Party, worker and peasant correspondents increasingly employed political jargon and terms encountered in education programmes. The result was often a jumbled, syncretic lexicon that distorted the political message and compromised the language of the streets with abstract categories.[63] Rather than structuring the language and world view of the worker and peasant, facilitating enlightenment and the articulation of perspectives, the unsystematised hybrid language that emerged reflected the growing gap between the Party élite and the masses, whether within or outside the Party. The fractured language became an object of aesthetic representation in the fictional works of writers like Boris Pil'niak, Mikhail Zoschchenko and Isaak Babel', with so-called *skaz* narration, in which the narrative voice is permeated by the stylistic peculiarities of characters, proving particularly

59   Clibbon 1993, pp. 161–71.
60   Maiakovskii 1959 [1926], p. 85.
61   Maiakovskii 1959 [1926], p. 84.
62   Maiakovskii 1959 [1926], p. 89.
63   For a discussion, see Gorham 1996.

effective. In such works, stylistic and ideological particularities were shown to be closely related. The technique was often used to comic effect, but sometimes, as in Babel''s portrayal of Cossack language or, as we shall see, Andrei Platonov's alienated proletarians, the results were rather more disturbing.

Linguistic Fragmentation

It was not long before the fractured language of the popular press became an object of analysis. In his 1924 study *The Newspaper and the Village*, Iakov Shafir found that literate peasants commanded a very limited vocabulary and that their speech relied heavily on analogies that were uncommon in the language of the press.[64] This was reflected in forms of popular etymology, so that, for instance, decorative [*dekorativnost'*] was understood to mean a wild plant [*dikoe rastenie*]; initiative [*initsiativa*] – a particular nationality; official [*ofitsial'nyi*] – good, correct and so on. He argued that the language of peasant newspapers should stay as close as possible to that of spoken language and use illustrations where appropriate. In a follow-up study, *Problems of Newspaper Culture* (1927), he argued that the rural reader did not understand the contractions, foreign words and unwieldy sentence constructions that commonly permeated the village press, and that these should be avoided where possible, with special training for a new corps of journalists who are closely tied to the masses.[65]

The problem was not only one of the press, however, since it became clear that even where formal instruction and training was taking place, the same fragmentation was occurring. One fascinating study of the problem was carried out by Isaak Shpil'rein and a group of researchers from the Psychotechnic section of the Institute of Experimental Psychology in Moscow in 1924–5. They analysed the language of worker and (mainly) peasant conscripts of the Moscow Garrison of the Red Army at various stages of their military careers, during which many progressed from almost totally illiterate and untutored raw recruits through two years of intensive training in literacy, basic education, military and political instruction.[66] Following the demobilisation at the end of the Civil War, educational practices had largely settled into a rut and the still-large numbers of recruits who passed through the army were not

---

64   Shafir 1924. For detailed discussions of the book and its reception, see Lehikoinen 1990, pp. 204–9; Gorham 2003, pp. 28–30, 33–5.

65   Shafir 1927, pp. 129–34.

66   Shpil'rein *et al.* 1928. For a fuller discussion of this work, see Brandist 2010.

emerging with the level of education that had been hoped. It was revealed that even towards the end of their time in the army, up to 75 percent of respondents misunderstood important borrowed or jargon terms such as *blokada* [blockade], *import* [import], *monopoliia* [monopoly] and *biurokrat* [bureaucrat]. The researchers traced this back to instructors not adjusting their methods to the sociological and experiential background of the recruits. Using the terminology of contemporary psychotechnics, the authors argued that instructors constantly needed to adjust their 'systematic', 'measured' and 'rationalised' 'influencing work' to the previous 'lexical experience' of the 'object of influence' (the soldier).[67] At the Kazan Institute of the Scientific Organisation of Labour, M.A. Iurovskaia carried out a follow-up survey of civilian students of political literacy and found problems in political development that could be traced back to similar, 'superficial-mechanical' associations, carelessness when instructors used foreign or jargon words and a general lack of appreciation among instructors of the need to attune instruction to the specific social environment and origins of the students.[68] Characteristic mistakes that were 'fatal' to political development included the following definitions: 1) Fascism – kingdom; 2) blockade – declaration of independence; 3) chauvinism – supporters of war in the West; 4) imperialism – German legislative organ; 5) trade union [*trediunion*] – abroad; 6) specialist-baiting [*spetseedstvo*] – food prescribed by a doctor.[69]

Throughout the NEP period, a number of studies emerged revealing the extent of linguistic and ideological fragmentation within Russia, and this began to shift the research agenda of linguists. As early as January 1919, Iakubinskii was drawing up plans at IZhS to collect the new material about the influence of the war and revolution on the Russian language, while a year later the dialectologist Vasilii Chernyshev was noting numerous phenomena that would reappear in a number of subsequent studies, the most famous being Afanasii Selishchev's *Language of the Revolutionary Epoch* (1928).[70] Acronyms, neologisms and stump compounds not only littered the speech of the streets, but also permeated the language of the new administration, which was made

---

67 Shpil'rein *et al.* 1928, pp. 116–17.

68 Iurovskaia 1928, pp. 29–40.

69 Iurovskaia 1928, p. 35.

70 RGALI (SPb) 82/1/22/520b; V.I. Chernyshev, 'Vliianie voiny i revoliutsii na russkii iazyk: Instruktsiia dlia sobraniia materialov' (1920), IRLI f.474, d.455, ll.1–25; Mazon 1920; Kartsevskii, 2000 [1923]; Selishchev 1928. One of the earliest considerations of the changes the war was bringing about was Vladimir Maiakovskii's article 'Voina i iazyk', of November 1914: Maiakovskii 1955 [1914]. For a recent discussion, see Lehikoinen 1990.

up of recently recruited persons with none of the training of the previous bureaucracy. Studies listed how, in the new situation, military jargon quickly spread throughout the urban environment and was used in a range of contexts, along with the emotional-expressive constructions often used in revolutionary propaganda, which inevitably lost their emotive force. At the end of the decade, one of Baudouin's former students, the Marxist linguist Evgenii Polivanov, sought to characterise the mechanism of 'evolutionary innovations' [*novshchestvo*], tracing the sources of new terminology and concepts that have entered official languages and 'collective consciousness' because of the October Revolution.[71] These are found, variously, in other national languages, social dialects or political discourse, the last of which had changed fundamentally.[72] However, Polivanov argued that structural changes in the Russian language had not been so great, but what was more significant was that the national language had now been transferred to a new 'social substratum'.[73] As we will see, philologists began to apply the methods of dialect geography to large cities, examining the relationship between the standard national language and other 'systems', such as varieties of argot and how one and the same speaker could simultaneously belong to a number of 'language collectives'. Funding for significant projects in this field led to an extremely rich body of sociolinguistic thought.[74]

As Michael Gorham has shown, by the mid-1920s a series of competing solutions were being formulated, ranging from the propagation of the language of the pre-revolutionary classics (favoured by Gorky and others), through investing the colloquial language [*govorenie*] with wider social functions and encouraging the emergence of a standard that was close to that spoken by the masses (favoured by the proletarian-culture movement, especially RAPP),[75] to an interventionist strategy through which radical intellectuals (poets, linguists and journalists) would act as linguistic technicians (favoured by the Futurists and given theoretical expression by Grigorii Vinokur), drawing on the linguistic creativity of the newly enfranchised masses to renew the public discourse and turn it into a medium of enlightenment.[76] After reviewing the various positions adopted in the debates, Riita Lehikoinen argues that most participants tended to conclude:

---

71   Polivanov 1974d [1931], p. 84.

72   Polivanov 1974c [1928], p. 197. Such studies clearly anticipated Gramsci's work on the sources and dissemination of linguistic and ideological innovations in the twenty-ninth notebook.

73   Polivanov 1974a [1927], p. 181.

74   See Brandist 2003.

75   See Dobrenko 2001, p. 281.

76   For an overview, see Gorham 2003, *passim*.

[I]t was necessary to maintain an orientation on the less-cultured mass reader, learn to speak to them in a language they found comprehensible, purge the language of newspapers of superfluous foreign words and difficult turns of phrase. Meanwhile, to simplify the Russian printed word did not mean merely bringing it closer to the spoiled language of the backward village.[77]

The focus should be on the middle-ability mass reader, with materials for the lowest abilities designed for stations to eradicate illiteracy and for newspapers that were read aloud. The newspaper materials should be designed to broaden the interests of the reader, 'from the small to the large, from the private to the general, from the concrete to the abstract, from the near to the far, from facts to theory'.[78] In any case, a critical and self-reflexive attitude to language use needed to be encouraged and the new lexicon stabilised. To this effect, a number of dictionaries of the new terminology began to appear in the mid-1920s and the standardisation spread as the ever-expanding corps of *rabkory* and *sel'kory* became more professionalised.[79]

These discussions all pertain to the hegemonic project according to which the intellectual leadership of the proletariat adjusted its language to that of the peasantry, while attempting to structure the latter's fragmented language and world view. This was underlain by an economic policy that subordinated industry to the peasant market, but which led to widening class differentiation in the countryside. As we have seen, many Party leaders, including Trotsky and Bukharin, were concerned with the delicate balance between the need to adjust the language of the press to the needs of the masses, and the need to raise the verbal skills of the masses. This was all accompanied by a general bureaucratisation of social life and the resultant dislocation between official political discourse and the experience of the general population, which meant that, for most workers and peasants, much socio-political terminology remained jargon.

Organisation of Labour

New arrivals from the countryside not only brought their non-standard linguistic forms with them but were also accustomed to patterns of working

---

77   Lehikoinen 1990, p. 238.
78   Ibid.
79   See Lehikoinen 1990, pp. 172–7 and the list of dictionaries (Lehikoinen 1990, pp. 264–5).

quite unsuited to industry. It is significant that the studies of Shpil'rein and Iurovskaia discussed above were carried out as part of a drive for the 'scientific organisation of labour' [*nauchnaia organizatsiia truda*, NOT], a movement launched to raise the productivity of labour in Soviet enterprises through the introduction of techniques of scientific management, such as the Taylor system. Although Lenin had championed the introduction of such measures, in no way did he present the system as an unambiguously positive phenomenon. Indeed, in 1918 he argued that the system, 'like all capitalist progress', is 'a combination of the refined brutality of bourgeois exploitation and a number of the greatest scientific achievements in the field of analysing mechanical motions during work, the elimination of superfluous and awkward motions, the elaboration of correct methods of work, the introduction of the best system of accounting and control, etc.'[80]

Such measures were a regrettable necessity brought about by economic collapse and, later, to buy time for the internationalisation of the revolution. Thus what was required was 'state capitalism', meaning private capitalism under state control, and Lenin was quite clear that this should not be presented as socialism. He insisted, against Bukharin and others, that '[w]e ... must tell the workers: Yes, it is a step back [from the dictatorship of the proletariat – CB], but we have to help ourselves to find a remedy'.[81] This intrinsic link between state capitalism and Taylorism was something that tended to disappear in subsequent discussions of the issue, so that the adoption of Taylorist methods ceased to be considered as a short-term necessity and was instead treated more like a permanent virtue. In his book-length study of Lenin's complex relationship to Taylorism, the French Maoist Robert Linhart argues that Lenin believed that the introduction of aspects of the Taylor system would allow workers to master *tekhnika* [technology and technique] and so better dominate the production process and, through the efficiencies achieved, allow for a reduction in the working day. This would facilitate an activist worker democracy that would provide an effective counter to the bureaucratisation of the state.[82] Linhart concluded, however, that such measures actually created their own forms of bureaucratisation by separating forms of mental and manual labour, and that this led to the rise of the productionist ideology that culminated in the Stakhanovite movement of the 1930s.[83] One does not need to accept Linhart's

---

80   Lenin 1972c [1918], p. 259

81   Lenin 1972d [1918], p. 301.

82   Linhart 1976, pp. 105–16. On Linhart's political background and his conception of Marxism, see Reid 2004.

83   Linhart 1976, p. 114.

apparent elision of the relations of production and of ideological factors to see that the struggle that developed within the movement for NOT could well be viewed as playing out this contradiction.

Shpil'rein was associated with the so-called 'Time League' [*Liga vremia*] led by the *Proletkul't* theorist Kerzhentsev, who argued that the involvement of workers in the creation and implementation of the processes of production, and their development through what Bogdanov had called 'comradely cooperation', would lead to the internalisation of time discipline among workers in the workplace. Workers must be able to appreciate the positive aspects of NOT, to overcome their 'organisational illiteracy',[84] to take control of their labour power and champion the restoration of the economy after the destruction of the Civil War. However, this was linked to the task of cultural hegemony, since the proletarian experience needed to be consolidated and generalised throughout social life, lest the alien culture of peasant life and bureaucracy come to predominate. As a mass movement, the Time League would act as a means for educating society in the values of proletarian culture – systematising, generalising and disseminating the organised social experience of the proletariat. Echoing Bogdanov's critique of Taylorism, which was republished after the revolution, Kerzhentsev contrasted the League's approach to NOT with that in the West, where 'positing a scientific approach to production was ... to increase the productivity of labour chiefly by means of its intensification ... the question of discipline was also posited only at the level of pressure on the proletariat from the administration of the enterprise'.[85] Rather than the worker being physically and psychologically dominated by the machine, 'the goal of socialism is to institute *the domination of the machine by labour*, for the worker to become the commander of the machine'.[86]

More importantly, the focus on time accentuated the fact that the pressure of socially necessary labour time as a determinant of production was proportional to the compulsion and restraints of capital. While time was currently (1924) a 'core issue in all kinds of socio-political and even economic plans and combinations', another writer in the League's journal noted that 'the exceptional significance that time acquires in the competitive struggle within capitalist states and between them on a world scale is significantly lessened with the transition of all human society to communism'.[87] While many of their publications were unsophisticated and their campaigns naive, the League thus

---

84   Kerzhentsev 1924, pp. 36–7.
85   Kerzhentsev 1990, p. 125. Bogdanov's text is Bogdanov 1918.
86   Katkyn' 1924, p. 8 [original emphasis].
87   Ibid.

focused attention on an important issue: the identification of socially necessary labour time as the crucial factor in determining the direction of social and economic development. Was this to remain an abstract form of social domination, an abstract compulsion which attested to the rule of capital, or was this to 'wither away' like the state with the coming of socialism? The fact that this was linked to the future of the international revolution was undoubtedly a reason why Trotsky sat on the editorial board of the League's journal, which to some extent determined the ultimate fate of the organisation and some of its members. Shpil'rein was executed for allegedly being a Trotskyist in 1938.

The League was pitted against Aleksei Gastev and his colleagues at the Central Institute of Labour, who aimed to create a technical intelligentsia able to systematise and generalise the new collective mentality that was created in mass industry. The struggle between the two trends, with the latter finally victorious, has been subject to a considerable amount of comment and so I will not present a general discussion here.[88] What is significant here was that Gastev sought to transform Marxism into a philosophy of technology, according to which technique in the sense of the German *Technik*, meaning the methods and procedures of material culture, is a force that shapes social organisation and consciousness.[89] In this he followed Plekhanov, Bogdanov and Bukharin in understanding Marx's *Produktionsweise* [mode of production] in a one-sided way, as being identical with *Arbeitsprozess* [labour process], and brought out certain implications that had not previously been recognised. Bukharin had adopted this notion of '*tekhnika*' as the engine of social change in his *Historical Materialism*, where he argued that 'technology [*tekhnika*] conditions the mode of production; the mode of production conditions the view of life; this chain uniting the material, human and mental system creates a certain type of society'.[90] As Georg Lukács noted in his critique of Bukharin:

---

88   See, *inter alia*, Lieberstein 1975; Bailes 1977, pp. 373–94; Sochor 1981a; Beissinger 1988; Stites 1989, pp. 145–64; Brunnbauer 2000.

89   As well as Oswald's 'energetics', this conception also had wider roots in the work of the German philosopher of technology, Ernst Kapp (see, for instance, Kapp 1877) and in the work of Noiré. For an example of the way in which these trends were presented together at the time, see the anthology edited by Plotnikov (Plotnikov (ed.) 1925).

90   Bukharin 1962 [1926], p. 233. The same rigid formulation is presented by Stalin in a 1938 article: 'First the productive forces of society change and develop, and then, depending on these changes and in conformity with them, men's relations of production, their economic relations, change. … however much the relations of production may lag behind the development of the productive forces, they must, sooner or later, come into correspondence

... this final identification of technique [*technik*] with the forces of production is neither valid nor Marxist. Technique [*technik*] is a part, a
moment, naturally of great importance, of the social productive forces,
but it is neither simply identical with them nor ... the final or absolute
moment of the changes in these forces. . . . if development is not explained
by the social forces of production (and this is what needs clarification), it
[*technik*] is just as much a transcendent principle, set over against man,
as 'nature', climate, environment, raw materials etc.[91]

Leaning heavily on Wilhelm Otswald's 'human energetics', which had also
been important for Bogdanov, Gastev treated Marx's abstract labour and
labour power as physiological categories that are fully absorbed into a 'science
of the installation of energy' [*nauka ustanovochnoi energetiki*].[92] In conditions
of machine technology, labour power is finally revealed to be just one form of
energetic, since human labour becomes an extension of the energetics of the
machine.[93] The modern factory revolutionises culture and psychology, 'standardising' the lives of the individual and of the social whole, creating new laws
and norms that do not depend on the will of individuals themselves.[94] The
machine becomes a social ideal, an example of organisation in every aspect of
life. *Tekhnika* is no longer limited to the factory, it organises the whole sense of
time and space of society according to objective criteria, rationalising psychological experience. A new reality is both revealed and created through mea-
surement, calculation and verification.

While Gastev's NOT thus provided the image of an extremely alienated society, his work had something in common with Bücher's diagnosis of the alienation of modern life. Bücher had argued that alienation was the psychological
consequence of a dislocation between the predominant mode of production
and the anthropological factors (rhythm of work, acquired psychological
framework) of a given society, its culture. Production and culture needed to be

---

with – and actually do come into correspondence with – the level of development of the
productive forces, the character of the productive forces'. Stalin 1976 [1938], pp. 859–60.

91   Lukács 1966 [1925]; Lukács 1969 [1925]. For a fair survey of the Russian reception of
      Bukharin's book, and of its relationship to Bogdanov's work, see Chagin 1971, pp. 75–82
      et passim. Bukharin did protest that he differed from Bogdanov on a number of issues in
      Bukharin 1923, p. 8.

92   Gastev 1973 [1918], p. 16. For an interesting discussion of this aspect of Gastev's work see
      Shearer 1979.

93   Gastev 1972 [1929], p. 245.

94   Gastev 1972 [1929], p. 241.

adjusted to one another.[95] For Gastev, however, such adjustment is one-sided, and it is the task of workers in the field of ideology (processing information, storing and communicating values) to help individuals to adapt to the social mechanism, to *tekhnika*. The principles of scientific management contribute to this adaptation and they needed to be applied to the cultural sphere as a whole, to organise the spatio-temporal experience of the population through the preparation of environmental factors. Both the direct process of production and culture now became the material of technical manipulation, with the technical intelligentsia creating a bureaucratised culture to match the rationalised world of production. Such a perspective had something in common with Grigorii Vinokur's ideas about the tasks of linguistic technicians (to be discussed below), but Gastev's aims were much more global and far less sophisticated. Socialism as a 'mode of production' was now transformed into a bureaucratic project. In separating abstract labour and labour power from the social and historical form of production, the control of production was stripped of significance and ultimately depoliticised. Analysis was flattened into discussion of a 'transition to "industrialism" *tout court*', rather than to industrial capitalism or to an alternative system, whose features were still indistinct.[96]

Gastev's vision of collectivism was far more extreme and soulless than the *Vperedists*, Bogdanov and Lunacharskii, had dared to imagine even at their most rhetorical moments, for their view was permeated with the spirit of the avant-garde in general and constructivism in particular.[97] In one early work, Gastev takes his arguments to quite absurd lengths, but completely devoid of any irony. All social differences would be levelled, thought would be mechanised and the objective psychology would undergo 'social standardisation' [*sotsial'noe normirovanie*]. In the future there would be an 'impossibility of individual thinking' in a world where there '. . . is no individual human face, but there are even, normalised steps, a face without expression, soul, and absence of lyrics, with emotion measured not by the cry [*krik*], not by laughter, but by a pressure gauge and a taxometer'.[98]

With the rise of a 'mechanised collectivism', individual thought would ultimately disappear into a general and objective social psychology. In the context of the time, Gastev's ideas clearly supported the cause of the burgeoning central bureaucracy and the subordination of the worker and production to

---

95   On the relationship of Bücher's work in this area to the neoliberalism of Wilhelmine Germany, see Smith 1991, pp. 199 ff.

96   Thompson 1991a [1967], p. 383.

97   See Bogdanov 1919. See also Susiluoto 1982, pp. 106–9.

98   Gastev 1919, p. 43; see also Bailes 1977.

the cause of capital accumulation. It is therefore unsurprising that such an approach found considerable support among economic planners.

The Cultural Substratum

In the first part of the 1920s, the rise of Gastev's brand of NOT was constrained by the residual commitment to a specifically proletarian dictatorship among the leadership. In the wake of the Civil War, Lenin noted that it was the 'enormous undivided prestige enjoyed by the small group which might be called the Old Guard of the Party' that maintained a policy oriented on the proletariat rather than 'the character of its membership' and noted that 'a slight conflict within this group will be enough, if not to destroy this prestige, at all events to weaken the group to such a degree as to rob it of its power to determine policy'.[99] Such a conflict soon broke out in the wake of the defeat of the German Revolution. The weakening of the proletarian orientation of policy was further aided by Lenin's withdrawal from actively participating in shaping that policy. The 'Lenin Levy' finally overwhelmed the 'old guard' with pliant careerists who owed their allegiance to what Lenin called the 'huge bureaucratic machine, that gigantic heap' that administered the state.[100] Speaking at the Eleventh Party Congress in March 1922, Lenin drew a provocative image:

> Something analogous happened here to what we were told in our history lessons when we were children: sometimes one nation conquers another, the nation that conquers is the conqueror and the nation that is vanquished is the conquered nation. This is simple and intelligible to all. But what happens to the culture of these nations? Here things are not so simple. If the conquering nation is more cultured than the vanquished nation, the former imposes its culture upon the latter; but if the opposite is the case, the vanquished nation imposes its culture upon the conqueror. Has not something like this happened in the capital of the R.S.F.S.R.?

The cultural substratum inherited from the previous regime, in the form of the bureaucrats who had been recruited into the administration, was systematised and powerful enough to exert a formative influence on the practices of the political leadership. As the preponderance and thus prestige of the 'old guard' declined, so the appeal of bureaucratic practices was heightened, easing the

---

99   Lenin 1965a [1922], p. 257.
100   Lenin 1965b [1922], p. 288.

path for 'functional' considerations in administering a unitary state encircled by hostile powers to triumph over political principle. Already in 1919, Lenin had been concerned at the way in which such practices were affecting attitudes among Party members when dealing with relations between the centre and periphery. He insisted that one must not argue that 'economic unity should be affected under all circumstances', since to do so is to lapse into Great Russian chauvinism.[101] Rather, such aims should be secured 'by propaganda, by agitation, by a voluntary alliance'.[102] As we shall see, such concerns faded from view over time. Conceptual adjustments would ultimately be necessary to justify bureaucratic practices in terms of Marxist principles, and this would lead to some crucial semantic shifts within the political lexicon.

The cultural and political issues discussed in this chapter were to frame a considerable amount of the cultural and linguistic research pursued in the USSR in the 1920s and beyond. As we shall see in the next chapter, the young scholars who had been trained by the prominent philologists of the late imperial period now began to rethink the relationship between linguistic phenomena and social environment in radically new ways. In so doing, they sociologised the thought of their predecessors, resulting in formulations that would not begin to emerge in the West until decades later.

---

101   Lenin 1974e [1919], p. 195.
102   Ibid.

The New Paradigm in Linguistic Science

By the middle of the 1920s, a root-and-branch rethink of the nature and tasks of the science of language had taken place when compared with the understanding prevalent at the turn of the century. This movement was not confined to Russia, and the paradigm shift completed by Saussure's *Cours de linguistique générale* [Course in General Linguistics, hereafter CLG] was clearly a crucial part of the transformation. Though a published translation of CLG appeared only in the 1930s, an incomplete translation was circulating among Russian scholars at the beginning of the 1920s.[1] However, as Vladimir Alpatov correctly argues, it was the fact that this shift coincided with the political and social changes inaugurated by the revolutions of 1917 that gave the development of Soviet linguistics its particular character.[2] The synchronic focus characteristic of the new paradigm clashed with the linguistic research of the late nineteenth century, which often focused on the ancient past, pursued the reconstruction of proto-languages or studied the dialects that diverged from the standard 'literary' language as relict forms. The generation that pursued such work was quickly replaced by a new generation that took the contemporary language as its object, but these scholars now found themselves in an institutional environment quite different to their predecessors. As Lev Zinder and Tat'iana Stroeva wrote about their time at one Leningrad institute:

> A characteristic feature of the time was an urge to derive something of *directly practical* usefulness from all research. And the field activity in this sense was vast: in the first place, the majority of languages were essentially unstudied and had no written form, the national language policy of the fledgling Soviet state introduced the study of a native language and in a native language; there was the spread of the literary language among the labouring masses: worker correspondents, peasant correspondents, agitators and propagandists; a method of teaching foreign European languages widely took root among the masses, a method that had to be decisively distinguished from the method of the

---

1 See Toddes and Chudakova 1981 and Reznik 2008.

2 Alpatov 2010.

'governess' (L.V. Shcherba). New types of grant were created in connection with all these tasks.[3]

The provision of resources for new types of research was fundamental, and clearly accelerated the development of applied linguistics. As I have argued elsewhere, this led directly to the development of a version of sociolinguistics decades before the rise of such a discipline in the West.[4] In this chapter, we focus in on the new perspectives on language that emerged in the 1920s and how they related to the linguistic dimensions of hegemony discussed above.

The relationship of Soviet scholars to the new synchronic paradigm is a significant topic in itself. While this is generally associated with CLG, Polivanov could write in 1929 that 'with regard to the famed posthumous book by de Saussure, one can assert with certainty that there are no new premises in it which would not already have been known to us from the teaching of Baudouin de Courtenay'.[5] With regard to many of Saussure's individual premises, one can have considerable sympathy for the view that it is difficult to find any that are completely original, although the way in which the CLG systematised the premises into a whole new definition of the object domain of linguistics, as opposed to general philology and psychology, was undoubtedly unprecedented. As Olga Amsterdamska has noted, while 'the distinction between synchrony and diachrony existed *in nuce*' in the works of Baudouin and Kruszewski, they regarded the adoption of synchronic and diachronic analyses as 'an entirely natural and unproblematic procedure' and thus did not fundamentally challenge the notion of language as a 'psycho-physical entity' that had been inherited from the neo-grammarians.[6] Saussure, on the other hand, regarded such a notion as but one possible way of conceiving language, contending that linguistic facts were not 'objective entities independent of the scientific mode of investigation' but creations of the particular perspective chosen by the observer'.[7] Saussure makes this point directly:

> The object is not given in advance of the viewpoint: far from it. Rather, one might say that it is the viewpoint adopted which creates the object.

---

3   Zinder and Stroeva 1999, p. 207.

4   Brandist 2003.

5   Polivanov 1974 [1929], p. 176.

6   Amsterdamska 1987, pp. 196–7.

7   Amsterdamska 1987, p. 219.

Furthermore, there is nothing to tell us in advance whether one of these ways of looking at it is prior to, or superior to, any of the others.[8]

Polivanov's comment was, however, symptomatic of how the idea of *langue* was long understood in the USSR and beyond. Paul Thibault describes the problem well:

> It is sometimes mistakenly thought that Saussure proposes a static and closed model of language. But this is to mistake an essentially *methodological* decision about how to delimit the study of the language system with Saussure's comprehensive knowledge of historical, geographical and dialectal factors, which are ever present in CLG.[9]

The error is at least understandable given that the model of *langue* that results from his methodological move is indeed 'static and closed', while Saussure does not provide a coherent alternative model based on a different methodological option.[10] Polivanov thus found nothing especially new in relation to these factors that would in any way challenge the fundamental principles of Baudouin's structural approach to language, and so remained largely indifferent to Saussure's work.

However, others did perceive the methodological innovation in *CLG* but then viewed the historical, geographical and dialectal factors discussed by Saussure as instantiations of *langue*. In such cases, the notion of *langue* was identified with the synchronic snapshot of the language of a given area as presented in the works of linguistic geographers, such as the widely-received works of Jules Gilléron. While, for Saussure, the prioritisation of the study of the 'internal principles of organisation of the language system' over the study of 'individual and social *uses* of language' rests on a distinction (*langue* and *parole*) in the theory of *linguistics*, most understood it to denote a distinction inherent in the 'concrete reality of language'.[11] The resultant misreading was as pervasive among those who championed Saussure's work as among those who rejected it. Moreover, once *langue* was ontologised as a system of *a priori* structures

---

8   Saussure 1983 [1916], p. 8. Quoted (using a different translation) in Amsterdamska 1987, p. 219. The implications of this move are not, however, discussed within the *Course in General Linguistics* itself, resulting in a certain tension throughout.

9   Thibault 1997, p. 5.

10   I am indebted to Peter Jones (personal communication) for this point.

11   Thibault 1997, p. 6.

and categories, Saussure's discussion of the relation of language and thought tended to be viewed as defining the conditions of the possibility of subjectivity and human experience, as well as of the ability of individual members of a community to perceive and act.

Such a conception had significant implications for the sort of applied linguistics that the new post-revolutionary environment required. Saussure's definition of *langue* as a 'social fact' was generally held to correspond to the Durkheimian conception, according to which a social fact is 'any way of acting, whether fixed or not, capable of exerting over the individual an external constraint; or which is general over the whole of a given society whilst having an existence of its own, independent of its individual manifestations'.[12] As we shall see, among many Soviet linguists, *langue* came to be seen as a social object external to, and coercing, the individual, with the result that language policy consisted in adjusting the system in such a way that the internalisation of such constraints could give rise to desired forms of subjectivity, perceptions and actions. However, others recognised that such a model essentially reified society which, after all, consists only of people, while language as a real, material presence can only be considered as the linguistic acts of persons and their results. Once this was recognised, then it could be asserted that, should *langue* so conceived be considered a reality, then it would render any linguistic policy an impossibility, and that, in light of the linguistic engineering that was taking place on an unprecedented scale in the USSR, the conception must be mistaken. The clearest statement of this position was in a paper by Iakubinskii delivered in October 1929, in which Saussure was held to claim that 'language changes in time according to objective causes' and that 'the subject of language – the bearer of a language – the language collective does not participate in these changes, its role is purely passive'.[13] If such a perspective is correct, concludes Iakubinskii, then Marx's advice to philosophers 'not only to study, but to change the world' does not apply to linguistics.[14]

There is a sense in which the opposition between the Moscow and Petersburg linguistic schools, which in the nineteenth century had been expressed in commitments to formalistic-positivist and psychologistic perspectives respectively,

---

12   Durkheim 1982, p. 59. The Durkheimian source of Saussure's idea has been challenged by, *inter alia*, Konrad Koerner, not least because Saussure himself refers to William Whitney as the source, and there is no evidence that Saussure engaged with Durkheim at all.

13   Iakubinskii 1986 [1929], p. 72.

14   Iakubinskii 1986 [1929], p. 73. Of course, Marx did not advise philosophers to change the world so much as point out the limitations of philosophy as such.

was transformed into an opposition between those committed and opposed to the Saussurean paradigm conceived in this manner. In each case, however, the Durkheimian-Saussurean conception could not be fully embraced or rejected because the revolutionary transformation that linguists were participating in was simultaneously popular, institutional and systematic. Even linguists most positively disposed towards the voluntarist model had to recognise that the structures of language impose limits on the speech acts performed by individuals. The pro-Saussurean orientation tended towards justifying a conception of linguistic policy that was bureaucratic and codified, while the oppositional currents tended toward a more voluntarist, or *laissez-faire*, orientation. Inevitably, however, the reality of linguistic research was much more complex, since the shortcomings of each approach were apparent to all concerned. In many ways, the theoretical approaches to language of the mid-to-late 1920s were attempts to find a way through this problem.

Specific features of the Soviet context were notable, however. One aspect was the category of the 'living word', as opposed to the written or printed word. As we have seen, living speech was not generally understood in the sense of individual expression, as one finds in the work of Romantic philosophers of the period, such as Benedetto Croce, Karl Vossler or psychologistic thinkers like Wilhelm Wundt. The 'living word' was ideologically replete, imbued with a collective sense that could be understood in national-popular terms (Ivanov etc.), in sociological terms (Bogdanov) or in some eclectic combination of the two (Lunacharskii). The relationship between the 'living' and 'printed' word could be understood as that between a living and reified or ossified form (Zelinskii and thinkers influenced by *Lebensphilosophie*, such as Iakubinskii) or as something that was complementary or strategic (Lenin). Ultimately, the need of the national minorities for the standardisation and codification of linguistic forms to enable them fully to participate in social life undermined the voluntarism of romantically-inclined linguists, since the standard form was to provide the conditions for socially effective speech activity. Similarly, the struggle against illiteracy within Russia itself clearly revealed knowledge of the standard language to be knowledge of an enabling structure as well as of a constraint on speech activity. However, the lexical changes brought about by the flood of non-standard forms of speech into the cities and administration clearly showed that the language was not immobile, but undergoing significant adjustments under the pressure of social changes. Empirical studies of the phenomenon, along with practical attempts to deal with the negative effects of the changes, inevitably required theoretical elaboration. As a consequence, reflection on the nature of linguistic science, and of language itself, took on a rather specific form.

New Directions in Research

1   *Leningrad*

The focus on the 'living word' that had characterised much linguistic research in Leningrad in the early years of the revolution did not so much fade away as shift to more narrowly practical areas. Erberg remained an important point of continuity and continued to work on the idea of the 'living word' throughout the 1920s at ILIaZV, where he made an important contribution to the 'Laboratory of Public Discourse' [*Laboratoriia publichnoi rechi*], which was first directed by Iakubinskii and then by Vladimir Kreps, a former graduate of IZhS and future director of the State Courses of Speech Techniques. The laboratory aimed to study the theory, history and methodology of public discourse and its various manifestations in different social spheres, such as the political, juridical and educational. This meant the study of the preparation, process of performance and results of public speech. Types of speech and its devices were to be classified, along with the lexicological, grammatical and audible characteristics of distinguished speakers, as found in the recordings of notable orators.[15] The most important results of this work still remain unpublished in Erberg's archive.[16]

Originally established as the Veselovskii Institute, ILIaZV continued to develop Veselovskii's idea of verbal art by treating social dialects and standard language, on the one hand, and folklore and literature on the other, as two sides of a single research programme. Veselovskii's students, Vladimir Shishmarev and Marr, held senior positions in the institute and one of its first projects was to complete the publication of Veselovskii's works.[17] Baudouin's students, Iakubinskii and Shcherba, also occupied senior positions, while Viktor Zhirmunskii had a foot in both linguistic and literary camps.

In the second half of the 1920s, as well as studying general questions of the study of language and literature, analysing their evolution, and collecting comments about language from the classics of Marxism, the institute had the following objects of study:

1)   Problems of international and intra-national linguistic and literary exchange on the basis of the socio-economic, political and general cultural interaction of peoples and countries.

---

15   RGALI (SPb) 288/1/27/70b–8.
16   See Brandist 2007. However, for one published article, see Erberg 1929.
17   RGALI (SPb) 288/1/13/10–100b.

a) The interaction of linguistic units (national and class languages, ethnic and social dialects and so on);

b) International literary exchange in connection with the social development of peoples and countries that are in literary interaction.

2) The study of the languages and the oral art [*tvorchestvo*] of the contemporary city, village and the national minorities of the USSR, along with the bordering peoples of East and West on the basis of their socio-economic, political and general-cultural development.[18]

Here we can see quite clearly the sociological reworking of the Veselovskii and Baudouin research programmes. The groups specialising in 'international literary exchange' and 'comparative studies of plot' [*sravnitel'naia siuzhetologiia*], led by Shishmarev, noted that the mutual influence of the literature and fine arts of one country on another was the result of a 'convergence of the social structures of those countries'.[19] This trend developed in connection with the application of certain aspects of Marr's semantic palaeontology, and will be dealt with later.[20] The other proposition that defined the aims of the group was the following statement by Plekhanov:

> A class that is engaged in struggle with his opponents gains a position for itself in the literature of its country. If the same class begins to move in another country, it assimilates the ideas and forms that have been created by its more advanced brethren. But it goes further, or modifies, or lags behind, depending on the differences between its position and the position of the class that serves as an example.[21]

It is by no means clear that this quotation pertains to artistic literature at all. However, it had a potentially valuable application in the third line of research: '[t]he study of the languages and oral art of the contemporary city, village and national minorities of the USSR, and the adjacent nations [*narody*] of the East and West on the basis of their socioeconomic, political and general cultural

---

18 RGALI (SPb) 288/1/39/10b.

19 RGALI (SPb) 288/1/27/100b–110b.

20 In general, see Brandist 2011; Clark and Tihanov 2011, pp. 131–43.

21 RGALI (SPb) 288/1/27/11. I have been unable to locate this quotation in the complete works of Plekhanov.

development'.[22] Clearly, the grounds were laid for significant research into hegemonic relations within the USSR and its neighbours, which were to operate on two levels: one related to literature and folklore and the other at the level of language and ideology more generally.

In Leningrad, the heritage of Baudouin was strong. The Humboldtian insistence that linguistic forms should not be considered separate from their conceptual implications was prominent. What had changed, however, was a clear understanding that the speech act bears characteristics of the social group to which the speaker belongs, and that these characteristics emerge in the social interaction that also shapes the speaker's psychology. This shift is already present in Iakubinskii's 1923 article 'O dialogicheskoi rechi' ['On Dialogic Speech'], written while he was still teaching at IZhS, in which the author attempts to present the complexities and dimensions of discursive interaction.[23] Characteristics of immediate face-to-face discursive interaction (dialogue) such as deictic expressions, bodily and facial gesture, elliptical phrasing and the like are contrasted with features typical of distanced, elaborated and, in certain instances, poetic interaction (monologue). The latter is linked to the high social status of the 'speaker', who is 'listened' to without interruption, while the former are linked to familiarity or 'solidarity'.

This was developed, according to some different philosophical principles, in the work of Valentin Voloshinov who, while working on a collective project about sociological poetics at ILIaZV, developed a model of the utterance in everyday conversation and the poetic work as two different types of utterance based on Karl Bühler's model of the speech act.[24] Here the sign is treated phenomenologically, as an object of the intentional consciousness, with the result that, in face-to-face interaction, the specific meaning that the sign acquires in a specific speech act must actively be inferred by the hearer against the linguistic context and spatio-temporal background of the utterance. Thus, the meaning of the sign depends on the specific configuration between speaker, hearer and the object or state of affairs that is being spoken about. In poetry, only the linguistic context is available to the hearer or reader. The sign is a social resource that enables the production of meaningful speech acts. However, while in his subsequent work, Bühler received Saussure's notion of *langue* positively, Voloshinov was to respond rather negatively in his next book, *Marxism and the Philosophy of Language*. Here, Voloshinov presented an account of language as social interaction in which the specific meaning that a word acquires

---

22   RGALI (SPb) 288/1/39/10b.

23   Iakubinskii 1986 [1923]. For a discussion, see Gulida 2010.

24   Voloshinov 1926. On this, see Brandist 2004.

in a concrete dialogue is shaped by the respective positions the interlocu-tors occupy in the social structure.[25] Indeed, on occasion Voloshinov comes close to adopting a voluntarist position, according to which the very linguistic meaning of a word is determined solely by context. The abstract system is a product of reflection upon language and derives from the practical and theo-retical need to study dead languages (philology) and to teach languages. The author associates this with Saussure's *langue*, and it appears as a dead and ulti-mately oppressive incrustation over the dynamic interaction that is the reality of the living language. Here, Voloshinov adopts and adapts a conception drawn directly from Georg Simmel's notion of the 'tragedy of culture', according to which forms produced in life ultimately crystallise as an 'objective culture' that exerts a repressive influence on social life.[26] For Voloshinov, Saussure's 'abstract objectivism' operates with a conception of language that is removed from the 'real units of the discursive stream – utterances' and is posited for the pur-pose of 'teaching of dead, alien languages preserved in written monuments'.[27] Applied to a living language, this is but a continuation of the rationalism of the Enlightenment, which champions abstract schemata over the living culture of social life and justifies the imposition of an inherited linguistic structure on the fluid discursive interaction of social life. Saussure had indeed noted that language is an 'inheritance from the past' and that '[i]t is because the linguistic sign is arbitrary that it knows no other law than that of tradition, and because it is founded on tradition that it can be arbitrary'.[28]

Here, Voloshinov detected a 'philologism' that has bequeathed to linguis-tics a veneration for a 'hierarchically-alien', 'priestly' language 'that brought civilization, culture, religion and political organization'.[29] Saussure was thus, in Voloshinov's interpretation, continuing the nineteenth-century characteri-sation of language as a remote or (to use a Chomskyan term) 'deep structure', impervious to the influence of the people who speak it, and only able to be per-ceived by the philologist armed with the appropriate conceptual tools. Instead of shaping the language, speakers were shaped by it. While Voloshinov identi-fied this with rationalism, it was at least as much the result of the Romanticism that viewed language as an organic emanation of the *Volk*.[30] In opposition to

25   Voloshinov 1995 [1929]; Vološinov 1973.
26   Simmel 1997 [1911]. For a discussion, see Tihanov 1998.
27   Voloshinov 1995 [1929], p. 286; Vološinov 1973, p. 71.
28   Saussure 1983 [1916], p. 74. I am indebted to Ken Hirschkop for drawing my attention to this passage from Saussure's *Course in General Linguistics*.
29   Voloshinov 1995 [1929], p. 290; Vološinov 1973, p. 75.
30   This recognition lay behind the objections to Voloshinov's thesis in Shor 1929.

this approach, Voloshinov cites Marr's discussion of Indo-European linguistics, which we will discuss later.[31] Philologism thus provides ideological cover for the ruling class's attempts to 'impart a supra-class, eternal character to the ideological sign, to extinguish or drive inward the struggle between social-value judgements that occurs in it, to make the sign uni-accentual'.[32] What Voloshinov is gesturing towards here, but does not discuss explicitly, is the role of philology in the formation of what Gramsci called 'written' or 'normative grammar' and its institutionalisation. This important issue requires careful institutional analysis, but this is not forthcoming in Voloshinov's work. Later, in his major 1934 essay 'Slovo v romane' ['Discourse in the Novel'], Voloshinov's colleague, Mikhail Bakhtin, comes close to identifying the abstract system with the standard, literary language, but again provides no account of the institutional mediation between these phenomena.[33]

Voloshinov's hostility to the Saussurean paradigm is contrasted with his extremely respectful, though critical, treatment of the 'individualistic subjectivism' of Benedetto Croce and Karl Vossler. While the subjectivism of this trend is clearly regarded as unacceptable, the tone of the critique is quite different and based on the contention that the subjectivists provide an account of linguistic activity devoid of the social form, or conditions, that make that activity possible. The conditions are provided by the utterances of others, which are encountered not as an abstract system of signs, but as articulated structures signifying something: 'true or false, good or bad, important or unimportant, pleasant or unpleasant and so on'.[34] The speaker and hearer relate intuitively to language, while *langue* is merely the product of *a posteriori* reflection on the process taken as an abstraction, reifying it as something real.[35] Iakubinskii makes the same point in his 1929 paper at the same institution as Voloshinov, arguing that one of the reasons Saussure is incorrect is that 'he thinks that the only possible knowledge about language is by means of reflection, contemplation from the side, forgetting about the subject of language, about the collective'.[36] Of course, there is a good deal of truth in this as a criticism of nascent structuralism but, as Roy Bhaskar notes in a different context, the categorisation of human action as intentionally directed involves precisely this

31   On Voloshinov's complex relationship to Marrism, see Lähteenmäki and Vasil'ev 2005.

32   Voloshinov 1995 [1929], p. 236; Vološinov 1973, p. 23.

33   Bakhtin 2012 [1934–5]; Bakhtin 1981 [1934–5].

34   Voloshinov 1995 [1929], pp. 284–5; Vološinov 1973, p. 70.

35   Voloshinov 1995 [1929], pp. 281–2; Vološinov 1973, pp. 67–8. For an interesting assessment of Voloshinov's critique of 'abstract objectivism', see Alpatov 2005, pp. 146–53.

36   Iakubinskii 1966 [1929] p. 81.

process of reflection having some effect on shaping human action, and therefore being real in a certain sense:

> This [intentionality – CB] seems to depend upon the feature that persons are material things with a degree of neurophysiological complexity which enables them not just, like the other higher order animals, to initiate changes in a purposeful way, to monitor and control their performances, but to monitor the monitoring of these performances and to be capable of a commentary upon them. This capacity for second-order monitoring also makes possible a retrospective commentary upon actions, which gives a person's account of his or her own behavior a special status, which is acknowledged in the best practice of all the psychological sciences.[37]

The language system that is posited by structured reflection on discursive interaction, and which is then propagated as a standard through the educational system, the media and so on, is thus something to which speakers orientate in specifically evaluative, that is, in intentional ways. Such an institutionalised standard has a social effectiveness and presence quite unlike the other forms of social language on which speakers reflect in their communicative activity. As Gramsci recognised in the *Notebooks*, this is a question of hegemony, because such a 'written grammar' is not only descriptive but a posited standard. Voloshinov essentially throws out the specific properties that make a language an *institution*, a social condition for institutionally effective discursive acts that is inherited from the past and (generally unconsciously) reproduced in utterances, along with the reified conception of *langue*. If it is to endure, the standard requires constant reproduction in discursive acts, and the error of reification appears only when this is forgotten. At the same time, however, while purposeful discursive activity may generally reproduce the standard, it may also, on occasion, and given the right circumstances, transform the structures that govern such activity. Voloshinov has a general understanding of this when he argues that it is only at times of revolutionary change that the struggle over meanings comes out into the open. However, while Voloshinov discusses the use of the same language by various social classes and the way in which this renders the sign 'multi-accentual', he does not discuss the fact that the availability of a recognisably single language to different classes presupposes it has already been, to some extent, institutionalised. Such crucial historical reflections are missing from Voloshinov's book. Various social groups all relate to, and interact with, a standard, prestige form in one way or another only when

---

37   Bhaskar 1998 [1979], p. 35.

socioeconomic developments have broken down the isolation of rural speech communities, and this is related to the rise of trade and the nation state. In the USSR this process was underway in a particularly self-conscious and theorised fashion.

It was in urban environments that relations between standard and non-standard forms proved particularly important as objects of study. The pioneer in this area was undoubtedly Boris Larin, who worked on both linguistic and literary projects at GIII as well as ILIaZV in the mid-1920s. Here he developed projects to study the language of the city. In an article based on research begun in 1924, presented at both institutes in 1926 but published two years later, Larin argued that the study of the urban language needs to be regarded as a special field, because the language of the city coincides neither with territorial dialects nor with the standard, national language.[38] The established habit of regarding the language of the city either as a debased form of the national language or an ennobled peasant conversational language presents two types of Procrustean bed on which the forms are made to lie. The urban language occupies an intermediary position between the standard and a dialect, but it has a fluidity that corresponds to that of the urban population itself. This was, of course, at the time of the reconstitution of the urban population after the devastation of the Civil War, with an influx of first-generation city dwellers under way. The most important specific feature of the urban population is its 'bilingualism', for there are always two or more language systems available to the citizen, who belongs to a variety of social groups, with their interrelated social dialects.

While Larin recognises that urban bilingualism may actually involve switching between different languages, what he is particularly interested in is what, in today's sociolinguistics, would be called diglossia: '[u]rban folklore, non-canonical types of written language, the conversational speech of various social groups of the urban population exert a direct and powerful influence on the normalised literary language, on its "higher" forms'.[39]

> In actual fact, here we have but the clearest example of the general and continual linguistic interaction of all strata of the urban population, a habitual employment of the 'other' discourses [*rech'*] of their social neighbours and antipodes, an example of the ceaseless search for new means of expression from the nearest sources (it is always successful when it turns to the rich 'linguistic depths' of the city). The historical

---

38   Larin 1929.
39   Larin 1929.

evolution of any literary language may be presented as a series of successive 'lowerings' [*snizhenii*], barbarisations, but it is better to say – as a series of concentric deployments.[40]

Urban argot is of particular interest here. Larin refutes the idea of the French linguists who studied argot as a deviant collection of secret terms and argued that it is a structured pattern of deliberate usage. What is significant about argot is that it is a conscious alternation between the standard language and a semantically distinct, socially specific and context-embedded pattern of speech. In this sense, argot represents a use of language that resembles that which Iakubinskii and Shklovskii highlighted in Lenin's form of argumentation, though obviously without the overtly political aim. Instead, as Larin's examples show, the aim is often deflationary humour. 'Fellow-traveller' writers, like Zoshchenko and Babel', had highlighted this in their satirical stories, presenting stylised images of precisely this linguistic phenomenon. Such discursive patterns provided evidence that what was taking place was a radical restructuring of the relationship between the official, standard language and the social groups that employed it. As another of Baudouin's students, Polivanov, argued, the standard language was being transferred to a new 'social substratum'.[41]

There is an implicit politics here: the standard language is being democratised from below. An erosion of the boundaries of the standard literary language is simultaneously the penetration of the conceptions of the non-standard 'depths' of society into the prestige form. Here we have the linguistic corollary of the relationship between hegemony and democracy that Gramsci discusses in Notebook 8 (1930–2), where he argues that, wherever democracy is present in a 'hegemonic system', then the legislative framework 'favors the [molecular] transition from the groups that are led to the leading group'.[42] In this context, it is significant that in an article Larin wrote on the same subject two years later, in 1928, he presents the relationship between the standard and non-standard languages as marked by conflict, and looks forward to a future of linguistic uniformity.[43]

Larin cites Charles Bally's 1913 book *Langage et la vie*, which was required reading for all students at ILIaZV: 'The conversational speech of ordinary people continues its onward march all the more securely for being underground

---

40   Larin 1929.

41   Polivanov 1974 [1927], p. 181.

42   Gramsci 2007, p. 345.

43   Larin 1977 [1928]. This point is well made by Gulida 2010, p. 66.

– it flows like living water under the thick ice of the literary conventional language; then one fine day the ice breaks and the noisy stream of popular language floods over the immobile surface, returning it to life and movement'.[44]

This image is strikingly similar to that which Bakhtin employs in '*Slovo v romane*' ['Discourse in the Novel'] when discussing the 'second stylistic line' in the development of the novel, which 'approaches the higher spheres of the literary language' from below, from the depths of the socially stratified language, *raznorechie*, which is generally translated into English as 'heteroglossia', and 'overwhelms them'.[45] Here there is a considerable development from Voloshinov's ideas, since the 'literary language' is now treated as a prestigious participant in the hierarchically structured linguistic processes in a society. As Mika Lähteenmäki and I have shown elsewhere, Bakhtin's conception of the socially stratified language and the emergence of a national standard was but a reworking of certain ideas developed by Leningrad linguists in the 1920s.[46] Particularly important here was the work of Lev Iakubinskii on the development of the Russian national language that appeared as a collection of popular-scientific articles in 1930 and 1931, in which the emergence of the national standard was shown to accompany the development of a national market and the emergence of capitalist relations of production in Russia.[47] Here, Iakubinskii was attempting to map the rise of the Russian national language onto the narrative about the rise of capitalism in Russia, presented by Lenin in his 1898 book *The Development of Capitalism in Russia*.[48] Despite several oversimplified formulations, which may derive from the popular orientation of the articles, a certain 'vulgar sociologism' when discussing relations between social and linguistic structures and the evident tailoring of the conclusions to support the Stalinist policy of promoting linguistic uniformity, the articles have considerable strengths in advancing a conception of the standard

---

44   Quoted, in Russian translation, in Larin 1929. Online at http://www.argotism.ru/works/
      larin-77a.htm (accessed 28 March 2012).

45   Bakhtin 2012 [1934–5], p. 155; Bakhtin 1981a [1934–5], p. 400. It should be noted that the
      use of '*slovo*' in this article does not fully correspond to the term 'discourse' and needs to
      be related to the discussion above about the '*slovo*' debates.

46   Brandist and Lähteenmäki 2010.

47   The articles were published in Maksim Gorky's journal, *Literaturnaia ucheba*, in 1930 and
      1931 and then published as a separate volume in 1932. Some of the articles were co-written
      with A.M. Ivanov and so the volume appeared in both their names as Iakubinskii and
      Ivanov 1932.

48   Lenin 1956.

language as a socio-political project.[49] In 1967 Viktor Zhirmunskii still referred to Iakubinskii's articles as 'the classical formulation of the formation of the common-national language of bourgeois society from the dialects of the feudal epoch' on the basis of the 'Marxist understanding of the social-historical process'.[50]

Iakubinskii discusses the linguistic consequences for the peasantry of the coming of the national market, in which the growth of towns and trade relations between them led to the development of a common national language that in turn impacts upon the peasantry. The development of capitalism ultimately leads to the hegemony of the towns over the countryside, which compels the peasantry to choose consciously between its old, local dialect and the new, urban language. This struggle is waged with the weapon of mockery and linguistic parody on both sides, but 'the history of the language of the peasantry under capitalism is the history of the active linguistic adaptation of the peasantry to the linguistic relations of capitalism'.[51] By this, Iakubinskii has in mind the effects of widening trade relations through the formation of a national market, the development of railways and of urbanisation. Such an adaptation is not uniform and even. Nor is it unilinear or devoid of battles and resistance, as the peasantry may seek to defend its own local dialect, along with its religion and ways of life as 'one of the moments of the struggle of declining feudalism with rising capitalism'.[52]

Stalinist ideological distortions become painfully evident, however, when Iakubinskii moves on to discuss the relationship between language and the dictatorship of the proletariat. With the dawn of the dictatorship, the pathologies of capitalism, which led the peasantry to resist the national language, fall away, and the new conditions 'open the widest possibilities for the development of public speech in the village, especially literary discourse', because 'writing becomes a mass phenomenon'.[53] Drawing on the earlier discussion of the rise of the living word, but now recast as the emergence of public discourse, Iakubinskii also discusses the various genres of spoken and written public discourse that come with the development of capitalist relations, as well as the way in which the intellectuals emerging from the proletariat seek to exploit

---

49   Zhirmunskii 1964; Desnitskaia 1974.

50   Zhirmunskii 1969.

51   Iakubinskii 1930a, p. 85.

52   Iakubinskii 1930b, p. 61. Here one can clearly see Iakubinskii's argument being adapted to the cause of collectivisation.

53   Iakubinskii 1930b, p. 63.

the opportunities that arise from these new situations.[54] The proletariat, as a collective that arises on the grounds of the division of labour rather than, as with the peasantry, a collection of dispersed producers, now develops a shared orientation on the language of the bourgeoisie through its collective organisation. This is given a conscious expression by means of the rise of political leaders who hone a specifically proletarian 'discursive method' in their oratory. This had been the focus of attention of the Laboratory of Public Discourse at ILIaZV, which was a generalisation of the 1924 studies of the language of Lenin, to which Iakubinskii had contributed. The proletariat thus begins to transform itself from a class in itself to a class for itself. The proletariat, therefore, has an objective interest in minimising linguistic variation, or at least confining it to the narrow bounds of specialised professional jargon in specific spheres of production, and this means following the lead of the specialists in developing the unified proletarian language, i.e. the Party. With the coming of socialism, therefore, the language of the proletariat, crystallised in the language of the Party, can become the common national language in the full sense.[55] This last, clearly Stalinist, elision of the distinction between the proletariat and the Party, found further expression in a work by one of Iakubinskii's most gifted students, Viktor Gofman, who argued that in the USSR of the time, political public speech can for the first time be combined with science, so that ultimately rhetorical, educational and scientific discourse can merge into a popular-scientific language.[56]

Despite the evident compromise formations that result from ideological genuflection in such work, there is no doubting the theoretical advances made in dealing with the relationship between the standard language, social dialects and the question of hegemony, even if the term 'hegemony' does not actually appear in these works. Avoiding, or at least minimising, such compromises generally meant shifting attention away from discussion of the linguistic situation in the USSR either by abstraction from concrete institutional coordinates (as in Bakhtin's 1934–5 essay mentioned above) or relocating the focus of discussion abroad. This latter path was adopted by Viktor Zhirmunskii in his 1936 book, *The National Language and Social Dialects*.[57] Although Zhirmunskii had begun his dialectological work studying the dialects of German colonists in the USSR, by the middle of the 1930s he shifted his attention to the German language in Germany. Zhirmunskii travelled to Germany twice, in 1925 and 1927,

54   Iakubinskii 1931a, pp. 22–33.

55   Iakubinskii 1931b; Iakubinskii 1931c.

56   Gofman 1932.

57   Zhirmunskii 1936.

in order to learn the techniques of dialectological and ethnographic research, and he met, among others, the leaders of German dialectological research and linguistic geography, Ferdinand Wrede and Theodor Frings.[58] In the 1930s he pursued parallel research in dialectology and folklore, as is indicated by the title of his 1932 article 'The Methodology of Social Geography (Dialectology and Folklore in the Light of Geographical Research)'.[59] Here, and in a 1934 article, 'The Problem of Folklore', he argued that the sociology of folklore is the study of 'living antiquity', the cultural relics of backward social groups that retain 'the transitional structure of economic and cultural existence and are usually the object of colonial or semi-colonial capitalist exploitation'. Similarly, dialects are the living relics of the territorially fragmented 'linguistic relations of the feudal epoch, characteristic of surviving social groups'. The object of study for ethnography, folkloristics and dialectology is therefore identical in its social nature.[60] In the 1936 book, Zhirmunskii presented a theoretical perspective based on his discussion of the French and, in particular, the German national languages. Following Iakubinskii, Zhirmunskii discussed the standard national language as the social dialect of the ruling class that had achieved hegemonic status. Thus, 'national languages' are 'late products of the convergent developments of dialects [...] [evolving] under definite historical conditions, after nations and national governments have been formed'. The fundamental difference between the national language and social dialects was not linguistic, but one of social function:

> The social dialects arising as a result of the class differentiation of society are in no way [the national language's] equals, and their interrelationship is not limited to mechanical co-existence: they are interconnected by complex interaction, by hierarchical subordinations and struggles evoked by the general direction of social evolution of the given epoch and country. In this interaction and struggle, the national language acts as a social norm which dominates all other social dialects.... The cultural hegemony of the ruling class in turn conditions its linguistic hegemony.[61]

---

58   RGALI SPb 288/1/29/83–830b. On Zhirmunskii's early research on German dialects, see Aumüller 2008. For a discussion of how this work fits in with his general intellectual development, see Brandist 2012b.

59   Zhirmunskii 1932. Here we can see the influence of two of Zhirmunskii's teachers, Veselovskii and Baudouin.

60   Zhirmunskii, 1934, pp. 198, 200.

61   Zhirmunskii 1936, pp. 15–16.

Zhirmunskii's analysis makes explicit what was implicit in the work of the Leningrad school: (non-Saussurean) synchronic linguistics deals with the standard language in relation to social dialects as an instance of the historical development of the nation state and the national language. This involves the emergence of a standard, prestige form that becomes the hegemonic form within society.

2   Moscow

The reception of the Saussurean paradigm in Moscow was generally more positive than in Leningrad, largely due to the heritage of the Moscow Linguistic School led by Fortunatov, whose proclivities for formalistic studies of language were shared by many of his students. Thus, the pioneers of phonology, Nikolai Trubetskoi, Roman Jakobson and Nikolai Iakovlev, each emerged from this school. A specialist in Caucasian languages and one of the founding members of the Moscow Linguistic Circle, Iakovlev developed formal analysis when he drew up phonetic tables and sought to develop a mathematical formula for the construction of alphabets.[62] Mikhail Peterson in particular continued the Moscow Linguistic School's 'paramount insistence on the search for general laws, for the problems of mind and language, and for the interrelations between verbal form and function'.[63] As early as 1923, we find him publishing a positive discussion of Saussure in *Pechat' i revoliutsiia*, which, under the editorship of Lunacharskii, was one of the most influential journals of the time.[64] In his article 'Language as a Social Phenomenon' [*Iazyk kak sotsial'noe iavlenie*], written in 1927, Peterson explicitly linked his general description of language to Durkheim's notion of 'social fact' and outlined the various social functions that language can play. This article is replete with references to the French social linguist, Antoine Meillet, and includes a bibliography of works on the sociology of language which directs the reader to, *inter alia*, Joseph Vendryes, Bally, Gillieron and Ascoli. Meillet was well known in Russia since becoming a corresponding member of the Russian Academy of Sciences in 1906, the very moment when his famous work on the social causes of semantic changes was appearing in Durkheim's *Année Sociologique*.[65] It should be recalled that it was Meillet who insisted that 'a language spreads only if it is the organ of a civilisation endowed with prestige' because it is regarded as superior, 'not

---

62   Iakovlev 1923; Iakovlev 1928.

63   Jakobson 1985, p. 282.

64   Peterson 1923.

65   Shcherba 1966, p. 97; see also Desnitskaia 1991. The work that was particularly influential was Meillet 1926 [1905–6].

necessarily of a material nature' but maybe also 'of a social organisation particularly adapted to the needs of a given period and region'.[66] Considering the
study of regional and social dialects, Peterson argues that 'the only difference'
is that the latter do not exist one around another, like dialects, but one above
another'.[67] However, in Moscow this influence of French sociological linguistics was combined with a particular phenomenology of discursive acts.

The particular way in which Saussure was received among linguists in
Moscow was, to a significant extent, due to the influence of the philosopher
Gustav Shpet, whose idiosyncratic blend of Russian orthodoxy and phenomenology stimulated much linguistic research.[68] Shpet had participated in the
work of the Moscow Linguistic Circle and then became the leader of the philosophy section of the *Gosudarstvennaia akademiia khudozhestvennykh nauk*
[The State Academy for Artistic Studies, hereafter GAKhN]. I do not intend to
investigate the peculiarities of Shpet's work in any detail here, but suffice it to
say that for him language [*iazyk*] and word [*slovo*, as *logos*] need to be differentiated rigorously. In the words of one of his students, Apollinaria Solov'eva, the
concept of the static language system is a 'posited, extensive cross-section' that
is 'devoid of the fullness of its being' and is comprised of 'assumed structural
articulations of an intentional character', while the word is a 'creative actuali-
sation of the potential implanted in language'.[69] This tortuous formulation is
characteristic of Shpet's own work, but the point was made much more clearly
by the Swiss phenomenologist, Anton Marty, whose notion of 'inner-speech
form' was particularly influential on the Shpet school.[70] Marty's model of language is simultaneously intentional and instrumental.[71] He decisively broke
with the psychologistic assumption that language is a direct outgrowth of
the mind and that the primary function of speech is self-expression, as held,
in various forms, by Wundt, Croce and Vossler, and instead prioritised the
communicative function. The speaker now relates to language in an empirical and teleological fashion. Aiming to invoke a meaning in the mind of an

---

66   Meillet 1967 [1925], pp. 31–2.

67   Peterson 1927, p. 41.

68   On this aspect of Shpet's work, see Cassedy 2009 and Nemeth 2009.

69   'Tezisy k dokladu A.K. Solov'evoi "O vzaimootnoshenii ekspressii razgovornogo i liter-
      aturno-khudozhestvennogo iazyka" '. GAKhN 941/14/27/14.

70   Hence the title of Shpet's rambling 1927 book, *Vnutrenniaia forma slova: Etiudy i variatsii
      na temy Gumbol'dta* [*The Inner Form of the Word: Studies and Variations on a Humboldtian
      Theme*]: Shpet 2006 [1927]. On the relationship between the philosophy of Shpet and
      Marty, see Venditti 2010, pp. 266–73.

71   Marty's main linguistic ideas were set out in a voluminous book (Marty 1908). Marty was
      also important for Voloshinov. On this, see Brandist 2004, pp. 98–101.

interlocutor, a speaker often finds an exact linguistic form unavailable and so employs a form that is contiguous or analogous, which he or she considers likely to 'trigger' [*auslösen*] the required meaning in a given context. This auxiliary concept (and every metaphor) is what Marty called, following von Humboldt (though his conception was quite different) the 'inner-speech form'. After repeated usage, the auxiliary form may supplant the original meaning entirely. This, for Marty, is the principle that governs semantic development. As one contemporary commentator put it:

> That means, hardly a word in the vocabulary of any language remains unaffected. It is not necessary, frequently not possible, in etymology to find one idea to cover all the meanings of a given form; it may come to convey, after repeated, chain-like use as 'inner form', the very opposite of its original meaning: 'quite a few' or 'eine schöne Geschichte' or 'awfully sweet' mean the contrary of what they seem to indicate.[72]

Language therefore generally develops in a fashion that is certainly unplanned, but which is nevertheless purposeful and teleological. Saussure's *langue* could now be viewed as the object of intentional consciousness, as a socio-cultural entity, a 'thing' which the intentional consciousness utilises in order to invoke a meaning.

In 1932 the erudite but eclectic linguist Rozaliia Shor, who had worked at *Institut iazyka i literatury* [The Institute of Language and Literature, hereafter IIaL], the sister institute of ILIaZV in Leningrad with, *inter alia*, Peterson and GAKhN (where she had direct contacts with, *inter alia*, Shpet), delivered a self-critical paper to the Institute of Linguistics in Moscow. Here she discussed the way in which the Saussurean, Durkheimian and phenomenological trends came together.[73] Shor claims to have been attracted to Saussure's work because of two fundamental elements that she found in his work: the insistence on a qualitative difference between social and natural phenomena and the primacy of the social over the individual. She regarded Saussure as adhering to a model of society that was fundamentally Durkheimian, that is, a unified, systematic totality in which class was not regarded as a fundamental concern. However, Shor argued that as both a literary scholar and linguist (which was not uncommon at the time), she had been influenced by Vladimir Friche's sociology of

---

72   Leopold 1929, p. 257. Marty's development of the concept is discussed at length in Funke 1924.

73   ARAN 677/3/107/23–34. For a balanced and sympathetic discussion of Shor's career, see Alpatov 2012, pp. 159–73.

literature, which was based on Plekhanov's ideas about literature as a reflection of the economic structure of society.[74] Shor had then tried to apply this to language, which she did through the notion of the inner form of the word developed from Marty and Shpet. The result was her 1926 book *Iazyk i obshchestvo* [*Language and Society*], in which the Saussurean *langue* was transformed by the introduction of a developmental model of language based on the structured character of the sign, the doctrine of the inner form and by posing the question of the reflection of social phenomena in language.[75] Shor's 1926 book presented a general description of the social stratification of the national language and argued that changes in the structure of society will lead to changes in the language of that society. The mechanism of such changes was Marty's notion of 'inner form', which she termed the establishment of 'co-meaning' [*soznachenie*] between interlocutors.[76] While, by 1929, Shor could argue that Saussure's ideas could be helpful for the creation of a Marxist linguistics if subjected to a 'fundamental restructuring', she was extremely hostile to the 'individualistic subjectivism' of the Croce-Vossler school, which she considered an 'apology for a-logicality and irrationality'.[77] Here, as Alpatov justly notes, was the diametrically opposite evaluation of the trends in contemporary linguistics presented by Voloshinov, and this was reflected in her evaluation of Voloshinov's book.[78]

In the early 1920s, the Moscow Linguistic Circle linguist, Grigorii Vinokur, had attempted to develop an interventionist approach to language by drawing on the same intellectual trends. He initially developed this in connection with the avant-gardistes gathered around the journal *LEF*. Here, the difference between word and language was recast as the difference between a 'social fact' and a social norm. In concrete usage, the speaker repeatedly employs the norm in a deviant fashion, which ultimately posits a new norm. This deviation is the object of poetics.[79] Such linguistic disciplines are, for Vinokur, phenomenological, in the sense of being closely descriptive rather than explanatory,[80] while the causes of semantic changes are the objects of sociology. Language

---

74   Friche was director of IIaL and played a leading role in RANION, to which both IIaL and
      GAKhN were affiliated. Relatively little has been written about this trend in scholarship,
      despite the fact that it was both original and influential. However, see Rakov 1986.

75   Shor 1926.

76   Shor 1926, pp. 92–7; ARAN 677/3/107/26.

77   Shor 1929, p. 154.

78   Alpatov 2005, p. 233.

79   See Reznik 2010 and Gorham 2010.

80   Vinokur 1923a.

is thus constantly being (re)built in connection with the various social contexts of its use, meaning that such construction can be deliberately and consciously organised by 'technicians' of language.[81] Such technicians can address the tendency for revolutionary phraseology to become stale, hackneyed and ultimately the object of mockery.[82] Here, Vinokur's concerns converged with the work of the Laboratory of Public Discourse at ILIaZV. As Vladislava Reznik notes, Vinokur adopted Saussure's 'fundamental precepts, such as the social primacy of language and its synchronic analysis, as the basis for the construction of a linguistic science of social utility, aimed, above all, at a conscious, guided influence on language by the speaking collective, the possibility of which was [in the view of Reznik – CB] utterly rejected by the author of the *Course*'.[83]

Though the heirs of the Moscow Linguistic School predominated numerically among Moscow linguists, their influence was tempered by representatives of the Baudouin school, who had relocated to Moscow. The linguistic section of IIaL was presided over by another of Baudouin's students, Polivanov, with the dialectologist Nikolai Karinskii as his deputy. The appointments were made by the head of RANION, V.M. Friche, specifically 'as a counterweight to representatives of the "Moscow Fortunatov School" '.[84] Karinskii had also studied at St. Petersburg University, attending lectures by, *inter alia*, Veselovskii and Baudouin.[85] The themes for research at the institute were 'Language and Society, the Revolution and Language and New Trends in Contemporary Linguistics'.[86] Polivanov was particularly productive at this time, working on general questions of the theory of language as well as on the problem of standardisation and forms of orthography for various hitherto unsystematised languages of the USSR. Polivanov worked on 'the evolution of language as a derivative of the social history of the collective and general questions of social dialectology and social language studies', while Karinskii investigated 'the evolution of language in places where there is a collision of linguistic groups belonging to closely related tribes [*plemena*] using material of Russian dialects

81   Vinokur 1923b.

82   Vinokur 1923c.

83   Reznik 2010, p. 31.

84   Leont'ev 1983, p. 14.

85   Karinskii's archive contains an undated copy of Baudouin's lectures (ARAN 468/1/30). Already at the turn of the century, Karinskii was making some initial forays into social dialectology. See, for instance, Karinskii 1898.

86   'Proizvodstvennyi plan i otchety o deiatel'nosti sektsii za 1924/25–1926/27g', GARF A-4655/1/324/16.

[*govor*] in connection with socio-cultural relationships'.[87] Towards the end of the 1920s, the subsection on social dialectology becomes of particular interest, for here the focus was on 'peasant dialects and the influence of the urban language on the language of the village'.[88] The plan of work in this area included the 'concretisation of the concept of the dialects of social groups, classes, professional and territorial dialects' and working out a theoretical perspective on 'the question of the interrelationships of socioeconomic life and linguistic phenomena'.[89] These plans, along with a number of scheduled publications, remained unfulfilled as the political situation changed drastically at the end of the 1920s, but Polivanov was able to conclude that 'in the struggle for the role of the literary dialect, the language of the village, of the less economically developed collective in general, never prevails over the language of the city of the region that is more generally developed in economic relations'.[90]

In his works of the 1920s, Polivanov stressed the social nature of language, treated speech [*rech'*] as a labour process and argued that language played crucial socioeconomic functions.[91] He also retained his teacher's distinction between the internal and external histories of language, and so was insulated against some of the worst types of 'vulgar sociologism' that emerged in the late 1920s. He thus distinguished between 'the technical laws of linguistic development' and extra-linguistic economic and political factors that interact and serve as an 'inner motor' of linguistic change. Thus, 'social change does not affect the direction (that is, the final result) of some specific historico-phonetic process.... For factors of a social (economic-political) character there is a much wider arena of action: on these [factors] may depend a radical question: will a given evolution in the language of a given collective come to be or not?'[92] In a 1929 article, Polivanov set out an 'immediate program of sociological linguistics' in seven basic subdivisions:

1) Definition of language as a socio-historical fact. Strictly speaking, the combination of linguist and Marxist in one person already presupposes a solution to this problem. But, nevertheless, a formulation is still necessary. Thus, this is only the first necessary step and no more.

---

87   GARF A-4655/1/389/10.
88   'Otchet o deiatel'nosti NII iazyka i istorii literatury za 1928–29gg', GARF A-4655/1/389/10.
89   ARAN 468/1/207/25.
90   Quoted in Alpatov 2012, p. 80.
91   Polivanov 1928b, pp. 20–42.
92   Leont'ev 1961, p. 118.

2)   Description of languages and dialects from the sociological point of view. First of all, of course, a methodology is needed (with new concepts on the order of social group dialects, etc.)

3)   Evaluative analysis of the given language as an instrument of intercourse.

4)   Study of the causal connections between socioeconomic and linguistic phenomena.

5)   Evaluative analysis of language (and its separate aspects) as a means of the struggle for existence.

6)   A general typological scheme of the evolution of language in connection with the history of culture.

7)   Applied questions of sociological linguistics: language policy.[93]

This sociolinguistic programme was nothing if not path-breaking, but it unfortunately appeared just as the socio-political situation and institutional structures were changing fundamentally. It also preceded the now famous clash between Polivanov and the advocates of Marr's 'new theory of language' at the Communist Academy in 1930, which resulted in the latter trend attaining quasi-official status as 'Marxism in linguistics'.

These theoretical developments were closely related to the practicalities of language policy on the ground, and this was not only related to the Russian language. Linguists began to question the universal applicability of traditional categories like the word, sentence and parts of speech. As Shcherba put it, '[o]ur problem...is that our linguistic thinking was inhibited by the Indo-European structure of languages... Our task is to free ourselves from this influence and understand that there are other languages that express the same as us otherwise'.[94] As a specialist in oriental languages, Polivanov questioned the applicability of received linguistic categories to Chinese and Vietnamese in the 1920s.[95] The Moscow linguists in particular were deeply involved in the huge language-building projects that were being undertaken in the USSR, and which required close attention to the synchronic descriptions and codifications of language as well as serious consideration of the relationship between standard languages and social dialects. Iakovlev and Polivanov were particularly closely involved in the formulation of standard languages and alphabets for the languages of the Caucasus and Central Asia respectively. As well as working at

---

93   Polivanov 1974b [1929], pp. 177–8.

94   Cited in Leont'ev 1983, p. 34.

95   For an overview, see Leont'ev 1983, pp. 31–45.

IIaL, Polivanov also worked at the *Kommunisticheskii universitet trudiashchikh-sia Vostoka* [Communist University of the Toilers of the East, KUTV], as well as at the *Institut Narodov Vostoka* [Institute of the Peoples of the East, INV], and from 1928 was a member of the Scientific Council for the All-Union Committee for the New Turkic Alphabet, VTsKNTA. Though a specialist in Indo-European languages (especially Sanskrit), Shor also played an important role in INV, where she worked on Georgian and Finno-Ugric languages, as well as Indian languages, before going to Azerbaijan to work on the Turkic languages of the region.[96] Leningrad linguists tended to be more focused on the languages of the western USSR, such as Finno-Ugric, German and Ukrainian. However, an important exception to this came in the form of the linguists associated with Marr's *Instutut Iazyka i Myshleniia* [Institute of Language and Thinking, IIaM], where Marr's general theoretical doctrines and the requirements of nationality policy came together. In these debates, the question of the relationship between language and hegemony could not but play an important role.

---

96   ARAN 677/3/107/102–6.

The Revolution in the West and East: Hegemony and the National Question

We have seen that the national question played a crucial role in discussions about language and hegemony in the pre-revolutionary period, when Lenin had argued that the proletariat needed to demonstrate that it was through its leadership that the oppressed nationalities could achieve self-determination. Lenin argued that by removing all compulsion and adopting policies to facilitate the social development of hitherto oppressed peoples, the proletariat could attract the oppressed to its cause. The proletariat's internationalism would ultimately break the oppressed from the influence of the nationalist bourgeoisie and the religious authorities, and the revolution would become an example to the oppressed colonies of the great powers. There is little doubt that this policy proved itself during the revolution itself and helped to bring significant numbers of indigenous peoples over to the side of the Bolsheviks in the struggle against the White armies.[1] Chaotic and regionally varied though the Civil War was, movements for national liberation generally found that what the White generals had in mind was not the national policy advocated by the Cadets, but the re-establishment of the Russian Empire. The Bolsheviks were, however, forced to defend most of the territory of the old Empire as if it were a single country and to introduce military-administrative divisions which cut across ethnographically distinct areas. Even in the aftermath of the Civil War, nations were incorporated into the USSR in a messy, complex series of struggles that involved competing geopolitical interests with a range of 'great powers', all of whom were keen to place the Soviet state in as great a danger as possible. Once a territory had been incorporated, efforts were made to ensure significant concessions were granted to win the trust of the local populations, but it was perhaps here that the shifting nature of the problematic of hegemony can be seen most clearly.

---

1 On the difficult relationship between the Bolsheviks and the central Asian reformists, see Khalid 1998.

Imperial and Anti-Imperial Tendencies

The Bolsheviks emerged from the War as leaders of an encircled one-Party state, ruling in the name of a proletariat that had since ceased to exist as a self-conscious entity. The new state was now subject to some of the same geopolitical, competitive pressures that had acted upon the tsarist state as a Eurasian power. The resulting pressures for institutional standardisation and centralisation ran counter to the motivations of most leaders of the Bolshevik Party, and the first years after the war show constant grappling between pragmatism and principle. As Jeremy Smith concludes, the Bolshevik nationality policy 'evolved haphazardly in response to specific circumstances', but according to a pattern that would lead to the prioritisation of the 'expansion of national education and the promotion of national culture' from 1923 until the end of the decade.[2] As effective power became more centralised, so the cultural autonomy of national territories increased, with significant transfers of resources from the metropolitan centre to the periphery. On the one hand, the hegemony of the Soviet state, which proclaimed itself to be synonymous with that of the proletariat, facilitated socio-cultural development and conferred considerable benefits. On the other hand, however, the formerly oppressed peoples were divided into administrative units, between which there was often considerable friction, and were thus rendered less able to resist the shift of power to the centre. As the decade progressed, hegemonic strategy shifted inexorably in the latter direction.

With the revolutionary wave in Europe having ebbed, the Party bureaucracy in the ascendency and the policy of 'socialism in one country' officially endorsed, nationality and language policy became fundamentally oriented on the development of administrative mechanisms for the creation of a 'harmonious multi-national state'. This in itself represented a significant change in nationality policy from the November 1917 'Declaration of the rights of the peoples of Russia', which had asserted that all peoples had the right to secede and that no frontiers would be drawn, and the principles of which were incorporated in the RSFSR Constitution, endorsed by the Fifth All-Russian Congress of Soviets on 10 July 1918. Emphasis now shifted to bureaucratic definition and delimitation of nationalities on the basis of the criteria of Stalin's 1913 *Marxism and the National Question*,[3] undertaken by the Comissariat of Nationalities, which he headed. The goal of liberation of the peoples became subordinated to defending the interests of the Soviet state, leading the Russian nationalist,

---

2   Smith 1999, p. 241.
3   Stalin 1953 [1913].

N.V. Ustrialov, a contributor to the famous 1921 *émigré* collection *Smena Vekh* [*Changing Landmarks*], to claim that the Soviet government, in the name of world revolution, would re-unite the centre with the distant lands and succeed where Denikin had failed, recreating Russia 'one and indivisible'.[4] In 1923, however, such centralising tendencies were still restrained by countervailing forces from the Communist Parties of the non-Russian territories who needed to secure resources and demonstrate their commitment to the native population. The bureaucratic drift of the regime gradually overcame the resistance of the national Communists, often by replacing them with more cooperative members of the Party. This was a process that was significantly assisted by the February-April 1924 'Lenin Levy'.

At the Twelfth Party Congress, Stalin made important concessions:

a) [I]n the building up of the central organs of the Union, equality of rights and duties of the individual republics should be ensured both in their relations with one another and in their relations with the central authority of the Union...

b) within the system of higher organs of the Union a special organ should be instituted that will represent all the national republics and national regions without exception on the basis of equality, providing as far as possible for the representation of all the nationalities within these republics....

c) the executive organs of the Union should be constructed on principles that will ensure the actual participation in them of representatives of the republics and the satisfaction of the needs and requirements of the peoples of the Union...

d) the republics should be accorded sufficiently wide financial and, in particular, budgetary powers, enabling them to display initiative in state administration and cultural and economic matters...

e) the organs of the national republics and regions should be staffed mainly with people from among the local inhabitants who know the language, manner of life, habits and customs of the peoples concerned...

f) special laws should be passed ensuring the use of the native languages in all state organs and in all institutions serving the local and national population and national minorities – laws that will

---

4 Ustrialov 1921.

> prosecute and punish with all revolutionary severity all violators of national rights, particularly the rights of national minorities.[5]

The specific measures adopted balanced the needs of the central apparatus with the aim of creating a formal equality of nationalities in terms of economic development, levels of literacy and formal education. The emergent imperial agenda already had an edge in the contest at this time, and the strengthening of the Party apparatus at the Twelfth Party Congress undoubtedly made this agenda likely to prevail unless there were significant developments abroad. However, it is a significant historiographical problem to present what was effectively the terms of a ceasefire, albeit one which reflected the advantage one side had gained, as a fully developed plan for a new type of imperial arrangement. In his well-documented 1954 book, *The Formation of the Soviet Union*, Richard Pipes established a trend in Western historiography in viewing the formation of the USSR as the systematic repression of national sovereignty by a Russian-dominated Communist state.[6] This approach has been challenged during the last thirty years by one that gives weight to the process of nation-building, in a series of meritorious studies led by US historians such as Ronald Grigor Suny and Terry Martin.[7] However, in most cases the Stalinist approach to the national question is generally identified with that of the Bolsheviks, and often with Marxism as a whole, with little attempt to review the real differences in conceptions between, say, Lenin and Stalin on the issue.[8] This also has the effect of separating the emergence of imperial practices in nationality policy from the encirclement of the Soviet state, the bureaucratisation of the revolution and of the rise of Stalinism in general. The most systematic attempt at effacement was made by Yuri Slezkine in an interesting 1994 article, where it is claimed that Lenin and Stalin shared 'assumptions about ontological nationalities endowed with special rights'.[9] As we have seen, such a conception hardly fits Lenin's conception at all, for whom the rise of national consciousness and of national oppression are inseparably linked to the uneven development of capitalism, something that needs to be addressed as political effects of real historical processes rather than treated as entities

---

5 Stalin 1954b [1923], pp. 279–80.

6 Pipes 1954.

7 Perhaps most representative are Suny 1993 and Martin 2001, pp. 3–20.

8 On the evolving approach to the national question in Marx and Engels see, *inter alia*, Lim 1992; Löwy 1998, pp. 20–9; Anderson 2010.

9 Slezkine 1994, p. 414.

with *bona fide* boundaries. It was Stalin who sought to define nations according to specific criteria and was able, with ever greater authority, to guide the development of nationality policy, especially after Lenin's opposition came to an end with his incapacitation. The idea of a relentless, centralising agenda riding roughshod over the rights of nations being present in the ideology that drove the revolution from its inception is a feature that has survived the repudiation of Pipes's approach, albeit in unexpected ways. Martin, for instance, presents the policies that emerged in 1923 as a 'highly theorised and coherent' plan that provided justifications for preferential treatment based on 'indigenousness' [*korennost'*] and 'cultural backwardness' [*kul'turno-otstalost'*] and that inaugurated an 'Affirmative Action Empire'.[10] According to Martin, 'Affirmative Action for all non-Russians necessarily implied reverse discrimination against Russians'.[11] As Hirsch notes, however, Martin's argument here 'misses the point', since the Soviet state 'did not make the Russians give up their language or culture, and the Russians remained the dominant nationality in the non-national territories of the Soviet Union'.[12] The old paradigm is replaced by the argument that nationality policy was driven *from the outset* by a Bolshevik determination to usher the entire population of the USSR along a pre-conceived Marxist evolutionary timeline of historical progression.

The problem with such work is not only that it involves a highly selective account of the history of Marxism, which assumes a unanimous adherence to a unilinear perspective, but that it severs the national question from the international context and from the wider political perspective within which policy emerged. An important virtue of Smith's *The Bolsheviks and the National Question* is that it allows the complexities of the emergence of nationality policy to be understood in this wider context. Hirsch also makes a significant contribution in showing that the period of 1921–3 involved extraordinarily painstaking discussions about the need to balance the needs of economic integration, which was necessary to hold the state together and provide some level of development, with the need to respect ethnographic distinctions and national autonomy:

---

10   Martin 2001, p. 23.

11   Ibid.

12   Martin 2001, p. 25; Hirsch 2005, p. 69, n. 29. The dominance of the Russians in this area was something that Rakovskii specifically argued against in his speech to the Twelfth Party Congress, proposing that no nations should have more than two-fifths of votes in the second tier of the Executive Committee. See Rakovsky 1980 [1923], pp. 86–7.

In actuality, the Soviet state took shape as it did because party leaders were unable to control Soviet state-formation and regionalisation. Party leaders could not reach a consensus in the early 1920s about how best to organise the Soviet state, let alone dictate all aspects of state-building in the RSFSR and republics.[13]

However, the issue was not only a competition between the conceptions of administrative agencies (in this case Gosplan and Narkomnats), but of the competing political conceptions of actors. There is a big difference between a policy requiring the Russian proletariat to make concessions to national minorities that had suffered social, political, religious and cultural repression in order to retain hegemony in a wider struggle against imperialism, on the one hand, and the conscious design of an imperial arrangement that disadvantaged Russians, or other nationalities, on the other. The problem is that proletarian hegemony and internationalism increasingly became identified with the unity of the Soviet state as such. At the Twelfth Congress, Rakovskii specifically warned that 'if we are to become the centre of the struggle of the oppressed nationalities outside the boundaries of the USSR, we must internally, within the boundaries of the USSR, make a correct decision on the national question'.[14] While it was undoubtedly an important fact that Stalin managed to have an amendment to the motion on the national question specifically detailing this rejected, the concessions he did make constrained the development of a specifically imperial arrangement until the end of the decade. This consolidation was itself driven by forces that were not wholly intrinsic to the Soviet Union itself.

Stalin's concessions of 1923 could ultimately only decelerate movement towards a new imperial relationship in the USSR. Those who wished to promote such a movement gradually became more confident, while those who feared the re-emergence of empire became increasingly alarmed. There were grounds for pre-revolutionary, pan-Russianist Orientalists, like Bartol'd, to find common cause with the Stalinist plan. As Sultan Galiev observed in an unpublished article of 1929, 'by means of the establishment of the USSR, the pan-Russianists would have liked to have revived, in fact, the unitary and indivisible Russia, that is, the hegemony of the Great Russians over other peoples [*narody*]', but this was blocked by loud protests at the centralising agenda of the 'pan-Russianists' in 1923.[15] Bartol'd was prepared to collaborate with the

---

13   Hirsch 2007, p. 158.
14   Rakovsky 1980 [1923], p. 85.
15   Sultan-Galiev 1995 [1929].

regime and found much in the emerging policies to commend, but he had clearly not changed his pan-Russian ideology, or his apologia for Russian imperialism. Thus, in a letter of 1918, he said he had agreed to write a history of the major Muslim powers 'on condition that they do not expect me to carry out any anti-imperialist tendencies; it is clear to me that without the world powers, there could have been no world culture'.[16] In 1927 he published a history of Turkestan in which he argued his familiar position that the 'realisation of historical tasks was impossible without conquests and subjugation, at least temporary, of some peoples by the others'.[17] In the subsequent period, official Soviet historians would support Bartol'd's insistence on the 'progressive consequences' of the incorporation of the Muslim nations into the Russian Empire.[18] In 1929 Galiev predicted, as Bartol'd may well have calculated, that ultimately *the authority of the Russians in Russia will be replaced by the collective power of 'nationals' [natsionalov], in other words the hegemony of the Russian nation [narod] over all the other nations [narody]'.*[19]

East and West

The logic of socialism in one country led to an important re-conceptualisation of the notions of East and West, and of the historical process in general. As Rakovskii's intervention showed, the term 'East' still retained an international significance in 1923, and this was expressed in more theorised terms by Mikhail Pavlovich, outlining the tasks of the newly-formed *Vserossiiskaia nauchnaia assotsiatsiia vostokovedeniia* [All-Russian Scientific Association of Orientalists, VNAV]. For Pavlovich, '[t]he East is not only the oppressed Asiatic world. The East is the whole colonial world, the world of oppressed nations [narod] not only of Asia, but also of Africa and South America . . . it is that world, the exploitation of which supports the power of the capitalist society in Europe and the United States'.[20] In his May 1925 speech 'The Political Tasks of the University of the Peoples of the East', however, Stalin specifically repudiated such a conception, arguing 'we have two Easts, living different lives, and developing under different conditions', and that the Communist University of the Toilers of the East therefore has two separate tasks: 'one line having the aim of creating cad-

---

16   Quoted in Bregel 1980, p. 388.
17   Ibid.
18   See Batunskii 2003, p. 160.
19   Sultan-Galiev 1995 [1929].
20   Pavlovich 1922, p. 9.

res capable of serving the needs of the Soviet republics of the East, and the other line having the aim of creating cadres capable of serving the revolutionary requirements of the toiling masses in the colonial and dependent countries of the East'.[21]

National education and the development of national culture were seen as crucial factors in maintaining proletarian hegemony in the territories of the former Empire, because imperial policies had left many areas with no standard, written, native language, extremely low levels of literacy, little or no local administrative experience and very low or non-existent levels of industrialisation. Where industry did exist, it had generally been administered either from Moscow or by foreign capital, with Russian settlers often forming the majority of the workforce. At the same time, the predominantly indigenous rural population had little systematic knowledge of the principles of hygiene or modern medicine, with the result that rapid urbanisation carried real dangers of epidemics.[22] This combination of inherited backwardness was generally spoken about as a 'low level of culture', which is problematic to modern Western ears, but needs to be understood in the sense in which it was meant at the time. Indeed, among Russian intellectuals at the time, 'culture' tended to mean 'technical civilisation' and 'material achievements' as much as language and literature.[23] This use is clear in one of Lenin's warnings about bureaucratic attitudes among some Party members in 1919, who adopted Russian-chauvinist positions:

> [I]n dealing with the national question one cannot argue that economic unity should be effected under all circumstances. Of course, it is necessary! But we must endeavour to secure it by propaganda, by agitation, by a voluntary alliance. The Bashkirs distrust the Great Russians because the Great Russians are more cultured and have utilised their culture to rob the Bashkirs. That is why the term Great Russian is synonymous with the terms 'oppressor', 'rogue' to Bashkirs in those remote places. This must be taken into account, it must be combated, but it will be a lengthy process. It cannot be eliminated by a decree. We must be very cautious in this matter. Exceptional caution must be displayed by a nation like the Great Russians, who earned the bitter hatred of all the other nations; we have only just learned how to remedy the situation, and then, not entirely.[24]

---

21   Stalin 1954c, p. 136.
22   See, for instance, Bairashevskii 1928 and the other papers in the same volume.
23   See Kenez and Shepherd 1998 (eds.), pp. 22–3.
24   Lenin 1974e [199b], p. 195.

While it is undeniable that such formulations involved an implicit 'civilising mission', it is important to recognise that 'cultural backwardness' specifically did *not* suggest that local, ethnic cultures were inferior so much as underdeveloped by the heritage of imperialism and needed to be helped to catch up if the bearers of that culture were to function effectively in the modern world. This was particularly true in the case of linguists. As we shall see, Marr's work was specifically oriented to destroying all notions of the cultural superiority of Indo-European cultures, while Nikolai Iakovlev made it especially clear that he used the term 'backward [*otstalyi*] cultures' with some unease, since 'we all know that any backward people [*narod*] sometimes has more cultural achievements than we have'.[25] The areas that were most clearly locked into this 'backward' condition were generally referred to as the *East*, while those areas of the former Russian Empire that were more advanced in these terms, and needed to make concessions in order to speed the development of the East, were referred to as the *West*.

The labels were not absolute, however, since significant areas in the 'West' were populated by hitherto oppressed national minorities, with the titular nationality often historically disadvantaged in comparison with the Russian population that lived in its midst. The majority of the population of Russia itself was also relatively backward in these terms, with persistently high levels of illiteracy or semi-literacy, and with cities populated by large numbers of recent arrivals from the village. In the last years of his life, Lenin repeatedly referred to the low cultural level of the Russian proletariat that made it reliant on the growing bureaucracy, arguing that this was the greatest danger facing the future of the revolution.[26] Moreover, at the Eleventh Party Congress in 1922, he specifically deplored the lack of 'culture among the stratum of the Communists who perform administrative functions' which had led the 'bureaucratic heap' to direct the Communist administrators.[27] 'Their culture is miserable, insignificant', declared Lenin, 'but it is still at a higher level than ours'.[28] Lenin's last works constitute increasingly desperate efforts to increase the level of education of the masses, to raise the administrative experience of the proletariat and, in so doing, undermine the burgeoning Party apparatus.[29] Unfortunately, the social basis of the regime increasingly turned out to be the

---

25   Iakovlev 1926, p. 224.
26   The classic account remains Lewin 1969, but also see, *inter alia*, Kagarlitsky 1988, pp. 64–71.
27   Lenin 1965b [1922], p. 288.
28   Ibid.
29   See especially Lenin 1965c [1923].

bureaucracy itself, and attempts to counter bureaucratic practices produced little more than more bureaucracy.

Delimitation

Once a particular course of *korenizatsiia* had been adopted, its implementation required very careful strategic and tactical adjustments both in general and in specific localities. The sheer complexity of working out a viable language policy that would remove the accumulated grievances of the non-Russian population during the tsarist period and fulfil the Bolsheviks' pledges of the pre-revolutionary period, but at the same time minimise the creation of new grievances among speakers of languages other than that of the titular nationality in particular regions, was staggering. The Communist parties of the national republics in the 1920s were compelled to facilitate analyses of the social bases of particular languages and their intersection with various forms of nationalist ideas, Russian and others, in specific and often varied situations, and to adjust their activities accordingly. The use of languages by particular social groups needed to be analysed, and an approach to the promotion of a particular national language as a public standard among that group to be carefully assessed and constantly revised in view of the responses of the local population. Where there was no standard form of the local language, this needed to be developed by the intervention of linguists working with the administration and local intelligentsia. Criteria for the selection of specific dialects as putative standards needed to be formulated, the dialects then codified and scripts developed. This by definition necessitated research into the relationship between social groups and language use on a huge scale.

A concerted drive to catalogue and explore the varied composition of the Russian Empire came from within the Imperial Academy of Sciences on the eve of the first revolution in February 1917, in response to concerns about the ethnographic surveys that were carried out by German and Austro-Hungarian researchers on prisoners of war from the Russian Empire.[30] The Commission for the Study of the Tribal Composition of the Population of the Russian Borderlands was transformed into the Commission for the Study of the Tribal Composition of the Population of Russia (and then of the USSR), KIPS, when the commission of academics – Ol'denburg, Bartol'd, M.A. D'iakonov, V.N. Peretts, E.F. Karskii, Shakhmatov and Marr – co-opted key members from the learned societies of Petrograd University, including A.D. Rudnev and

---

30   See, for instance, Evans 2003.

L.V. Shcherba from the Neophilological society. The Bolsheviks particularly needed the collaboration of the Orientalists, for as Mikhail Pavlovich noted in 1924, 'unfortunately Marxists studied the East very little because of a lack of knowledge of eastern languages and so its history, its past economic and spiritual life remained in the shade until now'.[31] The Civil War and the subsequent instability considerably hampered the work of the new commission until 1922, but then a considerable amount of the scant resources available were allocated for the work of KIPS. This had been outlined in February 1917 as 'the definition and mapping of the regional distribution of the peoples populating the Russian state, mainly based on linguistic data, religion, customs and the objective self-consciousness or self-definition of specific peoples, including their physical types (anthropological data)'.[32] The authority according to which linguistic and other boundaries would be drawn remained ambiguous until around 1926. The research of KIPS provided data that facilitated the demarcation of territories and cultures and this involved drawing what Barry Smith calls *fiat* boundaries in relation to certain *bona fide* 'landmarks'. *Fiat* boundaries are here defined as those 'induced through human demarcation',[33] while *bona fide* boundaries 'would exist (and did already exist) even in the absence of all delineating or conceptualising activity' on the part of the researcher or legislator. Demarcation involved the gluing together of 'heterogenous portions in fiat fashion in order to yield a boundary that is topologically complete'.[34] The same process was involved in delineating national languages. Among the tasks of the new commission was a significant expansion of dialect geography. In the context of the formation of the USSR in 1924, the ethnological mapping of the new state became an extremely complex procedure and was driven by the state's changing nationality policy. Dialect geography now merged with systematic studies of language contact, conflicts and planning on a large scale. The work of KIPS and other institutionally embedded researchers was, at the same time, increasingly viewed as providing tools for effective administration from the centre – their findings fed directly into the 1924 delimitation of national territories. As Hirsch concludes, '[t]he KIPS ethnographers, steeped in Western-European and imperial-Russian ideas about nationality and empire,

---

31   Cited in Pochta 1993, p. 82.

32   PFA RAN 135/2/245. It is important to stress that this characterisation of the tasks of KIPS
       pre-dated the October Revolution. See also Hirsch 1985, pp. 45–51.

33   Smith and Varzi 2000, p. 401; Smith 1995. Smith's distinction between fiat and *bona fide*
       objects broadly corresponds to Roy Bhaskar's distinction between transitive and intransi-
       tive objects as defined in Bhaskar 1998 [1979], pp. 9–13.

34   Smith 1995.

but with little formal training in Marxist thought, would continue to facilitate the process of internal transformation that shaped the new Soviet state'.[35] They would also shape the conceptual apparatus of the regime.

The Ukrainian *smychka*

The linguistic problems of the *smychka* in the non-Russian 'West' were particularly apparent in Ukraine. Here the predominant language of the proletariat and peasantry were different national languages that had already been standardised and had written forms (though disagreements about the standardised Ukrainian persisted). The implementation of *korenizatsiia*, in this case known as 'Ukrainisation', intersected in a fairly clear way with the need for the proletariat to make concessions to the peasantry. 'Active Ukrainisation' was understood by the local Party to involve 'a) the adoption of the [Ukrainian] language and the study of local conditions; b) Party direction of the construction of Ukrainian culture through direct involvement in work; c) the selection, Bolshevik education, and drawing of Ukrainians into work; d) the strengthening of the Ukrainian SSR as a state organism'.[36] Implementing this involved considerable difficulties, since the proletariat of the Ukrainian SSR was overwhelmingly Russian-speaking, with statistics collected in 1925–6 showing a mere 8.7 percent of trade-union members speaking Ukrainian and an even smaller amount of Party members among them.[37] The secretary of the Ukrainian Party Central Committee, Fedor Korniushin, explained this by referring to the fact that a Ukrainian peasant who entered industry or mining in tsarist times generally found himself working for a foreign, non-Russian capitalist and under a foreign administrative structure who had adopted the autocracy's Russification policies. Here the Ukrainian peasant, whose culture and language had been left undeveloped as a result of tsarist policies, mixed with Russian peasants and workers and adopted the Russian language as the bearer of a 'more developed culture', and as the language of those with whom he needed to unite in the face of foreign capital and tsarism.[38] As a result, the titular language was not that spoken by the proletariat but by the peasant masses. This was further complicated by the presence of significant enclaves of, *inter alia*, Yiddish, Romanian, Polish, Greek and German speakers, who were

---

35   Hirsch 2007, p. 161.
36   TSDAGOU 1/20/2255/62.
37   TSDAGOU 1/20/2255/6.
38   TSDAGOU 1/20/2255/7.

concentrated in specific localities and social functions. An example of the delicate policies that needed to be adopted concerned the language of the workplace. What language would be the main one used in an enterprise where there was an absolute majority of speakers of one non-Ukrainian language (generally Russian)? What language should be used when a majority of the workforce was non-Ukrainian-speaking but where there was no absolute majority of speakers of a single non-Ukrainian language? The issue was complex and there were several proposals discussed before adopting the general principle that Russian would predominate in the first case, but Ukrainian in the second.[39]

The resources and efforts expended to provide a native-language press and education for the national minorities were particularly impressive given the extraordinarily arduous economic situation in the early 1920s. In order for Ukrainian to be able to play the role of a general national language, an Institute of Ukrainian Scientific Language was founded in 1921 to establish a body of terminology for science, and between 1925 and 1928 a commission to unify the various forms of script was at work. From the middle of the decade, Ukrainian was the main language used at stations to eradicate illiteracy. By the end of the decade, the overwhelming number of schools worked in Ukrainian. The Ukrainian language press also grew precipitously during this period.[40] This growth encouraged Ukrainian intellectuals to talk about a national cultural renaissance. One important debate in the 1920s concerned the extent to which Ukrainian literature should be influenced by Russian literature and the extent to which it should make a unique contribution to European culture. The latter case was particularly made by Mikola Khvylevoi in his provocatively entitled pamphlet *Ukraine or Little Russia*, in which he discussed 'the struggle for the book market, for hegemony on the cultural front, between two fraternal cultures in the Ukraine – Russian and Ukrainian'.[41] He argued for measures to assist the rebirth of the national culture and for the Ukrainian intelligentsia to cast aside its subordinate habits and acknowledge that the Ukrainian path to socialism would proceed a little differently than that in Russia.[42] Khvylovoi found support from the Ukrainian Commissar of Enlightenment (1924–7), Aleksandr Shumskii, who argued that unless steps were taken to involve the proletariat actively in Ukrainisation, 'we will have a union [*smychka*] of the intelligentsia with the peasant masses rather than of the proletariat with

---

39   TsDAGOU 1/20/2251.

40   Borisenok 2006, pp. 109–11.

41   Quoted in Borisenok 2006, p. 130.

42   Ibid.

the peasantry'.[43] Stalin met to discuss the issue with Shumskii, but reported to the Ukrainian Central Committee that any attempt to replace the 'lengthy and spontaneous process' of the Ukrainisation of the proletariat with 'the forcible Ukrainisation of the proletariat from above would be a utopian and harmful policy, one capable of stirring up anti-Ukrainian chauvinism among the non-Ukrainian sections of the proletariat in the Ukraine'.[44] Resistance to such an idea was also strong among certain elements of the Russian-speaking intelligentsia who often regarded the Ukrainian language as a provincial dialect of Russian and resented Ukrainisation.

Already by the time of the Twelfth Congress, Dmitri Lebed', the Vice Chair of the Central Committee of the Ukrainian Party, was arguing that a 'struggle of two cultures', that of the city and of the village, Russian and Ukrainian culture respectively, was inevitable. What Lebed' meant by 'culture' was quite clear and reductionist: 'culture as the economics of the city and culture as the economics of the village, and for a Marxist language is its means [*sredstvo*]'.[45] The former was characterised by 'large industry', the latter was 'small-holding, almost natural peasant economy', and the Party must subordinate the latter to the former.[46] Russian-chauvinist ideas often entered the discussion in this guise, and were strengthened with the gradual removal of oppositionists, such as Rakovskii, from positions of influence within the republic.[47] The tactical problem was, simultaneously, to prevent the Ukrainian language becoming a cause of resentment among Russian speakers, and a vehicle for the formation of independent nationhood among Ukrainian speakers. Lebed' argued that it was important that the Party adopt the Ukrainian language so that it can go to the village to explain matters of concern to the peasants in a language that they understand, but 'we must not forget that for us language is not a means for conveying nationalism, but a means for conveying a Soviet, proletarian, communist influence'.[48] Lebed' then began to argue a case strongly reminiscent of that advanced by Bartol'd in the pre-revolutionary period:

---

43   Quoted in Borisenok, 2006, p. 175.
44   Stalin 1954d [1926], p. 160.
45   Quoted in Borisenok 2006, p. 147. See also Martin 2001, pp. 78–9.
46   Quoted in Borisenok 2006, p. 147.
47   Rakovskii was made Deputy Commissar of Foreign Affairs and sent to London in June 1923, probably in an effort by Stalin to remove potential opponents: Grosul 1988, p. 172. This also needs to be placed in the context of Stalin's move against Sultan-Galiev and against members of the Left Opposition, who had significant support within Ukraine at the same time. On the extent of support for Trotskyism in Ukraine at the time, see Skorkin 2011, pp. 275–82.
48   TsDAGOU 1/20/2255/11.

[F]or Communist internationalists, the national question does not exist
in principle, it is only one of the means for changing the pace of socialist
construction. When this is forgotten, mistakes are unavoidable. Our Party
must check whether, in Ukrainian conditions, the Ukrainian language
helps us to accelerate the cultural process among the Ukrainian people
[*narod*], especially among the backward peasantry, or whether it puts a
brake on the process, not helping the acquisition of culture, but obstruct-
ing it.[49]

The task, he argued, was to find a way to combine the correct theoretical solution to the problem (which had long been decided on by the Party) with 'a sober,
realistic plan for the party's practical mastery of cultural work in the countryside which is, at the same time, not harmful to socialist cultural construction'.[50]

The Ukrainian Party archives contain a particularly interesting paper by an
unnamed Central Committee member on the 'Problematic Nature of Ukrainian
Nationality', in which the social and political dangers of Ukrainisation are discussed with considerable subtlety.[51] The necessity of 'active Ukrainianisation'
to resolve national contradictions was clear, but such a policy raised the dangers of encouraging Russian and Ukrainian chauvinism, the social roots of
which needed to be analysed carefully. The first was rooted in the 'Russian
urban petty bourgeoisie and the intellectual-specialist stratum' that 'acutely
feels the degradation of Russian culture and the lowering of the cultural level.
With regards to Ukrainisation, the latter is focused on the issue of language
and spiritual culture, which puts into question its [the Russian intelligentsia's] social position (both in the sense of its ideological influence and in the
direct sense of its crust of bread)'. This was institutionally reinforced by the
'thousands of threads' that connect these ideologues with the central state
apparatus and was nourished by bureaucratisation. The Russian proletariat
was not subject to such influence, however, and at worst tended to be indifferent towards the national question. Chauvinism thus had no 'social roots'
among workers, but represented a survival of centuries of prejudice from the
'old world' and the influence of petty-bourgeois sloganeering.[52] The Party had
to engage in a determined struggle with the former, but in the case of the latter had to explain the social roots of Russian chauvinism and the proletariat's
responsibility to actively engage in Ukrainisation to strengthen the union

49   TsDAGOU 1/20/2255/11–12.
50   TsDAGOU 1/20/2255/12.
51   TsDAGOU 1/20/2255/58–69.
52   TsDAGOU 1/20/2255/64–5.

[*smychka*] with the Ukrainian peasantry. Ukrainisation must be practised decisively enough to ensure that the peasantry does not become anti-proletarian, but not so quickly that chauvinism is created among the Russified proletariat where it does not currently exist. The archives are replete with discussions about the experiences of local Party organisations and reflections on how to adapt tactically to specific conditions in localities, including how to combine agitation and propaganda among specific social groups.

Ukrainian chauvinism had more complex roots, however. These were to be found in three principal groups: 1) the strong village kulak (the bearer of a general property-owning provincialism); 2) the urban bourgeoisie (or more precisely its ideologue, the urban intelligentsia awaiting the rise of the bourgeoisie and oriented to Europe); and 3) a certain section of the rural poor that does not accept the NEP and 'intellectuals who are perplexed by the contradictions of socialist construction', who 'view communism through the prism of a romantic national rebirth'.[53] The first is quite content to continue making money under NEP and dreams of expansion, but is unconcerned with problems of the wider world and is, therefore, attracted by the idea of Ukraine for Ukrainians.[54] The second makes 'revolutionary gestures', condemns kulak provincialism and has 'followed Lenin's advice to learn from capitalist Europe', but is not content with acquiring technical knowledge and has developed a 'psychological dependence' on Europe as a counterweight to 'proletarian Moscow':

> His slogan is 'down with out-of-the-way provincialism, hold your head up, right hand to psychological Europe, left – to the Asian renaissance, face towards the Black Sea with its possibilities for import and export'. Quite logically, his back is to Moscow, and he finds the hold of Russian culture a hindrance. His concern is to develop the economic organism of Ukraine, leaving questions of building socialism to the Party and proletariat, and if there is to be socialism in one country, let it be in the Ukrainian SSR.[55]

The third factor, the disaffected and *declassé* rural poor that resents the NEP concession to the kulak, is a danger only in the context of the other two, since he is unable to organise himself politically but can provide the manpower for the others. In current circumstances, however, he dreams of a 'strong man from Europe', like the Polish dictator Pilsudskii, who will adopt his cause. The second factor was regarded as the biggest danger, since it had the capacity for

---

53   TsDAGOU 1/20/2255/65.

54   TsDAGOU 1/20/2255/66.

55   TsDAGOU 1/20/2255/66–7.

ideological elaboration and to link up with the first and third factors, requiring a determined effort by the Party on the ideological front, to strengthen Party cadre to confront the ideas of the 'Europeanists', which sometimes masked themselves with Marxist terms. This particularly required 'Marxist work on the question of Ukrainian history and cultures', central among which was the issue of language.[56] Here we see a striking example of how national, cultural and language policy all converged to compel practical, theoretical and historical consideration of the connections between language and social groups.

In the Ukrainian case, we can see that the policy of the hegemony of the proletariat required it to make very significant linguistic concessions to the peasantry – both in terms of Russian speakers learning Ukrainian and also by enduring a transfer of administrative, educational and other cultural resources to the Ukrainian peasant population. Where, from 1924, the official language of Poland, which incorporated a significant Ukrainian population, was Polish, in Soviet Ukraine from 1923 Russian and Ukrainian had equal status and, from January 1926, Ukrainian was adopted by all state institutions, with documentation in both languages. Ukrainisation not only addressed the question of hegemony within the Ukrainian Socialist Republic, but also provided a significant example of the benefits of the Soviet system to the non-titular nationalities of Central Europe.

The 'East': Azerbaijan and Beyond

The relationship between language policy and the *smychka* was much more complex in the East. As well as making substantial economic and political concessions, the Soviet regime provided significant resources for the creation of standard linguistic forms for the newly established national republics. The administrative requirements to draw up boundaries, determine titular nationalities and so make decisions about the promotion of certain languages to titular status in an ethnically complex region, were undoubtedly daunting. There is no doubting the skill which Stalin's Commissariat of Nationalities [Narkomnats] employed when negotiating between the work of ethnographers and linguists from central institutions, local intellectuals and linguists, and representatives of the newly promoted indigenous administrators. As with national delimitation, delineating the boundaries of the national language required the drawing of fiat boundaries in relation to those which already existed. Michael Smith correctly argues that the central government

---

56   TsDAGOU 1/20/2255/68.

'chose to promote selected patterns of linguistic and ethnic separation already in place', but what Stalin had in mind was something that would be ever less a federation and ever more a union.[57] The 1923 policy gave considerable space for local initiative and for the local determination of cultural policy, but the administrative arrangements also allowed for that autonomy to be gradually squeezed out through the selective promotion of local cadre. Moreover, whatever 'affirmative action' was taken in favour of the indigenous population, 'the Russian language remained a constant and heavy-handed imperative in Soviet life', since it remained an obligatory subject and students needed a certain level of proficiency in the language if they were to proceed to higher education.[58] Native peoples seeking career advancement sought to assimilate the Russian language, as Lenin had predicted, but the All-Union administrative structures were evolving in a way that made this a necessity rather than a choice.

In the East, the problem of the various Turkic languages spoken by millions of people in the vast area of Asia between Azerbaijan and Yakutsk undoubtedly posed the greatest challenge in terms of scale, but the extremely complex linguistic situation among the patchwork of small nations in the mountains and valleys of the Caucasus was no less challenging for other reasons. Throughout central Asia, research institutes were set up to study the natural, socioeconomic, ethnological and linguistic aspects of the national republics, in close collaboration with institutes in Moscow and Leningrad. Social and economic development in these areas required the construction of standard forms of language from the plethora of local dialects spoken, the development of sufficient technical terminology to facilitate education in the 'native' language and the working out of a written script that would not revive memories of Russian imperial impositions, but would not leave the population at the mercy of the Muslim establishment that was the sole bearer of Arabic literacy in the region. It was also generally accepted among linguists that the established Arabic alphabet imperfectly rendered the phonetics of Turkic languages in any case, while the Latin and Cyrillic alphabets proved more adaptable. Supporters of the Arabic alphabet did make significant advances in adapting the Arabic script and it found significant support in certain areas such as Tatarstan and Kazakhstan, leading both Polivanov and Iakovlev, two of the most significant people working on the creation of Latin-based alphabets for the 'peoples of the East', to recommend that policy makers respect the progress that had been made and not to rush ahead with the process of

57   Smith 1998, p. 50.
58   Smith 1998, p. 53.

Latinisation.[59] Meanwhile, Cyrillic was generally tainted by associations with tsarist Russification policies, and so the Azerbaijani government decided to support those committed to creating a Latin alphabet that would 'reflect all the living natural sounds found in the Azerbaijan dialect of the Turkish language and its southern variations'.[60] This task was given to the Committee of the New Turkish Alphabet of the local Party Central Committee (AzTsIK) in April 1922. The committee gradually established bases throughout the Caucasus and then throughout the wider Turkic areas. Each branch had autonomy but remained subordinate to the Central Committee in Baku. The introduction of the new alphabet was combined with the campaign to eradicate illiteracy in the region and it soon found wide acceptance among the Azerbaijani population at large, enabling the local government to scrap the Arabic alphabet.[61] In other areas, however, this was more problematic, and special attention needed to be given to local conditions. Nevertheless, the fact that the Kemalist Turkish regime, which was itself trying to implement a secular state oriented on Europe, decided to adopt the Latin alphabet on the model of the nascent USSR in the mid-1920s, bolstered the cause of Latinisation as best suited to the internationalist cause. It was, however, to count against that cause at the end of the decade, when the requirements of autarchy governed policy and fears of cross-border alliances grew.

In March 1924 the scale of the tasks being undertaken led one of the leading Leningrad Turkologists of the time, then Rector of the Petrograd Institute of Living Eastern Languages, Aleksandr N. Samoilovich, to raise the need for an All-Union Turkological Congress to the Central Committee of the New Azerbaijan Alphabet. He suggested that the Congress address three central issues: the development of a Latin alphabet for the whole Turkic world, the principles for the development of a literary language and the development of scientific terminology.[62]

Samoilovich argued that it was necessary to include in the list of invited speakers Bartol'd, Ol'denburg, Marr, Iakovlev and Polivanov, all of whom had

---

59   Alpatov 2000b, p. 67. For an overview of the work of the 'language builders', see Alpatov 2000b, pp. 51–60.

60   'Doklad o deiatel'nosti Komiteta Novogo Tiurkskogo Alfavita pri AZTsIKe c aprelia mesiatsa 1922 goda po 1 oktiabria 1925 goda' GAAR 103/1/1/39–42, l.39. On the political considerations, see also Polivanov 1923, p. 4.

61   GAAR 103/1/1/39–42.

62   GAAR 103/1/39/91–30b. Samoilovich became the director of the Institute of Oriental Studies of the USSR Academy of Sciences in 1927, but was shot on fabricated charges of acting as a Japanese spy and promoting counterrevolutionary pan-Turkism in 1938. On this, see Ashnin et al. 2002, pp. 7–20.

been centrally involved in the expeditions of KIPS. The event took place in Baku in March 1926, with 131 delegates from across the USSR, but with both Marr and Polivanov absent. While all the areas proposed by Samoilovich were discussed at the 1926 congress, and the Azerbaijani Latinisation campaign was endorsed, the event itself was somewhat broader than he had envisaged, with presentations on general ethnographical issues and even on the visual arts. While most papers delivered at the congress had to address questions of the relation between language construction and social conditions, it was the paper given by Iakovlev that systematically examined the relationship between Latinisation and the varied social bases for its introduction. Surveying the experience of introducing the Latin script into various areas, Iakovlev observed that the greater the profundity of the roots of Muslim culture, the greater popular resistance to attempts to replace the Arabic script. Furthermore, 'the higher the rate of literacy prior to the introduction of the Latin alphabet, the more difficult the introduction of the Latin alphabet'.[63] Thus, Azerbaijan had 1–1.5 percent literacy prior to 1917, Tartarstan 25 percent and Uzbekistan 11 percent. But other specifically sociological features were also evident: the extent of urbanisation (Azerbaijan 13 percent, Tartarstan 4.3 percent, Uzbekistan 16 percent) and its character. In Azerbaijan the presence of a relatively numerous and concentrated urban proletariat based on oil production within Azerbaijan aided Latinisation, but while the Tartar proletariat was no less numerous, its greater dispersal, often beyond the Tartar Republic, served, along with the relatively high proportion of literacy in Arabic, to obstruct the introduction of the Latin alphabet. In Uzbekistan the proletariat was almost completely absent, while the relatively large urban population was based on an urban merchant bourgeoisie and artisans, which combined with deep-rooted Muslim traditions to make the introduction of the Latin alphabet particularly complex. It was here that Polivanov was centrally engaged in language construction, and the experience undoubtedly contributed to his theoretical work. Other groups had their own specific sociological and ethnographic particularities that needed to be taken into consideration when formulating the script and introducing it on a mass scale.

This required considerable research, and Baku became an important regional centre for such work, with the most significant Union-wide linguists and ethnologists visiting on a regular basis. General research was initially centred on the Society for the Examination and Study of Azerbaijan, which was formed within the local Comissariat of Enlightenment in 1923, but which was transferred to the jurisdiction of AzTsIK in 1925, before becoming a fully fledged

---

63   Iakovlev 1926, p. 224.

Party research institute, AzGNII, in 1930. Here Japhetic linguists and more traditional Turkologists worked side by side, researching 'the history, contemporary state and the social dialectology of Azerbaijani, Turkish and other Turkic languages, languages of other peoples living in Azerbaijan, and also Japhetic and Iranian languages'.[64] This institute, and its forerunner, had close relations with the institutes in Moscow and Leningrad, with visits by figures such as Shor (in 1929–30) and Iakovlev from the Scientific Research Institute of the Ethnic and National Cultures of the Peoples of the East [*Nauchno-issledovatel'skii institut etnicheskoi i natsional'noi kul'tur narodov vostoka*, INV] in Moscow, and Marr and Meshaninov from IIaM in Leningrad. In most cases, the relationship between Moscow linguists and those indigenous linguists working on the formulation of national languages was advisory.

In her valuable book on the making of Soviet Turkmenistan, Adrienne Lynn Edgar shows how local linguists grappled with a range of problems about how to forge a standard national language from the variety of tribal dialects within the newly established national territory.[65] The linguists were particularly keen to ensure that the numerical preponderance of one tribal group, the Teke, was not reflected in the new language and so attempted to orchestrate a standard form that drew upon all the dialects of the region. This operation was clearly one that demanded significant diplomatic skill, since there were numerous struggles for social and political advantage taking place. Edgar characterises one linguist, Kumyshali Böriev, as concerned with certain advocates of the Teke dialect striving for 'linguistic hegemony'.[66] Nor did the matter end with internal conflicts, for local linguists also needed to settle the question of whether and how to borrow terminology from other languages, both Turkic and European, especially Russian. The very operation of drawing linguistic boundaries made the assimilation of terms from neighbouring Turkic languages particularly sensitive, and the linguists working in Turkestan were especially concerned about interference by linguists from other Turkic republics. The assertiveness of the Azerbaijani linguists was undoubtedly a major concern. Borrowing from Russian inevitably involved questions about the relationship between the centre and the regions of the union, but while the status of Russian as one of the official languages of the republic aroused discontent, borrowing from Russian does not seem to have been as sensitive an issue as borrowing from other Turkic languages. The question of borrowing preoccupied most of the newly standardised languages, since the extant dialects often had no terminol-

---

64   PFA RAN 77/1(1921–1929)/37/23.

65   Edgar 2004, pp. 129–64. See also Clement 2005.

66   Edgar 2004, pp. 151–2.

ogy to deal with technical and administrative issues.[67] Given the centralisation of policy that was taking place at the end of the 1920s, it is impressive that, when in 1930 a conference was held to settle the question of the Turkmen standard language, the questions were largely decided by local intellectuals, even if the decisions they made were often flouted by writers, journalists and teachers who had their own tribal biases.[68] Such autonomy quickly disappeared, however, and within three years many of the linguists found themselves purged and decisions about standardisation were being made by officials appointed by Moscow.[69]

The relationship between the regional and central institutes shifted towards subordination of the former to the latter or, in some cases, the absorption of the former into the structures of the latter. From the early 1930s, the Moscow Institute had been subordinated to Marr's Institute in Leningrad, ultimately becoming the Moscow branch of IIaM, while AzGII and IIaM were locked into 'socialist competition', through which plans and results were continually compared. Extensive fieldwork and theoretical developments fuelled each other, but the majority of the latter emerged at the central institutes in Moscow and Leningrad, where linguists reflected on the issues facing researchers as a whole. Institutional centralisation mirrored the increasing centralisation of language policy as a whole, which was partly pursued by the central agencies but was also impelled by competition and suspicion among the leaders of the new Turkic republics. As Andreas Frings has recently argued, the Azerbaijan committee consciously manoeuvred to bring about a situation in which Moscow had to intervene on the side of Azerbaijani-led Latinisation against those based in Kazan who were promoting the revised Arabic alphabet.[70] Concerns among some leaders of Turkic republics about attempts to establish 'Azerbaijani hegemony' over the process of Latinisation in Central Asia led to the Committee of the New Turkish Alphabet being reformed into the All-Union Committee for New Turkic Alphabet, VTsKNTA, which was placed under the funding and supervision of the Central Committee of the USSR in 1927.[71] VTsKNTA then endorsed the unification of all the Latin alphabets being developed for each of the Turkic languages. The shift of authority disarmed much of the opposition

---

67   Edgar 2004, pp. 143–8.

68   Edgar 2004, pp. 152–3.

69   These repressions were undoubtedly part of the campaign against both the intellectuals supporting national autonomy and, indeed, the former Russian intelligentsia during the 'Cultural Revolution'. This culminated in the fabricated case against the Slavists in 1933–4. On this, see Ashnin and Alpatov 1994.

70   Frings 2009, pp. 249–66.

71   Martin 2001, pp. 188–9.

among leaders of Turkic republics suspicious of Azerbaijani ambitions, but strengthened the hegemony of the central administration. All Soviet Turkic republics were to declare themselves in favour of Latinisation by mid-1928. In August 1929 the Latin script was made mandatory for all Turkic languages and, in 1930, VTsKNTA moved to Moscow, where it became a centrally administered body. All remaining opponents of Latinisation were now officially labelled 'reactionary' and even 'class enemies'.

Most researchers point out that the centralisation of language policy and the shift towards central institutions governing theoretical approaches to the relationship between the language and national questions was connected with the rise of Marrism to quasi-official status.[72] There is undoubtedly some truth in this, but one should recognise that most researchers went along with the changes, perhaps taking the rhetoric of national liberation, the equalisation and convergence of national cultures, at face value. Thus by 1928, when the Stalinist transformation of the USSR had begun in earnest with the so-called Cultural Revolution, a declared dimension of 'socialist transformation', Polivanov had left behind his caution about Latinisation, arguing in the journal *Novyi Vostok* that the adoption of the Latin alphabet by Soviet nationalities is the adoption of an international system facilitating the convergence of national cultures within the union and facilitating communication on an international scale. Latinisation, he concluded, allegedly paraphrasing Lenin from 1922, is the 'cultural revolution in the East'.[73] Encouraged by the success of the Latinisation campaign in Central Asia, in 1930 Iakovlev turned his attention to the Latinisation of other languages that already had their own forms of writing, such as Georgian, Belorussian and ultimately Russian. The areas still employing the Cyrillic alphabet, he claimed, were still employing a relic of autocratic oppression, the activity of Orthodox missionaries and Great Russian national chauvinism. This was now particularly anachronistic since it acted as a barrier between the 'revolutionary East' and the 'proletariat of the West'. Now that there was a 'general plan for the reconstruction of the country', constructing a new socialist culture and new ways of life, the 'Russian civil alphabet' no longer satisfied its citizens, even after the orthographical reforms that followed the revolution.[74] He strove to prove the 'material and

---

72   This is, for instance, suggested by Smith 1998, pp. 138–42; Edgar 2004, p. 154.

73   Polivanov 1928a, p. 315. The veracity of this alleged quotation from Lenin ('Latinisation is a great revolution for the East') cannot be verified and even if it were substantially correct it is far from clear what Lenin had in mind. For a discussion of this see Smith 1998, p. 124 and Martin 2001, p. 187.

74   Iakovlev 1930, pp. 35–6.

ideological gain' brought about by an immediate transition to a 'single international alphabet based on Latin' that should be part of the Five-Year Plan of the time.[75] While Iakovlev imbibed those aspects of Marrist theory that pertained to the origin of language in 'diffuse exclamations', he had no time for the elaborate and impractical 'analytic alphabet' the Marrists were trying to develop.[76] Nevertheless, the ambition to provide a medium for the international unification of the means of communication was the same, though Iakovlev clearly did not appreciate how times had changed, nor how the internationalist perspective he rather mechanically translated into linguistic terms no longer applied. Though in November 1929 a subcommission of *Glavnauka*, the Department of Science, was established to work on the Latinisation of Russian, by January 1930 Stalin had already spearheaded a Politburo resolution to 'order Glavnauka [the Department of Science] to cease work on the question'.[77] Three years later, discussion was already focusing on whether the whole project of Latinisation should be abandoned and whether Russian, a language now with quite a different 'class content' than before the Revolution, should bestow its own alphabet as a model for all the languages of the union. This did indeed come to pass on the eve of the 'Great Patriotic War'.

There is little doubt that the Marrists played an important role in undermining the credibility of the champions of Latinisation in the eyes of the all-Union authorities. Marr's absence from the 1926 congress had contributed to the minor role played by his theory in the discussions, with only one paper, delivered by A.N. Genko, devoted to the question of the relationship between Turkic and Japhetic languages and a resolution stating that the achievements of Japhetic theory should be taken into account when continuing research on the relation between Turkic and other language groups.[78] This led to a strong reaction against the conclusions of the congress among Marrists, who were keen to champion Marr's 'Analytic alphabet' over that developed by the leaders of the Latinisation movement. While Marr himself was already quite elderly and showing symptoms of mental illness, there were younger and belligerent advocates of Marrism who were well suited to the institutional politics at the end of the decade and who understood that, during the 'Cultural Revolution', statutory authority trumped scientific authority. This became especially clear when Polivanov, who, *inter alia*, was a linguist clearly associated with the

75 Iakovlev 1930, p. 43. On the idea of a unified alphabet, see Simonato-Kokochkin 2010.
76 Iakovlev 1931. For balanced discussions of the 'analytical alphabet', see Matthews 1953 and Smith 1998, pp. 140–1.
77 Alpatov 2012, p. 146.
78 Genko 1926, pp. 123–8.

Latinisation movement, unsuccessfully challenged the dominance of Marrism in 1929. Marr's *Institut iazyka i myshleniia* [Institute of Language and Thinking, IIaM] now became the main institute to which publishers referred manuscripts about linguistics pending publication, with reviewers continually demanding that the central tenets of Marrism be adopted.[79] At the beginning of the 1930s, Marrists like Iosif Kusik′ian used the journal *Prosveshcheniie natsional′nostei* [*The Enlightenment of Nationalities*] to launch vitriolic and ideological attacks on figures such as Iakovlev, arguing that the methodology of comparative-historical linguistics also provided the basis for 'national deviations' and 'Great Russian Chauvinism', since families of languages were identified with race.[80] The New Turkic Alphabet thus began to be associated with pan-Turkism, while other varieties of the Latin alphabet designed for, say, Finno-Ugric 'families', could promote a nationalist mentality among Karelians, Mordvins and the like.[81] Marr's analytical alphabet, on the other hand, was designed to be able to render the sounds of all languages. The fact that this alphabet was actually quite incapable of functioning in this way became a secondary consideration, for it promised to provide a medium for the unification of all the languages of the union, regardless of any distinctions of 'family'. When Japhetic theory achieved official endorsement in the early 1930s, some key participants in the 1926 congress were already being accused of promoting 'pan-Turkism' and bourgeois nationalism, and so of being enemies of internationalism.[82] The only 'internationalism' that now mattered, however, was that which transcended national distinctions within the USSR, and a theory that posited the gradual merging of all its languages fitted the agenda. In April 1935 IIaM was officially recognised as the centre for research into 'the cultural development of national languages' on an all-Union level, and accusations that came from that quarter undoubtedly contributed to the large numbers attending the 1926 congress who perished in the purges of the late 1930s, including the initiator of the conference, Samoilovich.[83]

It is highly unlikely that Bartol′d and other pre-revolutionary Orientalists would have supported the repression of the local intelligentsia, not least because a parallel persecution of some Russian intellectuals from the pre-revolutionary era was also occurring. However, there is little doubt that what

---

79   See, for instance, the demands made by V.I. Abaev and S.L. Bykhovskaia on Iakovlev's 'Grammatika Kabardinskogo iazyka' in July 1931 at PFA RAN (SPb) 77/1(1931)/14/1–30b.

80   See Alpatov 2004, pp. 102–5.

81   Martin 2001, p. 202.

82   PFA RAN (SPb) 77/1(1921–9)/37/154.

83   TsGAOU 1/20/6635/1. On the repressions, see Ashnin *et al.* 2002.

had emerged was precisely the hegemonic arrangement that the Rozen School Orientalists had pursued. It is quite possible, however, that the 'aggressive campaigns' of the regime against the local intellectuals could have been tolerated as 'unconscious steps on the road to the establishment of the ever more apparent historical mission of Russia'.[84] National languages and cultures were now being provided with the means for their development, while the study of the cultures of the peoples of the nations was being concentrated in research institutes in the metropolitan centres of Moscow and Leningrad, with local branches situated in the regions. Local intellectuals were no longer excluded from participation in research and nation building and were able to develop their careers as long as they accepted the primacy of the all-Union structures, implicitly recognising that 'we know them better than they know themselves'.[85] Moreover, the narrative employed to justify policy claimed that all the languages of the USSR, and ultimately humanity were, as Michael Smith puts it, 'developing according to the slow, spiraling formula of convergence and mergence toward proletarian unity [*edinstvo*]'. Indigenous people were now 'locked . . . within the upward stream of historical time' led by the most advanced people: the Russian proletariat.[86] While the proletarian gloss was quite alien to Bartol'd's world view, his idea of the convergence of all peoples through cultural exchange led by the most advanced nation was remarkably similar to the policy that emerged in the 1930s. This becomes less surprising when we recognise that one of the key contributors to the formulation of this narrative was Bartol'd's long-time colleague, Nikolai Marr. We will soon turn to the contradictory legacy of this extraordinary figure.

---

84 Bartol'd 1963b [1927], p. 432. See the discussion of this work in the earlier chapter.
85 Bartol'd 1963a [1900], p. 610.
86 Smith 1998, p. 88.

CHAPTER 7

Hegemony: The Decline and Fall of a Paradigm

If there is one event that led to the decline of the notion of hegemony as a critical resource dealing with the internal politics and culture of the USSR, it was the launch of the first Five-Year Plan. Policy was decisively reoriented toward break-neck industrialisation and forced collectivisation, with concessions to the peasantry no longer acceptable. While attacks on the national minorities were by no means as decisive, a dramatic shift towards coercion from the centre clearly took place. In some cases, such as in parts of Ukraine, resistance to collectivisation merged with a defence of national autonomy, with the result that breaking resistance to collectivisation also implied doing the same with national assertiveness. The *smychka* thus ceased to play a guiding role in Party discussion and the vitality of the notion of hegemony declined at the same time. Moreover, recent use of the term was particularly associated with both Zinov'ev and Bukharin, the influence of whom the Party now needed to expunge. As a result, at the Sixteenth Party Congress of June and July 1930, the term 'hegemony' was used almost exclusively in relation to the international situation.

This is not to say, however, that the term was, in principle, not applicable to the internal Soviet arrangement. While the balance of class forces shifted in decisive ways, the regime could not govern by force alone, and it was important to ensure that workers felt they had a stake in the system. The process of collectivisation also had to be moderated, as the consequences proved to be economically disastrous and the level of social dislocation completely unmanageable.[1] Although a dramatic employers' offensive was launched along with collectivisation itself, it was crucial that this did not lead to coordinated resistance among workers and that any resistance would not make connections with the struggles of the peasantry. It was, of course, quite likely that Party activists considered the offensive to threaten only sectional interests among workers and that, from the 'all-state' point of view, the interests of the proletariat were, in the long run, being promoted. However, these proletarian 'concessions' were not designed to win the support of the peasantry, but accompanied an offensive against the peasantry as such. The extension of the label 'kulak' to all peasants who resisted collectivisation served to obscure this fact, and rhe-

---

1 Stalin's famous 'Dizzy with Success' article of 20 March 1930 was indicative of this. Stalin 1954f [1930].

torical continuities with the period of the Civil War, in which unpopular grain requisitions kept the cities from complete starvation, appeared to gain more traction among the very different Party members of the late 1920s than the notion of hegemony was able to. To paraphrase Marx's *The Eighteenth Brumaire of Louis Bonaparte*, Party leaders anxiously conjured up the 'spirits of the past to their service, borrowing from them names, battle slogans, and costumes in order to present this new scene in world history in time-honoured disguise and borrowed language'.[2] To inspire heroic acts in order to achieve unheroic ends, they thus adopted the heroic forms of the past to conceal historical limitations from themselves and 'to keep their passion on the high plane of great historic tragedy'.[3]

In his prison notes on 'Americanism', written in 1929–30, Gramsci argues that in the United States production was being rationalised by combining 'force – destruction of trade-unionism – with persuasion wages and other benefits – so as to base the whole life of the nation on industry'.[4] Unlike in Europe, he concludes, '[h]egemony is born in the factory and does not need so many political and ideological intermediaries'.[5] This provides an interesting analogue to the new hegemonic arrangement that was being established in the USSR at the time. As the economy improved under NEP, workers experienced some of the benefits of the new trade-union laws, employment rights and a loosening of factory supervision, but as the crisis of the policy deepened, an employers' offensive loomed. The first Five-Year Plan finally ended the regime of proletarian hegemony. The workers lost the last of their institutional gains, the Troika, and were fully subordinated to the productive process itself, while the peasantry was dispossessed and brought under the control of the central bureaucracy by force. The bureaucracy, which was transforming itself into a ruling class, now exerted hegemony over the workers by combining force – the suppression of all vestiges of genuine trade unionism and residual forms of workers' control – with persuasion, including the setting of wages by the factory manager or the head of a particular branch of industry. In November 1928 the Sixteenth Party Congress approved the end of all vestiges of workers' power in enterprise in favour of 'streamlining the management of production, establishing one-man management [*edinonachalie*] and the reorganisation of the management of production, and demands the implementation of them

---

2 Marx 1979 [1851–2], pp. 104–5.
3 Marx 1979 [1851–2], p. 105.
4 Gramsci 1991, p. 169.
5 Ibid.

in life'.[6] In June 1931 Stalin declared the need to end 'the "Leftist" practice of wage equalisation', to increase wage differentials and maximise incentives.[7] The Commissar for Heavy Industry, Ordzhonikidze, cited Stalin to urge directors to no longer orient themselves on the 'average wage' and not to delegate decisions on pay, but to recognise that 'wages are the most powerful weapon in your hands'.[8] However, the ability to persuade the working class through high wages was severely limited in the USSR, where productivity remained very low. Differential access to scarce consumer goods through special outlets was to supplement wage differentials until the end of the Soviet era. The USSR was now passing through the stage of primitive accumulation and implementing a severe employers' offensive, meaning that the already bureaucratised apparatus of hegemony needed to be adapted to the new structures of power. Strategies to atomise the proletariat through competitive mechanisms, piecework and the like were accompanied by full-spectrum ideological dominance in all areas of social life. It was in this sense that the label 'totalitarian' could be applied to the USSR of the time with some justification. The new hegemony was indeed born in the factory, but the Party was determined to ensure that perception of any contradiction between the experience of workers in the productive process and the claims of the political leadership should not lead to oppositional ideological currents. This involved huge distortions of the political lexicon which, while the grounds for this had certainly been laid in some areas of political discourse in the period of the Civil War and the NEP, now took on a qualitatively new form. Agitation and propaganda were now decisively transformed into management techniques as the Party transformed itself into a collective of economic and political managers.

While Gastev's brand of NOT provided much that was appealing to the bureaucracy and political leadership in the context of a dramatic employers' offensive, there was one aspect of Gastev's ideas that raised concerns among the political leadership: the apparent championing of the rise of a privileged technical intelligentsia that could ultimately become the nucleus of a new ruling class. This prospect had been specifically raised by Bogdanov as early as 1919, and subsequently made its way into Bukharin's theory of cultural revolution, although Bukharin and Gastev had found common cause in the early 1920s.[9] A rising strike wave in the Donbass throughout 1927, coupled with

---

6   KPSS v rezoliutsiiakh i resheniiakh s"ezdov, konferentsii i plenumov Ts.K. 1898–1953, seventh edition (Moscow: Politicheskaia literatura, 1953), vol. 2, p. 591. See also Reiman 1987, pp. 110–12.

7   Stalin 1954g [1931], p. 58.

8   Ordzhonikidze 1957 [1934], p. 596.

9   Biggart 1990, p. 282; Biggart 1992; Bailes 1977, p. 387.

concern about the technical intelligentsia, led to the notorious 1928 Shakhty show trial [*Shakhtinskoe delo*], in which a group of engineers in the north Caucasus were arrested and tried for allegedly sabotaging coal production. As Reiman argues, the trial became a model for future show trials, in that it served as a means of 'relieving excess social and political tension while providing justification for an increased use of administrative and repressive models by the authorities'.[10] Industrial relations were now fundamentally restructured and the GPU began to penetrate into this area ever more deeply. Middle- and lower-level managers now became the targets of worker discontent, while '[t]he centers of political power were raised above society and above their own apparatus, gaining greater room for maneuver and greater possibilities for arbitrary and oppressive rule'.[11] From this time, we can trace an identifiable zig-zag in Stalinist policy, oscillating between a populist repudiation of 'bourgeois specialists' and attempts to raise their status in the productive process, corresponding to emphases on ideology and *tekhnika*.[12] Speaking at the First All-Union Conference of Leading Personnel of Socialist Industry in February 1931, Stalin argued that:

> The Shakhty affair showed that the Party organisations and the trade unions lacked revolutionary vigilance. It showed that our economic executives were disgracefully backward in technical knowledge [*tekhnika*]; that some of the old engineers and technicians, working without supervision, rather easily go over to wrecking activities, especially as they are constantly being besieged by 'offers' from our enemies abroad.[13]

In conclusion, he argued that '[i]t is time Bolsheviks themselves became experts. In the period of reconstruction, technique [*tekhnika*] decides everything'.[14]

Theory was adjusted *ad hoc* to legitimise policy. Once *tekhnika* had become accepted 1) as the principal determinant of the mode of production and consequently as the 'basis' of social psychology and culture, and 2) administrative control of that *tekhnika* had been established as a long-term feature of 'socialism', then the cause of proletarian hegemony, which Zinov'ev had regarded as the 'main, regulating idea of Bolshevism', was 'rendered inoperative' within the

---

10   Reiman 1987, p. 66.

11   Ibid.

12   On this, see the second half of Priestland 2007.

13   Stalin 1954i [1931], p. 38.

14   Stalin 1954i [1931], p. 43. On this see Priestland 2007, pp. 255–6.

USSR. The irony was that it was precisely the pioneers of the philosophy of technology in the revolutionary movement that had been the main champions of the 'cultural hegemony' of the proletariat. The defeat of the Time League was thus arguably the first defeat of the project of proletarian hegemony, the consequences of which would gradually be rolled out throughout the various spheres of social life. What began in the economic sphere ended in the cultural sphere with the institutionalisation of 'socialist realism' in state-regulated professional 'unions'. It was impossible now to speak coherently about the hegemony of the proletariat and so the conception gradually disappeared from Party discourse. None of this was implemented in a coherent fashion, however, as the leadership responded to events and the unintended consequences of each action. In such circumstances, the most immediate effect was social and institutional dislocation and the destruction of the sophisticated theoretical edifice that had emerged since the beginning of the century.

In essence, the paradigm of hegemony could not survive the pronouncement that the class struggle had ended within the USSR. The definitive statement to this effect was Stalin's speech on the draft constitution of the USSR in November 1936, at which it was announced that 'the complete victory of the socialist system in all spheres of the national economy is now a fact'.[15] The classes that exploited the proletariat and peasantry had been eliminated, leaving only the two 'friendly' classes of the proletariat and peasantry, as well as the stratum called the intelligentsia. The proletariat and peasantry were no longer as old, but new types had emerged, 'the like of which the history of mankind has never known before'. Moreover, the intelligentsia was not like that of old, but 'an equal member of Soviet society, in which, side by side with the workers and peasants, pulling together with them, it is engaged in building the new, classless, socialist society'.[16] Conspicuous by its absence was, of course, the party-state bureaucracy. Since the notion of hegemony pertained to alliances between classes, this was no longer of any relevance to Soviet society where 'the dividing lines between the working class and the peasantry, and between these classes and the intelligentsia, are being obliterated, and ... the old class exclusiveness is disappearing'.[17] Stalin made it clear that the whole basis for the applicability of such concepts was now disappearing:

---

15   Stalin 1978 [1936], p. 799.

16   Stalin 1978 [1936], p. 803.

17   Ibid. One may see here how Marr's idea of the convergence of all class languages could easily complement Stalin's contention.

What do these changes signify?

Firstly, they signify that the distance between these social groups is steadily diminishing.

Secondly, they signify that the economic contradictions between these social groups are declining, are becoming obliterated.

And lastly, they signify that the political contradictions between them are also declining and becoming obliterated.[18]

This also extended to the national question within the USSR, where the lack of exploitation, the ideas of internationalism, 'the actual practice of mutual aid among the peoples in all spheres of economic and social life; and, finally, the flourishing of the national culture of the peoples of the U.S.S.R., culture which is national in form and socialist in content – all these and similar factors have brought about a radical change in the aspect of the peoples of the U.S.S.R.; their feeling of mutual distrust has disappeared, a feeling of mutual friendship has developed among them, and thus real fraternal co-operation among the peoples has been established within the system of a single federal state'.[19] Along with this, there emerged a celebration of the leading role of Russia within the Union, and of the rehabilitation of heroes from the Russian Empire's past. The USSR was now presented not only as the product of the revolution, but as an heir to the great achievements of the imperial past.[20]

These monumental developments had crucial effects on the conceptions of language and culture in the USSR. While historical discussions of the transformation of the literary world and the general academic environment are numerous, discussion of how the end of the NEP period impacted on conceptions of language, culture and hegemony are sparse. Here we focus on these developments, beginning with the transformation of the institutions where the path-breaking research of the 1920s was carried out, before moving on to the development of a form of linguistic thought designed to correspond to the first Five-Year Plan and then to the changing nature of the struggle of groups of 'proletarian writers' for cultural hegemony. At each stage, we will see that the issues of language, culture and hegemony were closely related, even in the very process of the displacement of the Bolshevik project.

---

18   Stalin 1978 [1936], p. 803.

19   Stalin 1978 [1936], p. 805.

20   See, especially, Brandenberger 2002.

Institutional Transformations

The transformations of research and pedagogical institutions that accompanied the Five-Year Plan brought distortions of socio-political concepts and ensured that the effects of social dislocation would not become the object of critical research. Crucial in this was the effective annexation of state institutions by the Party institutions, with which they had enjoyed a parallel existence throughout the NEP period. After the defeat of the United Opposition in 1927, and of the Bukharin wing of the Party in 1928, the Central Committee set a goal of securing a majority of Party members among the 'scientific cadre' in the social sciences, while professorial and teaching staff were subject to 'reelection'.[21] Demands that all science, and scholarship generally, serve 'socialist construction' became ubiquitous, while 'specialist-baiting' of non-Party intellectuals became commonplace. The sheer scale of the constant re-organisation of institutions is bewildering for all researchers of the period, while representatives of the Worker and Peasant's Inspectorate, Rabkrin, were sent into institutions and set up 'Purge Commissions' to weed out hostile elements. Groups of intellectuals were organised into 'brigades' to pursue institutionally-set objectives, while 'socialist competition' between enterprises and units within enterprises became mandatory. The institutional and intellectual space that was a precondition for the pursuit of some of the most innovative research programmes of the 1920s was drastically curtailed, while an appeal to statutory, rather than scientific, authority became increasingly effective in the struggles that were being encouraged within institutions.

A good example of the changes was the *Institut rechevoi kul'tury* [the Institute of Discursive Culture, IRK, formerly ILIaZV] in Leningrad which, as we have seen, had been the locus of some of the most innovative and important research in language and literature throughout the 1920s. In 1930 RANION, the state body that had administered IRK and other institutes, was dissolved and the institute was rendered vulnerable to takeover by the Communist Academy. The focus of the institute narrowed sharply. In 1930 the older and new themes maintained an uneasy coexistence. The collective theme of the 'Office of General Linguistics' became the 'formation of national languages in the epoch of capitalism', and the theme of the newly-formed 'Office of Literary and Business [*delovoi*] Language' became 'the linguistic style of the proletariat (on the basis of the publicistic and scientific works of Lenin)'.[22] The former

---

21   David-Fox 1997, pp. 257–8.

22   'Otchet o rabote sektora metodologii lingvistiki GIRK za 1930–1 god', PFA RAN 827/3/93/59–60.

theme gave rise to Iakubinskii's articles about the Russian national language published in *Literaturnaia ucheba*, and Zhirmunskii's work on the German national language published in 1936, both of which were discussed in Chapter Five. The latter was symptomatic of the way in which the language of the Party was now becoming the explicit model for the newly standardised public language, and this was reinforced by the work of the Laboratory of Public Discourse, which was reorganised into brigades on the methods of oral agitation and the history of agitation, with collective themes on 'oral agitation for production' and 'proletarian oratorical style'.[23] These became the basis for the last of Iakubinskii's articles in *Literaturnaia ucheba* and Gofman's book *Slovo oratora*, with agitation now understood entirely in the spirit of management techniques. Soon after, in January 1931, the director of the Volodarskii Communist Institute of Agitation (the successor to the oratory section of the IZhS) and of the Laboratory of Public Discourse, Vladimir Kreps, made an attempt to take control of GIRK, to hand the literary section to the Communist Academy and to turn what remained into an entirely practical institute of applied linguistics. A Rabkrin 'purge commission' began to operate, concluding that there was inadequate ideological leadership, no sense of any 'socialist competition' and an absence of shock workers within the institute.[24] The commission decided to transfer the literary section, as recommended, and to transfer the laboratories of Public Discourse and the Physiology of Speech to the Institute of Agitation.[25] Following appeals and negotiations, including a particularly impressive petition by Zhirmunskii to Glavnauka,[26] a rump GIRK survived until the autumn of 1933, incorporating both reduced literary and linguistic sections led by Desnitskii and Iakubinskii respectively, before being absorbed into the Leningrad Institute of History, Philosophy, Literature and Linguistics [*Leningradskii institut istorii, filosofii, literatury i lingvistiki*, LIFLI], the semi-autonomous linguistic section of which was The Leningrad State Linguistic Institute [*Leningradskii gosudarstvennyi lingvisticheskii institut*, LGLI], which was directed by Iakubinskii.[27] In August 1937 the literary and linguistic faculties of LIFLI were merged into the philology faculty of Leningrad State University.[28]

---

23   PFA RAN 827/3/97/70.

24   PFA RAN 827/3/101/13–180b.

25   GARF A-4655/1/389/64–8; PFA RAN 827/3/101/11–12.

26   PFA RAN 1001/2/112/51–30b.

27   PFA RAN 302/1/91/45.

28   RGALI SPb 328/1/71/12.

This development followed a pattern that was repeated across the Soviet higher-education system.[29] The pyrrhic victory of the Communist Academy over the Academy of Sciences and RANION proved to be but an interlude before a conservative and extremely hierarchical system settled into place in the 1930s. The history of this episode has been told more than once and need not detain us here,[30] but we should be careful not to apply a too-monolithic view of Soviet academic life. After 1932 there was a gradual restoration of scientific authority in academic life and the re-emergence of an identifiable scientific field which, despite its very real limitations and distortions, continued to produce important work in areas relatively distant from political and administrative concerns.

The 'Proletarian Episode' in Linguistics[31]

During the first Five-Year Plan, changes in the governance of institutions led their agendas to become tied to pronouncements from within the Party far more directly than had ever been the case in the 1920s. There was a crucial shift in the effectiveness of appeals to statutory authority over scientific authority. At the end of 1929, Stalin called for ruthless struggle against the economic theories of Bukharin's 'Right Opposition', and this began a general offensive on the 'theoretical front', in which theories in economics, philosophy and history were to be brought into line with contemporary practice.[32] This was followed by two further interventions, one in connection with a philosophical discussion at the Institute of Red Professors in December 1930 and another in October 1931 regarding the history of the Party.[33] Again IRK provides a good example, for 'in connection with Comrade Stalin's letter' of 1931, a collection began to be prepared for publication called *Against the Theory and Practice of Trotskyism in Language* [*Protiv teorii i praktiki trotskizma v iazyke*].[34] The participation of a figure of Iakubinskii's status in such a collection was symptomatic of the

---

29   See, for instance, the fate of the path-breaking Institute of Buddhist Culture in Leningrad, as described in Ostrovskaia 2010.

30   The classic text is Graham 1967, since which there have been a significant number of studies in Russian and other languages. In English I draw the attention of the reader to Levin 1988; Shapiro 1976 and David-Fox 1997.

31   The title of this section alludes to the title of Brown 1971 [1953].

32   Stalin 1954e [1929].

33   Anon. 1930; Stalin 1954h [1931]. On the significance of this last document, see also Shapiro 1976, pp. 284–91.

34   PFA RAN 827/3/97/82.

time. It is no coincidence that it was now that attempts to construct a specifically 'Marxist linguistics' ceased to be a minority strand associated with
unsophisticated 'hotheads' within Soviet institutions. The main pretenders to
leadership in the construction of such a discipline were the Marrists and the
group of young radical linguists who organised under the banner of *Iazykfront*
[Language Front]. We will deal with Marrism in detail in the next chapter, but
here we will concentrate on the two attempts to present alternative models of
Marxism in linguistics. The first was Polivanov's celebrated attempt to block
the rise of Marrism to official status, which was less an attempt to claim leadership in the construction of a separate Marxist linguistics than to defend linguistics as an autonomous discipline, to which Marxists could make a valuable
contribution. His most elaborated statement on the question is undoubtedly
the 1931 collection of essays *For a Marxist Linguistics* [*Za Marksistskoe iazykoznanie*], in which he directly challenges the usurpation of scientific by statutory authority, stresses the importance of education in linguistic scholarship
regardless of the sociological origins of individual linguists, and declares the
need to build upon the achievements of 'bourgeois science'.[35] As he puts it in
his article on the relationship between linguistics and language policy:

> If ... we build our own science without all the achievements of bourgeois
> science of the type indicated, either simply rejecting them (that is, not
> desiring to know them) or denying them (because they are the product of
> the bourgeois world), we not only have not created any new science of
> *our own*, but we will simply transform ourselves into obscurantists. All
> this was understood very well by V.I. Lenin, who more than once warned
> against the authors of such meagre proletarian culture and meagre prole-
> tarian science, and I have had occasion to cite him for this reason more
> than once.[36]

Polivanov did move in the direction of trying to create a Marxist explanation of
such things as qualitative changes in language structure, and to present phonetic evolution as a 'labour process', but these were often attempts to recast
mutational theories of grammar and of the ideas of Baudouin about phonetics
into Marxist terminology. These concerns remained subordinate to his general attempt to bring the Marxist understanding of social structure and the

---

35   Polivanov 1931, pp. 3–4.
36   Polivanov 1931, p. 15; 1974e [1931], pp. 338–9. See also Alpatov 2010, pp. 31–3. See also the
      transcript of Polivanov's appearance at the Communist Academy in 1929: Polivanov 1991
      [1929].

historical process into analyses of sociolinguistic phenomena. Polivanov essentially rejected the terms of the new regime in linguistics, but was unable to withstand the ideological and institutional transformations that were occurring.

The next challenge was from within the parameters of the new regime. The leaders, Georgii Daniilov and Timofei Lomtev, were young and ambitious radicals with specialist training that was much less developed than the earlier generation of linguists like Polivanov, Iakubinskii and Shor. Daniilov had worked on social dialectology at IIaL, while Lomtev had recently graduated from Voronezh University, where he wrote an interesting, if immature, work on 'The Concept of Language in the Light of Marxism', in which he discussed the notion of the language system (Saussure's *langue*) in comparison with Marx's discussion of the capitalist system and the ideas of von Humboldt.[37] The work also included some interesting criticisms of Voloshinov's discussion of these ideas in *Marxism and the Philosophy of Language* (1929).[38] Unfortunately, these exploratory moves were soon eclipsed by a shift toward a polemical engagement with competing trends in linguistics, with a particularly hostile approach to 'formalist, metaphysical, idealist Indo-Europeanism', and condemnation of such figures as Peterson and Ushakov as 'representatives of pseudo-science'.[39] Polivanov was unambiguously consigned to the ranks of the Indo-Europeanists, while Marrism was credited with revealing the political agenda underlying the theory and with correctly positing language as part of the superstructure. In September 1930, the group *Iazykfront* was launched, with its name echoing that of the group *Litfront* that had just been formed within RAPP. The group involved around twenty-five young linguists, including the Esperantist Ernest Drezen and people who were to become significant figures in Soviet linguistics later, such as Nikolai Chemodanov, Sergei Bernshtein and Petr Kuznetsov.[40] Centred on the newly-founded Research Institute of Linguistics [*Nauchno-issledovatel'skii institut iazykoznaniia*, NIIaZ] in Moscow, the group sought to oppose the Marrists' claim to a monopoly position as the Marxists in linguistics, uncover the limitations of Japhetic theory, including its mechanistic formulations (especially the notorious four-element theory), its inability to pose

---

37   Lomtev 2011 [1930].

38   Voloshinov 1929.

39   Lomtev 2001 [1931]. See also Fedorova 2010.

40   The connection with RAPP is confirmed by the participation of Ian Loia, who had published a programmatic article under the name 'Linguist' (Lingvist 1929). The question of Esperanto in the early USSR is worthy of a study in its own right. On this see, especially, Lins 1999.

the question of class correctly and its fetishism of the paleontological method at the expense of addressing contemporary problems.[41] They tried to shift the focus of work towards 'the study of the language of the collective farmer, of the worker, the problems of planned influence on linguistic processes and the verification of theory by practice'.[42] They also proposed a whole range of ways in which linguists might intervene in the education of school children.[43] There is thus a sense in which, despite their compromises with the interests of the bureaucracy, *Iazykfront* was struggling to maintain the link of Marxist theory and practice that was in actuality being ineluctably severed. Marrist partisans fought back in particularly unpleasant ways, using their institutional positions and control of certain key publications. In their ideological struggle, they again recruited Iakubinskii to their cause.[44] Ultimately, however, it was the 'organisational position' of *Iazykfront* that began to concern the authorities more than its ideas. The concern was that the group 'presented a danger (in view of the absence of control and direction of "Iazykfront" from the side of leading Party organs)', and that it could 'grow into an anti-Party group or be penetrated by anti-Party elements'.[45] It was closed in May 1932 and NIIaZ followed suit the following year, leaving Marr's institutions as the dominant player in the field of linguistics. These institutions were to lead the subsequent course of linguistics in the USSR for almost another two decades.

Proletarian Culture

The one area where the concept of hegemony enjoyed a brief rise to prominence after 1929 was in the field of literature. One of the effects of the fall of Bukharin in 1928 was the removal of the constraints on the bellicose advocates of proletarian literature in their struggle to achieve 'hegemony' in the cultural sphere by administrative means.[46] Bukharin, it will be remembered, had specifically condemned VAPP, the forerunner of RAPP, for seeking control of the

---

41   'Iz stenogrammy torzhestvennogo sobraniia v NIIaZe, posviashchennogo godovshchine ego sushchestvovaniia, 2 marta, 1932g: Vystuplenie direktora instituta M.N. Bochachera', GARF A-2307/17/84.

42   Lomtev 1931, p. 161.

43   Ibid.

44   Iakubinskii 1932.

45   GARF A-2307/17/84/173.

46   Thus one of the leaders of RAPP, Vladimir Kirshon, could declare that proletarian literature was now the main trend and was clearly winning hegemony (*XVI S"ezd vsesoiuznoi kommunisticheskoi partii (b)* 1930, p. 281).

organs of the press under the guise of its campaign for proletarian hegemony in literature. When transferred to the struggle between institutions in these conditions, the term 'hegemony' ceased to describe the subtle adjustments to policy that the proletarian leadership needed to make in order to lead the peasantry and national minorities according to shared interests, and came to mean 'wide-ranging domination, political subordination, and control over activities and resources'.[47] The leaders of RAPP, especially Leopol'd Averbakh, now specifically targeted the 'students of Bukharin in the field of culture', while their anti-intellectual pronouncements chimed with those of the Party in the wake of the Shakhty affair.[48] As Averbakh put it, '[t]he struggle *for the cultural hegemony of the proletariat* – this is what interests us most of all, and it is from this point of view that we approach all questions'.[49] In an attempt to rewrite the history of the debates of the early 1920s, he claimed that when Lenin had polemicised against 'the term "proletarian culture"', he was actually attacking not the idea of proletarian culture itself, but the ideas of Bogdanov and Pletnev, who assumed that the cultural hegemony of the proletariat must precede both the achievement of political hegemony and state power.[50] Instead, proletarian culture must be understood as the 'class content of the cultural revolution, as the materialisation of the idea of the cultural hegemony of the proletariat'.[51] RAPP now led attacks on other theoretical approaches to literature purely on the basis of their merits to the new political situation and, famously, on fellow-traveller writers, but it was especially vitriolic in relations towards proletarian writers who did not present their work as in step with Party policy.

The bureaucratic distortion of the idea of proletarian culture, and of the political discourse in general, found one of its most profound presentations in the work of perhaps the most significant proletarian writer of the time, Andrei Platonov, whose own ideas had been significantly shaped by those of Bogdanov.[52] In his work of the first Five-Year Plan period, Platonov presented contrasting 'labour world views' of the poor worker and Party bureaucrat, the first of which, his 1929 story *Usomnivshiisia Makar* [*Doubtful Makar*], appeared in the RAPP journal *Oktiabr* (*October*). This proved particularly irritating to

---

47   David-Fox 1997, p. 192, n. 2. As we have seen, while this characterisation is appropriate for these debates, it is not an adequate characterisation of the general Bolshevik use of the term, as David-Fox seems to suggest.

48   Averbakh quoted in Perkhin 1997, p. 17.

49   Averbakh 1931 (original emphasis).

50   Averbakh 1931, p. 49.

51   Averbakh 1931, pp. 49–50.

52   See, *inter alia*, Seifrid, 1992; Bocharova 2003; Malygina 2005.

Stalin personally and led to a series of attacks on his work.[53] Here Platonov drew upon the disjuncture between the emerging official language and the patterns of reception among the peasantry and newly urbanised workers that had been the object of study by figures such as Shafir and Shpil'rein, and which had become the object of artistic representation during the NEP period in the work of Zoshchenko and others. Over-literal interpretations of metaphor and grotesque discursive hybridisations are now, however, symptomatic of a fundamental incompatibility between the 'labour world view' of the worker and that underlying the arbitrarily imposed, official political discourse.[54] Proletarian consciousness becomes a substratum which disrupts the ruling discourse. In this story, the different 'logics' of the worker and Party bureaucrat are explored in a deadly satire, in which the language of official propaganda is understood literally and presented in grotesque forms, ultimately undermining the whole bureaucratic system personified by a certain comrade Chumovoi, whose name derives from the Russian word for 'plague'. Platonov's hero particularly bemoans how general policy is indifferent to the spiritual needs of the individual proletarian. This class-based spirituality suggests a continuity between the author's pursuit of proletarian culture and the god-building ideas of Gorky, Lunacharskii and others.[55] Responding to the story, Averbakh viewed the inevitable product of such humanism to be an 'anarchistic anti-statism', declaring that 'our time does not tolerate ambiguity':

> Writers who want to be Soviet must understand clearly that *nihilistic dissoluteness and anarcho-individualistic opposition [fronda] is no less alien to the proletarian revolution than direct counterrevolution with fascist slogans.* This is what A. Platonov must understand.[56]

In the 1931 story, *Vprok (Bedniatskaia khronika)* [*For Future Use (A Poor-Peasant Chronicle)*], Platonov interspersed the class-war rhetoric of the collectivisation campaign with surreal images of collectivised peasants wandering around

---

53 Platonov 1988a [1929]. Platonov is notoriously difficult to translate, but a reasonable English translation is Platonov 1978 [1929]. The first critical response was Averbakh 1931 [1929].

54 Dhooge (Dhooge 2012) suggests Platonov's development of an unusual approach to language in his stories may have been due to the influence of LEF writers about language engineering and the work of Vinokur in particular. While the strategy might indeed have been so influenced, the structural issue of the labour world view remains fundamental.

55 Malygina 1995, pp. 17–18. On the religious dimension of earlier proletarian literature, see Steinberg 2002.

56 Averbakh 1931 [1929], pp. 70, 73 [original emphasis].

like latter-day holy fools.[57] This produced an outpouring of criticism from the guardians of proletarian literature, complaining that Platonov portrayed collectivisation as a 'bureaucratic invention' rather than the outcome of a proletarian policy.[58] Instead of viewing collectivisation as a conscious movement of poor peasants, and one which was opposed only by recalcitrant kulaks, that is, according to the official account, one reviewer complained that 'Platonov views the whole collective-farm movement as the result of a violent measure in relation to backward strata of the peasantry with a low level of consciousness, who go into the collective farms by force, without faith in, and unconvinced by, the success of the imposed experiment'.[59] In effect, the story was read as a veiled protest against the replacement of a policy of proletarian hegemony by bureaucratic *diktat*. It is open to question whether Platonov's story can justifiably be read in such unambiguous terms, but the reception among these administrative advocates of proletarian culture is significant in itself. Perkhin suggests, quite realistically, that one of the attacks on Platonov's story deliberately echoed Stalin's 1929 speech on the agrarian question discussed above, likening Platonov to the economist and utopian Aleksandr Chaianov, the publication of whose works Stalin had condemned.[60] In the short 1930 novel, *Kotlovan* [*The Excavation*], which remained unpublished until 1987, the comic satire of Makar has given way to a tragic portrayal of the alienation and intellectual subordination of the worker.[61] The extraordinary, contorted language that results from the disjuncture between the official ideology and the 'labour world view' of the worker is now contained by an implied and sometimes open portrayal of state violence and a pervasive sense of proletarian exhaustion and resignation. The central symbol of the novel is how work on a projected tower of living space results only in a pit that serves as a grave. Nina Malygina reasonably suggests that Platonov may have been alluding to the imagined tower that had appeared in Gastev's poetic works.[62] Indeed, there is a sense in which Platonov's work presents an implicit critique of the replacement of the

---

57   Platonov 1988c [1931].

58   See, *inter alia*, Fadeev 1931; Selvanovskii 1931. For an overview, see Perkhin 1997, pp. 16–21.

59   Quoted in Perkhin 1997, p. 20.

60   Perkhin 1997, p. 19. It is notable that Platonov was subject to significant attention from the
       GPU. On this, see Shentalinsky 1993, pp. 209–19. Chaianov, it should be noted, had been
       arrested in 1930.

61   Platonov 1988b [1930]. There are two English translations, both of which struggle with
       Platonov's revealingly tortuous prose: Platonov 1978 [1930] and Platonov 1994 [1974].

62   Malygina 1995, pp. 17–18; Malygina 2005.

humanist ideals of proletarian culture, as developed within *Proletkul't*, with the bureaucratic-technological conception of proletarian culture championed by Gastev.

While RAPP played a significant role in destroying the organisational capacities of most other groups of writers, it soon faced attacks on its own positions from its competitors for the mantle of the Party's cultural vanguard and attracted criticism from the Party for its sectarianism and harsh administrative conduct, especially towards non-Communist writers.[63] The passing of the anti-intellectual wave and attempts to rehabilitate the technical intelligentsia and 'bourgeois specialists' rendered RAPP out of step with the Party's own policy zig-zags. Ermolaev is probably correct to argue that, however close the RAPP agenda remained to Party policies during the first Five-Year Plan, it could not ultimately continue to exist once the Party resolved to create a socialist society at the Seventeenth Party Congress.[64] Now the Party was set on a policy of 'gradually deemphasising the proletarian nature of the Soviet state and bringing out its socialist character', and so on 23 April 1932 all proletarian-culture organisations were dissolved by decree.[65] In place of 'proletarian literature', there would ultimately be 'socialist realism', presenting images of the assured arrival of a classless society where there was no longer any need to discuss strategies of hegemony.

The role of Gorky who, it will be remembered, championed the adoption of the language of the nineteenth-century classics as a model in the debates about the new public discourse of the mid-1920s, is significant here. Having spent most of the 1920s in Italy, from where he had made his interventions in earlier debates, Gorky was personally invited by Stalin to return to the USSR in 1932. He quickly renewed his mentoring of fledgling Soviet writers, promoting the '*tekhnika* of literary work', which pertained most of all to the study of the literary language.[66] He thus spearheaded an attempt to bring the organisation of culture in line with that of the rest of social life. Bukharin was to echo this in his speech to the August 1934 Soviet Writers' Congress, when he argued that 'poetics is the *tekhnika* of poetic craftsmanship'.[67] Gorky regarded the language of the classics to be a guide for writers in the present, who had to deal with a lexis that had undergone considerable changes under new economic

---

63   Brown 1971 [1953], pp. 106–18; Sheshukov 1984 pp. 302–13.

64   Ermolaev 1963, p. 120.

65   Ermolaev 1963, p. 123. The document can be found in Clark and Dobrenko 2007, pp. 151–2.

66   Gor'kii 1953a [1933].

67   Gorky *et al.* 1977 [1934], pp. 185–6.

and social relations. Writers had a responsibility not only to recognise and understand the changes, but also to play a role in organising the language 'to find appropriate verbal forms to reveal the heroism of reality'.[68] In his article 'On Language', which was published in *Pravda* in March 1934, Gorky retained vestiges of his earlier association with *Vpered*, but he forced Bogdanov's ideas about language together with the new bureaucratic agenda. He reminded the reader that 'words contain concepts, organised by enduring work experience', and called for 'a struggle for the purity, the precision of meaning, for the sharpness of language', which is a struggle for the 'weapon of culture'.[69] He now argued for a struggle against 'ungainly phrases' and 'verbal nonsense', because it was now 'beyond dispute' that soiling the language with such factors is 'a reflection of class hostility in as much as it takes the form of contempt, scorn, mockery and irony'.[70] The linguistic grotesqueries of Platonov's alienated proletarians, chafing against the outward, extrinsic linguistic and ideological order, which acted as a fetter on their intellectual and spiritual growth, had no place in such a literature.[71]

---

68   Muratova 1958, p. 333.

69   Gor'kii 1953b [1934].

70   Gor'kii 1953b [1934].

71   Gorky regarded Platonov as 'a gifted man, spoiled by the influence of [the modernist] Pil'niak and by collaboration with him' (Primochkina 1998, p. 63).

Ideology Critique, Positivism and Marxism: The Paradoxical Legacy of Nikolai Marr

The particular variety of sociological linguistics that developed in the USSR in the 1920s facilitated path-breaking reflections on the relationship between the sociolects of different social strata and on the relationship between the putative standard and non-standard forms of language. Such work was to decline, however, at the same time as the paradigm of hegemony declined. In place of these approaches to language, and in the face of the resistance of some important linguists, there followed the rise to prominence of the ideas of Nikolai Marr in linguistics, which was to render the central considerations of the linguists of the 1920s of secondary importance at best. Marr's work stretches across all the periods discussed in this book, emerging from the old schools of philology that were concerned with the remote past of various languages, and with etymological questions as a primary focus. In some respects he returned the focus of Soviet linguistics to precisely these questions. Yet Marr rejected the search for original proto-languages and combined the concerns of philology with the positivist narrative of the passage from myth to science, and of the gradual convergence of cultures in the upward stream of evolutionary development that, as we have seen, concerned the school of Orientalists from which he emerged. Thus, while the sociological linguists placed questions associated with the hegemony of the proletariat over the peasantry, the towns over the countryside and the formation of national languages over tribal and local dialects at the forefront of their research, Marr's work viewed such issues largely as irrelevant, given that evolution itself was leading to the merging of various systems of languages into a single language, quite unlike all those languages that had gone before, and that this accompanied the breaking down of the class structure of society under socialism. For this reason, Marr's ideas proved highly compatible with Stalin's drive for the homogenisation of national languages, and his claim to be building socialism in the USSR, especially in the mid-1930s. Questions of the way in which workers and peasants employed linguistic forms assimilated from social groups who exerted cultural prestige which was to prove crucial in considerations of hegemony were now rendered trivial, not least because the 'crossing' of languages could be projected back into the distant past. Rather, what now came to the fore was the struggle between a conception of language developed in the interests of colonialism and one which furthered the interests of subject peoples to break free of the intellectual hegemony of their oppressors. These ultimately mapped onto the struggle between the capitalist world and the USSR, where the imperial distinctions between West and East were allegedly 'melting away'.

No work dealing with theories of language in Russia in the 1920s and 1930s can avoid the issue of Marrism. Marr's 'Japhetic theory', later renamed and transformed into the 'new theory of language', achieved official recognition as 'Marxism in linguistics' in 1932 and remained dominant until 1950. It was promoted, and then officially denounced, by Stalin himself. Yet as interesting as the official, institutional history of Marrism is, it is only part of a larger, deeply paradoxical story. Marr was often regarded as either a genius or a madman by some of the most significant specialists in the humanities at the time. The dominance of Marrism in language studies was undoubtedly extremely destructive, but at the same time it enabled significant theoretical advances in studies of literature and folklore.

While Marrism was leading to some of the most extraordinary 'quackery' in one area, it stimulated some of the most important work in literary and cultural studies of the inter-war period. This is a challenging phenomenon to explain, and while one or another side of the paradox has been subject to sustained and valuable study, the source of the paradox has remained elusive.

Recent discussions of Marr in Russia might be divided into two trends exemplified by Vladimir Alpatov's 1991 (second enlarged edition 2004) book, *Istoriia odnogo mifa: Marr i marrizm* [*The History of a Myth: Marr and Marrism*], and Ia. V. Vasil'kov's major 2001 article, 'Tragediia akademika Marra' ['The Tragedy of Academician Marr'].[1] Both works have considerable strengths and present excellent research, but each is one-sided. Alpatov tackles Marr's work from the point of view of a linguist, criticising his evident incompetence in matters of general linguistics and attempting to explain both the appeal of his 'New Theory' during its period of dominance and the relief with which the demise of the doctrine was greeted by linguists in 1950. Alpatov rightly highlights the extremely destructive activities of Marr's most belligerent followers and the way in which some of the most talented linguists of the period and their valuable research projects were harassed, denounced and in some cases physically eliminated. While briefly acknowledging Marr's valuable work outside linguistics, Alpatov regards Marr's most perceptive insights into language to be fatally flawed due to persistent and unproductive theorising from the beginning of his career. The ultimate victory of Marrism, according to this argument, needs to be understood as the triumph of a myth supported by interested powers

---

1 Alpatov 2004; Vasil'kov 2001.

akin to the dominance of Lysenko in genetics. Vasil'kov is rather more sympathetic towards Marr and tries to take a more rounded view of his career as an archaeologist, philologist and finally linguist, giving due attention to his achievements at each stage. For Vasil'kov, Marr's work took a qualitatively new and mistaken turn with the declaration of the 'new theory' in 1923, which was a result of Marr trying to reform his ideas according to a Marxist agenda and thereby abandoning true scholarship for ideological mystification. Alpatov's approach makes it rather difficult to understand how Marrism managed to inform valuable work outside the realm of linguistics, while that of Vasil'kov presents a rather naïve view of the relationship between scholarship and ideology, which Marr himself sought to undermine and, as we shall see, fails to show that the 'new theory' was a variant of Marxism in linguistics. Alpatov, much more convincingly, shows both that Marr was not a Marxist and that Marxism was not incompatible with rigorous linguistic scholarship, but fails to appreciate the force of Marr's critique of the ideology behind Indo-European philology.

It is important to recognise that Marrism was certainly not a systematic doctrine, but was (to echo Brennan's description of Said's work above) a 'patented eclectic amalgam' that was unstable and under constant revision up until Marr's death in 1934. From this time, various scholars continued to develop certain aspects of Marr's ideas, often bringing order and rigour to Marr's own diffuse suggestions and peregrinations, but this often led in directions and to discoveries that were not in accordance with expectations. Moreover, specific episodes in Marr's life coincide with certain transformations in his works in such a way as to make any consideration of his ideas problematic without significant biographical references. Among these are Marr's volatile personality, his personal encounters with Indo-European linguists and their reception of his early work, the loss of the archaeological centre he had laboured to build for 15 years when the part of Armenia in which it was located was handed to Turkey as part of the Brest-Litovsk Peace Treaty and fire destroyed most of the archive, Marr's consequent separation from the material he had studied and on which he had based his empirical work, and the death of his favourite son in 1921.[2] One of the strengths of Vasil'kov's work is that he integrates biographical and ideological factors, while Alpatov is rather stronger in recognising the institutional dimension of Marrism. Increasing psychological instability, combined with growing official indulgence as the 1920s progressed, encouraged Marr's ever less restrained and abstract theorising as he threw himself into

---

2   On Marr's biography, Mikhankova 1949; Platonova 1998; Platonova 2002; Ilizarov 2012.

intensive administrative work and fervid writing that often crossed the border between theorising and graphomania.

Along with Bartol'd and Ol'denburg, Marr emerged from the Rozen School of Orientalists and shared their general, positivist orientation towards the tasks of Russian Orientalism and the critical approach towards the orientation developed by the thinkers working within the institutions of the Western powers. He was loyal to the tsarist regime and its institutions, being elected an elder of the official Georgian church in St. Petersburg and serving as a censor of Armenian books. He was untouched by pre-revolutionary campaigns against left professors. Marr was nevertheless critical of the regime's policies towards the national minorities, an issue about which he was particularly sensitive as a Georgian, but his position never moved beyond the liberal promotion of schools for national minorities, similar to that of the other pre-revolutionary Orientalists we have already discussed.[3] Like them, he also bemoaned the way in which non-European cultures of the Empire were poorly studied, but was particularly scathing about the lack of attention given to the languages and cultures of the Caucasus. As Alpatov correctly argues, if one takes Marr's work from any period of his career, one finds it 'full of declarations about the global role of Caucasian peoples and that science, especially linguistics, had suppressed discussion of this role'.[4] Like Bartol'd, Marr wanted to reorient and promote Russian imperial Orientalism in contradistinction to that practised in the rest of Europe, but he was particularly focused on the promotion of the cultures of the Caucasus. As Tolz has shown, during World War I and before the October Revolution, he presented the work of French and German archaeologists and ethnographers who were working in areas close to the border of the Russian Caucasus as enemies, looking forward to Russian victory in both fields.[5] It appears that after the October Revolution and the Civil War, Marr perceived an opportunity to complete this reorientation by undergirding it with an ideological and political structure that he gleaned from contemporary statements about imperialism and the class nature of science. This certainly helped him to achieve the institutional bases he craved, beginning with the establishment of the *Gosudarstvennaia akademiia istorii material'noi kul'tury* [State Academy for the History of Material Culture, GAIMK] in 1919, but any assimilation of Marxism was limited to the eccentric application of Marxist-sounding phraseology. Stalin was certainly correct when, in 1950, he argued

---

3   Alpatov 2004, p. 21.

4   Alpatov 2004, p. 14.

5   Tolz 2011, pp. 92–3. See Marr 1917, pp. 964–5. The article is recorded as having been submitted on 6 September 1917 and the issue of the journal is dated 1 October.

that Marr was unable to become a Marxist, but only a 'simplifier and vulgariser of Marxism, like the Proletkul'tists or RAPPists'.[6] In 1922 the head of the newly established VNAV, Mikhail Pavlovich, defined the tasks of Soviet Oriental studies in opposition to those of the West, but at the same time he worked to minimise the divisions between the late imperial Orientalists and the new Soviet Orientalism.[7] While societies for the study of the East in Britain, France and Germany subordinated scholarly study of the East to doing whatever they could to help their governments conquer Asian territories, the 'All-Russian Scientific Association of Oriental Studies must be the higher scientific organ, studying the East, spreading scientific knowledge about the East to the wider popular mass and simultaneously helping Soviet power to determine the correct policy with regard to the peoples of the East'.[8] Marr quickly picked up on such programmatic statements and presented his own theories as exemplary of a unitary 'anti-imperialist', 'proletarian' Soviet scholarship against an equally unitary 'imperialist', 'bourgeois' scholarship of the West. This proved a very useful analogue for Stalin's 1925 contention that 'we have two Easts, living different lives, and developing under different conditions' and for the autarchic policies of the Stalin regime at the end of the 1920s.[9] Marrism ultimately facilitated the effacement of the difference between the liberal imperialism of the pre-revolutionary Orientalists and the anti-imperialism of the original Bolshevik programme, while the contrast between Soviet and European Orientalism was highlighted.

This was undoubtedly a significant factor determining the outcome of the discussion at the Communist Academy in February 1929, when Polivanov challenged Marrist claims that Japhetic theory was Marxism in linguistics.[10] While showing an appreciation for Marr's early comparative studies of south Caucasian languages, Polivanov convincingly picked apart Marr's more controversial claims (to be outlined below) on the basis of their being unsupported by factual data, insisted on the historical reality of proto-languages and cast considerable doubt on Marr's credentials as a Marxist. Polivanov argued that it was insufficient to claim, as Marr did, that one particular pattern of development in language was determined by one set of economic conditions without proving that an alternative pattern emerges from other economic conditions.

---

6   Stalin 1972 [1950], p. 31.
7   Ol'denburg 1927, p. xxv.
8   Pavlovich 1922, pp. 5, 10.
9   Stalin 1954c, p. 136.
10   The transcript of Polivanov's contributions to the discussion, as well as some of the responses, are published in Polivanov 1991 [1929].

As Ilizarov argues, 'Polivanov soberly and in detail attempted to establish a bridge between European and Soviet scholarship', but by this time the scientific validity of the criticism was beside the point.[11] The newspaper *Vecherniaia Moskva* [*Evening Moscow*] reported the exchange, noting that Marr's supporters accused Polivanov of attempting to 'hitch-up his reactionary theory to Marxist phraseology'.[12] Polivanov failed to halt the rise of Marrism to semi-official status as 'Marxism in linguistics', despite the fact that his own knowledge of Marxism was far superior to that of Marr who, as we shall see, really did hitch his own ideas up to a pseudo-Marxist phraseology.

The critique of the entanglement of European Orientalism with the imperial projects of the states in which they emerged developed in the work of the pre-revolutionary Orientalists nevertheless did have important strengths. What Marr was to do was to refocus this critique specifically on philology. There were specific reasons why Marr endeavoured to do this, not least his aim to promote the study of the languages of the Caucasus and his driving ambition to be recognised as a great scholar. Before Marr's work reached its final, extravagant proportions, however, he made some of the first studies of the language and culture of the Caucasus region. Marr had established himself as a formidable presence in philology with his monumental three-volume critical edition of the Armenian *Parables of Vardan* (1899), for which the Russian Geographic Society awarded him a gold medal.[13] Here Marr illustrated many parallels between Armenian and Arabic and Syrian literary monuments, which led him to hypothesise genetic relations between Caucasian and Semitic cultures. Rather than remaining within this very productive area of philology, Marr then tried to integrate his insights into a wider theory that the languages of the Caucasus, beginning with Georgian, were related to Semitic languages.[14] While able to provide descriptive grammars of previously unstudied Caucasian languages, Marr's more global propositions were based on intuitive insights rather than systematic linguistic analysis. Rozen and his colleagues were already concerned about Marr's linguistic hypotheses at the turn of the century, and the former had long tried to dissuade the latter from publishing his claims. In this connection, Ol'denburg wrote to Rozen from Paris in 1894 that he was personally pleased (though sorry for Marr) that, on meeting Antoine

---

11   Ilizarov 2012, p. 151.

12   Quoted in Lartsev 1988, p. 85.

13   Marr 1899.

14   Marr's sharpest and most perceptive critic, Polivanov, was quite prepared to acknowledge Marr's 'great achievement' in the area of the languages of the South Caucasus region. See Polivanov 1991 [1929], p. 511.

Meillet, he had told him that he unconditionally rejected Marr's linguistic theories, saying that they were ' "striking fantasies in which there is no linguistics"
but, on the other hand, he was very sympathetic in reviewing his philological
knowledge'. Ol'denburg suggested Rozen should tell Marr about this because
'perhaps he will listen more to the judgement of a very clever linguist than to
us philologists'.[15] Marr's response was evidently one of outrage that a specialist in Indo-European linguistics presumed to pronounce on such matters, and
it appears he regarded the dispute over whether Armenian was, as most linguists thought, fundamentally an Indo-European language or, as he thought,
one related to Georgian, as an attempt by European scholarship to colonise the
Caucasus. While this appears rather paranoiac, it should be remembered that
during the nineteenth century, German Orientalists like Bernhard Dorn and
Julius Klaproth had linked Indo-European language forms to certain physical
attributes and had posited the Caucasus as the probable original homeland
[*Urheimat*] of the Indo-European peoples. Klaproth had even marshalled linguistic and facial evidence to suggest that Ossetian was a lost branch of the
Indo-Germanic family and the Ossetes an ancient 'Medo-German' colony.[16]
Unable conclusively to prove his case, Marr studied the various dialects of
Armenian and concluded that standard Armenian was a result of the crossing
of the languages of the indigenous 'Japhetic' peoples with those of princely
[*kniazheskii*] Indo-European invaders. The living dialects of the simple people
[*prostonarody*] of Armenia thus had more in common with those of simple
people in Georgia than with the language of the aristocratic Armenians.[17]

Here was the beginning of Marr's much ridiculed idea about the class-nature
[*klassovost'*] of languages, according to which different classes speak different languages. However, it also had another effect: it questioned the generally
assumed identification of a single people with a single language, which can be
traced back to the French Enlightenment philosopher Etienne de Condillac,
but finds its definitive statement in the work of Herder, von Humboldt and the
German Romantics.[18] While Indo-European linguists like Meillet were to begin
to undermine this idea at the end of the nineteenth century, it was indeed
exported through colonialism, and Marr was particularly concerned that the

---

15   Cited in Mikhankova, p. 31, n. 2.

16   For an overview, see Benes 2004 and Benes 2008, pp. 88–95. It should be noted that such
      scholars were actually sought and employed by the tsarist state.

17   Marr 1933 [1910], p. 39, n. 3. For a cogent overview and balanced evaluation of Marr's ideas
      about Armenian, see Thomas 1957, pp. 18–34.

18   Woolard 1998, pp. 16–17.

same conception should not be adopted by scholars in the Caucasus.[19] He thus entered into a series of conflicts with Georgian scholars on this very issue.[20] Marr was thus one of the first to recognise the importance of ideological factors in defining linguistic boundaries and, as such, delineated an area of concern that has only recently become a live issue under the name of 'linguistic ideology'.[21] Moreover, this led him to an even more controversial observation, namely that the same ideological factors that determine linguistic boundaries often do the same for disciplinary boundaries.[22] These were important and progressive insights which, had they been developed judiciously, could have led to some extremely valuable advances. Unfortunately, however, Marr was more inclined to develop his insights extravagantly, with little regard for methodological rigour, and the more he was indulged, the more global his hypotheses became. The fact that Marr had few competitors with a detailed knowledge of Caucasian languages inclined many otherwise sober and careful thinkers to take his assertions at face value and to be dazzled by the bold implications that Marr was to draw.

Marr's *bête noir* was Indo-European linguistics *in toto*, which he approached in a way that clearly anticipated Edward Said's approach to the work of Western Orientalists.[23] For Said, Orientalism is a trend which naturalised Eurocentrism, rendered European culture 'hegemonic both in and outside Europe', and in so doing served to legitimise and authorise imperialism.[24] Moreover, Said argued it was 'the extraordinarily rich and celebrated cultural position' of philology that 'endowed orientalism with its most important technical characteristics'.[25] There was, it seems, a genetic link between Said's *Orientalism* and the work of the Russian and Soviet Orientalists. As Vera Tolz has shown, this was due to Said's debt to the Egyptian Marxist Anouar Abdel-Malek's 1963 article 'Orientalism in Crisis', which was, in turn, indebted to the Soviet Orientalists.[26]

---

19   For a fascinating discussion of the relationship between Indian and European studies of Sanskrit, see Krishnaswamy 2005.

20   See, especially, Cherchi and Manning 2002. The reception of Marr's ideas in Georgia was, however, by no means uniform. Different scholars responded in various ways to various aspects of his work. For a valuable discussion see Tuite 2011.

21   For an overview see Woolard and Schieffelin 1994.

22   Gal and Irvne 1995.

23   The terms 'Indo-European', 'Indo-Germanic' and 'Indo-Aryan' were all in common circulation throughout the nineteenth century, according to the developing national traditions of scholarship. On the history of the terms, see, *inter alia*, Norman 1929 and Shapiro 1981.

24   Said 1995 [1978], p. 7.

25   Said 1995 [1978], p. 131.

26   Tolz 2006, pp. 132–3. The article in question is Abdel-Malek 1963.

The link between Indo-Europeanism and imperial ideology was systematically pursued in Maurice Olender's now famous study, *Languages of Paradise*,
in 1989.[27] Here the complex relationship between European colonialism,
Christianity, anti-Semitism and linguistic scholarship was uncovered once
more, this time achieving scholarly respectability. Olender catalogues how,
in nineteenth-century philology, belonging to an Indo-European culture was
often viewed as synonymous with belonging to a chosen people, destined to
dominate the world, while all other languages and cultures were rendered
peripheral at best. As Revathi Krishnaswamy puts it, 'through the systematic
contrast between the Indo-European and other language families, comparative philology constructed a grand supranational tribal prehistory that posi-
tioned white Christian Europe at the center of contemporary world history'.[28]
It was precisely this feature that aroused Marr's hostility to Western linguistics.

A whole series of Indo-European philologists, from Herder and Friedrich
von Schlegel, through Adolphe Pictet, Ernest Renan to Rudolph Grau, sought
to combine race psychology, mythology and comparative philology to advance
the cause of Eurocentrism and Christian superiority. By the 1870s and 1880s,
philological evidence was routinely adduced to promote racist arguments. The
original Aryans were increasingly described as blonde-haired and blue-eyed
and the putative original Indo-European homeland shifted towards Europe,
being variously posited as Germany, south-western Russia, Scandanavia and
even the North Pole.[29] Increasingly tenuous connections were often supported
by strained etymological hypotheses of a sort that were no less eccentric than
Marr's later speculations.[30] Even those philologists who opposed direct correla-
tions of language and race tended to assume that the original Indo-Europeans
had a special place in history and that this underlay their imperial mission.
Max Müller was exemplary in this regard:

> The Aryan nations ... have been the prominent actors in the great drama
> of history, and have carried to their fullest growth all the elements of
> active life with which our nature is endowed. They have perfected society
> and morals; and we learn from their literature and works of art the ele-
> ments of science, the laws of art, and the principles of philosophy. In con-
> tinual struggle with each other and with Semitic and Turanian races,
> these Aryan nations have become the rulers of history, and it seems to be

---

27   Olender 1992 [1989]. See also Arvidsson 1999 and Bernal 1987.
28   Krishnaswamy 1985, p. 67.
29   McGetchin 2009, pp. 141–66.
30   McGetchin 2009, pp. 154–5.

their mission to link all parts of the world together by the chains of civilisation, commerce and religion.[31]

Müller further argued that comparative philology proved the kinship of the English armies then subduing hostile Indian groups and the 'Brahmical people... of Arian origin' who had conquered India in antiquity. The British had returned to their 'primordial soil, to accomplish the glorious work of civilization, which had been left unfinished by their Arian brethren'.[32]

In his early work, Marr joined those, mainly Jewish, researchers who sought to undermine the caricatures of race psychology by turning to an alternative form of nascent social psychology: the *Völkerpsychologie* that had been developed by Steinthal and Lazarus. These thinkers had precisely aimed to counter the anti-Semitism implicit and often explicit in Indo-Aryan studies by showing that, however different the culture of diverse peoples may appear, the same laws govern the 'life of the soul' of all.[33] This fitted well with the argument of British positivist thinkers, such as Spencer, that the laws of thought are everywhere the same. In common with a whole generation of Russian Oriental scholars and philologists of the time, Marr absorbed the principles of *Völkerpsychologie* and mined the trend for its potential to undermine colonial ideology.[34] Marr first attempted to subvert Indo-Europeanism by proposing an alternative centre to Sanskrit, from which he would consider the relations between languages. Emboldened by Carl Meinhof's then widely supported studies of 'Hamitic' African languages, which he connected to the languages of the Caucasus, and Wilhelm Schmidt's studies of the languages of Oceana and Australia, which he posited as an 'Austric' group of languages, Marr held the Georgian language to belong to a distinct family related to Semitic languages, which he labelled Japhetic.[35] He also raised the anomalous positions of Basque and Etruscan, languages spoken at the heart of Europe, but allegedly having more features in common with Caucasian than Indo-European languages, in order to disrupt

---

31   Müller, quoted in Voigt 1967, p. 6.

32   Müller, quoted in Benes 2008, p. 214.

33   See, for instance, Kalmar 1987 and Bunzl 2003. On the use of these ideas by Jewish philologists, see Olender 1992 [1989], pp. 116–24.

34   On Marr's debt to *Völkerpsychologie*, see Brandist 2005. On the *völkerpsychologische* prelude to Soviet sociological linguistics in general, see Brandist 2006. On the anti-colonial agenda of pre-revolutionary Russian Orientalists, including Marr, see Tolz 2005 and Tolz 2006.

35   These influences were specifically cited by Marr 1936a [1927], p. 3. Meinhof did, however, continue the tendency to adduce philological and facial evidence in his speculations, which Marr specifically opposed.

the coherence of the Indo-European narrative.[36] In accordance with the principles of *Völkerpsychologie*, he then proceeded to argue that Indo-European linguists were unable to understand Japhetic languages, since Japhetic has its own laws, psychology and mode of evolution that is at odds with European languages.[37] Marr here also drew upon the work of Franz Boas, who had argued that Eurocentric preconceptions had blinded linguists to important aspects of native-American languages.[38] As long as Indo-European linguists remained wedded to race psychology, Marr contended, they would be unable to understand Japhetic languages, since, in order to recognise the universal 'laws of the soul', they would need to abandon their ideological framework.

When Marr invoked the name of Japeth, Noah's favourite son, to designate Caucasian languages, he plugged into a history of linguistic speculation that underlay Indo-European linguistics. The idea that Japeth had preserved the original, prelapsarian language in its purity and had laid the foundations of European languages, independent of Semitic influence, was well ingrained by the beginning of the nineteenth century.[39] Marr thus aimed to undermine the very foundations of Indo-European linguistics by providing an alternative narrative of the relations between European and Semitic that was no more speculative or ideological than the narrative that lay behind that of the Indo-European philologists discussed above. By 1908 Marr was arguing that Japhetic and Indo-European languages had separate origins, which sometimes 'crossed' to form such languages as Armenian, where the Japhetic and Indo-European elements corresponded to the languages of the oppressed and oppressor peoples respectively.[40] This attempt to specify the role played by the 'Japhetites' in history led, in 1921, to the assertion that they were the most ancient inhabitants of the Mediterranean and Middle East and that to them belong the main cultural achievements of the ancient world:

---

36   The hypothesis of links between Basque and Caucasian languages predates the work of Marr and still attracts adherents. Symptomatic of this was the publication of Marr 1987.

37   As Steinthal had argued, national languages 'depicted objects "entirely and exclusively based on their own laws ... which arise from the nature of their own goals and means, and are not dictated by the objects being represented"'. Quoted in Benes 2008, p. 257.

38   Marr 1936a [1927], p. 3 noted the influence of Boas quite explicitly. He probably had in mind Boas 1974 [1889]. See also Jakobson 1944.

39   See Olender 1994.

40   Marr here may have followed Meinhof's 1899 discussion of Bantu as a 'mixed language [*Mischsprache*], so to speak, descended of a Hamitic father and Negro mother', in Meinhof 1932 [1899, 1910], p. 164.

it has already been established that it was the Japhetic family, the Japhetic literary milieu [*pis'mennaia sreda*] that created and developed the first foundations of modern civilisation, that it was mixing with the Japhetites that passed on cultural nobility to the Indo-European race, that it was crossing with them that produced the Greeks and Romans, the early appearance of civil society [*grazhdanstvennost'*] on the world arena, which was historically known in later times to the Romance and Germanic peoples.[41]

What distinguished Marr's work from that of the Indo-European philologists and linguists discussed above was, therefore, not the entwinement of linguistics and ideology, but the low level of technical competence (and, in some cases, indifference) with which Marr went about validating his linguistic claims. On meeting with the Germanist F.A. Braun in Leipzig at the end of 1920 (Marr had known Braun since the days of their mutual involvement in the Neo-Philological Society), Marr noted that rarely in his life had he spent time with such a refined Indo-European linguist, and he marvelled at the care with which Braun explained to his audience the need to consider the dual nature of the origins of the German people.[42] While Marr was certainly a more than competent philologist when providing general descriptions of certain languages of the Caucasus, his grounding in general linguistic theory was questionable to say the least. Yet this did not restrain him from making increasingly extravagant generalisations. Thus, Marr's Japhetic family became ever more extended, sometimes without the newly annexed languages having been subject to any systematic study.[43] During World War I the family moved beyond the Caucasus, and Basque and Etruscan were added in 1920, with *ad hoc* methodological adjustments being made along the way.

Marr's Sources

Marr's foundational ideas did not differ to any great extent from the other pre-revolutionary Orientalists associated with the Rozen School and the ideas of Veselovskii. In each case, there was a combination of positivist ideas of social and cultural evolution and *völkerpsychologische* ideas about collective

---

41   Marr 1933c [1923], p. 177. See also Vasil'kov 2001, pp. 399–401.

42   PFA RAN 909/5/46/9.

43   Thomas 1957, pp. 35–60 provides an excellent and detailed account of the extension of the Japhetic family.

psychology. The only real difference was the increasingly arbitrary way in which these were applied to specific instances and the unrestrained generalisations that he drew. Marr absorbed many important ideas through his close relationship with Veselovskii during his association with the Neo-Philological Society, of which Marr was a member from 1907, but the meetings of which he may have attended earlier.[44] One participant outlined the approach of the society as follows:

> Neo-philology is that science that, for the resolution of questions about the processes and laws of the spiritual development of man, addresses itself to the observation of the immediate, real phenomena of life and, on the basis of these, reaches conclusions about suggested analogous phenomena in the past; on the basis of the study of contemporary dialects [*govor*] and newly formed words it works on questions about the birth [*zarozhdenii*] and development of languages; on the basis of the observation of general [*obshche*] psychological processes, of associations and differentiations of representation, it establishes the laws of poetic creation. Various branches of culture enter into its orbit, for it is one unified by the commonality of the main object of study, that is, man in the different forms of his spiritual activity. Neo-philology studies monuments of the past, but does not isolate this past from the present; it deals with what is ancient but, in contradistinction to archaeology, primarily with 'living antiquity'.[45]

Such global concerns, and Veselovskii's universalistic approach to the comparison of widely dispersed literary and pre-literary material, undoubtedly emboldened Marr's own inclinations in the same direction. In the commentaries to a volume of Veselovskii's work on folklore published in 1938, Boris Kazanskii argued that while the idea of a proto-language still persisted in bourgeois linguistics, such a conception had been destroyed in the fields of myth and folklore studies by the positivist scholars of the 1860s and 1870s.

---

44   Anon. 1914, p. 82. The most sustained discussion of the issue is Shishmarev 1937, pp. 325–6. In the most extensive biography of Marr, written in the wake of the reaction against Veselovskii during the anti-cosmopolitanism campaign and on the eve of Stalin's denunciation of Marr, the influence of Veselovskii on Marr is considerably understated. See Mikhankova 1949, pp. 66–8.

45   ARAN SPb 208/4/3a/30b. The document is entitled 'Po povodu pervogo desiatletiia Neofilologicheskogo Obshchestva (byvshego Otdeleniia po romano-germanskoi filologii) pri S. Peterburgskom universitete' by F.D. Batiushkov (1897).

Revealing the inadequacies of the linguistic conception was held to be Marr's achievement.[46]

The situation was really much more complex, however. While, as we have seen in the case of Veselovskii, comparative mythology suffered a heavy defeat at the hands of Lang and his followers, it is clear that important weaknesses in the armour of the anthropological school were revealed. Müller had forced Lang to retreat on several important issues by acquainting himself with the ethnological material on which Lang depended for his critique, but at the same time pointed out that the anthropologists, and Lang himself, had failed to turn their attention to the languages of the peoples they studied.[47] It is also interesting to note that the line of defence of one of the mythologists, Robert Brown, was to argue that 'Semitic Asia had contributed at least as many divinities to the Greek pantheon as had Aryan India!'[48] Thus, where Müller could lambast his critics for their lack of attention to Sanskrit, Brown could defend comparativism by insisting on the centrality of Semitic languages as a source of European culture. This is precisely where Marr began, and it is clear that Brown was not the only comparativist to insist on the importance of Semitic languages. Marr was clearly familiar with Renan's *Histoire générale et système comparé des languages sémitiques* [*General History of Semitic Languages* (1855, 1858, 1863)], which he adduces in an article of 1924, and Marr certainly shared some of Renan's aims as described by Said: 'to bring the Semitic languages into sharp and glamorous focus *à la* Bopp, and in addition to elevate the study of these neglected inferior languages to the level of a passionate new science of mind *à la* [Balzac's] Louis Lambert'.[49] Renan's orientation was, however, quite the opposite to that of Marr. For Renan, Semitic languages lacked the syntactical features necessary for reason and science, proving 'absolutely incapable of giving birth to mythology'.[50] Philosophy and mythology thus had their roots in India and Greece. By associating Caucasian with Semitic languages, Marr shared Renan's aim to 'elevate' their study, and he certainly hoped to establish a 'passionate science of the mind', but the alleged inferiority of these languages was something Marr was determined to challenge. Marr therefore needed to

---

46   Kazanskii 1938, p. 263.

47   Dorson 1955, pp. 401–5.

48   Brown 1877–8, vol. 1, pp. vi, 11, 334; quoted in Dorson 1955, p. 408.

49   Said 1995 [1978], p.139. Marr cites Renan's study in Marr 1935 [1924], p. 144. Renan's twelve-volume collected works were published in Russian translation in Renan 1902–4. Marr's colleague, Izrail' Frank-Kamenetskii, engaged systematically with Renan's work in Frank-Kamenetskii 1925.

50   Benes 2008, pp. 226–7.

develop his own etymological procedures if he was to dethrone Indo-European linguistics, and this he did by degrees.

Where thinkers like Müller were profoundly anti-evolutionary and some were wedded to race psychology (of which Müller was not guilty), Marr followed Spencer and Tylor in adapting their ideas to an evolutionary agenda. Tylor used Müller's work to develop his own evolutionary perspective, arguing that it has 'the merit of having taken up the problem [of language and mythology – CB] on the principle applied with such success to geology by Sir Charles Lyell, that of working back from the processes whose action we can trace in modern times and under similar conditions, and arguing that, where we find like effects in late and early periods of history, it is probable that the causes we know to produce them in the one case were also at work producing them in the other'.[51] While Tylor thought comparative theology could coexist with his own comparative method, his followers, led by Lang, sought to use evolutionism to undermine the claims that an original body of myths had been disseminated through Indo-European cultures from the original Indo-European homeland, degenerating in the process. For Lang, comparing the myths and folklore of widely dispersed peoples showed such abundant parallels that one can conclude that similar cultural formations derive from similar conditions of life, and that the stadial development of human culture is as open to paleontological analysis as material culture. One would not be surprised to find similarly shaped arrow heads in archaeological excavations on each side of the globe, so why should one not find similar mythical figures and plot lines? We have seen how Veselovskii accepted this argument, as did Marr.

Marr clearly over-generalised wildly about Indo-European philology.[52] Some of the very features that Marr developed in his own work on language in order to combat the claims of Indo-Europeanism can actually be found in the works of these very scholars, though made to serve different ends. Pictet, for instance, embarked 'on a journey of "linguistic paleontology", tracking the destiny of words. His mission: to revive Indo-European memories in a Christian Europe that is in search of an even brighter future'.[53] Müller also employed the technique to reveal the 'mythopoetic age', when truly noble conceptions of

---

51   Quoted in Stocking 1987, p. 61.

52   Said also over-generalised rather extravagantly in his characterisation of Orientalism, though not to the near-pathological level of Marr. See for instance Ahmad 1992, pp. 159–242; Habib 2005.

53   Olender 1992, p. 95. Said (1995 [1978], p. 142) argues that the writings of founder of vertebrate paleontology, Georges Cuvier, provided a model for many linguists of the period, including Renan. See also Joseph 2012, pp. 147–52.

the Aryan gods first arose, as well as the gradual degeneration of these conceptions through the 'disease of language'. This took two forms, *polyonymy*, where
one word carried plural conceptions, and *homonymy*, where one idea became
attached to different words. Marr's own 'semantic palaeontology' was certainly
not as radical a break with the Indo-European doctrine as he and his followers generally liked to claim, even if the way Marr developed the method sub-
verted the aims of Pictet and Müller.[54] Here Marr was following Spencer, who
inverted Müller's idea to argue that 'verbal signs being at first so inadequate
that gesture-signs are needful to eke them out, the distinction between metaphor and fact cannot be expressed, much less preserved in tradition'.[55] Mental
evolution and linguistic evolution thus develop from an 'extreme vagueness'
and 'indefiniteness' to the precision and definiteness of modern speech.[56] In
Marr's formulation, Müller's processes of *polyonymy* and *homonymy* were
replaced with the emergence of *polysemy* from primordial 'diffuse' or amor-
phous sounds. It was not without reason that Marr noted that Spencer exerted
a strong influence on his thinking from an early age.[57] What Marr added to
Spencer's reformulation of Müller was the idea, taken from Geiger and Noiré,
and subsequently adopted by Bogdanov, that language first develops through
the transfer of meanings from labour activity to the product of that activity, and
the transfer of names from one object to another according to their function.

  Marr was thus trying to weld together British positivism, German monism
and neo-Kantianism, with convenient aspects of Marxist work that he had
picked up along the way. To this he even recruited selected ideas from his
adversaries – particularly what Marr's followers were to call 'dissident Indo-
Europeanism'. This referred to figures who were sceptical of the possibility of
reconstructing proto-languages, posited links between language and material
culture and talked about the mixing of languages. Among those who had been
critical of the neo-grammarians were Schuchardt, Meillet and Ascoli (whose
influence he acknowledged), as well as Baudouin (whose influence he never
acknowledged). It is very tempting to see a first attempt to create a post-
colonial 'adversary epistemological current' here.

---

54   See also Tchougounnikov 2005, pp. 295–310.
55   Spencer 1882, p. 362. Spencer specifically criticises Müller and other mythologists for
      'tracing the genesis of beliefs from above downwards, instead of tracing it from below
      upwards' in an appendix to the same volume (Spencer 1882, pp. 815–24, 816).
56   Spencer 1882, pp. 362, 85.
57   Marr 1935, p. 127.

The Break with Comparative Linguistics

Braun was based in Leipzig from 1920, where for three years he acted as a propagandist for Japhetic theory in Western Europe.[58] His interest in considering ethnological and linguistic issues together had been fostered by his time in the Neo-Philological Society, and he had independently reached the conclusion that a significant portion of German words derived from earlier inhabitants of Europe that preceded the arrival of Indo-Europeans. When he encountered Marr's then new ideas about Japhetic inhabitants and the crossing of languages, Braun was immediately struck by the convergence and began to introduce Japhetic terms into his work. Braun and Marr worked out a plan to 'acquaint the West European world of scholars with Japhetic theory by means of a series of publications *Japhetitische Studien für Sprache und Kultur Eurasiens*'.[59] The alliance could not last long, however. While Braun counselled diplomacy in relations with Indo-European linguists, Marr became increasingly belligerent in his relations with anyone who doubted his assertions and demanded firm evidence that Japhetites were the original inhabitants of Europe. In support of his policy of a constructive dialogue with Indo-Europeanists, Braun reported that some linguists, like Eduard Sievers (then Chair in Germanic and Romance philology at Lepizig), 'admitted the possibility' of the presence of Japhetic elements in Indo-European languages, but that 'he regarded it to be unproven'.[60] Braun suggested to Marr that the main reason Western specialists were unconvinced by Japhetic theory was the absence of a general work on the theory, and he particularly recommended a 'comparative grammar of Japhetic languages', the absence of which Meillet had repeatedly raised.[61]

Other linguists were, however, more hostile, even when they were on thin ice themselves. As Braun reported:

> With significant persistence the fool Meyer announced that he would believe [Japhetic theory] only when there lay before him a completed

---

58 Particularly interesting in this regard is the unpublished correspondence between Marr and Braun in these years. An account is given in Mikhankova 1949, pp. 314–31. A more extended, but unpublished, account is held in the archive of I.A. Orbeli: PFA RAN 909/5/46. See also Tukhina 2000.

59 PFA RAN 909/5/46/9. The first volume was Braun 1922. An abridged Russian version was also published in Berlin and appeared as Braun 1924. The second was to be a German translation of Marr 1933b [1920].

60 PFARAN 909/5/46/21.

61 PFARAN 909/5/46/24–5.

dictionary of Japhetic languages. I replied that I was afraid he would have to wait a rather long time for that, and that I was surprised that he could work on Indo-European linguistics not having a completed comparative dictionary of Indo-European languages in front of him.[62]

Marr responded with considerable indignation that a textbook, especially written in a foreign language, should be required of someone holding a doctorate in the corresponding languages, a member of the Academy of Sciences and a professor of the Faculty of Oriental Studies in order to be considered competent to pronounce on such matters.[63] It was certainly not beyond the realms of possibility that hostility among conservative German scholars towards the USSR, and the political trend it represented in contemporary Germany, contributed to the hostile reception of Marr's ideas. More concerning, however, were repeated objections by German philologists to the term 'Japhetic family' on the grounds that such a term pertains only to 'old Jewish tradition' rather than 'having Europe in view'. Such a conception was allegedly limited to 'a Semitic cultural horizon'. Not unreasonably, Braun concluded: 'there is undoubtedly a certain anti-Semitism there'.[64] By the end of 1922, Braun was increasingly pessimistic about the prospects for Japhetic theory in the absence of support among Western scholars:

> 'Marr's theory', as they call it, must be transformed into 'Japhetic theory' or it will be exhausted as soon as you leave the stage. It will remain merely an 'episode' in the history of science. An interesting episode for sure, one that raised many questions, but did not provide a final answer to any of the questions it raised in the eyes of its readers.[65]

Marr was content to let the theory develop free from those who may want to 'smother or translate it'.[66] The break was now complete, but when the theory did so develop, Marr's ideas were still to face sustained opposition at home.

A combination of Marr's intellectual hubris, volatile character and the hostile reception of his work by Western scholars, some of whom in many ways

---

62   Mikhankova 1949, p. 324, n. 2; PF ARAN 909/5/46/23. It is not entirely clear who was being referred to here, but it was probably K.H. Meyer, author of *Slavische und indogermanische Intonation* (Meyer 1920).

63   Mikhankova 1949, pp. 327–8; PFARAN 909/5/46/26–8.

64   Mikhankova 1949, pp. 322–3; PFARAN 909/5/46/20.

65   PFA RAN 909/5/46/36.

66   Ibid.

confirmed Marr's own preconceptions about them, made any meaningful dialogue between the two trends impossible. In 1923 Marr publicly announced his complete break with Indo-European linguistics by proclaiming that 1) Indo-European languages mark a stage in linguistic development and not a special racial family of languages;[67] and that 2) Indo-Europeanism is 'flesh and bone' the product of 'expiring bourgeois sociality' that had been 'built on the oppression of the peoples of the East by the murderous colonial policies of European nations'.[68]

The 'New Theory'

It was now that Marr fully adopted the comparative, evolutionary method of Tylor, Lang and others, counterposing this to the established methods of comparative linguistics and mythology. Semantic material was pronounced to be immortal and the doctrine of survivals was adopted to claim that traces of earlier stages could be found in the strata of modern languages. This was now named 'paleontological analysis' and the Japhetic family began to annex Indo-European languages more aggressively and with little or no evidence adduced. Finally, paleontological analysis led Marr to conclude that the very notion of families of languages had to be abandoned, along with the thesis of the proto-language, since in actuality languages were evolving from diverse origins toward unity. Japhetic theory had now become the 'new theory of language'. Marr's opponents were dismayed and some looked for the origins of these ideas in unconventional places, finding parallels that suggest certain of his ideas were actually widespread. *Iazykfront* leaders, G.K. Danilov and Timofei P. Lomtev, found features of Marr's paleontological method anticipated in the work of the eccentric Ukrainian linguist-ethnographer Platon Lukashevich, though they never suggested direct borrowing.[69] Danilov did suggest, however, that when Marr inverted the Indo-Europeanist narrative, according to which a variety of languages developed from a single proto-language, to argue that all languages were developing from variety to unity, he was echoing the work of Renan.[70] While Danilov presents no textual evidence, Renan did argue that the

---

67 Marr 1933d [1924].
68 Marr 1934a [1924], p. 1.
69 Danilov 1931, pp. 9–12; GARF A-4655/2/586/71–88. The suggestion was rebutted in the review of Danilov's short book in the journal of Marr's institute (see Zborovskii 1932). A selection of the work of Lukashevich has recently been published (Lukashevich 2008).
70 Danilov 1931, p. 23.

distinctiveness of races, understood as 'a group of people who spoke a common language or related dialects', gradually fades and will ultimately disappear: 'the future will see a homogeneous humanity in which all the native rivulets will coalesce into a great stream, and all memory of diverse origins will be lost'.[71]

However, the conception has more probable roots in the idea that all societies were evolving through a process of ever-greater convergence that we saw was a core concern of the Rozen school of Orientology, to which Marr had belonged and which, as we have already seen, was operative in the work of Bartol'd. It was also convenient for Marr that the conception was shared by Kautsky, as detailed in his then well-known 1908 article, 'Nationality and Internationality':

> In the origins of humanity, we . . . have to accept that there isn't a single language, but rather numerous original languages. We should therefore presume that at the beginning of humanity there was not a single *Ursprache*, but rather numerous original languages.[72]
>
> In a similar way we may also presume that, in terms of language, the same linguistic forms were created under the same conditions, and that under similar conditions, similar linguistic forms were created. That is to say that the languages that sprang into existence completely independently of each other amongst different hordes, but under equal conditions in the same area, exhibit a certain similarity or a relationship to each other. . . . On the other hand it can also happen that peoples with different languages come into permanent contact with each other and that, in so doing, take over so much of the other language that their languages become, if not the same, then similar or you could say, related.[73]
>
> Languages do not generally develop from unity to plurality, but actually the other way around.[74]

With the establishment of the 'new theory', rigour and restraint was abandoned, with bizarre and even crackpot formulations beginning to emerge. The obvious example of such extremities is the notorious 'four-element' theory, according to which all words in all languages were held to have derived from

---

71   Quoted in Bierer 1953, p. 378.
72   Kautsky 2009 [1908], p. 381.
73   Kautsky 2009 [1908], pp. 381–2.
74   Kautsky 2009 [1908], p. 382.

four primordial 'diffuse exclamations' – *sal, ber, yon* and *rosh*.[75] The linguistic paleontologist could 'excavate' all linguistic phenomena until these totemic elements were revealed, and in the 1930s and 1940s a whole generation of linguists were trained to do precisely this. A passing remark by Gramsci about positivist scholarship is appropriate in this case: 'To reconstruct a megatherium or a mastodon from a tiny bone was Cuvier's special gift, but it may also happen that from a piece of a mouse's tail one might reconstruct a sea-serpent'.[76] Marr certainly remained a talented, intuitive thinker. Ilizarov is certainly justified to argue that '[h]is historical-linguistic associations would have been the envy of any philosopher, poet and myth-maker'.[77] One might particularly raise Marr's prize-winning 1899 work on the *Parables of Vardan*, in which connections between Caucasian and Semitic folktales were discussed as an example of this. Not unreasonably, Alpatov suggests that Marr may have even been a genius (as many of his contemporaries thought), noting that he had an extraordinary capacity for organisational work and made some 'remarkable conjectures'.[78] But Marr was so confident in his methodological principles that he rarely restrained himself from placing each item in its proper place according to a preconceived totality and thereby tended to 'reconstruct' sea serpents.

Positivism and Marxism

The worst aspects of Marr's positivist way of thinking, which had been relatively restrained in his early work on linguistics, now came to the fore in Marr's work.[79] Emile Durkheim's characterisation of Spencer as (like Auguste Comte) 'a philosopher, whose sole concern was to verify "the grand hypothesis he has conceived and which must explain everything", namely the law of evolution', seems doubly appropriate for describing Marr.[80] Indeed, there is a strong case

---

75 Marr never provided anything approaching a systematic account of this theory. This was left to Marr's most prominent student, Meshchaninov (Meshchaninov 1934, pp. 7–31).

76 Gramsci 1994, vol. 1, p. 302.

77 Ilizarov 2012, p. 44.

78 Alpatov 2004, p. 262.

79 Spencer may safely be regarded as an early positivist for the purposes of the current argument, despite his disagreements with Comte, as detailed in Spencer 1864. Both thinkers shared an evolutionary view of social progress through various stages, with natural science providing the solution to man's problems and sociology emerging as the supreme science of sciences.

80 Quoted in Lukes 1973, p. 83. Marr's voluminous and unreflective writing also resembled that of Spencer, while his single-minded determination and prodigious capacity for work

for arguing that it is Spencer's combination of von Bauer's epigenesis and Lamarckism that underlies Marr's historical narrative.[81] The former defined the course of change from homogeneity and generality to the heterogenous and special, the main exemplification of which we find in Marr's insistence that all words and linguistic systems evolved from the combination of four diffuse sounds. The latter can specifically be seen in Marr's contention that 1) certain areas of a language strengthen due to high levels of use, while others fall into disuse and 2) functionally produced semantic modifications are preserved and reproduced in a language. Linguistic change is thus to be explained primarily through the inheritance of environmentally induced modifications, just as for Spencer 'the inheritance of functionally-produced modifications is the chief factor throughout the higher stages of organic evolution, bodily as well as mental'.[82] Adam Kuper argues that the Lamarckian paradigm also led anthropologists to regard change from one stage of development to another to be punctuated by leaps and transmitted genetically.[83] This certainly applies to Marr, who not only characterised semantic change in precisely this way, but also, in common with Spencer and other thinkers of the time, made no distinction between organic and cultural evolution. Joseph Carrol notes that Spencer took an abstract formal process, 'complexification', and passed every field of knowledge through it. Marr did precisely the same for linguistics. We thus have 'an advance from a diffused, indeterminate and uniform distribution of matter, to a concentrated, determinate, and multiform distribution of it', that is, 'from a confused simplicity to an orderly complexity'.[84] A mechanistic formula thus takes the place of the complexities of history. Rather than beginning with study of each item that has been uncovered, each item serves only as a detail to confirm the accuracy of an established general picture. Thomas notes that Marr's early work on Caucasian languages was already marked by a tendency to 'make individual facts subservient to the main purpose' and 'to arrange facts in a "logical" order which does not correspond to reality, and even to create forms to fill the gaps in the "logical" (an aprioristic) order'.[85] All restraint was now left behind. The results were often outlandish, and the most technically

---

followed the recommendations of the other early influence on Marr, the Scottish moralist, Samuel Smiles (1812–1904). See Marr 1935, p. 127.

81   On Spencer's combination, see Haines 1988.

82   Spencer 1884, p. 446. See also Freeman 1974, where this quotation from Spencer is adduced and discussed (p. 216).

83   Kuper 1988, p. 3.

84   Carrol 2003, p. 34.

85   Thomas 1957, p. 11.

accomplished linguists of the time often recognised the inadequacies of Marr's formulations, but they achieved extraordinary currency among many thinkers of the time. This is something that needs to be explained.

As Gramsci noted about the 'crude positivism, opportunism, perverse think-ing and careless scholarship' of the Italian professor of economics Achille Loria, the presence of such figures is not necessarily of great importance, and is not unusual.[86]

> But the fact that he became a pillar of culture, a 'master', and that he 'spontaneously' found an enormous audience – this is what makes one reflect on the weakness of the bulwarks of criticism which existed even during periods of normality. One should think on how easy it is during abnormal times of uncontrolled passion for individuals like Loria, sup-ported by interested powers, to overwhelm every bulwark and to trans-form an environment of intellectual culture which is still weak and frail into a swamp for decades to come.[87]

Like Loria, Marr was not 'a teratological individual case', but rather 'the most complete and perfect exemplar of a series of representatives of a certain stra-tum of intellectuals from a certain period'.[88] Marr was certainly supported by 'interested powers', which gave his formulations added authority, but his ideas were more than simply the product of an indulged, active individual fan-tasy. Marr's ideas are inseparable from the intellectual climate in which they emerged, for he drew sustenance from the ideas around him and his ideas found a resonance precisely because they echoed contemporary concerns. During the 'abnormal times' of the first Five-Year Plan, Marrism achieved something approaching official status, but the grounds for this had been laid during the relatively 'normal' times of NEP period, when Marr was among the positivist ethnographers and Orientalists who had served the regime.

As in the case of Loria, Marr also came to be seen as developing Marxism, even though his real intellectual roots lay elsewhere. It is now quite clear that Marr's foundational ideas were in place before he began consciously to connect his ideas with Marxism, even though some discerned an 'elemental' or 'spon-taneous' Marxism earlier. In 1925 Marr wrote that 'Japhetic Linguistics . . . is not Marxism any more than it is a theory, and if it contains principles which

---

86   Buttigeig 1990, p. 61.
87   Quoted in Buttigeig 1990, p. 69. The passage derives from the first section of Gramsci's
      Prison Notebook, 28, the English translation of which has still not been published.
88   Gramsci 1991, p. 116.

confirm the Marxist doctrine, so much the better for it (that is, the doctrine), in my opinion, and so much the worse for its opponents'.[89] Boris Unbegaun reported Marr saying something similar in 1927, from which time he began to pepper his works with quotations from various Marxist sources, while ignoring the substance of Marx's and Engels's opinions about language.[90] Marr had associates who were versed in the forms of the emerging official ideology, however, and Marr included the theses of one such person, the historian Sergei Kovalev, in the publication arising from his famous lectures at Baku University in 1927. This work became central in the presentation of Marr's theory as 'Marxism in linguistics'. Among Kovalev's theses we find the following:

> 38. Marxism does not have its own special linguistic theory.
>
> 39. Engels only made general statements about the development of language from the labour process ('The Role Played by Labour in the Transition from Ape to Man').
>
> 40. Therefore L. Noiré's views about the origin of language from the collective labour of primitive man was accepted and popularised by a series of Marxists (Plekhanov, Bogdanov, Bukharin and others).
>
> 41. Being in the process of continual development, Japhetic theory is to a great extent more a method than a 'theory' in the proper sense of the word. . . .
>
> 65. Having the same methodological points of departure and a great proximity on a whole series of individual positions, it is inescapable that Marxism and Japhetic theory must unite. Japhetic theory needs to accept Marxism openly as its general philosophical and sociological basis; Marxism needs to accept Japhetic theory as its special linguistic section. The conjecture of the genius Noiré cannot play such a role in that it is only a hypothesis and that it operates on the material and methods of Indo-European linguistics. Marr has developed a series of Noiré's fundamental positions completely independently, and has developed them with full scientific persuasiveness and exhaustive breadth.[91]

Kovalev concludes by arguing that the unification of Marxism and Japhetic theory, in that it is opposed to 'great-power', Indo-European linguistics, is a

---

89   Quoted in Matthews 1950, p. 17.

90   Alpatov 2004, p. 68.

91   Kovalev 1936 [1927], pp. 114, 118. After Marr's death, Konstantin Megrelidze, one of his most talented students, attempted to further provide a Marxist foundation for Marr's theory in Megrelidze 1935.

'powerful weapon in the cultural liberation' of the peoples who imperialism had left with no written language. Marr subsequently seized on Stalin's comments at the Sixteenth Party Congress that in the future, after the international victory of socialism, national languages would merge, as echoing his own formulations. The identical formulations were not due to borrowing, claimed Marr, but because 'by means of one and the same Marxist method', the 'politician-revolutionary' and the 'Japhetologist-linguist' reached the same 'scientific-organisational' conclusion about organising the 'linguistic material of the whole world'.[92] A.O. Tamazishbili argues that, in this way, Marr 'acted soberly, calculatedly and purposefully, having fully utilised the favourable conditions for the achievement of his strategic goal – the recognition of his theory of language as the only genuinely Marxist theory, and therefore the only true theory'. Moreover, Marr could argue that Japhetic theory had become 'a political party directive at least for linguistics'.[93]

In his serious study of Marr's ideas, Thomas indicates certain Marxist-like formulations in Marr's writings from 1923 onwards, when the 'new theory' was proclaimed, specifically his adoption of the dialectical method and his contention that 'semantics, like morphology derives from ... economically formed social conditions'.[94] However, as Thomas himself hints, this actually proves little except that Marr was writing in the USSR at the time and adapting the terms of his argument to the dominant paradigm. A certain dialectical method was present in *Völkerpsychologie*, which Marr readily assimilated, and the way in which Marr used the dialectic to discuss successive semantic bifurcations is more akin to a vulgarised Hegelian formulation than anything specifically Marxist.[95] Similarly, the championing of economic determinations in morphology and syntax has no roots in classical Marxism, while the recognition of social and economic determinants in social consciousness is, again, not specifically Marxist. Rather, we have the assimilation of certain Marxist categories into a pre-established, positivist scheme that increasingly resonated with the development of Soviet Marxism itself. As Iurii Sokolov noted in a 1938 survey of the development of folklorics:

---

92 Quoted in Tamazishbili 2000, pp. 93–4. This passage from Marr's 1931 pamphlet *Iazykovaia politika iafeticheskoi teorii i udmurtskii iazyk*, which was published immediately following Stalin's speech, was not included in the version published as Marr 1935c [1931].

93 Tamazishbili 2000, p. 94.

94 Thomas 1957, p. 92; Marr 1933d [1924], pp. 31–2.

95 See especially Marr 1936b [1931].

The doctrine of the oneness of the human mind, the oneness of the laws of development of human culture, of the single animistic essence of religious beliefs, of the presence of 'cultural survivals' in the life and creative work of civilized peoples, seemed altogether too general a principle, and, in the main, devoid of a materialistic basis. What guides the regularity of human development, in what, concretely, this regularity consists, what is the nature of the sequence of stages in the cultural growth of mankind – this is not explained in Tylor's and Lang's theory. The most fruitful observations made by the representatives of the 'anthropological' and 'animistic school' could be clearly interpreted only when there was placed under them a firm foundation in the materialistic doctrine of Marxism on social-economic formations as the determining principle of human history from the most ancient eras down to our own time.[96]

With unusual clarity, Sokolov here outlines how the positivist narrative only needed to be mapped onto the logical progression of 'modes of production' that now passed for Marxism. It was, however, in folklore studies and historical poetics that Marrism was able to play perhaps its most positive role in providing a more robust, sociological foundation for the methods pioneered by Veselovskii.[97]

Jairus Banaji provides a trenchant outline of the fundamental revision of Marxism that occurred. Following behind Plekhanov, Soviet Marxists of the 1930s sought to *verify* laws they regarded as implicit in the 'materialist conception of history', rather than to *determine* the 'laws of motion' regulating different historical epochs, which had been Marx's actual aim.[98] The dialectic became a 'cosmological principle prior to and independent of science', rather than 'the principle of rigorous scientific investigation of historical processes' it had been for Marx:

> For the materialist conception of history, it substituted a theory of history 'in general', 'converting historical epochs into a logical succession of inflexible social categories'. Finally, this rubber-stamp conception of history it represented as a history *déjà constituée*, open therefore only to the procedures of verification. This lifeless bureaucratic conception, steeped in the methods of formalism, produced a history emptied of any

---

96   Sokolov 1966 [1938], p. 96.

97   Azadovskii 1935; Frank-Kamenetskii 1935; Desnitskii 1938; Moss 1984; Tihanov 2012.

98   Banaji 2010, p. 47.

specifically historical content, reduced by the forced march of simple formal abstractions to the meagre ration of a few volatile categories.[99]

Marr easily assimilated, or at least simulated, this approach. His historico-philological research provided facts designed to verify pre-established laws of history. In this, his work bolstered the reversion of historical materialism to a variant of the positivist, evolutionary narrative that had underlain the work of many scholars of the pre-revolutionary period, including the Orientalists of the Rozen School. As head of the department of the History of the Ancient World at Leningrad University (1934–58) and at GAIMK (1930–7), Kovalev was one of the main Soviet historians to forge the orthodox stadial theory of socioeconomic development as it pertained to the ancient world, and was the author of some of the main textbooks on the history of Ancient Greece and Rome that were to be used throughout much of the Soviet period.[100] Indeed, it was at GAIMK that some of the main work to create the Stalin-era conception of 'a Marxist doctrine of historical laws in social development, a serial succession of socioeconomic formations, logically arising and succeeding one another' with reference to the ancient world was carried out not only by 'Marxists' like Kovalev and Aleksandr Tiumenev, but also by scholars whose intellectual formation had been under positivist historians before the revolution, such as Vasilii Struve (a student of Mikhail Rostovtsev (Rostovtzeff)), and by some of the main classicists of the pre-revolutionary period, such as Sergei Zhebelev.[101] Together, such figures were more than able to match facts to the stadial universal history that was now accepted to be Marxism.[102] It was thus hardly surprising that, in the 1930s, the work of positivist historians like Bartol'd could readily be assimilated into the framework of Stalinist history, especially once the supposedly beneficial effects of Russian domination of the dominions of the Empire had been accepted by the regime.

As an intellectual trend and as an institutional phenomenon, Marrism thus served to subordinate all sociological considerations of linguistic borrowing and influence to a unitary developmental narrative that placed any such encounters in the distant past. In such quasi-positivist scholarship, hegemony effectively became a non-issue and the idea was invoked only when

---

99   Banaji 2010, p. 48.

100   Kovalev 1936. On Kovalev's work and its place in the development of Soviet Marxist historiography, see Frolov 1986.

101   Frolov 1986, p. 6. On the perceived importance of Marrism for the development of Soviet history, see Matiurin 1933. For overviews, see Podol' 2008, pp. 201 ff. and Krikh 2012.

102   In this regard, Buzeskul 1929–31 provides a wealth of intriguing material.

Marrists argued that the Soviet, Japhetic paradigm in linguistics struggled for hegemony with the Indo-Europeanism of the bourgeois world. At the same time, the struggle of what Stalin would declare in November 1936 to be the 'fully formed multinational Socialist state' with the capitalist states effectively removed hegemony as an issue within the USSR itself and dominant usage reverted back to the sense it had maintained in international politics throughout the nineteenth century.[103] Together, these developments seriously reduced the impact of the undoubted insights about the entwinement of scholarship with ideological constructions and the institutional forms which engendered them that Marr and the other Orientalists had developed. The identification of the official Soviet scholarship that emerged with the first Five-Year Plan with critical, emancipatory social science inevitably required serious distortions of Marxism by requiring attention to be turned away from historical evidence that did not fit the pre-set scheme that the USSR was declared to be following. Thus was the first attempt to construct an 'adversary epistemological current' against the cultural and intellectual realities of imperialism subordinated to the interests of a state soon to embark on its own imperial project.

---

103   Stalin 1978 [1936], p. 163.

Conclusion

Our study thus reaches its conclusion. The concept of hegemony remained a crucial, dynamic and multifaceted one in Russian Marxism for the first thirty years of the twentieth century, at the end of which it underwent a process of vulgarisation and ultimately became an irrelevance. Initially coined to delineate the leading role of the proletariat in achieving the tasks of the bourgeois revolution in the Russian Empire, a whole complex of issues began to coalesce around the concept, leading to complex and sophisticated analyses of the dynamics of revolutionary leadership. While linguistic and cultural dimensions were recognised and theoretically developed in the period before 1917, these remained subordinate to the immediate struggles of the day and few expected the revolution of February 1917 rapidly to lead on to a socialist revolution. When this did indeed occur, the idea of hegemony was transferred to the nature and maintenance of the *smychka* between the proletariat and the peasantry, in which the linguistic and cultural aspects that had only weakly been understood in the pre-October period demanded systematic elaboration. Now it was not only political leaders who were involved in reflecting on the various dimensions of hegemony, but fellow-travelling intellectuals, whose formation had taken place independently of Marxist theory and practice. These 'traditional intellectuals', in the Gramscian sense, brought a great deal of sophistication to linguistic and cultural analysis, informing and participating in the development of some of the most progressive social and cultural policy ever witnessed. For a brief period, Soviet linguists and literary scholars led the world in the development of sociologically based scholarship, precisely because the institutional framework that developed in the 1920s facilitated the Marxist reformulation of the leading paradigms of the time. The need to maintain proletarian hegemony in a predominantly peasant society and, further, in a multi-ethnic, multi-lingual, multi-faith state in which the legacy of imperialism needed to be addressed, was fundamental in shaping the agendas of early Soviet scholars.

Among the many achievements of this time was the development of an elaborated form of sociolinguistics, an ideology critique of dominant trends in philology and the rise of new ways of conceptualising the relationship between structures of power and knowledge. But all this took place in an isolated and severely battered revolutionary state that was experiencing chronic institutional and political degeneration. In these circumstances, positivist and imperial trends, which had never been entirely expunged, gradually reasserted themselves through a series of compromise formations that tended to subordinate open, flexible and detailed work to abstract schemata and *a priori* theoretical constructions. There was no simple reversion to earlier paradigms but, rather, emerging paradigms were forced into combinations with them, degenerating as if down a spiral. Marrism was an exemplary form of this, since from the outset it had been an eclectic combination of ideas which incorporated aspects of Marxism and then sought to subordinate Marxist work on language to its own agenda. This was largely achieved because Marr and his followers opportunistically made common cause with the emerging nationality policies of the Stalin regime. Even here, however, we find extremely valuable insights compromised by adherence to abstract schemata and *a priori* constructions.

As the Stalin regime moved toward final consolidation, we saw that the notion of hegemony was consigned to the realm of an allegedly ascendant proletarian culture, where it was vulgarised almost beyond recognition, before this itself gave way to the assertion of a unitary bureaucratic formulation. Meanwhile, in the work of Platonov, probably the most talented proletarian writer of all, hegemonic reflections in literary form not only traced the containment of proletarian culture by the bureaucratic apparatus, but the way in which the new hegemonic relationship led to moral and political passivity among the alienated masses. Such reflections could not but attract the ire of the self-proclaimed guardians of proletarian hegemony in culture. Yet even here, the notion of hegemony could not withstand the Party's decision to implement socialism in the USSR. The concept lived on to some extent in justifications of the popular-front strategy then being promoted among Communist Parties abroad, but here too the class distinctions were 'obliterated' and alliances with 'progressive' elements of the bourgeoisie to safeguard the interests of the USSR were being advocated. It is from here that the seed of the Eurocommunist and 'neo-Gramscian' conception of hegemony was planted, but it had nothing to do with Gramsci.

Beyond Gramsci?

While adopting the surface of Gramsci's terminology about hegemony, the dominant trend within cultural studies and post-colonial studies has been consciously to go beyond Gramsci. Assuming Gramsci had some new insights into the dynamics of popular consciousness and the exercise of cultural power, which he discussed under the rubric of hegemony, many have assumed that these insights need to be liberated from their residual Leninism, or even from Marxism in general, in order to be able adequately to account for the contestation of cultural authority and the legacies of colonial domination. Post-structuralist ideas and the invocation of the clichés of postmodernism were to stand in for any serious historical reflection on the categories of analysis, generating an image of Marxism as something based on a Eurocentric universalism, the naïve valorisation of scientific truth and a quasi-mystical faith in historical progress. With searching critiques of Eurocentrism now presented as something new, graduate students could be expected to rehearse a repertoire of post-structuralist categories (which usually had a history of their own that was generally overlooked) and stereotypes about intellectual history, in order to build academic careers. Gramsci, along with selected Soviet thinkers like Bakhtin and Vygotsky, now appeared as forerunners of a radically new paradigm, intermittently able to transcend the dreary progressivism of their intellectual environment.

In this study, we have seen that engagements in revolutionary Russia with what are now the object domains of cultural and post-colonial studies already went far beyond Gramsci – both before and while he was engaged in his own analyses. The image of Marxism that permeates much work produced within these disciplines simply cannot survive anything approaching a fair-minded acquaintance with these debates. Yet such an acquaintance is problematic because this image is a fundamental part of the foundational myth of intellectual trends that are well embedded in the institutions of the academic world. Myth, as many thinkers have shown, functions in such a way as to render itself impervious to refutation, and so it is only those who are already sceptical of these trends that will be open to the arguments that have been presented here. Fortunately, such scepticism is in the ascendant due to the decreasing returns of the postmodern paradigm, the fading legacies of Stalinism, the fundamental shifts in patterns of global power and the inescapably systemic nature of the crisis of the capitalist system. Analysing the contemporary world increasingly demands a new engagement with the valuable critical-intellectual resources that were accumulated in the era of wars and revolutions at the beginning of the twentieth century. As we have seen, there were important engagements with the question of the active relationship between popular consciousness in its linguistic embodiment and forms of intellectual authority, between class experience and ideological elaborations, between the languages and cultures of the colonial and post-colonial world with those of the major imperial powers, and the production and function of knowledge about the 'East' (what today would be called the 'Global South'). All this occurred, however, in the context of a crucial question: how can a democratic mode of political leadership be developed that is capable of leading the labouring masses, the workers and peasants, and the oppressed peoples of the world to victory over the forces of exploitation and oppression? This needed to be based on an understanding of the dynamics of the capitalist system that was becoming ever more integrated, but was still characterised by a hierarchy of states. The linguistic and cultural forces operative within that dynamic were of crucial importance. This was the problematic of hegemony, and in one way or another it occupied the work of many Soviet thinkers and all international Marxists for at least the first third of the century. Gramsci was but one of these thinkers. Like every participant in the debates of the time, he was limited in terms of scope and purview, but he occupied a unique position that also allowed him to develop a particular perspective on the issues raised.

In many respects, Zinov'ev was correct to argue that the hegemony of the proletariat was the 'main regulating idea of Bolshevism', the 'nodal point [*uzlovoi punkt* – CB]', around which Bolshevism differed from all other trends.[1] The rise, development and fall of each clearly coincided. This is why the idea achieves such prominence in Gramsci's work, for it is around the winning of proletarian hegemony that the very project of the Bolshevised Communist Party must be organised. To win state power, the proletariat must achieve hegemony over kindred classes, which requires the leadership to understand the way in which the northern bourgeoisie and southern landowners exert their hegemony. The political, linguistic and wider cultural dimensions of bourgeois hegemony constitute the terrain which the proletariat must contest if it is to achieve its own hegemony. In Russia, the hegemonic apparatus of the bourgeoisie was at most embryonic, and the workers' state had to develop its own 'hegemonic apparatus' from the beginning, an achievement which was sufficient in itself to make Lenin the greatest theoretician of hegemony in these terms.[2]

The institutional apparatus that maintained the *smychka* throughout the NEP period was, for Gramsci, an example of how the workers could establish and maintain a viable revolutionary state in Italy. At the Fourth Congress of the Comintern, which Gramsci attended, Zinov'ev had stressed the significance of NEP for other countries, for 'the proletariat in every country must weigh its strength against that of the peasantry and clearly establish a relationship between the industrial proletariat and a large part of the rural population'.[3] After a period in which the Russian proletariat had driven forward at a rapid tempo, it 'then had to recognise that, in order not to lose touch with the great mass of the peasantry … it had to take measures that later received the name

---

1 Zinov'ev 1924 [1923], p. 301; Zinoviev 1973 [1923], p. 216.
2 Gramsci 1971, p. 365.
3 Riddell (ed.) 2012, p. 71.

of New Economic Policy'.[4] Yet, as Gramsci was to argue, while in Russia the conquest of power was relatively easy, but maintaining it was extremely difficult, the inverse would be true in Italy. Italy was different. Not least because in that country, detailed thinking about linguistic, cultural and religious questions could not wait until state power had been secured, but was a precondition of the conquest of the state itself, for important ideological battles would take place precisely there. Thus Gramsci incorporated into his understanding of hegemony, as a revolutionary strategy, aspects that had been addressed by the Russian Party only as it was forced to grapple with the unforeseen consequences of governing alone in a multi-national, peasant-based society.

This is why the difference between bourgeois and proletarian hegemony is a constant refrain throughout his *Notebooks*. Hegemony does not simply mean rule by consent rather than force, but the very mode of political authority characteristic of certain forms of class leadership and rule. Force and consent are aspects of a 'dual perspective', dialectically interpenetrating opposites that never exist in isolation but are integrated at a 'molecular' level, as it were.[5] Political state power and civil society are the institutional forms of class rule, which exist in a dynamic relationship, and the prominence of which vary from state to state and at different moments in the history of certain states. The Soviet state under the NEP was, for Gramsci, an example of an apparatus designed to 'keep the dispossessed reactionary forces within the bounds of legality, and to raise the backward masses to the level of the new legality', as opposed to the rule of the bourgeoisie, especially in its fascist form, which carries out 'its policing function in order to conserve an outward, extrinsic order which is a fetter on the vital forces of history'.[6] The bourgeoisie had to 'reconstruct the hegemonic apparatus of the ruling group, an apparatus which disintegrated as a result of the [1914–18 – CB] war, in every state throughout the world'.[7] In all cases, force was needed, and the specific combination of legal and illegal forces employed varied according to the specificities of each state, with Italy requiring a particularly high proportion of illegal force. Once in place, the hegemonic apparatus operates through intellectual subordination, inducing 'moral and political passivity' among the masses by preventing the conception of the world, implicit in its practice as a class, from achieving coherence and structure. The classic example of this, for Gramsci, is the Catholic counter-reformation, which aimed to 'leave the "simple" in their

---

4   Riddell (ed.) 2012, p. 72.
5   Gramsci 1971, pp. 169–70.
6   Gramsci 1971, p. 155.
7   Gramsci 1971, p. 228.

primitive philosophy of common sense ... and preserve unity at the low level of the masses'.[8] This was, of course, backed up by a very real and active apparatus of coercion. The Soviet example was the complete opposite, for it sought 'to construct an intellectual-moral bloc which can make politically possible the intellectual progress of the mass and not only of small intellectual groups'. The establishment of such an apparatus of hegemony requires that the proletariat recognise itself as the leading part of a movement to overthrow the hegemonic apparatus of the bourgeoisie:

> Critical understanding of self takes place therefore through a struggle of political 'hegemonies' and of opposing directions, first in the ethical field and then in that of politics proper, in order to arrive at the working out at a higher level of one's own conception of reality. Consciousness of being part of a particular hegemonic force (that is to say, political consciousness) is the first stage towards a further progressive self-consciousness in which theory and practice will finally be one.[9]

Here, and throughout the *Notebooks*, one can see Gramsci synthesising some of the strands that had run through the Russian debates, from Lenin and Plekhanov's thinking about the concept of hegemony being crucial in the transition of the proletariat from a collection of guilds to a class, through Bogdanov's conception of a class's world view being implicit in its productive activity, to the complex working out of the means through which the *smychka* could be maintained. In some cases, this was a conscious process, but in other cases Gramsci drew theoretical conclusions from considering the way different problems had been addressed. I would therefore argue that not only is it impossible to understand Gramsci's conception of hegemony without understanding the concept's history in Russian Marxism, but that it is also impossible to understand Gramsci's own contribution to political thought more broadly.

Gramsci began to weave together the various strands running through debates and struggles within Russian Marxism of the first thirty years of the twentieth century into something approaching a coherent fabric. This was possible not only because he was removed from active political engagement at a crucial moment, which was undoubtedly the case, but also because he was able to maintain an external perspective on the Soviet experience, viewing the contours of argument in a way that would have been impossible to those embedded in the intense struggles of the time. Thus some of the theoretical

---

8   Gramsci 1971, p. 332.
9   Gramsci 1971, p. 333.

perspectives that were embedded in direct political engagements were raised to a new level of elaboration. But for Gramsci, this relative detachment was not that of an academic observer but of a participant in a related struggle, who needed to distil what was essential in the Soviet experience, so as to operate as a revolutionary in distinct historical circumstances. It is certainly true that Gramsci drew upon important Italian sources, including his own linguistic training. As we have seen, however, early Soviet intellectuals were at the forefront of work on the social and political dimensions of culture and of language more specifically. They also reflected upon the relationship between language and hegemony. In most cases, however, Soviet linguists did not have a very profound understanding of Marxism, and just as work was reaching a significant level of theoretical elaboration, the institutional and ideological environment distorted both Marxism and the research programmes in which they were involved. Beginning with 'philological' investigations of various issues, in his last years in prison Gramsci began to weave his short notes together into more sustained analyses, moving between the current Italian situation, European history and the recent experience of the USSR. The surviving texts are far from complete – their terminology is related to specific texts, debates and events with which Gramsci engaged, and remain open to significant misinterpretation if this historicity is obscured. This makes it all the more important to establish the way in which the political, cultural and more specifically linguistic dimensions of hegemony were developed prior to Gramsci's own employment of the term and development of the idea.

However significant Gramsci's achievement, it is a mistake to view the Soviet debates about hegemony solely through the prism of his work. There was a significant 'surplus' in these debates, of which Gramsci was, after all, only partially aware. The Bolshevik era, which we might define as the first thirty years of the twentieth century, yielded a great many intellectual riches, many of which remain unstudied, or have been perceived in a one-sided fashion, according to ideological preconceptions. These constitute only partially-uncovered resources not just for scholars, but for those seeking to forge political concepts and movements appropriate for our own era of wars and revolutions. If the current study has provided an insight into some of these resources and facilitates further investigation and critical reflection on a crucial period in world history, then it will have succeeded in its aim.

Glossary of Names

Abaev, Vasilii Ivanovich (1900–2001) Russian linguist. An advocate of Marr's 'new theory of language' in the 1920s–40s. Among his works are publications about Ossetian and Iranian etymology, Ossetian folklore, Iranian studies and general linguistics.

Annenskii, Innokenti Fedorovich (1855–1909) Russian poet and dramatist. His influential *Lectures on Ancient Greek Literature* were published in the year of his death.

Aptekar', Valerian Borisovich (1899–1937) Russian linguist and propagandist of Marr's 'new theory of language'. Arrested and shot in 1937.

Ascoli, Graziado Isaia (1829–1907) Italian linguist who became especially well known for his study of Italian dialects and disagreement with Alessandro Manzoni about the latter's contention that the Florentine dialect should become the basis of standard Italian. He was the founder of the so-called 'substratum theory', according to which previous languages spoken by a community affect the way in which a new language is adopted.

Avanesov, Ruben Ivanovich (1902–82) Russian linguist, co-founder of the Moscow Phonological School, along with Nikolai F. Iakovev, Vladimir I. Sidorov and Alexandr A. Reformatskii. Known for his works in Russian phonetics, orthography and dialectology.

Averbakh, Leopol'd Leonidovich (1903–37) Soviet literary critic and one of the leaders of RAPP, whose journal, *Na literaturnom postu*, he edited. Arrested and shot in 1937.

Babel, Isaak Emmanuilovich (1894–1940) Russian-language Jewish author and journalist. Best known for his cycles of short stories *The Odessa Tales* and *Red Cavalry* (Babel 2002). Arrested in 1939 and shot.

Bachofen, Johann Jakob (1815–87) Swiss jurist and anthropologist. Particularly well known for his 1861 book, *Das Mutterrecht: eine Untersuchung über die Gynaikokratie der alten Welt nach ihrer religiösen und rechtlichen Natur* [*Mother Right: An Investigation of the Religious and Juridical Character of Matriarchy in the Ancient World*] (Bachofen 1861), which was influential on, *inter alia*, Marx and Engels.

Bakhtin, Mikhail Mikhailovich (1895–1975) Russian philosopher and literary theorist.

Bally, Charles (1865–1947) French linguist and co-editor of Saussure's *Cours* (Saussure 1983 [1916]). Bally's book, *Le Langage et la Vie* (Bally 1826 [1913]) was required reading for linguists at ILIaZV in the 1920s.

Bartol'd, Vasilii Vladimirovich (1869–1930) Russian historian who specialised in the history of Central Asia and of Islam. Elected to the Russian Academy of Sciences in 1913.

Bartoli, Matteo (1873–1946) Italian linguist and opponent of the neo-grammarians. He founded so-called 'Neolinguistics', which mapped the diffusion of linguistic elements between sign communities. He supervised the uncompleted doctoral dissertation of Antonio Gramsci.

Baudouin de Courtenay, Jan (in Russian, Ivan Aleksandrovich Boduen de Kurtene, 1845–1929) Polish-Russian linguist. Established the Kazan and the Petersburg Linguistic Schools. Polivanov, Iakubinskii, Larin and Shcherba, *inter alia*, participated in the latter. He emigrated to Poland in 1918.

Belinskii, Vissarion Grigor'evich (1811–48) Russian literary critic. Founder of the Russian 'civic criticism' of the nineteenth century.

Belyi, Andrei (pseudonym of Boris Nikolaevich Bugaev, 1880–1934) Russian poet, novelist and literary theorist of the symbolist movement. A leading participant in *Vol'fila*.

Benfey, Theodor (1809–81) German philologist who, *inter alia*, traced the relationship between Sanskrit and European languages and literature.

Berdiaev, Nikolai Aleksandrovich (1874–1948) Russian religious and political philosopher. Participated in the 1909 symposium, *Vekhi* (Berdyaev *et al.* 1977 [1909]). Expelled from the USSR in 1922, he settled in Paris.

Bernshtein, Sergei Ignat'evich (1892–1970) Russian linguist, a student of Baudoun, Shakhmatov and Shcherba. Worked at a number of institutes, including IZhS, where he developed new approaches to the study of the sound of languages.

Blok, Aleksandr Aleksandrovich (1880–1921) Prominent Russian poet. Participated in *Vol'fila*.

Boas, Franz (1858–1942) German-American anthropologist often regarded as the father of American anthropology. Among his works were descriptive studies of native-American languages and considerations of the problems in classifying them according to categories inherited from Indo-European linguistics.

Bogdanov, Aleksandr Aleksandrovich (pseudonym of Aleksandr Aleksandrovich Malinovskii, 1873–1928) Russian philosopher, author, physician, revolutionary and leading member of the Bolshevik faction of the Russian Social Democratic Labour Party until 1909. He remained very influential on Soviet thought despite his high-profile disagreements with Lenin. His 1922 book, *Tektologiia*, is now regarded as a forerunner of systems theory.

Bopp, Franz (1791–1867) German linguist, one of the main developers of the comparative method in linguistics. Published extensively on the comparative history of grammatical forms in Indo-European languages. Among his most influential works is *Vergleichende Grammatik des Sanskrit, Zend, Griechischen, Lateinischen, Litauischen, Gotischen und Deutschen* [*Comparative Grammar of Sanskrit, Zend (Avestan), Greek, Latin, Lithuanian, Gothic and German*] (Bopp 1833–52).

Böriev, Kumyshali (1896–1932) Soviet linguist and cultural activist. Vice-chair of VTsKNTA in 1927 and then participated in a range of Latinisation initiatives in Central Asia. Arrested in 1932, charged with promoting Pan-Turkism and then shot.

Braun, Fedor Aleksandrovich (1862–1942) Russian Germanist, professor at St. Petersburg University. He travelled to Germany in 1922 and remained there, becoming a professor at Leipzig University in 1922.

Bücher, Karl (1847–1930) German economist. Chiefly known for his books, *Die Entstehung der Volkswirtschaft* [The Rise of the National Economy (Bücher 1893)]; and *Arbeit und Rhythmus* [Labour and Rhythm (Bücher 1896)], which was translated into Russian in 1899 and reprinted in 1923.

Bühler, Karl Ludwig (1879–1963) German psychologist and theorist of language. His numerous works on psychology and language were well known in the early USSR and influenced, *inter alia*, Voloshinov and Vygotskii.

Bukharin, Nikolai Ivanovich (1888–1938) Russian revolutionary and a leading Bolshevik who held a number of prominent Party and governmental positions, including editor of *Pravda* 1918–29 and Chair of the Comintern 1926–9. A supporter of Stalin after Lenin's death, he opposed the forced collectivisation of the peasantry in 1929 and lost much of his very considerable influence. He was arrested and subjected to a prominent show trial with other 'old Bolsheviks' before being shot in 1938.

Bulgakov, Sergei Nikolaevich (1871–1944) Russian Orthodox theologian, philosopher and economist. Initially a so-called 'legal Marxist', he became an idealist critic of the October Revolution and participated in the symposium *Vekhi* [*Landmarks*] in 1909 (Berdyaev et al. 1977 [1909]). He was expelled from the USSR and lived in Paris from December 1922.

Buslaev, Fedor Ivanovich (1818–98) Russian philologist and chief representative of the 'mythological school' in Russia. Influenced by Jacob Grimm and Theodor Benfey and teacher of, *inter alia*, Aleksandr Veselovskii.

Chaianov, Aleksandr Vasil'evich (1888–1937) Russian economist, sociologist, writer of utopian fiction, a member of the cooperative movement after the February 1917 Revolution and Gosplan worker in the early 1920s. He was arrested in 1930 and executed in 1937.

Chemodanov, Nikolai Sergeevich (1903–86) Russian philologist, specialist in Germanic and general linguistics. A participant in the activities of the *Iazykfront* group and an organiser of the Moscow *Rabkor*. Later became a professor at Moscow State University.

Chernov, Viktor Mikhailovich (1873–1952) Russian revolutionary and founder of the Socialist-Revolutionary Party, of which he was its main theoretician.

Chernyshevskii, Nikolai Gavrilovich (1828–89) Russian revolutionary, critic, materialist philosopher. He had a significant influence on the work of, *inter alia*, Plekhanov and Lenin, who derived the title of his 1902 work *What is to be Done?* from Chernyshevskii's novel of the same name.

Chuzhak, Nikolai Fedorovich (real surname Nasimovich, 1876–1937) Russian revolutionary, journalist and literary critic. Associated with the journal *Lef*, champion of the ideas of 'art as the creation of life' and of 'factography'.

Cohen, Hermann (1842–1914) German Jewish philosopher. Founder of the Marburg School of neo-Kantianism.

Comte, Auguste (1798–1857) French philosopher, often held to be the founder of sociology and of the doctrine of positivism.

Condillac, Etienne Bonnot de (1715–80) French philosopher who viewed language as a means through which emotions and sense impressions are transformed into higher mental functions.

Croce, Benedetto (1866–1952) Italian idealist philosopher who viewed linguistics as a sub-division of aesthetics. His linguistic ideas were well known in Russia.

Curtius, Georg (1820–85) German philologist whose work on classics and Indo-European languages was fundamental to the study of the Greek language.

Danilov, Georgii Konstantinovich (1896–1937) Russian linguist, specialist in African languages and founder of the *Iazykfront* group, which opposed Marr's 'new theory of language' being granted the status of Marxism in linguistics. In 1931–2 he was deputy director of the Moscow-based Research Institute of Linguistics (1931–3). He was arrested and shot in 1937.

Deratini, Nikolai Fedorovich (1884–1958) Russian classical philologist.

Derzhavin, Nikolai Sevast'ianovich (1877–1953) Russian slavist, director of ILIaZV (1923–32) and advocate of Marr's 'new theory of language'.

D'iakonov, Mikhail Aleksandrovich (1855–1919) Russian historian. A member of the Russian Academy of Sciences from 1912.

Diderot, Denis (1713–84) French philosopher and writer, one of the leaders of the Enlightenment. One of the editors of the monumental *Encyclopédie, ou dictionnaire raisonné des sciences, des arts et des métiers* [Encyclopaedia or a Systematic Dictionary of the Sciences, Arts and Crafts] (Diderot and d'Alembert 1757–72).

Dorn, Johannes Albrecht Bernhard (Also known as Boris Andreevich Dorn, 1805–81) German Orientalist specialising in the languages of Russia, Iran and Afghanistan. Taught at the universities of Leipzig, Kharkov (where he was head of the Department of Oriental Languages), and St. Petersburg. A corresponding member of the Russian Academy of Sciences from 1835.

Doroshevskii, Vitol'd Ian (Doroszewski Witold Jan, 1899–1976) Polish linguist, specialist in Slavonic languages and dialectology.

Drabkina, Elizaveta Iakovlevna (1901–74) Russian revolutionary and writer. Author of novels, memoirs and analytical works, she was arrested as an alleged Trotskyist in 1928 and 1936.

Drezen, Ernest Karlovich (1892–1937) Latvian Esperantist, leader of the Union of Soviet Esperantists. The leading proponent of Esperanto in the USSR. Arrested for alleged espionage and counter-revolutionary activity and shot in 1937.

Durnovo, Nikolai Nikolaevich (1876–1937) Russian linguist and member of the Moscow Dialectology Commission, the forerunner of the Moscow Linguistic Circle. Spent 1924–8 in Prague, working with the Prague Linguistic Circle. Worked and published on Russian dialectology, the history of Russian and Slavonic languages, Russian morphology, the theory of grammar and ancient Russian literature. Was arrested and shot in 1937.

Eikhenbaum, Boris Mikhailovich (1886–1959) Russian literary scholar and one of the most prominent Russian Formalist critics.

Erberg, Konstantin Aleksandrovich (real surname Siunnerberg, 1871–1942) Russian symbolist philosopher and theorist of art. After the October Revolution he became director of the oratory section of IZhS and then worked at ILIaZV.

Fortunatov, Filipp Fedorovich (1848–1914) Russian linguist and founder of the Moscow Linguistic School known for its formal approach to the study of linguistic data.

Frank-Kamenetskii, Izrail' Grigor'evich (1880–1937) Lithuanian-born Jewish Orientalist, philosopher, biblical scholar and linguist. One of the most talented collaborators of N.Ia. Marr, whose ideas he imbibed selectively.

Friche, Vladimir Maksimovich (1870–1929) Soviet literary and art critic, one of the founders of the 'sociological method'. Held many influential positions in Soviet educational and research institutions and became a member of the Academy of Sciences of the USSR in 1929.

Frings, Theodor (1886–1968) German linguist. A specialist in German dialect geography.

Frunze, Mikhail Vasil'evich (1885–1925) Soviet political figure, Party member from 1904, commander in the Red Army during the Civil War and Commissar for War in 1924–5, during which time he introduced important reforms.

Gastev, Aleksei Kapitonovich (1882–1939) Russian revolutionary, poet, writer, participant in the *Proletkul't* movement, proponent of the scientific organisation of labour (NOT) and the director of the Central Organisation of Labour. Arrested in 1938 and shot the following year.

Genko, Anatolii Nestorovich (1896–1941) Soviet linguist, ethnographer and leading specialist in the languages and cultures of the Caucasus. He worked with Nikolai Marr at a number of institutes in Leningrad.

Gershenzon, Mikhail Osipovich (1869–1925) Russian essayist and publicist. Participated in the symposium *Vekhi [Landmarks]* in 1909 (Berdyaev *et al.* 1977 [1909]).

Gilléron, Jules (1854–1926) Swiss linguist and pioneer in dialect geography, who is best known for his landmark, *Atlas linguistique de la France [Linguistic Atlas of France*, 1902–12] (Gilléron and Édmont 1902–12).

Gofman, Viktor Abramovich (1899–1942) Russian philologist, a student of Boris Eikhenbaum and Lev Iakubinskii. He is best known for his work on the language of Russian Symbolists and on the relationship between politics and oratory.

Gorky [Gor'kii], Maksim (pseudonym of Alexei Maximovich Peshkov 1868–1936) Russian writer and political activist. Lent financial support to the RSDLP before the October Revolution and cooperated with the *Vpered* group. Hosted the RSDLP school at his villa on the Italian island of Capri. Returned to the USSR after his second exile in 1932, when he championed the cause of 'socialist realism'.

Gramsci, Antonio (1891–1937) Italian political theorist and activist, leader of the Communist Party of Italy (PCI) in 1923–6 before being arrested. He then wrote his now famous *Prison Notebooks*, in which the relation between language and politics plays a key role. He was a PCI delegate to the Comintern in Moscow 1922–3 and visited Moscow again in 1925.

Grande, Bentsion Meerovich (1891–1974) Russian-Jewish linguist and specialist in Semitic languages. A follower and advocate of the ideas of N.Ia.Marr.

Grau, Rudolph Friedrich (1835–93) German protestant theologist, among whose works was the widely-received *Semiten und Indogermanen. Eine Apologie des Christentums vom Standpunkte der Völkerpsychologie [Semites and Indo-Germans. An Apology for Christianity from the Standpoint of Völkerpsychologie]* (Grau, 1867 [1864]).

Grimm, Jacob (1785–1863) German philologist whose histories, grammars and dictionary of the German language, development of a theory of non-trivial sound changes in language and collection (with his brother Wilhelm (1786–1859)) of German folktales exerted a formative influence on philology across Europe, including Russia.

Gumilev, Nikolai Stepanovich (1886–1921) Russian poet, translator and critic. Participated in the work of IZhS but was arrested in connection with the so-called Tagantsev military conspiracy soon after the Kronstadt mutiny and shot. He was posthumously rehabilitated in 1992.

Herder, Johann Gottfried (1744–1803) German philosopher, poet, theologian and literary critic. His 1772 *Treatise on the Origin of Language* (Herder 2002 [1772]), proved to be a foundational text in the formation of comparative philology.

Holbach (Paul-Henri Thiry, Baron d'Holbach) (1723–89) French-German philosopher and a prominent figure of the French Enlightenment. His materialist philosophy and atheism were particularly influential in Russia.

Humboldt, Wilhelm von (1767–1835) German government functionary, diplomat, philosopher, particularly remembered as a linguist who made important contributions to the philosophy of language and to the theory and practice of education. His book, *The Heterogeneity of Language and its Influence on the Intellectual Development of Human Species* (Humboldt 1999 [1836]), in which he defined language as a rule-governed system that embodies a world view, was particularly influential in Russia.

Iakovlev, Nikolai Feofanovich (1892–1974) Russian linguist, played a key role in the formation of the Moscow Phonological School. Made a significant contribution to the codification of the phonetics of several Caucasian languages in the USSR and in the development of Latin scripts for those languages in the 1920s. He attempted to incorporate elements of Marr's theories into his work from the late 1920s.

Iakubinskii, Lev Petrovich (1892–1945) Russian linguist and, early in his career, a literary scholar connected with OPOIaZ. His work on dialogue and the development of the Russian national language was very influential in the 1920s and 1930s. A student of Baudouin de Courtenay, he supported Marr's 'new theory of language' from the late 1920s.

Il'inskii, Grigorii Andreevich (1876–1937) Russian linguist, specialist in the history and etymology of Slavonic languages. Professor at Kharkov, Saratov and the first Moscow Universities. Between 1899 and 1906 he was Secretary of the Linguistic Section of the Neo-Philological Society of the St. Petersburg University. He was a staff member of the Moscow-based Research Institute of Language and Literature, a member of the Dialectology Commission. Arrested in 1934 and sentenced to ten years hard labour, which was subsequently commuted to exile in Slavgorod (Western Siberia); he was repeatedly arrested and finally shot in 1937.

Il'minskii, Nikolai Ivanovich (1823–91) Russian Orientalist, missionary-pedagogue and corresponding member of the Academy of Sciences. He promoted the teaching of Orthodox Christianity in the native languages of the peoples of the Russian Empire.

Ivanov, Viacheslav Ivanovich (1866–1949) Russian symbolist poet and philosopher. A classical scholar influenced by the early works of Nietzsche, he promoted the idea that Russian culture had inherent connections to Classical Greece and promoted the classical ideal. Collaborated with TEO Narkomprosa after the October Revolution, but emigrated in 1924 and settled in Rome.

Ivanov-Razumnik (pseudonym of Razumnik Vasil'evich Ivanov, 1876–1946) Russian literary scholar, sociologist and writer. He was politically close to the Left SRs and collaborated with Andrei Bely in the formation of *Vol'fila*.

Jespersen, Otto (1860–1943) Danish linguist specialising in English grammar.

Kalinin, Mikhail Ivanovich (1875–1946) Russian Bolshevik, member of the Politburo from 1926.

Kamenev, Lev Borisovich (1883–1936) Russian Bolshevik and a member, with Stalin and Zinov'ev, of the 'Triumvirate' following Lenin's incapacitation. Joined the United Opposition in 1926 but capitulated when it was defeated. He was arrested and, after a show trial, was shot in 1936.

Karinskii, Nikolai Mikhailovich (1873–1935) Russian philologist, palaeographer, Slavist and dialectologist. Worked on Russian regional dialects but, after the October Revolution, increasingly connected these to sociological factors. From 1931 he was a prominent member of the Dialectology Commission at Marr's Institute of Language and Thinking.

Karskii, Evfemii Fedorovich (1860–1931) Russian philologist, ethnographer and a member of the Russian Academy of Sciences from 1916. He specialised in the language and culture of the Belorussian people.

Kautsky, Karl Johann (1854–1938) Czech-German Marxist theoretician and political activist.

Kazanskii, Boris Vasil'evich (1889–1962) Russian philologist and professor at Leningrad University. Participated in the activities of the Petrograd formalists.

Kerzhentsev, Platon (1881–1940) Russian dramatist and theorist of the arts. He was a leading member of the *Proletkul't* movement and applied his ideas about collective activity to the rationalisation of labour.

Khvylevoi, Mikola (pseudonym of Nikolai (Mikola) Grigor'evich Fitilev, 1893–1933) Ukrainian author. An enthusiastic supporter of Ukrainisation. Committed suicide.

Kirshon, Vladimir Mikhailovich (1902–38) Soviet dramatist and one of the leaders of RAPP. He played a leading role in campaigns against fellow-traveller writers. He was arrested and shot for allegedly belonging to a Trotskyist literary group.

Klaproth, Julius Heinrich von (1783–1835) German Orientalist and linguist. Appointed to the St. Petersburg Academy, he made an extensive ethnographic and linguistic exploration of the Caucasus (1807–8), publishing his two-volume *Reise in den Kaukasus* [*Journey to the Caucasus*] in 1814 (Klaproth 1814).

Kogan Petr Semenovich (1872–1932) Russian literary historian. He was the president of GAKhN in 1921–30.

Koni, Anatolii Fedorovich (1844–1927) Russian jurist, social activist, memoirist and professor at Petrograd University in 1918–22. He defended the revolutionary Vera Zasulich in a celebrated trial of 1878. Taught at IZhS 1918–24.

Kondakov, Nikodim Pavlovich (1844–1925) Russian historian of Byzantine and ancient-Russian art and archaeologist. He emigrated to Bulgaria (via Istanbul) in 1920, where he became a professor at Sofia University.

Korniushin, Fedor Danilovich (1893–1938) Russian revolutionary. Member of the Central Committee of the Ukrainian Communist Party in 1924–30. Arrested and shot in 1938.

Kovalev, Sergei Ivanovich (1886–1960) Soviet historian of antiquity and professor at Leningrad University (LGU) in 1924–56. He created the department of the History of Ancient Greece and Rome at LGU in 1934. Among his publications were the first Soviet Marxist textbooks published under the rubric of the *History of the Ancient World* (1936).

Kovalevskii, Maksim Maksimovich (1851–1916) Russian historian, jurist, ethnologist and sociologist. He was personally acquainted with Marx and Engels, both of whom drew on his work in their later ethnographic writings.

Kremer, Arkadii (1865–1935) Lithuanian-born Jewish Marxist and member of the Central Committee of the Bund. Author, with Martov, of the pamphlet *On Agitation* [*Ob agitatsii*] (Kremer and Martov 1983 [1896]).

Kreps, Vladimir Moiseevich (1903–84) Soviet applied linguist and author. Director of the Volodarskii institute of Agitation and of the Laboratory of Public Discourse at ILIaZV. He subsequently worked as a writer of film scripts and as an author of children's books.

Krohn, Julius (1835–88) Finnish poet and literary scholar who established the 'historical-geographical method' for the study of folklore. Father of Kaarle Krohn.

Krohn, Kaarle (1863–1933) Finnish folklorist and developer of the historical-geographical method for the study of folklore. His 1926 book, *Die folkloristiche Arbeitsmethode* [*Folklore Methodology*], became the standard reference work on the question. Son of Julius Krohn.

Krupskaia, Nadezhda Konstantinovna (1869–1939) Russian revolutionary, head of Glavpolitprosvet in 1920–30, wife of V.I. Lenin.

Kruszewski, Mikołaj (1851–87) Polish linguist who, with Baudouin de Courtenay, established the Kazan school of linguistics and developed an innovative, systematic approach to the phonological structure of language.

Kudriavskii, Dmitri (1867–1920) Russian linguist and political activist.

Kusik'ian, Iosif Karpovich (1890–1964) Armenian linguist, specialist in the history of Armenian language, literature and folklore, a supporter of Marr's 'new theory of language'.

Kuznetsov, Petr Savvich (1899–1968) Russian linguist, co-founder and one of the key theorists of the Moscow Phonological School, along with Nikolai F. Iakovlev, Ruben I. Avanesov, Vladimir N. Sidorov and Aleksandr A. Reformatskii. Member of the Moscow Dialectology Commission, specialist in Russian phonetics, orthography, dialectology and the history of the Russian language. A participant in the *Iazykfront* group.

Labriola, Antonio (1843–1904) Italian Marxist theorist.

Lang, Andrew (1844–1912) Scottish man of letters and specialist in folklore.

Larin, Boris Aleksandrovich (1893–1964) Russian linguist and, in his early career, literary scholar. His work on urban dialects and argot in the 1920s was well known in the USSR.

Lazarus, Moritz (1824–1903) German philosopher and psychologist, founder, with Haymann Steinthal, of *Völkerpsychologie* [cultural psychology], and, in 1860, the journal *Zeitschrift für Völkerpsychologie und Sprachwissenschaft*. He was an outspoken opponent of anti-Semitism.

Lebed', Dmitri Zakharovich (1893–1937) Russian Bolshevik. Between 1920 and 1924 he served as Second Secretary of the Central Committee of the Communist Party of Ukraine and in 1925–30 was vice-chair of Rabkrin. Accused of Ukrainian nationalism, he was arrested and shot in 1937.

Leont'ev, Aleksei Nikolaevich (1904–79) Russian psychologist, early colleague of Vygotskii and Luria and founder of activity theory in psychology.

Liapunov, Boris Mikhailovich (1862–1943) Russian Slavist, specialist in the history and comparative grammar of Slavonic languages, a former student of Aleksandr A. Potebnia and Aleksei I. Sobolevskii, professor at Novorossiisk and Leningrad universities. He took an active part in discussions of the post-revolutionary Russian orthography in the mid-1930s.

Likhachev, Dmitri Sergeevich (1906–99) Russian philologist. His early work was related to the Marrist paradigm in linguistics and was developed at the Institute of Language and Thinking in Leningrad. He later became one of the foremost researchers of Old Russian language and literature.

Loia, Ian Viliumovich (1896–1969) Latvian Soviet linguist. A Party member from 1915 and a participant in the October Revolution, Lomtev graduated from Moscow State University before pursuing an academic career in

Moscow, Leningrad and Gor'kii. He participated in the group *Iazykfront*. He published more than one hundred and thirty works.

Lomtev, Timofei Petrovich (1906–72) Russian linguist and one of the founders of *Iazykfront*. After the defeat of the group, he worked at the Institute of Linguistics of the Academy of Sciences in Minsk, but returned to Moscow in 1943 where he worked as a professor at Moscow State University.

Loria, Achille (1857–1943) Italian political economist. A critic of Marx's political economy, whose work he attempted to improve by combining it with ideas from, *inter alia*, Herbert Spencer. Loria was criticised by Engels and, in Gramsci's *Prison Notebooks*, is treated as representative of the parlous influence of positivism.

Lunacharskii, Anatolii Vasil'evich (1875–1933) Russian revolutionary, Marxist and first Commissar of Enlightenment 1917–29. A dramatist and participant, with Bogdanov and Gorky, in the *Vpered* group and an enthusiast for proletarian culture before the October Revolution.

Marr, Nikolai Iakovlevich (1864/5–1934) Georgian archaeologist, philologist and linguist whose controversial Japhetic Theory, later recast as the 'new theory of language', achieved considerable official support in the 1930s and 1940s. The dominance of Marr's ideas in Soviet linguistics was brought to an abrupt end in June 1950, when they were denounced by Stalin.

Martov, L. (pseudonym of Iulii Osipovich Tsederbaum, 1873–1923) Russian Jewish socialist, leader and chief ideologue of the Menshevik wing of the RSDLP. Author, with Arkardii Kremer, of the pamphlet *On Agitation* [*Ob agitatsii*] (Kremer and Martov 1983 [1896]).

Marty, Anton (1847–1914) Swiss philosopher who wrote on ontology, psychology and the philosophy of language. His application of Franz Brentano's descriptive psychology to language in *Untersuchungen zur Grundlegung der allgemeinen Grammatik und Sprachphilosophie*, vol. 1 [*Studies of the Foundation of Universal Grammar and the Philosophy of Language*] (1908) (Marty 1980) was well known among early Soviet linguists.

Megrelidze, Konstantin Romanovich (1900–44) Georgian philosopher, psychologist and sociologist. A collaborator, with N. Ia. Marr, he is now chiefly known for his *Osnovnye problem sotsiologii myshleniia* [*Fundamental problems of the Sociology of Thinking*], completed in 1938 but published only in 1965.

Meierkhol'd, Vsevolod Emil'evich (Karl Kasimir Theodor Meyergold, 1874–1940) Russian theatre director, theorist and one of the organisers of TEO Narkomprosa. Arrested in 1939 and shot the following year.

Meillet, Antoine (1866–1936) French linguist and founder of the sociological school, which sought to combine linguistics with Durkheimian sociology.

From 1906 he was a corresponding member of the Russian Academy of Sciences and he wrote works on Slavonic languages.

Meinhof, Carl Friedrich Michael (1857–1944) German linguist and specialist in African languages. As well as developing comparative grammars of Bantu languages, he posited the existence of a 'Hamitic' group of languages, which connected certain African and Caucasian languages. He also advocated the centrality of language mixing.

Mehring, Franz Erdmann (1846–1919) German Marxist politician and historian, a biographer of Karl Marx.

Mill, John Stuart (1806–73) British philosopher and political economist.

Morgan, Lewis Henry (1818–81) American anthropologist and social theorist. His works on kinship and the family were influential on Marx and Engels and widely received in the USSR.

Müller, Friedrich Max (1823–1900) German philologist and Orientalist, specialist in Indology and comparative religion. In 1846 he moved to Britain and between 1868 and 1875 he was the first Professor of Comparative Philology at Oxford University.

Noiré, Ludwig (1829–89) German philologist and monist philosopher. His work on the origin of language as lying in labour organisation was influential among Russian Marxists in the 1920s and 30s.

Ol'denburg, Sergei Fedorovich (1863–1934) Russian Orientalist specialising in Buddhism and Indology. One of the students of Viktor Rozen. A founding member of the Cadet Party and a confidant of Lenin. From 1904 to 1929 he served as Permanent Secretary of the Academy of Sciences.

Ordzhonikidze, Grigorii Konstantinovich (1886–1937) His Party nickname was Sergo. A Georgian Bolshevik, member of the Central Committee 1912–17, 1921–7 and 1934–7. From 1922–6 he was prominent in the North Caucasus Party Regional Committee. He held several significant positions, including Commissar for Heavy Industry from 1930.

Otswald, Friedrich Wilhelm (1853–1932) Latvian-born German chemist. Supporter of philosophical monism and eugenics.

Ozhegov, Sergei Ivanovich (1900–64). Russian lexicographer and Director of the Institute of Russian Language of the Soviet Academy of Sciences.

Pavlovich, Mikhail Pavlovich (pseudonym of Mikhail Lazarevich Vel'tman, 1871–1927) Also wrote under the pseudonym 'Volonter' before the revolution, when he was associated with the *Vpered* group. He had contacts with revolutionaries from Turkey, Iran, India, China and other Asian countries while in exile and wrote works about imperialism. After the October Revolution he worked in Narkomnats, the Commissariat of Nationalities where, *inter alia*, he established the *Vserossiiskaia nauchnaia assotsiatsiia vostokovedeniia*

[All-Russian Scientific Association of Orientalists, VNAV] and served as the editor of its journal *Novyi Vostok* [*The New East*].

Peretts, Vladimir Nikolaevich (1870–1935) Specialist in the history of Russian and Ukrainian medieval and early-modern literature, theatre and folklore. Professor at Kiev and St. Petersburg Universities, staff member of the Institute for the Comparative History of the Literatures and Languages of the West and East (ILIaZV). Arrested and sent into exile to Saratov in 1934, where he died the following year.

Peshkovskii, Aleksandr Matveevich (1878–1933) Russian linguist, a former student of Filipp F. Fortunatov and an author of *Russian Syntax in Scientific Representation* (1914), a popular textbook of Russian grammar for schools, the practical and academic value of which proved to be unsurpassed for several decades. In his works, Peshkovskii successfully combined formal and functional approaches to the study of language, which helped to narrow the methodological gap between the two. Peshkovskii's works also contain publications on Russian post-revolutionary orthography, stylistics and prosody.

Peterson, Mikhail Nikolaevich (1885–1962) Russian linguist who emerged from the Moscow Linguistic School, a member of the Moscow Linguistic Circle and a supporter of Saussure's linguistic theory. He is best remembered for his work on the Lithuanian language and on Russian syntax.

Pictet, Adolphe (1799–1875) Swiss linguist. Apart from introducing Saussure to philology, Pictet is best known for his monumental *Origines indo-européennes ou les Aryas primitifs: Essaie de paléontologie linguistique* (Pictet 1859–63), in which he attempted to reconstruct the world of the ancient Indo-Europeans.

Piłsudski, Józef Klemens (1867–1935) From November 1918, when Poland regained independence, until 1922, Piłsudski was Poland's Chief of State, commanding Polish forces in the 1919–21 Polish-Soviet War. He withdrew from politics in 1923, only to return to power in a *coup d'etat* in May 1926, in which he became the *de facto* ruler of Poland.

Platonov, Andrei (pseudonym of Andrei Platonovich Klimentov, 1899–1951) Russian proletarian writer, member of *Proletkul't*. His works from the first Five-Year-Plan period were subject to considerable criticism and many were not published until the 1980s.

Plekhanov, Georgii Valentinovich (1856–1918) Russian revolutionary and Marxist theorist. Established the first Russian Marxist group, the Emancipation of Labour Group [*Gruppa Osvobozhdenie Truda*], in 1883 and played a major role in Russian politics until shortly after the 1905 Revolution.

Pletnev, Valerian Fedorovich (1882–1942) Russian writer and critic, one of the leaders of *Proletkul't*. A member of the Bolsheviks from 1904, his article 'Na ideologicheskom fronte' ['On the Ideological Front'], published in *Pravda* in 1922, drew sharp criticisms from Lenin for fetishising proletarian life.

Polivanov, Evgenii Dmitrevich (1891–1938) Russian linguist, Orientalist and opponent of Marr's 'new theory of language'. He publicly opposed Marr's theory at a special session of the Communist Academy in Moscow in 1929, after which he worked in Uzbekistan. He played an important role in the codification and standardisation of several Turkic languages in the USSR, including the development of Latin scripts for those languages. He was arrested in 1937 and shot the following year.

Poppe, Nikolai Nikolaevich (1897–1991) Soviet, German and American linguist, specialist in Altaic languages spoken on the territory of the USSR. Poppe was the author of some significant publications on Bashkir, Chuvash, Mongolic, Altaic and Sakha languages, to the codification of many of which he actively contributed in the 1920s–30s. In 1944 he emigrated to Germany and then to the USA, where he continued his research work at Washington University.

Porzhezinskii Viktor Karlovich (Porzeziński Jan Viktor, 1870–1929) Russian and Polish linguist, a student of Fortunatov and a specialist in Baltic languages. Co-founder and the first Chairperson of the Moscow Linguistic Society (1918–23).

Potebnia, Aleksandr Afanasievich (1835–91) Russian linguist, ethnographer and literary critic. Representative of the Humboldtian and *völkerpsychologische* trends in Russia.

Pott, August Friedrich (1802–87) German linguist. As professor of General Linguistics at the University of Halle from 1833, Pott developed modern etymological studies on the basis of the correspondence of sounds occurring in related words in the Indo-European languages.

Radtsig, Sergei Ivanovich (1882–1968) Russian classicist and philologist.

Rakovskii, Khristian Georgievich (1873–1941) Bulgarian revolutionary and Bolshevik. Chairman of the Provisional Revolutionary Government of the Workers and Peasants of Ukraine 1919–23. An activist in the Left Opposition.

Rask, Rasmus (1787–1832) Danish philologist who established the connection of Northern and Gothic languages with Lithuanian, Slavonic, Greek and Latin.

Renan, Joseph Ernest (1823–92) French Orientalist, philosopher and philologist. Known especially for his histories of early Christianity.

Riazanov, David (pseudonym of David Borisovich Goldendakh, 1870–1938) Russian-Jewish Marxist revolutionary and scholar. A member of the Bolshevik Party from August 1917, he was the founder of the Marx-Engels Institute in 1921 and editor of the works of Marx and Engels. He was a prominent victim of the Stalinist terror.

Romm, Aleksandr Il'ich (1898–1945) Russian philologist and poet. A member of the Moscow Linguistic Circle, he produced the first Russian translation of Saussure's *Cours*, but this was not completed.

Rostovtsev, Mikhail Ivanovich (1870–1952) Russian and American historian and classicist. A specialist in the economic history of the Black Sea region. A member of the Petrograd Academy of Sciences in 1917, he emigrated the following year, settling in the United States in 1920.

Rozen, Baron Viktor Romanovich (1849–1908) Russian Orientalist, founder of the St. Petersburg School of Oriental Studies, member of the Russian Academy of Sciences from 1890.

Rozenberg, Otton Ottonovich (1888–1919) Russian Buddhologist.

Rudnev, Andrei Dmitrovich (1878–1938) Russian Orientalist and Mongolist.

Samoilovich, Aleksandr Nikolaevich (1880–1938) Russian Orientalist, specialist in Turkic languages. Organiser of the First Turkological Congress in 1926. Arrested in 1937 and shot the following year. Rehabilitated in 1956.

Shcherba, Lev Vladimirovich (1880–1944) A former student of Baudouin de Courtenay, a founder of the Leningrad Phonetic School, professor at St. Petersburg/Leningrad University and a school pedagogue, Shcherba published extensively on the sound systems of European languages, as well as on the general questions of language theory and practice. Like Baudouin, he was also interested in the problem of the mixing of non-related or distantly related languages. He actively contributed to the process of codification of post-revolutionary Russian.

Schleicher, August (1821–68) German linguist who presented linguistics as a natural science and viewed language as an organism. Also wrote a *Compendium of the Comparative Grammar of the Indo-European Languages* (Schleicher 1874), in which he attempted to reconstruct the Proto-Indo-European language.

Schmidt, Wilhelm (1868–1954) Austrian ethnographer, anthropologist and linguist who studied the languages of south-east Asia and posited the existence of an 'Austric' group of languages.

Serge, Viktor (Pseudonym of Viktor L'vovich Kibal'chich, 1890–1947) Belgian-born Russian revolutionary and writer. Originally an anarchist, he became a Bolshevik on arrival in Petrograd in 1919. He joined the Left Opposition, was expelled from the Party and arrested in 1928 before leaving the USSR and finally settling in Mexico, where he died.

Selishchev, Afanasii Matveevich (1886–1942) Russian linguist and philologist, worked on the history of the Russian language, the comparative grammar of Slavonic languages, Slavonic dialects in the Balkans and on Slavonic palaeography. In the early years after the revolution, he was best known for his study of changes in the Russian language in the wake of World War I, the October Revolution and the Civil War. He was arrested in 1934 but returned to Moscow three years later.

Shafir, Iakov Moiseevich (1887–?) Soviet journalist, author of books on the language of the press.

Shakhmatov, Aleksei Aleksandrovich (1864–1920) Russian philologist and historian who worked to establish the historical study of the Russian language and ancient-Russian literature. Though a member of the Moscow Linguistic School, in later years Shakhmatov moved to St. Petersburg, where he participated in the post-revolutionary orthographic reforms of the Russian language and worked on questions of language and thought.

Shcherbatskoi, Fedor Ippolitovich (1866–1942) Russian Orientalist, specialising in Buddhism, India and Tibet. A member of the Russian Academy of Sciences from 1918.

Shishmarev Vladimir Fedorovich (1874–1957) Russian philologist and a senior student of Veselovskii. Specialist in Romance languages and cultures. Member of the USSR Academy of Sciences from 1946.

Shklovskii, Viktor Borisovich (1893–1984) Russian literary critic and author. One of the founders of the Society for the Study of Poetic Language (OPOIAZ).

Shor, Rozaliia Osipovna (1894–1939) Russian linguist, literary historian and Orientalist. Her main works were on German and ancient-Indian linguistics, general linguistics and the history of linguistics. She initiated the publication of a series of translations of Western linguists in the 1930s, leading to the first Russian publications of Sapir, Vendryes and Saussure.

Shneider, Aleksandr Karlovich (1889–1938) Russian literary scholar. Specialised in the 'living word', working at IZhS, IS and GAKhN.

Shpet, Gustav Gustavovich (1879–1937) Russian philosopher, psychologist, theoretician of the arts and translator. He studied under, *inter alia*, Edmund Husserl and went on to develop a somewhat idiosyncratic, phenomenological approach to language that was to have a significant influence in the early USSR. He was arrested for alleged participation in an anti-Soviet organisation and shot in November 1937.

Shpil'rein, Isaak Naftulovich (1891–1937) Russian psychologist and leader of psychotechnics in the USSR. A participant in *Liga Vremia*. The author of a significant number of works about applied psychology, most notably *The Language of the Red Army Soldier* in 1928. He was arrested and shot as a Trotskyist in 1937.

Shumskii, Aleksandr Iakovlevich (1890–1946) Soviet state and Party figure. An active participant in the policy of Ukrainisation. Arrested in 1933 and sent to the GULAG.

Simmel, Georg (1858–1918) German sociologist and philosopher whose anti-positivist works were influential on many Russian Marxists.

Sobolevskii, Aleksei Ivanovich (1856/7–1929) Russian Slavist, specialist in Russian ethnography, palaeography, the history of the Russian literary language and the historical dialectology of Slavonic languages.

Sokolov, Boris Matveevich (1889–1930) Soviet folklorist whose book (written with his brother Iurii (1889–1941)) *Russian Folklore* (Sokolov 1966 [1938]) became the standard textbook on the question for use in Russian universities. On publication, the book bore only the name of the surviving brother, Iurii.

Spencer, Herbert (1820–1903) British philosopher, sociologist and political theorist. Particularly influential in Russia because of his theories of social evolution.

Spitzer, Leo (1887–1960) Austrian Romance philologist. A member of the Vossler school of literary stylistics before emigrating in 1933. Spitzer's stylistics was influential on literary scholars in Russia in the 1920s and some of his articles were translated into Russian.

Steinthal, Haymann (1823–99) German philologist and philosopher. Joint founder, with his brother-in-law Moritz Lazarus, of *Völkerpsychologie* [cultural psychology] and, in 1860, the journal *Zeitschrift für Völkerpsychologie und Sprachwissenschaft*.

Stroeva, Tatiana Viktorovna (1907–81) Russian philologist, a student of Zhirmunskii and Shcherba.

Struve, Peter Berngardovich (1870–1944) Russian economist, philosopher and publicist. Began his career as a 'legal Marxist' before becoming a liberal. He joined the White movement and left Russia for Paris in 1920.

Struve, Vasilii Vasil'evich (1889–1965) Russian Orientalist (Egyptologist and Assyriologist). A founding figure in the creation of the school of Soviet historians of the ancient East. A member of the USSR Academy of Sciences from 1935.

Sultan-Galiev, Mirsaid (1892–1940) Tatar revolutionary who joined the Bolsheviks in November 1917 and was one of the chief architects of Muslim national communism. He played an important role during the Russian Civil War, but in the early 1920s he came into conflict with Stalin's nationality policies and was briefly arrested, before being expelled from the Party. He supported the Left Opposition and was arrested again in 1928 and in 1937. He was shot in January 1940.

Tiumenev, Aleksandr Il'ich (1880–1959) Russian Marxist historian, a specialist in the history of the ancient world. A Research Fellow at the Leningrad Communist Academy (1928–31) and at GAIMK (1931–8). A member of the USSR Academy of Sciences from 1932.

Tomashevskii, Boris Viktorovich (1890–1957) Russian literary scholar, at different times active in both the Moscow and Petrograd trends of Russian Formalism.

Tomson, Aleksandr Ivanovich (1860–1935) Russian linguist, a member of Fortunatov's Linguistic Circle, a specialist in diachronic and experimental phonetics, the history of Slavic and Armenian languages and Russian orthography.

Trubetskoi, Nikolai Sergeevich (1890–1938) Russian linguist who emigrated to Prague after the Revolution, where he developed the sub-discipline of phonology. He was also involved in the Eurasian movement.

Tylor, Edward Burnett (1832–1917) British anthropologist, particularly influential in Russia and elsewhere for his theories of cultural evolution. His works *Primitive Culture* (Tylor 1871) and *Anthropology* (Tylor 1881) were translated into Russian and republished several times in the Soviet period. His so-called 'doctrine of survivals' was particularly influential on Marrism.

Tynianov, Iurii Nikolaevich (1894–1943) Russian novelist, literary critic, theorist and translator. Tynianov became perhaps the leading figure in the development of the so-called 'formal method' in the late 1920s in Leningrad, developing, *inter alia*, an influential theory of literary evolution.

Uhland, Ludwig (1787–1862) German poet, philologist and literary historian. One of the founders of historical philology.

Ul'ianova, Mariia Il'inichna (1878–1937) Russian revolutionary and younger sister of Lenin. One of the main organisers of the *Rabsel'kor* movement after the revolution.

Ushakov, Dmitri Nikolaevich (1873–1942) Russian linguist, a member of Fortunatov's Linguistic Circle, Head of the Moscow Dialectology Committee (later – the Dialectology Committee at Narkompros), a member of the Orthography Committee at Narkompros, the author of the first post-revolutionary dictionary of the Russian language, also known as The Ushakov Dictionary (Ushakov 1935–40). Ushakov played a key role in the codification of the Russian language in the 1930s. In his works on the topic, he argued for the importance of a balanced combination of the new linguistic elements of the Soviet period with the well-established classical traditions of the Russian literary language.

Ustrialov, Nikolai Vasil'evich (1890–1937) Russian jurist, philosopher and political activist, regarded as the founder of Russian 'National Bolshevism' as represented by the 1921 collection, *Smena Vekh* [*Changing Landmarks*] (Kliuchnikov *et al.* 1921). The idea behind the collection was that the October

Revolution should be accepted because it had managed to conserve a unified and powerful Russian state.

Vendryes, Joseph (1875–1960) French linguist who developed the ideas of the French sociological school that had been established by Meillet.

Veselovskii, Aleksandr Nikolaevich (1838–1906) Russian literary historian, member of the Russian Academy of Sciences from 1877. One of the most influential figures in Russian philology, he taught a large number of early Soviet literary specialists and was one of the founders of the discipline of comparative literature.

Vinokur, Georgii Osipovich (1896–1947) Russian linguist and literary scholar who was particularly concerned with the stylistics of the Russian language and its relationship to socio-historical factors. Vinokur was an early member of the Moscow Linguistic Circle and went on to work at a number of significant Moscow institutes.

Volodarskii, V. (pseudonym of Moisei Markovich Goldshtein, 1891–1918) Russian revolutionary and renowned orator. Became a Bolshevik in July 1917 and was assassinated in June 1918.

Voloshinov, Valentin Nikolaevich (1895–1936) Russian linguist and literary scholar. A member of the Bakhtin Circle and senior researcher at ILIaZV in 1925–32. Best known for his 1929 book, *Marxism and the Philosophy of Language* (Vološinov 1973 [1929]), in which verbal interaction is foregrounded.

Vossler, Karl (1872–1934) German linguist and specialist in Romance philology. Several of his works were translated into Russian in the period before 1929 and his development of literary and linguistic stylistics proved influential for a number of Russian scholars, including Viktor Zhirmunskii and members of the so-called Bakhtin Circle.

Vsevolodskii-Gerngross, Vsevolod Nikolaevich (1882–1962) Russian actor and historian of the theatre. Founding director of IZhS.

Vygotskii, Lev Semenovich (1896–1934) Russian psychologist and leader of the so-called 'cultural-historical school'. Vygotskii's work on psychological theory, child development, 'defectology' (disability studies) and the psychology of language were key developments in Soviet psychology and continue to exert a significant influence in the discipline internationally.

Wrede, Victor Karl Paul Ferdinand (1863–1934) German linguist. Pioneer of German dialect geography.

Winckler, Hugo (1863–1913) German archaeologist and historian. Wrote extensively on Assyria and Babylonia and conducted important excavations of the Hittite civilisation.

Wundt, Wilhelm (1832–1920) German psychologist and philosopher.

Zasulich, Vera Ivanovna (1849–1919) Russian Populist, socialist and writer. In 1883 she became a Marxist and joined Plekhanov's Emancipation of Labour group. She translated some works of Marx and Engels and corresponded with Marx at the end of his life.

Zelinskii Faddei Frantsevich (1859–1944) Polish-Russian classicist, promoter of the idea of the 'Third Renaissance'. Collaborated with TEO Narkomprosa after the revolution but emigrated in 1920.

Zhebelev, Sergei Aleksandrovich (1867–1941) Russian philologist and classicist, a specialist in ancient history and archaeology. A Professor at St. Petersburg and Leningrad University in 1904–27 and a member of the USSR Academy of Sciences from 1927, from which time he worked at GAIMK, directing study of the northern Black Sea region in antiquity.

Zhirmunskii, Viktor Maksimovich (1891–1971) Russian linguist and literary scholar. Member of the Academy of Sciences of the USSR from 1966.

Zinder, Lev Rafailovich (1904–95) Russian philologist, a student of Zhirmunskii. A specialist in the phonetics of German.

Zinov'ev, Grigorii Evseevich (pseudonym of Grigorii Evseevich Radomyl'skii Apfel'baum, 1883–1936) Russian-Jewish revolutionary and leading Bolshevik. One of the closest confidants of Lenin before the October Revolution, he occupied a number of key governmental and Party positions after 1917, including Chair of the Executive Committee of the Comintern in 1917–26. After opposing the Left Opposition in 1923–4, he joined with Kamenev and Trotsky in the 'United Opposition', which was defeated in 1927. He was arrested and shot in 1936.

Zoshchenko, Mikhail Mikhailovich (1895–1958). Soviet author and satirist. A pioneer of *skaz* narration.

Institutions

AzGNII (*Azerbaidzhanskii gosudarstvennyi nauchno-issledovatel'skii institut*) [Azerbaijan State Scientific Research Institute]. Originally founded as the Society for the Examination and Study of Azerbaijan within *Narkompros* in 1923, it was brought under the jurisdiction of the Central Committee of the Azerbaijan Communist Party (AZTsIK) in 1925 and became a Party research institute in 1930.

GAIMK (*Gosudarstvennaia akademiia istorii material'noi kul'tury*) [State Academy for the History of Material Culture]. Established as the *Rossiiskaia* *akademiia istorii material'noi kul'tury* [Russian Academy for the History of Material Culture, RAIMK] in 1919 and reorganised as GAIMK in 1926. It was the original basis for Marrist scholars after the revolution. The institute subsequently became the *Institut istorii materialnoi kul'tury* [Institute of the History of Material Culture, IIMK] of the Soviet Academy of Sciences in 1937.

GAKhN (*Gosudarstvennaia akademiia khudozhestvennykh nauk*) [State Academy for Artistic Studies]. Opened in October 1921 on the initiative of Lunacharskii as *Rossiiskaia akademiia khudozhestvennykh nauk* [Russian Academy for Artistic Studies], with the sociologist of literature P.S. Kogan as President and the philosopher G.G. Shpet as Vice-President. Reorganised and purged in 1930.

Glavnauka (*Glavnoe upravlenienauchnymi, nauchno-khudozhestvennymi i muzeinymi uchrezhdeniiami*) [Chief Direction of Scientific, Scholarly-Artistic and Museum Establishments]. State body coordinating the research profiles in science and culture in the USSR 1921–30. It was originally established as the Academic Centre of Narkompros in 1921.

Glavpolitprosvet (*Glavnyi politiko-prosvetitel'nyi komitet Respubliki*) [The Chief Political Enlightenment Committee of the Republic]. Narkompros committee established in November 1920 to conduct political enlightenment among the adult masses, including the eradication of illiteracy, adult education, clubs, libraries and Party education. The chair was Lenin's wife, Nadezhda Krupskaia. In June 1930 it was reorganised as a sector for mass work in Narkompros.

IIaL (*Institut iazyka i literatury*) [Institute of Language and Literature]. Moscow institute administered by RANION from 1925 as the sister institute of ILIaZV.

IIaM (*Institut iazyka i myshleniia AN SSSR*) [Institute of Language and Thinking of the Academy of Sciences of the USSR], founded in Petrograd by N.Ia Marr as the *Institut Iafeticheskikh issledovanii* [Institute of Japhetic Research] in 1921, *Iafeticheskii Institut* [Japhetic Institute] 1922–1930. IIaM functioned until 1950 when it was merged with the *Institut russkogo iazyka* [Institute of the Russian Language] into a unitary *Institut iazykoznaniia AN SSSR* [Institute of Linguistics of the Academy of Sciences of the USSR].

ILIaZV (*Nauchno-issledovatel'skii institut sravnitel'noi istorii literatur i iazykov Zapada i Vostoka*) [Scientific Research Institute for the Comparative History of the Literatures and Languages of the West and East]; *Institut im. A.N. Veselovskogo* [Aleksandr Veselovskii Institute] 1921–3; *Gosudarstvennyiinstitut rechevoi kul'tury* [State Institute for Discursive Culture] 1930–3. Research institute organised within Petrograd University, but falling within the orbit of RANION in 1925. Eventually became the philology faculty of Leningrad State University.

INV (*Nauchno-issledovatel'skii institut narodov vostoka*) [*Scientific Research Institute of the Peoples of the East*]. Moscow institute administered by RANION from 1927. Originally *Nauchno-issledovatel'skii institut etnicheskoi i natsional'noi kul'tur narodov vostoka* formed within Glavnauka Narkompros in 1924.

IS (*Institut slova*) [Institute of the Word]. Moscow institute originally formed as the *Kursy diktsii i deklamatsii* [Courses in Diction and Declamation] in Moscow 1913–19, reorganised as the *Gosudarstvennyi institut deklamatsii* [State Institute of Declamation] in the autumn of 1919 and renamed as IS in the autumn of 1920. Closed in 1922, when it was incorporated into the structures of GAKhN. The institute came under the orbit of *TEO Narkomprosa* and trained actors, public readers and specialists in oratory.

IZhS (*Institut zhivogo slova*) [Institute of the Living Word]. Petrograd institute originally formed within *TEO Narkomprosa* in 1919. Subsequently the oratory section became *Goskursy tekhniki rechi* [State Courses in Speech Techniques] in 1924 and *Institut agitatsii im. V. Volodarskogo* [Volodarskii Institute of Agitation] in 1930.

Narkompros (*Narodnyi Kommissariat Prosveshcheniia*) [People's Commissariat of Enlightenment]. State body administering the cultural and state-educational sphere in the USSR in the 1920s and 1930s. Formed immediately after the October Revolution with Lunacharskii remaining its head until 1930.

NIIaZ (*Nauchno-issledovatel'skii institut iazykoznaniia*) [Scientific Research Institute in Linguistics]. Moscow research institute within the Commissariat of Enlightenment 1931–3. The institutional base for the group *Iazykfront*, it was closed soon after their unsuccessful challenge against Marrism.

Proletkul't (*Proletarskie kul'turno-prosvetitel'nye organizatsii*) [Proletarian Cultural-Enlightenment Organisations]. A mass movement of cultural-enlightenment and literary-artistic organisations for workers' self-activity. Formed a week before the October Revolution, it was subordinated to Narkompros in 1920. It existed from 1917–32, but underwent significant decline from 1922.

RANION (*Rossiiskiia assotsiatsia nauchno-issledovatel'skikh institutov obshchestvennykh nauk*) [Russian Association of Scientific Research Institutes in the Social Sciences]. State body administering a range of non-Party social-science institutes in 1925–30.

RAPP (*Rossiiskaia assotsiatsiia proletarskikh pisatel'ei*) [Russian Association of Proletarian Writers]. Literary group originally formed as VAPP, *Vserossiiskaia assotsiatsiia proetarskikh pisatel'ei* [All-Russian Association of Proletarian

Writers] in 1925. From 1926 it published the journal *Na literaturnom postu,* which was subsequently renamed *Na postu.* The General Secretary was L.L. Averbakh. RAPP was liquidated by decree in April 1932.

TEO **Narkomprosa** (*Teatral'noe otdelenie Narkomprosa*) [Theatrical Section of the Commissariat of Enlightenment] established by Anatolii Lunacharskii in 1918. Reorganised and ceased to exist as such in 1920.

VNAV (*Vserossiiskaia nauchnaia assotsiatsiia vostokovedeniia*) [All-Russian Scientific Association of Orientalists]. Formed within the Commissariat of Nationalities (Narkomnats) in 1921 to study the East and to help the Soviet government adopt the correct policy towards its people.

Vol'fila (*Vol'naia filosofskaia assotsiatsiia*) [Free Philosophical Association]. Petrograd-based association created on the initiative of Ivanov-Razumnik and Belyi, but involving many prominent intellectuals in the period 1918–24. Its mission was to work on problems of cultural creativity 'in the spirit of philosophy and socialism'.

VTsKNTA (*Vsesoiuznyi tsentral'nyi komitet novogo tiurkskogo alfavita*) [All-Union Central Committee of the New Turkic Alphabet]. All-Union body set up in 1927 on the basis of the *Komitet novogo tiurksogo alfavita* [Committee for the New Turkic Alphabet] in Baku (1922–7), to coordinate the Latinisation of Turkic alphabets in the USSR. It moved to Moscow in 1930.

Bibliography

Archival Sources

References given in the text correspond to the acronym for the repository followed by the number of the fond, the inventory [*opis'*], the file [*delo, edinitsa khraneniia*] and the sheet [*list*] with ob. [*oborotnoe*] indicating the verso of a sheet. In cases where a specific title of an archival document is significant and available, this is also provided.

Russia
Arkhiv rossiiskoi akademii nauk. ARAN (Moscow)
Fond #397 Institut mirovoi literatury
Fond #468 Karinskii, Nikolai Mikhailovich
Fond #677 Institut iazyka i pis'mennosti narodov SSSR
Fond #678 Institut iazyka i myshleniia im. N.Ia. Marra

Gosudarstvennyi arkhiv rossiiskoi federatsii. GARF (Moscow)
Fond #A-2306 Narkompros
Fond #A-2307 Glavnauka Narkomprosa;
Fond #A-4655 Rossiiskaia assotsiatsiia nauchno-issledovatel'skikh institutov obshchestvennykh nauk (RANION)

Otdel' arkhivnykh dokumentov rossiiskoi natsional'noi biblioteki OADRNB (St. Petersburg)
Fond #10 Lichnyi sostav

Rossiiskii gosudarstvennyi arkhiv literatury i iskusstva. RGALI (Moscow)
Fond #941 Gosudarstvennaia akademiia khudozhestvennykh nauk
Fond #1230 Proletkul't
Fond #2238 Shneider, Aleksandr Karlovich
Fond #2889 Kreps, Vladimir Mikhailovich

Rossiiskii gosudarstvennyi arkhiv sotsial'no-politicheskoi istorii. RGASPI (Moscow)
Fond #495 Ispolnitel'nyi komitet Kominterna
Fond #513 Kommunisticheskaia partiia Italii

Rukopisnyi otdel' instituta rossiiskoi literatury (Pushkinskii dom). RO IRLI (St. Petersburg)
Fond #474 Siunnerberg, Konstantin

Sankt Peterburgskii filial arkhiva rossiiskoi akademii nauk. PFA RAN (St. Petersburg)

Fond #77 Institut iazyka i myshleniia im.N.Ia. Marra

Fond #135 Institut po izucheniiu narodov SSSR AN SSSR

Fond #208 Ol'denburg, Sergei F.

Fond #302 Leningradskoe otdelenie tsentral'nogo instituta iazyka i pis'mennosti narodov SSSR (LOTsIIaP)

Fond #800 Marr, Nikolai Iakovlevich

Fond #827 Derzhavin, Nikolai

Fond #853 Frank-Kamenetskii, Izrail' Grigor'evich

Fond #909 Orbeli, I.A.

Fond #1001 Zhirmunskii, Viktor Maksimovich

Fond # R.IV op 24 Neofilologicheskoe obshchestvo pri petrogradskom universitete

Tsentralnyi gosudarstvennyi arkhiv (Sankt Peterburg) TsGA (St. Petersburg)

Fond #2551 Teatral'nyi otdel Narkomprosa

Tsentralnyi gosudarstvennyi arkhiv literatury i iskusstva. TsGALI (St. Petersburg)

Fond #288 Nauchno-issledovatel'skii institut sravnitel'noi istorii literatur i iazykov Zapada i Vostoka (ILIaZV)

Fond #328 Leningradskii institut istorii, filosofii, literatury i lingvistiki.

Tsentral'nyi gosudarstvennyi arkhiv istoriko-politicheskikh dokumentov. TsGAIPD (St. Petersburg)

Fond #8720 Institut agitatsii im. Volodarskogo

Azerbaijan

Gosudarstvennyi arkhiv azerbaizhanskoi respubliki. GAAR. (Baku).

Fond #57 Narkompros Azerbaizhanskoi SSR (1920–43)

Fond #103 Tsentral'nyi komitet novogo azerbaizhanskogo alfavita pri AzTsIK (1922–6)

Fond #389 Obshchestvo obsledovaniia i izucheniia Azerbaizhana pri Narkomate Prosveshcheniia Azerbaizhanskoi SSR (1923–5); Obshchestvo obsledovaniia i izucheniia Azerbaizhana pri ATsIK (1925–9); Obshchestvo obsledovaniia i izuche-niia pri Azerbaizhanskom gosudarstvenyu nauchno-issledovatel'skii institut (AzGII, 1930–2)

Fond #387 Azerbaizhanskii gosudarstvennyi nauchno-issledovatel'skii institut (AzGII, 1929–32)

Ukraine

Tsentral'nyi derzhavnii arkhiv gromads'kikh ob'edhan' Ukraïni (TsDAGOU). Kiev.

Fond #1. Tsentral'nii komitet komunistichnoï partii Ukraïni.

Tsentral'nyi derzhavnii arkhiv vishchikh organiv vladi Ukraïni (TsDAVOVU). Kiev.
Fond #166. Narkompros Ukrainskogo SSR.

Published Sources

Dates of publication of the editions used are given, followed by the date of the original
text in square brackets where appropriate. This is particularly important in cases
where the date of the original has historical importance for the narrative of the study.

Abaev, Vasilli Ivanovich 2006 [1934], 'Iazyk kak ideologiia i iazyk kak tekhnika', in *Stat'i po teorii i istorii iazykoznaniia*, Moscow: Nauka.

Abdel-Malek, Anouar 1963, 'Orientalism in Crisis', *Diogenes*, 11: 103–40.

Agard, Frederick B. *et al.* (eds.) 1983, *Essays in Honor of Charles F. Hockett*, Leiden: Brill.

Ahmad, Ajaz 1992, *In Theory: Classes, Nations, Literatures*, London: Verso.

Alapuro, Risto 1988, *State and Revolution in Finland*, Berkeley: University of California Press.

Alferov, N.N. 1970, *Vozniknovenie i razvitie rabsel'korovskogo dvizheniia v SSSR*, Moscow: Mysl'.

Alpatov, Vladimir Mikhailovich 2000a, 'What is Marxism in Linguistics?' in Brandist and Tihanov (eds.) 2000.

—— 2000b, *150 iazykov i politika 1917–2000*, Moscow: KRAFT + IV RAN.

—— 2004, *Istoriia odnogo mifa: Marr i Marrizm*, second edition, Moscow: URSS.

—— 2005, *Voloshinov, Bakhtin i lingvistika*, Moscow: Iazyki slavianskoi kul'tury.

—— 2010, 'Soviet Linguistics of the 1920s and 1930s and the Scholarly Heritage', in Brandist and Chown (eds. 2010).

—— 2012, *Iazykovedy, vostokovedy, istoriki*, Moscow: Iazyki slavianskikh kul'tur.

Amirova, T.T., *et al.* 1975, *Ocherki po istorii lingvistiki*, Moscow: Vostochnaia literatura.

Amsterdamska, Olga 1987, *Schools of Thought: The Development of Linguistics from Bopp to Saussure*, Dortrecht: Reidel.

Anderson, Kevin B. 2010, *Marx at the Margins: On Nationalism, Ethnicity, and Non-Western Societies*, Chicago: University of Chicago Press.

Anderson, Perry 1976, 'The Antinomies of Antonio Gramsci', *New Left Review*, I/100: 5–80.

—— 1979 [1976], *Considerations on Western Marxism*, London: Verso.

Andreeva, M.S. 1968, 'Kommunisticheskaia partiia-initsiator sozdaniia i rukovoditel' Glavpolitprosveta (1920–3 gg.)', *Voprosy istorii KPSS*, 6: 80–98.

Andrew, Edward 1983, 'Class in itself and Class against Capital: Karl Marx and His Classifiers', *Canadian Journal of Political Science*, 16, 3: 577–84.

Anon. 1914, 'Spisok chlenov Neofilologicheskogo obshchestva', *Zapiski Neofilologicheskogo Obshchestva pri Imperatorskom S.-Peterburgskom Universitete*, 1: 79–84.

———— 1920, 'Mezhdunarodnoe Biuro Proletkul'ta', *Proletarskaia kul'tura*, 17–19: 5.

———— 1923, *VAPP*, 'Ideologicheskii front i literatura', online at http://www.teencity.ru/projects/myaeots/bibl_11/manifest/proletcult/proletcult3.htm.

———— 1925, 'On The Policy Of The Party In The Sphere Of Artistic Literature', online at http://www.sovlit.com/decreejuly1925/.

———— 1930, 'Vazhneishii istoricheskii dokument: Itogi filosofskoi diskussii (Rezoliuciia Biuro iacheiki IKPF. i E. ot 29 dekabria 1930 g.)', *Pod znamenem Marksizma*, 10–12.

Anikeev, Nikolaj P. 1969, *Modern Ideological Struggle for the Ancient Philosophical Heritage of India*, Calcutta: Indian Studies Past and Present.

Aristotle 1991, *On Rhetoric*, Oxford: Oxford University Press.

Arvidsson, Stefan 1999, 'Aryan Mythology as Science and Ideology', *Journal of the American Academy of Religion*, 67, 2: 327–54.

Ashnin, F.D. and V.M. Alpatov 1994, *'Delo Slavistov' 30-e gody*, Moscow: Nasledie.

———— *et al.* 2002, *Repressirovannaia tiurkologiia*, Moscow: Vostochnaia literatura.

Aumüller, Mattheus, 2008, 'Viktor Žirminskij and German *Mundartforschung*', *Studies in East European Thought*, 60, 4: 295–306.

Avanesov, Ruben Ivanovich (ed.) 1981, *Teoriia iazyka, metody ego issledovaniia i prepodavaniia*, Leningrad: Nauka.

Averbakh, Leopol'd Leonidovich 1929, *Spornye voprosy kul'turnoi revoliutsii*, Moscow: Gosizdat.

———— 1931 [1929], 'O tselostnykh masshtabakh i chastnykh Makarakh', in *Iz RAPPovskogo dnevnika*, Leningrad: Izd. Pisatelei v Leningrade.

———— 1931, *Za gegemoniiu proletarskoi literatury*, Moscow: GIKhL.

Axelrod, Pavel 1898, *K voprosu o sovremennykh zadachakh i taktike russkikh sotsialdemokratov*, Geneva: Soiuz russkikh sotsial-demokratov.

Azadovskii, Mark K. 1935, 'Pamiati N.Ia. Marra', *Sovetskii fol'klor*, 2, 2: 5–20.

Babel, Isaak 2002, *Collected Stories*, New York: Norton.

Bachofen Johann, 1861, *Das Mutterrecht: eine Untersuchung über die Gynaikratie der alten Welt nach ihrer religiösen und rectlichen Natur*, Stuttgart: Krais & Hoffmann.

Bachtin, Nicholas M. 1963, *Lectures and Essays*, Birmingham: University of Birmingham.

———— 1963a, 'The Russian Revolution As Seen By a White Guard', in Bachtin 1963.

———— 1963b, 'The Symbolist Movement in Russia', in Bachtin 1963.

Backhaus, Jürgen (ed.) 2000, *Karl Bücher: Theory–History–Anthropology–Non Market Economies*, Metropolis: Marburg.

Bagrinskaia, Nina, 2004, 'Slavianskoe vozrozhdenie antichnosti', in S.N. Zenkin (ed.) *Russkaia Teoriia 1920–1930-e gody*, Moscow: RGGU.

Bailes, K. 1977, 'Aleksej Gastev and the Soviet Controversy over Taylorism, 1918–1924', *Soviet Studies*, 29, 3: 373–94.

Bairashevskii, O.A. 1928, 'Bolezni azerbaidzhanskogo naseleniia i rol' shkoly v ego ozdorovlenii', *Izvestiia Obsledovaniia i Izucheniia Azerbaidzhana*, 6: 224–43.

Bakhtin, Michail M. 1981, *The Dialogic Imagination: Four Essays*, University of Texas Press: Austin.

———— 1981a [1934–5], 'Discourse in the Novel', in Bakhtin 1981.

———— 2012 [1934–5], 'Slovo v romane', in *Sobranie sochinenii*, Vol. 3, Moscow: Iazyki slavianskikh kul'tur.

Balibar, Etienne and Immanuel Wallerstein 1991, *Race, Nation, Class: Ambiguous Identities*, London: Verso.

Bally, Charles 1926 [1913], *Le Langage et la Vie*, Paris: Payot.

Banaji, Jairus 2010, *Theory as History: Essays on Modes of Production and Exploitation*, Leiden: Brill.

Baron, Samuel H. 1963, *Plekhanov: The Father of Russian Marxism*, Stanford: Stanford University Press.

Bartol'd, Vasilii Vladimirovich 1963a [1900], 'Rech' pered zashchitoi dissertatsii', in *Sobranie sochinenii*, Vol. 1, Moscow: Vostochnaia literatura.

———— 1963b [1927], 'Istoriia kul'turnoi zhizni Turkestana', in *Sobranie sochinenii*, Vol. 2, Part 1, Moscow: Nauka.

———— 1964 [1918], 'Ulugbek i ego vremia', in *Sobranie sochinenii*, Vol. 2, Part 2, Moscow: Nauka.

———— 1966a [1918], 'Kul'tura Musul'manstva', in *Sobranie Sochinenii*, Vol. 6, Moscow: Nauka.

———— 1966b [1903], 'Teokraticheskaia ideia i svetskaia vlast' v musul'manskom gosu-darstve', in *Sobranie sochinenii*, Vol. 6, Moscow: Nauka.

———— 1968 [1896], 'Retsenzia na Léon Cahun *Introduction à la historoire de l'Asie. Turcs et Mongols des origins à 1405*', in *Sobranie sochinenii*, Vol. 5, Moscow: Nauka.

———— 1977a [1911], 'Istoriia izucheniia vostoka v Evrope i Rossii', in *Sobranie sochine-nii*, Vol. 9, Moscow: Nauka.

———— 1977b [1914], 'Zadachi russkogo vostokovedeniia v Turkestane', in *Sobranie sochinenii*, Vol. 9, Moscow: Nauka.

Bassin, Mark 1992, 'Geographical Determinism in Fin-de-siecle Marxism: Georgii Plekhanov and the Environmental Basis of Russian History', *Annals of the Association of American Geographers*, 82, 1: 3–22.

Batunskii, M.A. 2003, *Rossiia i Islam*, Vol. 3, Moscow: Progress-aTraditsiia.

Baudouin de Courtenay, J.N. 1972, *A Baudouin de Courtenay Anthology*, Bloomington: Indiana University Press.

———— 1972a [1889], 'On the Tasks of Linguistics', in Baudouin 1972.

———— 1972b [1901], 'On the Mixed Character of All Languages', in Baudouin 1972.

———— 1972c [1904], 'Linguistics of the Nineteenth Century', in Baudouin 1972.

Bayerlein, Bernard H. 1999, 'The Abortive "German October" 1923. New Light on the Revolutionary Plans of the Russian Communist Party, the Comintern and the German Communist Party', in McDermott and Morison (eds.) 1999.

Baziiantz, A.P. 1986. 'Dve vstrechi S.F. Ol'denburga s V.I. Leninym i razvitie sovetskogo vostokovedeniia', in Skriabin and Primakov (eds.) 1986.

Bazylev, V.N. and V.P. Neroznak (eds.) 2001, *Sumerki lingvistiki: Iz istorii otechestvennogo iazykoznaniia*, Moscow: Academia, 2001.

Beiser, Frederick 2003, *The Romantic Imperative: The Concept of Early German Romanticism*, Cambridge: Harvard University Press.

Beissinger, Mark R. 1988, *Scientific Management, Socialist Discipline, and Soviet Power*, London: I.B. Tauris.

Belichkov, N.F. (ed.) 1974, *Sovremennye problemy literaturovedeniia i iazykoznaniia*, Moscow: Nauka.

Belinsky, Vissarion 1963, 'Thoughts and notes on Russian literature', in Matlaw (ed.) 1963.

Belkin, S.M. 2002, 'Tema Tsitserona v tvorchestve F.F. Zelinskogo', *Mnemon: Issledovanie i publikatsii po istorii antichnogo mira*, 1: 357–70.

Belous, V.G. (ed.) 2005, *Vol'fila. Issledovanie po istorii russkoi mysli*, St. Petersburg: Tri kvadrata.

––––––– 2007, *Vol'fila ili Krizis kul'tury v zerkale obshchestvennogo samosoznaniia*, St. Petersburg: Mir.

Belykh, A.A. 1990, 'A.A. Bogdanov's Theory of Equilibrium and the Economic Discussions of the 1920s', *Soviet Studies*, 42, 3: 571–82.

Benes, Tuska 2004, 'Comparative Linguistics as Ethnology: In Search of Indo-Germans in Central Asia, 1770–1830', *Comparative Studies of South Asia, Africa and the Middle East*, 24, 2: 117–32.

––––––– 2008, *In Babel's Shadow: Language, Philology and the Nation in Nineteenth-Century Germany*, Detroit: Wayne State University Press.

Berd, R. (Bird, R.) 2006, 'Viach. Ivanov i massovye prazdnestva rannei sovetskoi epokhi' (2006), online at: http://imwerden.de/pdf/berd_vjach_ivanov_i_massovye_prazdnestva_2006_text.pdf.

Berdiaev, Nikolai 1909, 'Philosophic Truth and Moral Truth', in Berdyaev *et al.* 1977 [1909].

Berdyaev, Nikolai *et al.* 1977 [1909], *Landmarks: A Collection of Essays on the Russian Intelligentsia*, New York: Karz Howard.

Berezin, F.M. 1976, *Russkoe iazykoznanie kontsa XIX–nachala XX.*, Moscow: Nauka.

Bernal, Martin 1987, *Black Athena: The Afroasiatic Roots of Classical Civilization*, Vol. 1, *Fabrication of Ancient Greece 1785–1985*, London: Free Association Books.

Bezlepkin, N.I. 2002, *Filosofiia iazyka v Rossii*, St. Petersburg: Iskusstvo.

Bhaskar, Roy 1998 [1979], *The Possibility of Naturalism: A Philosophical Critique of the Contemporary Human Sciences*, London: Routledge.

Biebuyck, B. and Nell Grillaert 2003, 'Between God and *Übermensch*: Viacheslav Ivanovich Ivanov and His Vacillating Struggle with Nietzsche', *Germano-Slavica*, 14: 55–73.

Bierer, D. 1953, 'Renan and His Interpreters: A Study in French Intellectual Warfare', *Journal of Modern History*, 25, 4: 375–89.

Biggart, John 1981, ' "Anti-Leninist Bolshevism": The *Forward* Group of the RSDRP', *Canadian Slavonic Papers*, 23: 134–53.

———— 1982, 'Marxism and Social Anthropology – A Proletkul't Bibliography on the "History of Culture" (1923)', *Studies in Soviet Thought*, 24: 1–3 and 89–93.

———— 1987, 'Bukharin and the Origin of the "Proletarian Culture" Debate', *Soviet Studies*, 39, 2: 229–46.

———— 1990, 'Alexander Bogdanov and the Theory of a "New Class" ', *Russian Review*, 49, 3: 265–82.

———— 1992, 'Bukharin's Theory of Cultural Revolution', in *The Ideas of Nikolai Bukharin*, edited by A. Kemp-Welch, Oxford: Clarendon Press.

———— et al. (eds.) 1998, *Alexander Bogdanov and the Origins of Systems Thinking in Russia*, edited by John Biggart et al., Aldershot and Brookfield: Ashgate.

Biukher, K. [Bücher, K.] 1923, *Rabota i ritm*, Moscow: Novaia Moskva.

Blackledge, Paul 2006, 'Karl Kautsky and Marxist Historiography', *Science and Society*, 70, 3: 337–59.

———— (ed.) 2010, 'Symposium on Lars Lih's *Lenin Rediscovered*', *Historical Materialism*, 18, 3: 25–174.

Boas, Franz 1974 [1889], 'On Alternating Sounds', in Stocking (ed.) 1974.

Bocharova, N.A. 2003, 'A. Bogdanov i A Platonov: K postanovke voprosa', *Izvestiia Rossiiskogo gosudarstvennogo pedagogicheskogo instituta im. A.I. Gertsena*, 3, 5: 162–9.

Boduen de Kurtene, Ivan Aleksandrovich. [Baudouin de Courtenay, Jan Niecislaw Ignacy] 1906, *Proekt osnovnykh polozhenii dlia resheniia pol'skogo voprosa*, St. Petersburg: Sadovaia.

———— 1913, *Natsional'nyi priznak v avtonomii*, Moscow: Stasiulevich.

———— 1963 [1901], 'O smeshannom kharaktere vsekh iazykov', in *Izbrannye trudy po obshchemu iazykoznaniiu*, Vol. 1, Moscow: Akademiia nauk.

———— 1963a [1904], 'Iazykoznanie', in *Izbrannye trudy po obshchemu iazykoznaniiu*, Vol. 2, Moscow: Akademiia nauk.

———— 1963b [1904], 'Iazyk i iazyki', in *Izbrannye trudy po obshchemu iazykoznaniiu* Vol. 2, Moscow: Akademiia nauk.

———— 1963c [1908], 'Blatnaia muzyka', in Boduen de Kurtene, I.A. [Baudouin de Courtenay, J.N.], *Izbrannye trudy po obshchemu iazykoznaniiu*, Vol. 1, Moscow: Akademiia nauk.

Bogdanov, Alexander A. 1899, *Osnovnye elementy istoricheskogo vzgliada na prirodu*, St. Petersburg: Izdatel'.

―――― 1901, *Poznanie s istoricheskoi tochki zreniia*, St. Petersburg: Leifert.

―――― 1904, *Iz psikhologii obshchestva*, St. Petersburg: Dobratovskii.

―――― 1910, *Padenie Velikogo fetishizma (Sovremennyi krizis ideologii). Vera i nauka*, Moscow: Doboratovskii i Charushnikov.

―――― 1914, *Nauka ob obshchestvennom soznanii (kratkii kurs ideologicheskoi nauki v voprosakh i otvetakh)*, Moscow: Pisateli v Moskve.

―――― 1918, *Mezhdu chelovekom i mashinoiu*, second revised edition, Moscow: Volna.

―――― 1919, 'O tendentsiiakh proletarskoi kul'tury: otvet Gastevu', *Proletarskaia kul'tura*, 9–10: 46–52.

―――― 1923a [1913], *Filosofiia zhivogo opyta*, third edition, Moscow and Petrograd: Kniga.

―――― 1923b, 'Taina smekha', *Molodaia gvardiia* 2, 1923, online at www.bogdinst.ru/vestnik/v02_04.htm.

―――― 1925, 'Uchenie o refleksakh i zagadki pervobytnoe myshlenie', *Vestnik kommunisticheskoi akademii*, 10: 67–96.

―――― 1989 [1922], *Tektologiia: Vseobshchaia organizatsionnaia nauka*, 2 Vols., Moscow: Ekonomika, 1989.

―――― 1999 [1911], *Poznanie s istoricheskoi tochki zreniia: izbrannye psikhologicheskie trudy*, Moscow and Voronezh: Izd. Moskovskii psikhologo-sotsial'nyi institut.

―――― and I.I. Skvortsov-Stepanov 2011 [1925], *Kurs politicheskoi ekonomiki dokapitalisticheskoi epokhi*, Moscow: Librokom.

―――― and L.B. Krasin 1934 [1909], 'Otchet tovarishcham bol'shevikam ustranennykh chlenov rasshirennoi redaktsii "Proletariata" ' (July 1909), in *Protokoly soveshchaniia rasshirennoi redaktsii "Proletariia"*, Moscow: Partizdat, online at http://az.lib.ru/s/shuljatikow_w_m/text_1010.shtml.

Boothman, Derek 2008, 'The Sources for Gramsci's Concept of Hegemony', *Rethinking Marxism*, 20, 2: 201–15.

―――― 2010 'Translation and Translatability: Renewal of the Marxist Paradigm', in Ives and Lacorte (eds.) 2010.

Bopp, Franz 1868, *Vergleichende Grammatik des Sanskrit, Zend, Griechischen, Lateinischen, Litauischen, Gotischen und Deutschen*, Berlin: Dümmler.

Bordiugov, G.A. (ed.) 1995, *A.A. Bogdanov i gruppa RSDRP 'Vpered' 1908–1914*, Moscow: Airo-xx.

Borisenok, Elena 2006, *Fenomen sovetskoi ukrainizatsii*, Moscow: Evropa.

Brandenberger, David 2002, *National Bolshevism: Stalinist Mass Culture and the Formation of Modern Russian National Identity, 1931–1956*, New Haven: Harvard University Press.

Brandist, Craig 2003, 'The Origins of Soviet Sociolinguistics', *Journal of Sociolinguistics*, 7, 2: 213–33.

—— 2004, 'Voloshinov's Dilemma: On the Philosophical Roots of the Dialogical Theory of the Utterance', in Brandist *et al.* (eds.) 2004.

—— *et al.* (eds.) 2004, *The Bakhtin Circle: In the Master's Absence*, Manchester: Manchester University Press.

—— and Galin Tihanov (eds.) 2005, *Materializing Bakhtin: The Bakhtin Circle and Social Theory*, Houndmills: Macmillan.

—— 2005, 'Le marrisme et l'héritage de la *Völkerpsychologie* dans la linguistique soviétique', *Cahiers de l'ILSL*, 20: 39–56.

—— 2006, 'The Rise of Soviet Sociolinguistics From the Ashes of *Völkerpsychologie*', *Journal of the History of the Behavioral Sciences*, 42, 3: 261–77.

—— 2008, 'Sociological Linguistics In Leningrad: The Institute for the Comparative History of the Literatures and Languages of The West and East (ILJAZV) 1921–33', *Russian Literature* LXIII (II/III/IV): 171–200.

—— 2010, 'Psychology, Linguistics and the Rise of Applied Social Science in the USSR: Isaak Shpil'rein's *Language of the Red Army Soldier*', in Brandist and Chown (eds.) 2010.

—— and Mika Lähteenmäki 2010, 'Early Soviet Linguistics and Mikhail Bakhtin's Essays on the Novel of the 1930s', in Brandist and Chown (eds.) 2010.

—— and Katya Chown (eds.) 2010, *Politics and the Theory of Language in the USSR*, London: Anthem Press.

—— 2011, 'Semantic Paleontology and the Passage from Myth to Science and Poetry: The Work of Izrail' Frank-Kamenetskij (1880–1937)', *Studies in East European Thought*, 63: 43–61.

—— 2012a, 'The Cultural and Linguistic Dimensions of Hegemony: Aspects of Gramsci's Debt to Early Soviet Cultural Policy', *Journal of Romance Studies*, 13, 3: 24–43.

—— 2012b, 'Viktor Žirminskij on Evolution, Diffusion and Social Stratification in Literary Studies and Linguistics', *Russian Literature*, 72, 3–4: 385–423.

Brandist, K. (Brandist, C.) 2007, 'Konstantin Siunnerberg (Erberg) i issledovanie i prepodavanie zhivogo slova i publichnoi rechi v Leningrade 1918–1932gg', *Ezhegodnik rukopisnogo otdela Pushkinskogo doma 2003–2004*, St. Petersburg: Dmitri Bulanin.

Braun, Fedor A. 1922, *Die Urbevölkerung Europas und die Herkunft der Germanen*, Berlin: W. Kohlhammer.

—— 1924, *Pervobytnoe naselenie Evropy*, Berlin: Epokha.

Bregel, Yuri 1980, 'Barthold and Modern Oriental Studies', *International Journal of Middle East Studies*, 12, 3: 385–403.

Brennan, Timothy 2006, *Wars of Position: The Cultural Politics of Left and Right*, New York: Columbia University Press.

Broué, Pierre 2006 [1971] *The German Revolution, 1917–1923*, Chicago: Haymarket.

Brown, Edward J. 1971 [1953], *The Proletarian Episode in Russian Literature, 1928–1932*, New York: Octagon Books.

Brown, Robert 1877–8, *The Great Dionysiak Myth*, Vol. 1, London: Longmans.

Brown, Stephen 1995, 'Communists and the Red Cavalry: The Political Education of the *Konarmiia* in the Russian Civil War, 1918–1920', *Slavonic and East European Review*, 73, 1: 82–99.

Brunnbauer, U. 2000, '"The League of Time" (*Liga Vremia*): Problems of Making a Soviet Working Class in the 1920s', *Russian History/Histoire Russe*, 27, 4: 461–95.

Buci-Glucksmann, Christine 1980, *Gramsci and the State*, London: Lawrence and Wishart.

Budgen, Sebastian *et al.* (eds.) 2007, *Lenin Reloaded: Towards a Politics of Truth*, Durham: Duke University Press.

Bücher, Karl 1893, *Die Entstehung der Volkswirtschaft*, Tübingen: Lapp'sche Buchhandlung.

————— 1899, *Arbeit und Rhythmus*, Leipzig: Tübner.

Bühler, Karl Ludwig 1990, *Theory of Language: The Representational Function of Language*, Philadelphia: John Benjamins.

Bukhareva, M.A. 1977, 'E. Meier i konservativnoe napravlenie v burzhuaznoi istoricheskoi mysli xix–xxv', in Shofman (ed.) 1977.

Bukharin, Nikolai Ivanovich 1921, *Teoriia istoricheskogo materializma: Populiarnyi ocherk marksistskoi sotsiologii*, Moscow: Gosizdat.

————— 1922, 'Burzhuaznaia revoliutsiia i revoliutsiia proletarskaia', *Pod znamenem Marksizma*, 7–8: 61–82.

————— 1923, 'K postanovke problem teorii istoricheskogo materializma', *Vestnik sotsialisticheskoi akademii*, 3: 3–15.

————— 1926 [1924], *O rabkore*, Moscow: Pravda.

————— 1962 [1926], *Historical Materialism: A System of Sociology*, London: Allen and Unwin.

————— 1988 [1925], 'Novoe otkrovenie o sovetskoi ekonomike ili kak mozhno pogubit' raboche-krest'ianskii blok: K voprosu ob ekonomicheskom obosnovanii trotskizma 1925g.', in *Izbrannye proizvedeniia*, Moscow: Politicheskaia literatura.

————— 1993 [1925], 'Proletariat i voprosy khudozhestvennoi politiki', in *Revoliutsiia i kul'tura: Stat'i i vystupleniia 1923–1936 godov*, Moscow: Fond imeni N.I. Bukharina.

Bulgakov, Sergei Nikolaevich 1977 [1909], 'Heroism and Asceticism: Reflections on the Religious Nature of the Russian Intelligentsia', in Berdyaev *et al.* 1977.

Bunzl, M. 2003, '*Völkerpsychologie* and German-Jewish Emancipation', in Glen Penny and Bunzl (eds.) 2003.

Burbank, Jane *et al.* (eds.) 2007, *Russian Empire: Space, People, Power, 1700–1930*, Bloomington: Indiana University Press.

Bürger, Peter 1984, *The Theory of the Avant Garde*, Manchester: Manchester University Press.

Buttigeig, Joseph A. 1990, 'Gramsci's Method', *Boundary 2*, 17, 2: 60–81.

Buzeskul Vladislav Petrovich 1929–31, *Vseobshchaia istoriia i ee predstaviteli v Rossii XIX i nachale XX veka*, Leningrad: Akademiia nauk.

——— 1931, 'Eduard Meier: Nekrolog', *Izvestiia akademii nauk SSSR. Otdelenie Obshchestvennykh nauk*, 3: 259–68.

Byford, Andy 2005, 'The Rhetoric of Aleksandr Veselovskii's "Historical Poetics" and the Autonomy of Academic Literary Studies in Late Imperial Russia', *Slavonica*, 11, 2: 115–32.

Bykovskii, Sergei (ed.) 1932, *Protiv burzhuaznoi kontrabandy v iazykoznanii*, Leningrad: GAIMK.

Cadiot, Juliette 2005, 'Searching for Nationality: Statistics and National Categories at the End of the Russian Empire (1897–1917)', *Russian Review*, 64, 3: 440–55.

Callinicos, Alex 1985, 'The Politics of Marxism Today', *International Socialism*, 2, 29: 128–68.

——— 1995, *Theories and Narratives: Reflections on the Philosophy of History*, Oxford: Polity.

Carneiro, Robert L. 2003, *Evolutionism in Cultural Anthropology*, Boulder: Westview.

Carr, Edward Hallet 1969, *The Interregnum 1923–1924*, Harmondsworth: Penguin.

——— 1970, *Socialism in One Country 1924–1926*, Harmondsworth: Penguin.

Carrol, Joseph 2003, 'Introduction', in Charles Darwin, *On the Origin of Species by Natural Selection*, Toronto: Broadview Press.

Cartledge, Paul, 1996, 'Comparatively Equal', in Ober and Hendrick 1996.

Cassedy, Steven 1990, *Flight from Eden: The Origins of Modern Literary Criticism and Theory*, Berkeley: University of California Press.

——— 2009, 'Gustav Shpet and Phenomenology in an Orthodox Key', in Tihanov (ed.) 2009.

Cassirer, Ernst 1955 [1925], *The Philosophy of Symbolic Forms 2, Mythical Thought*, New Haven: Yale University Press.

Chagin, B.A. 1971, *Ocherk istorii sotsiologicheskoi mysli v SSSR (1917–1969)*, Leningrad: Nauka.

Chattopadhyaya, Debuprasad 1969, 'Introduction', in Stcherbatsky 1969.

Cherchi, Marcello and H. Paul Manning 2002, *Disciplines and Nations: Niko Marr vs. His Georgian Students on Tblisi State University and the Japhetidology/Caucasology Schism*, Carl Beck Papers no. 1603.

Chernov, Viktor 1911, 'Otkrovennaia kniga (A. Morskoi "Iskhod Russkoi revoliutsii 1905g i pravitel'stvo Nosaria)', *Sovremennik*, 7: 181–214.

Chibber, Vivek 2013, *Postcolonial Theory and the Specter of Capital*, London: Verso.

Chown, E. and Craig Brandist, 2007, 'Iz predistorii Instituta zhivogo slova: protokoly zasedanii kursov khudozhestvennogo slova', *Novoe literaturnoe obozrenie*, 86: 96–106.

Chuzhak, Nikolai 1923, 'Partiia i iskusskvo (K stat'e tov. Trotskogo v No. 209 "Pravdy")', *Gorn*, 9: 81–8.

Clark, Katerina and Evgeny Dobrenko (eds.) 2007, *Soviet Culture and Power: A History in Documents, 1917–1953*, New Haven: Yale University Press.

———— and Galin Tihanov 2011, 'Soviet Literary Theory in the 1930s: The Battles of Genre and the Boundaries of Modernity', in Dobrenko and Tihanov (eds.) 2011.

Clarke, Bruce and Linda Dalrymple (eds.) 2002, *From Energy to Information: Representation in Science and Technology, Art, and Literature*, Stanford: Stanford University Press.

Clement, Victoria 2005, *Rewriting the 'Nation': Turkmen Literacy, Language, and Power, 1904–2004*, Ph.D. diss., Ohio State University.

Clibbon, Jennifer 1993, *The Soviet Press and Grass-roots Organization: The Rabkor Movement, NEP to the First Five-Year Plan*, Ph.D. diss., University of Toronto.

Cliff, Tony 1986, *Lenin: Building the Party 1893–1914*, London: Bookmarks.

Cloeren, Hermann J. 1988, *Language and Thought: German Approaches to Analytic Philosophy in the 18th and 19th Centuries*, New York: Walter de Gruyter.

Coe, Steven 1996, 'Struggles for Authority in the NEP Village: The Early Rural Correspondents Movement, 1923–1927', *Europe-Asia Studies* 48, 7: 1151–71.

Cowan, Micheal J. 2008, *Cult of the Will: Nervousness and German Modernity*, Pennsylvania: Pennsyvania State University Press.

Danilov, Georgii Konstantinovich 1931, *Kratkii ocherk istorii nauki o iazyke*, Moscow: Izd. 1go MGU.

Danziger, Kurt 1983, 'Origins and basic principles of Wundt's *Völkerpsychologie*', *British Journal of Social Psychology*, 22: 303–13.

David-Fox, Michael 1997, *Revolution of the Mind: Higher Learning Among the Bolsheviks 1918–1929*, Ithaca: Cornell University Press.

———— et al. (eds.) 2006, *Orientalism and Empire in Russia*, Bloomington: Slavica.

Day, Richard B. 1990, 'The Myth of the "Super-Industrializer": Trotsky's Economic Policies of the 1920s', in Ticktin and Cox (eds.) 1990.

———— and Daniel Gaido (eds.) 2009, *Witnesses to Permanent Revolution: The Documentary Record*, Chicago: Haymarket.

Dement'eva, N.V. 1971, 'O nekotorykh ocobennostiakh estetiki i gnoseologii Proletkul'ta (Bogdanovskaia kontseptsiia "kollektivnogo opyta")', *Pisatel' i zhizn'*, 4: 124–37.

Desnitskaia, A.V. 1951, 'O roli antimarksistskoi teorii proiskhozhdeniia iazyka v obshchei sisteme vzgliadov N.Ia Marra', in Vinogradov and Serebrennikov (eds.) 1951.

——— 1974, 'Kak sozdavalas' teoriia natsional'nogo iazyka', in Belichkov (ed.) 1974.

——— 1981, 'O traditsiiakh sotsiologizma v russkom iazykoznanii', in Avanesov (ed.) 1981.

——— 1991, 'Frantsuzskie lingvisty i sovetskoe iazykoznanie 1920–1930kh godov', *Izvestiia akademii nauk SSSR: seriia literatury i iazyka*, 50, 5: 474–85.

——— *et al.* (eds.) 1969, *Voprosy sotsial'noi lingvistiki*, Leningrad: Nauka.

Desnitskii Vasilii A. 1938, 'A.N. Veselovskii v russkom literaturovedenii', *Izvestiia akademii nauk SSSR otdelenie obshchestvennykh nauk*, 4: 67–84.

Deutscher, Isaac 1982, 'The Tragedy of the Polish Communist Party', *The Socialist Register*, 19: 125–63.

Dhooge, B.W. 2012, 'G.O. Vinokur's "New Class Approach". A Possible Model for A.P. Platonov's Poetic Language?', *Russian Literature*, 72, 2: 153–200.

Diderot, Denis and Jean le Rond d'Alembert (eds.) 1757–72, *Encyclopédie, ou dictionnaire raisonné des sciences, des arts et des métiers*, Paris: André le Breton, Michel-Antoine David, Laurent Durand, and Antoine-Claude Briasson.

Dietzgen, Joseph 1906 [1870–5], *Philosophical Essays*, Chicago: Charles H. Kerr.

——— 1906a [1870–5], 'The Religion of Social Democracy', in Dietzgen 1906 [1870–5].

Dittmar, Norbert 1976, *Sociolinguistics: A Critical Survey of Theory and Application*, London: Edward Arnold.

Dmitrieva, N. 2007, *Russkoe neokantianstvo: 'Marburg' v Rossii*, Moscow: ROSSPEN.

Dobrenko, Evgeny Aleksandrovich 2001, *The Making of the State Writer: Social and Aesthetic Origins of Soviet Literary Culture*, Stanford: Stanford University Press.

——— and Galin Tihanov (eds.) 2011, *A History of Russian Literary Theory and Criticism: The Soviet Age and Beyond*, Pittsburgh: University of Pittsburgh Press.

Dorson, Richard M. 1955, 'The Eclipse of Solar Mythology', *The Journal of American Folklore*, 68, 270: 393–416.

Douglas, Charlotte 2002, 'Energetic Abstraction: Otswald, Bogdanov, and the Russian Post-Revolutionary Art', in Clarke and Dalrymple Henderson (eds.) 2002.

Drabkina, Elena 1932, 'O gegemonii proletariata v burzhuazno-demokraticheskoi revoliutsii v sviazi s programmoi bol'shevizma po natsional'nomu voprosu', *Istorik-Marksist*, 4–5: 9–36.

Durkheim, Émile 1982, *The Rules of the Sociological Method*, New York: Free Press.

Durov, V.S. (ed.) 1997, *MOUSEION: Professoru Aleksandru Iosifovichu Zaitsevu ko dniu semidesiatiletiia*, St. Petersburg: SPBGU.

Dzhioev, O.I. 1973, 'Problemy sotsiologii myshleniia v trudakh K. Megrelidze', in *Sotsial'naia priroda poznaniia: materialy k vsesiuznomu simpoziumu 10–12 oktiabria 1973g*, Moscow: Institut filosofii AN SSSR.

——— 1980, ' "Net v mire bogatstva, ravnogo chelovecheskoi zhizni . . ." ', *Literaturnaia gruziia*, 12: 174–82.

—— 1989, 'Aktual'nost' sotsiologii myshleniia K.R. Megrelidze', *Filosofskaia i sotsiologicheskaia mysl'*, 2: 86–93.

Eagleton, Terry 1990, *The Ideology of the Aesthetic*, Oxford: Blackwell.

Edgar, Adrienne Lynn 2004, *Tribal Nation: The Making of Soviet Turkmenistan*, Princeton: Princeton University Press.

Embleton, Sheila *et al.* (eds.) 1999, *The Emergence of the Modern Language Sciences: Studies on the Transition from Historical-Comparative to Structural Linguistics in Honour of E.F.K. Koerner*, Philadelphia: John Benjamins.

Engel'gardt, Boris M. 1924, *Aleksandr Nikolaevich Veselovskii*, Petrograd: Kolos.

Engels, Frederick 1940 [1876], *Dialectics of Nature*, London: Lawrence and Wishart.

—— 1940a [1876], 'The Part Played by Labour in the Transition from Ape to Man', in Engels 1940.

—— 1975a [1841], 'Ernst Moritz Arndt', in Marx and Engels 1975–2004, Vol. 2.

—— 1975b [1842], 'Centralization and Freedom', in Marx and Engels 1975–2004, Vol. 2.

—— 1977 [1848], 'The Debate on Jacoby's Motion', in Marx and Engels 1975–2004, Vol. 7.

—— 1985 [1865], 'The Prussian Military Question and The German Workers' Party', in Marx and Engels 1975–2004, Vol. 20.

—— 1989 [1877], 'Karl Marx', in Marx and Engels 1975–2004, Vol. 24.

—— 1990 [1887–8], 'The Role of Force in History', in Marx and Engels 1975–2004, Vol. 26.

Erberg, Konstantin 1929, 'O formakh rechevoi kommunikatsii', *Iazyk i literatura*, 3: 156–79.

Eremina, V.I. 2011, 'A.M. Veselovskii o zakonomernostiakh literaturnogo protsessa, genezise i evoliutsii narodnogo soznaniia i poeticheskikh form', part 1, *Russkaia literatura*, 2: 13–45, and part 2, *Russkaia literatura*, 3: 3–36.

Ermakova, Tat'iana V. 1995, 'Issledovanie buddizma v Rossii (konets XIXv–nachalo XXv)', *Vostok*, 5: 139–47.

—— 1998, *Buddiskii mir glazami rossiiskikh issledovatelei xix-pervoi treti xx veka (Rossiia i sopredel'nye strany)*, St. Petersburg: Nauka.

Ermolaev, Herman 1963, *Soviet Literary Theories 1917–1934: The Genesis of Socialist Realism*, Berkeley: University of California Press.

Esaulov, Ivan A. 1995, *Kategoriia sobornosti v russkoi literature*, Petrozavodsk: Izd. Petrozavodskogo Universiteta.

Evans, A.D. 2003, 'Anthropology at War: Racial Studies of POWs During World War 1', in Penny and Bunzl (eds.) 2003.

Fadeev, Aleksandr Aleksandrovich 1931, 'Ob odnoi kulatskoi khronike', *Krasnaia nov'*, 5–6: 206–9.

Fedorova, Kapitolina 2010, 'Language as a Battlefield: the Rhetoric of Class Struggle in Linguistic Debates of the First Five-Year Plan Period', in Brandist and Chown (eds.) 2010.

Fitzpatrick, Sheila 1979, *Education and Social Mobility in the Soviet Union 1921–1934*, Cambridge: Cambridge University Press.

Frank, A.U., Kuhn W. and D.M. Mark (eds.) 1995, *Spatial Information Theory. Proceedings of COSIT '95*, Berlin: Springer Verlag, online at http://ontology.buffalo.edu/smith/articles/drawing.html.

Frank-Kamenetskii, Izrail' Grigor'evich 1925a, *Proroki-chudotvortsy: o mestnom proiskhizhdenii mifa o Khriste*, Leningrad: Seiatel'.

―――― 1925b, ' "Gruzinskaia parallel' " k drevneegipetskoi povesti "O dvukh brat'iakh" ', *Iafeticheskii sbornik*, 4: 39–71.

―――― 1929, 'Pervobytnoe myshlenie v svete iafeticheskoi teorii i filosofii', *Iazyk i literatura*, 3: 70–155.

―――― 1934, 'Zhenshina-gorod v bibleiskoi eskhatologii', in Krachkovskii (ed.) 1934.

―――― 1935a, 'K voprosu o razvitii poeticheskoi metafory', *Sovetskoe iazykoznaniie*, 1: 93–145.

―――― 1935b, 'Akademik N.Ia.Marr', *Front nauki i tekhniki*, 1: 109–14.

―――― 1938, 'Adam i Purusha: makrokosm i mikrokosm v iudeiskoi i indiiskoi kosmogonii', in I.I. Meshchaninov (ed.) 1938.

Freeman, Derek 1974, 'The Evolutionary Theories of Charles Darwin and Herbert Spencer', *Current Anthropology*, 15, 3: 211–37.

Fridman, Sh. (ed.) 1972, *Indiiskaia kul'tura i buddizm*, Moscow: Nauka.

Friedrich, Janette 1993, *Der Gehalt der Sprachform Paradigmen von Bachtin bis Vygotskij*, Berlin: Akademie Verlag.

Frings, Andreas 2009, 'Playing Moscow Off Against Kazan: Azerbaijan Maneuvering to Latinization in the Soviet Union', *Ab Imperio*, 4: 249–66.

Frisby, David 1984, 'Georg Simmel and Social Psychology', *Journal of the History of the Behavioral Sciences*, 20: 107–27.

―――― and Mike Featherstone (eds.) 1997, *Simmel on Culture*, edited by D. Frisby and M. Featherstone, London: Sage.

Frolov, E.D. 1995, 'Eduard Meier i russkaia nauka o klassicheskoi drevnosti', *Problemy istorii, filologii, kul'tury*, 2: 91–7.

―――― 1986, 'S.I. Kovalev i ego "Istoriia rima" ', in Kovalev 1986.

Frostini, F. 2010, 'On "Translatability" in Gramsci's Prison Notebooks', in Ives and Lacorte (eds.) 2010.

Funke, Otto 1924, *Innere Sprachform, eine Einführung in A. Martys Sprachphilosophie*, Reichenberg: Kraus.

Gal, Susan, and Judith T. Irvine, 1995, 'The Boundaries of Languages and Disciplines: How Ideologies Construct Difference', *Social Research*, 62, 4: 967–1001.

Gastev, Aleksei 1919, 'O tendentsiiakh proletarskoi kul'tury: kontury proletarskoi kul'tury', *Proletarskaia kul'tura*, 9–10: 35–45.

—— 1972 [1929], 'Normirovanie i organizatsiia truda', in *Kak nado rabotat'*, Moscow: Ekonomika.

—— 1973 [1918], *Poeziia rabochego udara*, Moscow: Khudozhestvennaia literatura.

Geldern, James von, 1993, *Bolshevik Festivals, 1917–1920*, Berkeley: University of California Press.

Genko, Anatolii Nestorovich 1926, 'Ob otnoshenii turetskikh iazykov k iafeticheskim iazykam', in *Pervyi vsesoiuznyi tiurkologicheskii s"ezd 26 fevralia–5 marta 1926g. (Stenograficheskii otchet)*, Baku: obsledovaniia i izucheniia Azerbaidzhana.

Gensini, S. 2010, 'Linguistics and the Political Question of Language', in Ives and Lacorte (eds.) 2010.

Gershenzon, M. 1977 [1909], 'Creative Self-Cognition', in Berdyaev *et al.* 1977.

Giasi, Francesco (ed.) 2008, *Gramsci nel suo tempo*, Rome: Carocci.

Gibbon, Peter 1983, 'Gramsci, Eurocommunism and the Comintern', *Economy and Society*, 12, 3: 328–66.

Gilléron, Jules and Édmond Édmont 1902–12, *Atlas linguistique de la France*, Paris: Champion.

Ginzburg, Carlo 1999, *History, Rhetoric and Proof*, Hanover: University Press of New England.

Glen Penny, H. and Matti Bunzl (eds.) 2003, *Worldly Provincialism: German Anthropology in the Age of Empire*, Ann Arbor: University of Michigan Press.

Gluckstein, Donny 1994, *The Tragedy of Bukharin*, London: Pluto Press.

Gofman, V.A. 1932, *Slovo Oratora (ritorika i politika)*, Leningrad: Izdatel'stvo pisatelei v Leningrade.

Gorham, Michael 1996, 'Tongue-Tied Writers: The Rabsel'kor Movement and the Voice of the "New Intelligentsia" in Early Soviet Russia', *Russian Review*, 55, 3: 412–29.

—— 2003, *Speaking in Soviet Tongues: Language Culture and the Politics of Voice in Revolutionary Russia*, DeKalb, Ill: Northern Illinois University Press.

—— 2010, 'Language Ideology and the Evolution of *Kul'tura iazyka* ("Speech Culture") in Soviet Russia', in Brandist and Chown (eds.) 2010.

Gor'kii, Maksim 1953a [1933], 'O sotsialisticheskom realizme', in *Sobranie sochinenii v tritsati tomakh*, Vol. 27, Moscow: GIKhL.

—— 1953b [1934], 'O iazyke', in *Sobranie sochinenii v tritsati tomakh*, Vol. 27, Moscow: GIKhL, online at http://az.lib.ru/g/gorxkij_m/text_11934_0_yazyke.shtml.

Gorky, Maksim, *et al.* (eds.) 1977 [1934], *Soviet Writers' Congress 1934: The Debate on Socialist Realism and Modernism*, London: Lawrence and Wishart.

Görs, Britta *et al.* (eds.) 2005, *Wilhelm Ostwald at the Crossroads Between Chemistry, Philosophy and Media Culture*, Leipzig: Leipziger Universitätsverlag.

Gorskii, I.K. 1975, *Aleksandr Veselovskii i sovremennost'*, Moscow: Nauka.

Graham, Loren R. 1967, *The Soviet Academy of Sciences and the Communist Party, 1927–1932*, Princeton: Princeton University Press.

Gramsci, Antonio 1971, *Selections from The Prison Notebooks*, translated and edited by Quintin Hoare and Geoffrey Nowell Smith, London: Lawrence and Wishart.

———— 1975, *Quaderni del carcere*, Turin: Einaudi.

———— 1985, *Selections from the Cultural Writings*, London: Lawrence and Wishart.

———— 1991, *Prison Notebooks*, Vol. 1, New York: Columbia University Press.

———— 1994, *Letters from Prison*, New York: Columbia University Press.

———— 2007, *Prison Notebooks*, Vol. 3, New York: Columbia University Press.

———— *et al.* 2012 [1922], 'The Proletcult Institute', *Journal of Romance Studies*, 12, 3: 97–107.

Gramshi, Antonio [Gramsci, Antonio], *et al.* 1922, 'Institut Proletkul'ta', *Gorn*, 1, 6: 121–7.

Grau, Rudolf, 1867 [1864], *Semiten und Indogermanen in ihrer Beziehung zu Religion und Wissenschaft: eine Apologie des Christentums vom Standpunkt der Völkerpsychologie*, Stuttgart: Liesching.

Gray, Ann and Jim McGuigan (eds.) 1977, *Studies in Culture: An Introductory Reader*, London: Arnold.

Grigor'eva, I.V. 1998, 'Rossiiskie stranitsy biografii Antonio Gramshi (1922–1926) po dokumentam arkhiva kominterna', *Rossiia i Italiia*, 3: 96–123.

Grille, Dietrich 1966, *Lenins Rivale Bogdanov und seine Philosophie*, Köln: Verlag Wissenschaft und Politik.

Grosul, V.Ia. 1988, 'Kh.G. Rakovskii – revoliutsioner, diplomat, publitsist', *Novaia i noveishaia istoriia*, 6: 151–75.

Guha, Ranajit 1997, *Dominance Without Hegemony: History and Power in Colonial India*, Cambridge: Harvard University Press.

Gulida, Victoria B. 2010, 'Theoretical Insights and Ideological Pressures in Early Soviet Linguistics: The Cases of Lev Iakubinskii and Boris Larin', in Brandist and Chown (eds.) 2010.

Gusev, S.S. 1995, 'Ot "zhivogo opyta" k "organizatsionnoi nauke" ', in Gusev (ed.) 1995.

———— (ed.) 1995, *Russkii pozitivizm: V.V. Lesevich, P.S. Iushkevich, A.A. Bogdanov*, St. Petersburg: Nauka.

Habib, Irfan 2005, 'In Defence of Orientalism: Critical Notes on Edward Said', *Social Scientist*, 33, 1–2: 40–6.

Hagen, Mark von, 1990, *Soldiers in the Proletarian Dictatorship: The Red Army and the Soviet Socialist State, 1917–1930*, London: Cornell University Press.

Haines, Valerie A. 1988, 'Is Spencer's Theory an Evolutionary Theory?', *American Journal of Sociology*, 93, 5: 1200–23.

Hall, Stuart *et al.* (eds.) 1980, *Culture, Media, Language: Working Papers in Cultural Studies, 1972–79*, London: Routledge.

Halliwell, S. 1994, 'Philosophy and Rhetoric', in Worthington (ed.) 1994.

Harding, Neil and Richard Taylor (ed.) 1983, *Marxism in Russia: Key Documents 1879–1906*, Cambridge: Cambridge University Press.

Harman, Chris 1977, 'Gramsci versus Eurocommunism', *International Socialism*, 1, 98: 23–6 and 1, 99: 10–14.

Harris, Nigel, 1978, *The Mandate of Heaven: Marx and Mao in Modern China*, London: Quartet.

———— 1990, *National Liberation*, London: I.B. Tauris.

Hatch, John B. 1989, 'The "Lenin Levy" and the Social Origins of Stalinism: Workers and the Communist Party in Moscow, 1921–1928', *Slavic Review*, 48, 4: 558–77.

Hautala, Jouko 1968, *Finnish Folklore Research 1828–1918*, Helsinki: Finnish Academy of Science.

Herder, Johann, 2002 [1772], 'Treatise on the Origin of Language', in *Philosophical Writings*, Cambridge: Cambridge University Press.

Hicks, Jeremy 2007, 'Worker Correspondents: Between Journalism and Literature', *Russian Review*, 66, 4: 568–85.

Hirsch, Francine 2005, *Empire of Nations: Ethnographic Knowledge and the Making of the Soviet Union*, London: Cornell University Press.

———— 2007, 'State and Evolution: Ethnographic Knowledge, Economic Expediency, and the Making of the USSR 1917–1924', in Burbank *et al.* (eds.) 2007.

Hoare, Quintin and Geofferey Nowell Smith 1971, 'General Introduction', in Gramsci 1971.

Hodgen, M.T. 1931, 'The Doctrine of Survivals: The History of an Idea', *American Anthropologist*, 33, 3: 307–24.

———— 1933, 'Survivals and Social Origins: The Pioneers', *American Journal of Sociology*, 38, 4: 583–94.

Hoffman, D. 1972, 'Bukharin's Theory of Equilibrium', *Telos*, 14: 126–36.

Howe, S. 2007, 'Edward Said and Marxism: Anxieties of Influence', *Cultural Critique*, 67: 50–87.

Humboldt, Wilhelm von 1999 [1836], *On Language: On the Diversity of Human Language Construction and its Influence on the Mental Development of the Human Species*, Cambridge: Cambridge University Press.

Iakovlev, Nikolai Feofanovich 1923, 'Tablitsy fonetiki kabardinskogo iazyka', *Trudy podrazriada issledovaniia kavkazskikh iazykov pri institute Vostokovedeniia v Moskve*, Moscow: Institut vostokovedeniia.

———— 1926, 'Voprosy alfavita v sviazi s sotsial'nymi i kul'turnymi usloviami sushchest-vovaniia tiurkskikh natsional'nostei i problema ustanovleniia sistemy pis'ma', in

Pervyi vsesoiuznyi tiurkologicheskii s"ezd 26 fevralia–5 marta 1926g. (*Stenograficheskii otchet*), Baku: Institut obsledovaniia i izucheniia Azerbaidzhana.

———— 1928, 'Matematicheskaia formula postroeniia alfavita', *Kul'tura i pismennost' vostoka*, 1: 41–64.

———— 1930, 'Za latinizatsiiu russkogo alfavita', *Kul'tura i pis'mennost' vostoka*, 6: 27–43.

———— 1931, ' "Analiticheskii" ili "novyi" alfavit?', *Kul'tura i pis'mennost' Vostoka*, x: 43–60.

Iakubinskii, L.P. 1924, 'O snizhenii vysokogo stilia u Lenina', *Lef*, 1, 5: 71–80.

———— 1986 [1923], 'O dialogicheskoi rechi', in *Izbrannye raboty: Iazyk i ego funktsionirovanie*, Moscow: Nauka.

———— 1930a, 'Klassovyi sostav sovremennnogo russkogo iazyka: iazyk krest'ianstva. Stat'ia chetvertaia', *Literaturnaia ucheba*, 4: 80–92.

———— 1930b, 'Klassovyi sostav sovremennogo russkogo iazyka: iazyk krest'ianstva. Stat'ia chetvertaia', *Literaturnaia ucheba*, 6: 51–66.

———— 1931a, 'Klassovyi sostav sovremennogo russkogo iazyka: iazyk proletariata. Stat'ia piataia', *Literaturnaia ucheba*, 7: 22–33.

———— 1931b, 'Russkii iazyk v epokhu diktatury proletariata', *Literaturnaia ucheba*, 9: 66–76.

———— 1931c, 'O nauchno-populiarnom iazyke', *Literaturnaia ucheba*, 1: 49–64.

———— 1932, 'Protiv "Danilovshchiny" ', in Bykovskii (ed.) 1932.

———— 1986 [1929], 'F de Sossiur o nevozmozhnosti iazykovoi politiki', in *Izbrannye raboty: Iazyk i ego funktsionirovanie*, Moscow: Nauka.

———— and A.M. Ivanov, 1932, *Ocherki po iazyku dlia rabotnikov literatury i dlia samoobrazovaniia*, Moscow and Leningrad: Gosudarstvennoe izdatel'stvo khudozhestvennoi literatury.

Ignatovich, A.N. 1991, 'O.O. Rozenberg i ego trudy po buddizmu', in Rozenberg 1991.

Ilizarov, Boris S. 2012, *Pochetnyi akademik Stalin i akademik Marr*, Moscow: Veche.

Isaacs, Harold 2009 [1938], *The Tragedy of the Chinese Revolution*, Chicago: Haymarket Press.

Iurovskaia, M.A. 1928, 'Psikhotekhnicheskaia proverka znanii v shkole politgramoty', *Psikhofiziologiia truda i psikhotekhnika*, 1, 2: 29–40.

Ivanov, Viacheslav Ivanovich 1974 [1906], 'Predchuvstviia i predvestiia. Novaia organicheskaia epokha i teatr budushchego', in *Sobranie socheneniia*, Vol. 2, Brussels: Foyer Oriental.

Ivanova, E.V. 1993a, 'Beseda o proletarskoi kul'tury v Vol'file', *De Visu*, 7, 8: 5–27.

———— 1993b, 'Blok v Teatral'no-literaturnoi kommissii i TEO Narkomprosa', in Shcherbina (ed.) 1993, Vol. 5.

———— 2010, *Vol'naia filosofskaia assotsiatsiia 1919–1924*, Moscow: Nauka.

Ivanova, Irina 2003, 'Razvitie poniatie "zhivoe slovo" v russkoi kul'ture kontsa XIX – nachala XX veka', in Sériot (ed.) 2003.

Ives, Peter 2004a, *Gramsci's Politics of Language: Engaging the Bakhtin Circle and the Frankfurt School*, Toronto: University of Toronto Press.

—— 2004b, *Language and Hegemony in Gramsci*, London: Pluto Press.

—— and Rocco Lacorte (eds.) 2005, *Gramsci, Language, and Translation*, Lanham: Lexington Books.

Jakobson, Roman 1944, 'Franz Boas's Approach to Language', *International Journal of American Linguistics*, 10, 4: 188–95.

—— 1971, 'The Kazan' School of Polish Linguistics and its Place in the International Development of Phonology', in *Selected Writings*, Vol. 2, The Hague Mouton.

—— 1985, 'Toward the History of the Moscow Linguistic Circle', in *Selected Writings*, Vol. 7, Berlin: de Gruyter.

Janaček, G. 1981, 'Baudouin de Courtenay versus Kručenych', *Russian Literature*, 10: 17–30.

Jarah, N. 1999, 'Edward Said Discusses "Orientalism", Arab Intellectuals, Reviving Marxism, and Myth in Palestinian History', *Al Jadid Magazine*, 5, 28, online at http://www.aljadid.com/content/edward-said-discusses-%E2%80%98orientalism%E2%80%99-arab-intellectuals-reviving-marxism-and-myth-palestinian.

Jason, Heda 1970, 'The Russian Criticism of the "Finnish School" in Folktale Scholarship', *Norveg*, 14: 285–94.

Jensen, K.M. 1978, *Beyond Marx and Mach: Aleksandr Bogdanov's Philosophy of Living Experience*, Reidel: Dortrecht.

Jessop, Robert *et al.* 1984, 'Authoritarian Populism, Two Nations, and Thatcherism', *New Left Review*, 1, 147: 32–60.

Joseph, John 2012, *Saussure*, Oxford: Oxford University Press.

Kagarlitsky, Boris 1988, *The Thinking Reed: Intellectuals and the Soviet State from 1917 to the Present*, London: Verso.

—— 2008, *Empire of the Periphery: Russia and the World System*, London: Pluto Press.

Kalb, Judith E. 2008, *Russia's Rome: Imperial Visions, Messianic Dreams, 1890–1940*, Madison: University of Wisconsin Press.

Kalmar, Ivan 1987, 'The *Völkerpsychologie* of Lazarus and Steinthal and the Modern Concept of Culture', *Journal of the History of Ideas*, 48, 4: 671–90.

Kamenev, Lev 2003 [1906], 'Proletarskaia gegemoniia i burzhuaznaia puglivost'', in *Mezhdu dvumia revoliutsiiami*, Moscow: Tsentropoligraf.

Kandel', E.P. *et al.* (eds.) 1969, *Literaturnoe nasledstvo K. Marksa i F. Engel'sa. Istoriia publikatsii i izucheniia v SSSR*, Moscow: Politizdat.

Kapp, Ernst 1877, *Grundlinien einer Philosophie der Technik: Zur Entstehungsgeschichte der Kultur aus neuen Gesichtspunkten*, Braunscheig: G. Westermann.

Karinskii, Nikolai Mikhailovich 1898, 'O nekotorykh govorakh: po techeniiu rek Lugi i Oredezha', *Russkii filologicheskii vestnik*, 40: 92–124.

Karpov, A.V. 2009, *Russkii Proletkul't: ideologiia, estetika, praktika*, St. Petersburg: SPbGUP.

Kartsevskii, Sergei Iosifovich 2000 [1923], 'Iazyk, voina i revoliutsiia; Iz nabliudenii nad russkim iazykom poslednikh let', in *Iz lingvisticheskogo naslediia*, Vol. 1, Moscow: Iazyk russkoi kul'tury.

Kasarov, G.G. 1986, 'Kritika V.I. Leninym liberal'no-burzhuaznykh i melkoburzhuaznykh vzgliadov na voprosy gegemonii proletariat v pervoi rossiiskoi revoliutsii', in Ushakov (ed.) 1986.

Katkyn', A. 1924, 'Vremia, kak ekonomicheskii faktor', *Vremia*, 1: 7–11.

Kautsky, Karl 1983 [1906], 'The Driving Forces of the Russian Revolution and its Prospects, with a Preface by V.I. Lenin', in Harding and Taylor (eds.) 1983.

———— 2009a [1906], 'The American Worker', in Day and Gaido (eds.) 2009.

———— 2009b [1906], 'The Driving Forces of the Russian Revolution and its Prospects', in Day and Gaido (eds.) 2009.

———— 2009 [1908], 'Nationality and Internationality', Part 1, translated by Ben Lewis, *Critique*, 37, 3: 371–89.

———— 2010 [1908], 'Nationality and Internationality', Part 2, translated by Ben Lewis, *Critique*, 38, 1: 143–63.

Kazanskii, B.F. 1938, Commentary to 'Zametki i somneniia o sravnitel'nom izuchenii srednevekovogo eposa', in Veselovskii 1938.

Kelley, Catriona 2002, ' "A Laboratory for the Manufacture of Proletarian Writers": The *Stengazeta* (Wall Newspaper), *Kul'turnost'* and the Language of Politics in the Early Soviet Period', *Europe-Asia Studies*, 54, 4: 573–602.

Kelly, Donald R. 1984, 'The Science of Anthropology: An Essay on the Very Old Marx', *Journal of the History of Ideas* 45, 2: 245–62.

Kelly, Louis G. 2002, *The Mirror of Grammar: Theology, Philosophy and the Modistae*, Philadelphia: John Benjamins.

Kenez, Peter 1985, *The Birth of the Propaganda State: Soviet Methods of Mass Mobilization 1917–1929*, Cambridge: Cambridge University Press.

———— and David Shepherd (eds.) 1998, *Russian Cultural Studies: An Introduction*, Oxford: Oxford University Press.

Kerzhentsev, Platon M. 1920, *Tvorcheskii teatr*, Petrograd: Gosizdat.

———— 1924, *Bor'ba za vremia*, Moscow: Krasnaia nov'.

———— 1990, 'NOT. Nauchnaia organizatsiia truda', in Zhukova (ed.) 1990.

Khalid, Adeeb 1998, *The Politics of Muslim Cultural Reform: Jadidism in Central Asia*, Berkeley: University of California Press.

Khamaganova, E.A. 1998, 'Pis'ma iz Atsagata (Iz perepiski E.E. Obermillera s akademikom F.I. Shcherbatskoi', *Orient almanakh*, 2–3: 113–27.

Khoruzhii, S.S. 1994, 'Transformatsii slavianofil'skoi idei v xx veke', *Voprosy filosofii*, 11: 52–62.

Khudiakov, M.G. 1935, 'Graficheskie skhemy istoricheskogo protsessa v trudakh N.Ia. Marra', *Sovetskaia etnografiia*, 1: 18–41.

Kibbee, Douglas A. 1999, 'The "People" and their Language in 19th Century French Linguistic Thought', in Embleton *et al.* (eds.) 1999.

Kim, Mi Gyung 2008, 'Wilhelm Ostwald (1853–1932)', *HYLE – International Journal for Philosophy of Chemistry*, 12, 1: 141–8.

Klaproth, Julius von 1814, *Reise in den Kaukasus und nach Georgien: Unternommen in den Jahren 1807 und 1808*, Halle and Berlin: Hallischen Waisenhauses.

Kleberg, Lars 1993, *Theatre as Action: Soviet Russian Avant-Garde Aesthetics*, London: Macmillan.

Kleinbort, L.M. 1923, *Ocherki rabochei intelligentsia*, Moscow: Nachatkii znanii.

Kliuchnikov, Iu.V. *et al.* 1921, *Smena Vekh. Sbornik statei*, Prague: Politika.

Koerner, E.F.K. 1973, *Ferdinand de Saussure: Origins and Development of His Linguisic Thought in Western Studies of Language*, Braunchweig: Vieweg.

———— 1997, 'Linguistics vs Philology: Self-Definition of a Field or Rhetorical Stance?' *Language Sciences*, 19, 2: 167–75.

———— 2002, 'William Labov and the Orgins of Sociolinguistics', *Folia Linguistica Historica*, 22, 1–2: 1–40.

Kondratenko D.P. 2005, *Samoderzhavie, liberaly i natsional'nyi vopros v Rossii v kontse xix–nachale xx veka*, Kirov: Viatskii Gosudarstvennyi Gumanitarnyi Universitet.

Koni, A.F. 1933 [1904], *Vospominaniia o dele Very Zasulicha*, Moscow: Academia.

Kostomarov, Vitalii Grigor'evich and L.I. Skvortsov (eds.) 1970, *Aktual'nye problem kul'tury rechi*, Moscow: Nauka.

Kovalev, Sergei I. 1936 [1927], 'Marksizm i iafeticheskaia teoriia', in Marr 1936a [1927].

———— 1936b, *Istoriia antichnogo obshchestva*, t.1, *Gretsiia*; t.2, *Ellenizm. Rim*, Leningrad GAIMK.

———— 1986, *Istoriia Rima. Kurs lektsii*, Leningrad: LGU.

Kozlov, Nicholas N. and Eric D. Weitz 1989, 'Reflections on the Origins of the "Third Period": Bukharin, the Comintern, and the Political Economy of Weimar Germany', *Journal of Contemporary History*, 24, 3: 387–410.

Krachkovskii, I.Iu. (ed.) 1935, *Sergeiu Fedorovichu Ol'denburgu k piatidesiatiletiiu nauchno-obshchestvennoi deiatel'nosti 1882–1932*, Leningrad: AN SSSR.

———— 1947, *Pamiati akademika V.R. Rozena: Stat'i i materialy k sorokaletiiu ego smerti (1908–1948)*, Moscow and Leningrad: Akademiia nauk.

Kreindler, Isabelle 1977, 'A Neglected Source of Lenin's Nationality Policy', *Slavic Review*, 36, 1: 86–100.

Kremer, Arkady and Julius Martov 1983 [1896], 'On Agitation', in Harding (ed.) 1983.

Krikh, S.B. 2012, *Obraz drevnosti v sovetskoi istoriografii*, Moscow: URSS.

Krishnaswamy, R. 2005, 'Nineteenth-century language ideology: A postcolonial perspective', *Interventions: International Journal of Postcolonial Studies*, 7, 1: 43–71.

Krohn, Kaarle 1926, *Die folkloristische Arbeitsmethode: Begründet won Julius Krohn und weitergeführt won nordischen Forschern*, Oslo: Instituttet for Sammenlignende Kulturforskning.

Krois, John Michael *et al.* (eds.) 2007, *Embodiment in Cognition and Culture*, Amsterdam and Philadelphia: John Benjamins.

Krupskaia, Nadezhda 1921, 'Glavpolitprosvet i iskusstvo', *Pravda*, 13 February 1921.

Kudriavskii, Dmitri N. 1912, *Vvednie v iazykoznanie*, Iu'ev: Pechat' vyshikh zhenskikh kursov.

Kulikova, A.M. 2001, 'Nauchnye sviazi akademika-literaturoveda A.N. Veselovskogo (1838–1906) s vostokovedami (po epistliarnym materialam', in *Rossiiskoe vostokovedenie XIX veka v litsakh*, St. Petersburg: Peterburgskoe vostokovedenie.

Kuklick, Henrika (ed.) 2008, *A New History of Anthropology*, London: Blackwell.

Kuper, Adam 1988, *The Invention of Primitive Society: Transformations of an Illusion*, London, Routledge.

Laclau, Ernesto 1979, *Politics and Ideology in Marxist Theory*, London: Verso.

———— and Chantal Mouffe 1985, *Hegemony and Socialist Strategy*, London: Verso.

Lacorte, Rocco 2010, 'Translatability, Language and Freedom in Gramsci's *Prison Notebooks*', in Ives and Lacorte (eds.) 2010.

Lähteenmäki, M. and N.L. Vasil'ev 2005, 'Retseptsiia "novogo ucheniia o iazyke" N.Ia. Marra v rabotakh V.N. Voloshinova: iskrennost' ili kon"iunktura?' *Russian Linguistics*, 29, 1: 71–94.

Lang, Andrew 1904 [1884], *Custom and Myth*, London: Longman, Green and co.

———— 1899, *Myth, Ritual and Religion*, London: Longman, Green and co.

Lappo-Danilievskii and A.B. Shiskin (eds.) 2010, *Viacheslav Ivanov: Issledovaniia i materialy*, Vol. 1, St. Petersburg: Izd. Pushkinskogo Doma.

Larin, Boris Aleksandrovich 1928, 'K lingvisticheskoi kharakteristike goroda: neskol'ko predposylok', *Izvestiia gosudarstvennogo pedagogicheskogo Instituta im. A.I. Gertsena*, 1: 175–85.

———— 1929, 'O lingvisticheskom izuchenii goroda', *Russkaia rech'*, 3: 61–75.

Lartsev, V.G. 1988, *Evgenii Dmitrievich Polivanov: Stranitsy zhizni i deiatel'nosti*, Moscow: Vostochnaia literatura.

Lavrov, A. and R. Timenchik (eds), *Ot slov k telu: Sbornik statei k 60-letiiu Iuriia Tsiv'iana*, Moscow: Novoe literaturnoe obozreniie.

Lazarus, M. 1851, 'Über den Begriff und die Möglichkeit einer Völkerpsychologie', *Zeitschrift für Literatur, Kunst und Öffentlichkeitsleben*, 1: 112–26.

———— and H. Steinthal 1851, 'Einleitende Gedanken über Völkerpsychologie, als Einladung zu einer Zeitschrift für Völkerpsychologie und Sprachwissensschaft', *Zeitschrift für Völkerpsychologie und Sprachwissensschaft*, 1: 1–73.

Leach, Robert 1994, *Revolutionary Theater*, London: Routledge.

Lehikoinen, Riita 1990, *Slovar' revoliutsii – revoliutsiia v slovare: Abbreviatury i inoia-zychnaia leksika v russkom iazyke pervogo poslerevoliutsionnogo desiatiletiia*, Helsinki: Neuvostoliittoinstituutin vuosikirja 32.

Lenček, R.L. 1977, 'Jan Baudouin de Courtenay on the Dialects Spoken in Venetian Slovenia and Rezija', *Society for Slovene Studies Newsletter*, Michigan: University of Michigan.

Lenin, Vladimir Ilych 1960–79, *Collected Works*, Moscow: Foreign Languages Publishing House.

—————— 1961 [1902], 'What is to be Done? Burning Questions of Our Movement', in Lenin 1960–79, Vol. 5.

—————— 1962a [1905], 'Working Class and Bourgeois Democracy', in Lenin 1960–79, Vol. 8.

—————— 1962b [1905], 'Two Tactics of Social-Democracy in the Democratic Revolution', in Lenin 1960–79, Vol. 9.

—————— 1962c [1906], 'Guerrilla Warfare', in Lenin 1960–79, Vol. 11.

—————— 1962d [1907], 'The Elections to the Duma and the Tactics of the Russian Social-Democrats', in Lenin 1960–79, Vol. 12.

—————— 1962e [1915], 'Socialism and War: The Attitude of the Russian Social-Democratic Labour Party Towards the War', in Lenin 1960–79, Vol. 21.

—————— 1964a [1916], 'The Socialist Revolution and the Right of Nations to Self-Determination: Theses', in Lenin 1960–79, Vol. 22.

—————— 1964b [1916], 'The Discussion on Self-determination Summed Up', in Lenin 1960–79, Vol. 22.

—————— 1965a [1922a], 'Conditions for Admitting New Members to the Party', in Lenin 1960–79, Vol. 33.

—————— 1965b [1922b], 'Political report of the Central Committee to the Eleventh Congress of the RCP(b), 27 March 1922', in Lenin 1960–79, Vol. 33.

—————— 1965c [1923], 'Better Fewer, But Better', in Lenin 1960–79, Vol. 33.

—————— 1972 [1907], 'The Agrarian Programme of Social-Democracy in the First Russian Revolution, 1905–1907', in Lenin 1960–79, Vol. 13.

—————— 1972 [1913], 'Critical remarks on the National Question', in Lenin 1960–79, Vol. 20.

—————— 1972a [1914], 'The Right of Nations to Self-Determination', in Lenin 1960–79, Vol. 20.

—————— 1972b [1914], 'Is a Compulsory Official Language Needed?', in Lenin 1960–79, Vol. 20.

—————— 1972c [1918], 'The Immediate Tasks of the Soviet Government', in Lenin 1960–79, Vol. 27.

—————— 1972d [1918], 'Sessions of the All-Russia C.E.C.', in Lenin 1960–79, Vol. 27.

—————— 1974a [1911], 'Old Truths that are Ever New', in Lenin 1960–79, Vol. 17.

———— 1974b [1911], 'Those Who Would Liquidate Us', in Lenin 1960–79, Vol. 17.

———— 1974c [1911], 'Reformism in the Russian Social-Democratic Movement', in Lenin 1960–79, Vol. 17.

———— 1974d [1919a], ' "Democracy" and Dictatorship', in Lenin 1960–79, Vol. 28.

———— 1974e [1919b], 'Speech Closing the Debate on the Party Programme', in Lenin 1960–79, Volume 29.

Lentin, Ronit (ed.) 2008, *Thinking Palestine*, London: Zed Books.

Leont'ev, Aleksei Alekseevich 1961, 'I.A. Boduen de Kurtene i peterburgskaia shkola russkoi lingvistiki', *Voprosy iazykoznaniia*, 4: 116–24.

———— 1966, 'Boduen i frantsuzskaia lingvistika', *Izvestiia akademii nauk SSSR, seriia literatury i iazyka*, 30, 4: 329–32.

———— 1983, *Evgenii Dmitrevich Polivanov i ego vklad v obshchee iazykoznanie*, Moscow: Nauka.

Leopold, W. 1929, 'Inner Form', *Language*, 5, 4: 254–60.

Levin, A.E. 1988, 'Expedient Catastrope: A Reconsideration of the 1929 Crisis at the Academy of Sciences', *Slavic Review*, 47, 2: 261–79.

Levchenko, M. 2007, *Industrial'naia svirel': Poeziia proletkul'ta 1917–1921gg.*, St. Petersburg: PBGUTD.

Lewin, Moshe 1969, *Lenin's Last Struggle*, London: Pluto Press.

Lieberstein, Samuel 1975, 'Technology, Work, and Sociology in the USSR: The NOT Movement', *Technology and Culture*, 16, 1: 48–66.

Liebman, Marcel 1975, *Leninism under Lenin*, London: Merlin Press.

Lih, Lars T. 2005, *Lenin Rediscovered: What is to Be Done? in Context*, Chicago: Haymarket.

———— 2011a, 'The Ironic Triumph of Old Bolshevism: The Debates of April 1917 in Context', *Russian History*, 38, 2: 199–242.

———— 2011b, 'Zinoviev: Populist Leninist', in *Zinoviev and Martov: Head to Head in Halle*, edited by Ben Lewis and Lars Lih, London: November Publications.

Lim, Jie-Hyun 1992, 'Marx's Theory of Imperialism and the Irish National Question', *Science & Society*, 56, 2: 163–78.

Lingvist (Ian Loia) 1929, 'Osnovnye napravleniia v iazykoznanii', *Na Literaturnom postu*, 20: 55–7.

Linhart, Robert 1976, *Lénine, les paysants, Taylor: Essai d'analyse matériel historique de la naissance du sistém productif soviétique*, Paris: Éditions du seuil.

Lins, U. 1999, *Opasnyi iazyk. Kniga o presledovaniiakh Esperanto*, Moscow: Impeto.

Litman, A.D. 1972, 'Vklad F.I. Shcherbatskogo v izuchenie indiiskoi filosofii', in Fridman (ed.) 1972.

L'iuis, D.G. and D.S. Mill' 1867, *Ogiust Kont i polozhitel'naia filosofiia*, St. Petersburg: Tiblena.

Loia, Ian 1929, 'Protiv sub"ektivnogo idealizma v iazykovedenii', in Marr (ed.) 1929.

Lomtev, Timofei Petrovich 1931, 'Rezoliutsiia po dokladu T.P. Lomteva – "Ocherednye zadachi marksistskoi lingvistiki" ', *Russkii iazyk v sovetskoi shkole*, 5: 160–1.

―――― 2001 [1931], 'Za marksistskuiu lingvistiku', in Bazylev and Neroznak (eds.) 2001.

―――― 2011 [1930], 'Poniatie iazyka v marksistskom osveshchenii', in Orekhov (ed.) 2011.

Lo Piparo, Franco 1979, *Lingua Intellettuali Egemonia in Gramsci*, Bari: Laterza.

―――― 2010, 'The Linguistic Roots of Gramsci's Non-Marxism', in Ives and Lacorte (eds.) 2010.

Lowe, Heinz-Dietrich 1992, 'Russian Nationalism and Tsarist Nationalities Policies in Semi-Constitutional Russia, 1905–1914', in McKean (ed.) 1992.

Löwy, Michael 1976, 'Marxists and the National Question', *New Left Review*, 1, 66: 81–100.

―――― 1998, *Fatherland or Mother Earth: Essays on the National Question*, London: Pluto Press.

Lukács, Georgy 1925, 'Literaturbericht, N. Bucharin, Theorie des historischen Materialismus. Gemeinverständliches Lehrbuch der marxistischen Soziologie, 1922', *Archiv für die Geschichte des Sozialismus und der Arbeiterbewegung*, 11: 218–24.

―――― 1966 [1925], 'Technology and Social Relations', *New Left Review*, 1, 39: 27–34.

―――― 1969 [1925], 'Über Bucharins "Theorie des historischen Materialismus" ', in Negt (ed.) 1925.

Lukashevich, Platon 2008, *Pervobytnyi slavianskii iazyk, otkrytyi Platonom Lukashevichom*, Moscow: Belye Al'vy.

Lukes, Steven 1973, *Émile Durkheim, His Life and Work: A Historical and Critical Study*, Harmondsworth: Penguin.

Lunacharskii, Anatolii V. 1908 and 1911, *Religiia i sotsializm*, St. Petersburg: Shipovnik.

―――― 1925, *Ot Spinozi do Marksa*, Moscow: Novaia Moskva.

―――― 1965 [1920], 'Peredovoi otriad kul'tury na zapade', in *Sobranie sochinenii*, Vol. 5, Moscow: Khudozhestvennaia literatura.

―――― 1981 [1920], 'Na otkrytii Gosudarstvennogo instituta deklamatsii', in *O massovykh prazdnestvakh, estrade, tsirke*, Moscow: Iskusstvo.

Lur'e, I. 1940, 'Sorokletie nauchnoi i obshchesvenno-pedagogicheskoi deiatel'nosti akademika N.M. Nikol'skogo', *Vestnik drevnei istorii*, 3–4: 258–66.

Maiakovskii, Vladimir Vladimirovich 1955 [1914], 'Voina i iazyk', *Polnoe sobranie sochinenii*, Vol. 1, Moscow: Khudozhestvennaia literatura.

―――― 1959a [1926], 'Kak delat' stikhi', *Polnoe sobranie sochinenii*, Vol. 12, Moscow: Khudozhestvennaia literatura.

―――― 1959b [1927], 'Rasshirenie slovesnoi bazy', *Polnoe sobranie sochinenii*, Vol. 12, Moscow: Khudozhestvennaia literatura.

Maksimov N. (A.A. Bogdanov) 1909, *Ko vsem tovarishcham*, Paris: Soiuz.

Mally, Lynn 1990, *Culture of the Future: The Proletkult Movement in Revolutionary Russia*, Berkeley: University of California Press.

Malygina, N.M. 1995, *Khudozhestvennyi mir Andreia Platonova*, Moscow: MPU.

———— 2005, *Andrei Platonov: poetika 'vozvrasheniia'*, Moscow: Teis.

Marot, John 1990, 'Alexander Bogdanov, Vpered, and the Role of the Intellectual in the Workers' Movement', *Russian Review*, 49, 3: 241–61.

——— 1991, 'Politics and Philosophy in Russian Social Democracy: Alexander Bogdanov and the Sociotheoretical Foundations of *Vpered*', *Canadian Slavonic Papers*, 33, 3–4: 263–84.

Marr, Nikolai Iakovlevich 1899, *Sborniki pritch Vardana*, Vols. 1–3, St. Petersburg: Tipografiia Imperatorskoi Akademii Nauk.

——— 1915, 'O religioznykh verovaniiakh abkhazov (k voprosu ob iafeticheskom kul'te i mifologii', *Khristianskii Vostok*, 4, 1: 113–40.

——— 1917, 'Zapiska akademika N.Ia. Marra o Kavkazskom Istoriko-Arkhiologicheskom Institute', *Izvestiia Rossiiskoi Akademii Nauk* (VI seriia) 13: 962–94.

——— 1926, 'K voprosu o pervobytnom myshlenii v sviazi s iazykom v osveshenii A.A. Bogdanova', *Vestnik kommunisticheskoi akademii*, XVI: 133–9.

——— 1927, *Iafeticheskaia teoriia. Programma obshchego kursa ucheniia ob iazyke*, Baku: Izd. vostochnogo fakul'teta Azerbaidzh. gos. Universiteta.

——— (ed.) 1929, *Iazykovedenie i materialism*, Leningrad: Priboi.

——— 1933a [1910], 'O chanskom iazyke', in *Izbrannye raboty*, Vol. 1, Leningrad: GAIMK.

——— 1933b [1920], 'Iafeticheskii Kavkaz i tretii etnicheskii element v sozidanii srednizemnomorskogo kul'ture', in *Izbrannye raboty*, Vol. 1, Leningrad: GAIMK.

——— 1933c [1923], 'Chem zhivet iafeticheskoe iazykoznanie?' in *Izbrannye Raboty*, Vol. 1, Leningrad: GAIMK.

——— 1933d [1924], 'Indoevropeiskie iazyki Srednomor''ia', in *Izbrannye Raboty*, Vol. 1, Leningrad: GAIMK.

——— 1933e [1930], 'Iafetidologiia v leningradskom gosudarstvennom universitete' [1930], in *Izbrannye Raboty*, Vol. 1, Leningrad: GAIMK.

——— 1934a [1924], 'Ob iafeticheskoi teorii', in *Izbrannye raboty*, Vol. 3, Moscow and Leningrad: Gosudarstvennoe sotsial'no-ekomomicheskoe izdatel'stvo.

——— 1934b [1926], 'K voprosu o pervobytnom myshlenii v sviazi s iazykom v osveshenii A.A. Bogdanova', in *Izbrannye raboty*, Vol. 3, Moscow and Leningrad: Gosudarstvennoe sotsial'no-ekomomicheskoe izdatel'stvo.

——— 1935a, 'Avtobiografiia N.Ia. Marra', *Problemy istorii dokapitalisticheskikh obshchestv*, 3–4: 126–30.

——— 1935b [1924], 'Terminy iz abkhazo-russkikh etnicheskikh sviazei "loshad'" i "trizna"', in *Izbrannye raboty*, Vol. 5, Moscow and Leningrad: Gos. Sotsial'no-ekomicheskoe izdatel'stvo.

—— 1935c [1931], 'Iazykovaia politika iafeticheskoi teorii i udmurtskii iazyk', *Izbrannye raboty*, Vol. 5, Moscow and Leningrad: Gos. Sotsial'no-ekonomicheskoe izdatel'stvo.

—— 1936a [1927], 'Iafeticheskaia teoriia. Programma obshchego kursa ucheniia ob iazyke', in *Izbrannye raboty*, Vol. 2, Moscow and Leningrad: Gosudarstvennoe sotsial'no-ekomomicheskoe izdatel'stvo.

—— 1936b [1931], 'K paleonotlogicheskoi palentologii v iazykakh neiafeticheskikh sistem', *Izbrannye raboty*, Vol. 2, Moscow and Leningrad: Gosudarstvennoe sotsial'no-ekomomicheskoe izdatel'stvo.

—— 1987, *Bassko-kavkazskie leksicheskie paralleli*, Tblisi: Metsnieba.

Martin, Terry 2001, *The Affirmative Action Empire: Nations and Nationalism in the Soviet Union, 1923–1939*, London: Cornell University Press.

Marty, Anton 1908, *Untersuchungen zur Grundlegung der allgemeinen Grammatik und Sprachphilosophie, 1. Band*, Halle: Niermeyer.

Martynov, Alexandr 1905, *Dve diktatury*, Geneva: RSDRP.

Marx, Karl 1979 [1851–2], 'The Eighteenth Brumaire of Louis Bonaparte', in Marx and Engels 1975–2004, Vol. 11.

—— 1984 [1861], 'The North American Civil War', in Marx and Engels 1975–2004, Vol. 19.

—— 1987 [1866], 'Marx to Engels 7 July 1866', in Marx and Engels 1975–2004, Vol. 42.

—— 1989 [1886], 'Letter to *Otechestvenniye Zapiski*', in Marx and Engels 1975–2004, Vol. 24.

—— and Frederick Engels 1975–2004, *Collected Works*, Moscow: Progress Publishers.

—— 1976 [1845–7], 'The German Ideology', in Marx and Engels 1975–2004, Vol. 5.

—— 1989 [1882], 'Preface to the Second Russian Edition of the *Manifesto of the Communist Party*', in Marx and Engels 1975–2004, Vol. 24.

Matejka, Ladislav 1987, 'Sociological Concerns of the Moscow Linguistic Circle', in Pomorska *et al.* (eds.) 1987.

Matiurin, N.M. 1933, 'N.Ia. Marr i istoricheskaia nauka', *Sovetskaia etnografiia*, 5–6: 3–13.

Matlaw, Ralph E. (ed.) 1963, *Belinsky, Chernyshevsky and Dobrolyubov: Selected Criticism*, New York: Dutton.

Matthews, W.K. 1950, 'Soviet Contributions to Linguistic Thought', *Archivum Linguisticum*, 2: 1–23 and 97–121.

—— 1953, 'Marr's Analytical Alphabet', *Archivum Linguisticum*, 5: 65–74.

Mauro, T. de 2010, 'From Nature to History', in Ives and Lacorte (eds.) 2010.

Mazon, André 1920, *Lexique de la guerre et de la révolution en Russie (1914–1918)*, Paris: E. Champion.

McCarthy, Conor 2008, 'The State, the Text and the Critic in a Globalized World: The Case of Edward Said', in Lentin (ed.) 2008.

McDermott, Kevin and John Morison (eds.) 1999, *Politics and Society under the Bolsheviks: Selected Papers From the Fifth World Congress for Central and East European Studies Warsaw 1995*, Basingstoke: Macmillan.

McGetchin, Douglas T. 2009, *Indology, Indomania and Orientalism: Ancient India's Rebirth in Modern Germany*, Madison: Fairleigh Dickinson University Press.

McKean, Robert (ed.) 1992, *New Perspectives in Modern Russian History*, New York: St. Martin's Press.

McNally, Mark 2011, 'Revisiting the Gramsci-Bukharin relationship: Neglected symmetries', *History of European Ideas*, 37, 3: 365–75.

Megrelidze, Konstantin [Kita] Romanovich 1935a, 'O khodiachikh sueveriiakh i "pralogicheskom" sposobe myshleniia (replica Levi-Briuliu)' in Meshaninov (ed.) 1935.

———— 1935b, 'N.Ia. Marr i filosfiia marksizma', *Pod znamenem marksizma*, 3: 35–52.

———— 1989, 'Dva slova ob ottse', *Filosofskaia i sotsiologicheskaia mysl'*, 2: 93–106.

———— 2007 [1936], *Osnovnye problemy sotsiologii myshleniia*, Moscow: URSS.

Meillet, Antoine, 1926 [1905–6], 'Comment les mots changent de sense', in *Linguistique historique et linguistique générale*, Paris: Librarie ancienne honoré champion.

———— 1967 [1925], *The Comparative Method in Historical Linguistics*, Paris: Honore Champion.

Meinhof, Carl 1932 [1899, 1910], *Introduction to the Phonology of the Bantu Languages*, Berlin: Reimer.

Meiskins Wood, Ellen and John Bellamy Foster (eds.) 1997, *In Defence of History: Marxism and the Postmodern Agenda*, New York: Monthly Review Press.

Mellor, A. *et al.* 1976, 'Writers and the General Strike', in Morris (ed.) 1976.

Meshchaninov, Ivan Ivanovich 1934, 'Osnovnye lingvisticeskie elementy', *Iazyk i myshlenie*, 2: 7–31.

———— (ed.) 1935, *Akademiku N.Ia. Marru*, Moscow-Leningrad: ANSSSR.

———— (ed.) 1938, *Pamiati akademika N.Ia. Marra*, Moscow and Leningrad: AN SSSR.

Meyer, Karl H. 1920, *Slawische und indogermanische Intonation*, Heidelberg: Winter.

Meyer-Kalkus, Reinhart 2007, 'Work, Rhythm, Dance: Prerequisites for a Kinaesthetics of Media and Arts', in Krois *et al.* (eds.) 2007.

Mikhankova, Vera Andreevna 1949, *Nikolai Iakovlevich Marr*, third edition, Moscow and Leningrad: Izd. AN SSSR.

Molyneux, John 1978, *Marxism and the Party*, London: Pluto Press.

Mommsen, Wolfgang J. and Jürgen Osterhammel 1987, *Max Weber and His Contemporaries*, London: Unwin Hyman.

Montenyohl, E.L. 1988, 'Andrew Lang's Contributions to English Folk Narrative Scholarship: A Reevaluation', *Western Folklore*, 47, 4: 269–84.

Morgan, Lewis Henry 1871, *Systems of Consanguinity and Affinity of the Human Family*, Washington: Smithsonian Institution.

———— 1877, *Ancient Society*, New York: Henry Holt.

Morley, David and Chen Kuan-Hsinh (eds.) 1996, *Stuart Hall: Critical Dialogues in Cultural Studies*, London: Routledge.

Morris, Margaret (ed.) 1976, *The General Strike*, London: Journeyman Press.

Moss, Kevin 1984, *Olga Mikhailovna Freidenberg: Soviet Mythologist in a Soviet Context*, Ph.D. dissertation, Cornell Unversity, UMI.

Mouffe, Chantal (ed.) 1979, *Gramsci and Marxist Theory*, London: Routledge.

Mueller, Julie Kay 1998, 'Newspapers and Training Journalists in Early Soviet Russia', *Journal of Social History*, 31, 4: 851–73.

Mulhern, Francis 1997, 'The Politics of Cultural Studies', in Meiskins Wood and Bellamy Foster (eds.) 1997.

Mühlfried, Florian and Sergey Sokolovskiy (eds.) 2011, *Exploring the Edge of Empire: Soviet Era Anthropology in the Caucasus and Central Asia*, Münster: LIT-Verlag.

Müller, Friedrich Max 1878, 'On the Origin of Reason', *The Contemporary Review*, 31: 465–93.

———— 1885, *Lectures on the Science of Language*, London: Longmans, Green and co.

———— 1887, *The Science of Thought*, London: Longmans, Green and co.

Muratova, K.D. 1958, *M. Gor'kii v bor'be za razvitie sovetskoi literatury*, Moscow and Leningrad: AN SSSR.

Murphree, I.L. 1961, 'The Evolutionary Anthropologists; The Progress of Mankind: The Concepts of Progress and Culture in the Thought of John Lubbock, Edward B. Tylor, and Lewis H. Morgan', *Proceedings of the American Philosophical Society*, 105, 3: 265–300.

Murphy, Kevin Joseph 2005, *Revolution and Counterrevolution: Class Struggle in a Moscow Metal Factory*, Chicago: Haymarket Press.

Negt, Oskar (ed.) 1969, *N. Bucharin/A. Deborin, Kontroversen über dialektischen und mechanistischen Materialismus*, Frankfurt am Main: Suhrkamp.

Neitzsche, Friedrich, 1967 [1878], *The Birth of Tragedy*, New York: Vintage Books.

Nemeth, Thomas 2009, 'Shpet's Departure from Husserl', in Tihanov (ed.) 2009.

Nikolaev, Nikolai Ivanovich 1997, 'Sud'ba tret'ego vozrozhdeniia', in Durov (ed.) 1997.

Nikol'skii, Nikolai Mikhailovich 1923, *Religiia kak predmet nauki*, Minsk: Beltrestpechat'.

———— 1938, 'Problemy kritiki biblii v sovetskom nauke', *Vestnik drevnei istorii*, 1: 30–44.

Nikonova, A.A. 2003, *Problemy arkhaicheskogo soznaniia i stanovlenie otechestvennoi kul'turologicheskoi mysli (20–30e gody XX v)*, Kandidatskaia dissertatsia, St. Petersburg: SPbGU.

Noiré, Ludwig, 1877a, *Der Ursprung der Sprache*, Mainz: Zabern.

———— 1877b, *Aphorismen zur monistischen Philosophie*, Leipzig: F.A. Brockhaus.

———— 1877c, *Einleitung und Begründung einer monistischen Erkenntnistheorie*, Leipzig: F.A. Brockhaus

—— 1880, *Das Werkzeug und seine Bedeutung für die Entwicklungsgeschichte der Menschheit*, Mainz: Diemer.

Noskova, Ol'ga G. 1999, 'A.A. Bogdanov i psikhologicheskaia nauka', in Bogdanov 1999.

Norman, F. 1929, ' "Indo-European" and "Indo-Germanic" ', *The Modern Language Review*, 24, 3: 313–21.

Novikov M.V. and T.B. Perfilova 2011, 'Professional'noe stanovlenie F.F. Zelinskogo i ego sud'ba', *Iaroslavskii pedagogicheskii vestnik*, 1, 3: 7–17.

Nuare, L. [Noiré, L] 1925, *Orudie truda i ego znachenie v istorii razvitiia chelovechestva*, Kiev: Gosizdat.

Obatnin, G. 2010, 'O "ritmicheskom zheste" ', in Lavrov and Timenchik (eds.) 2010.

Ober, Josiah 1998, *Political Dissent in Democratic Athens: Intellectual Critics of Popular Rule*, Princeton: Princeton University Press.

—— and Hendrick, Charles (eds.) 1996, *Dēmokratia: A Conversation on Democracies Ancient and Modern*, Princeton: Princeton University Press.

Ol'denburg, Sergei Fedorovich 1915, ' "Ne dovol'no": K vos'midesiatletiiu Grigoriia Nikolaevicha Potanina 21 sentiabria 1915 goda', *Russkaia mysl'*, 1: 1–11.

—— 1927, 'Pamiati M.P. Pavlovicha', *Novyi Vostok*, 18: 24–6.

Olender, Maurice 1992 [1989], *The Languages of Paradise: Aryans and Semites, a Match Made in Heaven*, New York: Other Press.

—— 1994, 'Europe, or How to Escape Babel', *History and Theory*, 33, 4: 5–25.

Olmsted, D.L. and L.A. Timm 1983, 'Baudouin de Courtenay as a Sociolinguist', in Agard *et al.* (eds.) 1983.

Ordzhonikidze, Grigorii Konstantinovich 1957 [1934], 'Mobilizirovat' rezervy tiazheloi promyshlennosti, vypolnit' i perevypolnit' godovoi plan', in *Stat'y i rechi v dvukh tomakh*, Vol. 2, Moscow: Politicheskaia literatura.

Orekhov, Boris (ed.) 2011, *Khronotop i okrestnosti. Iubileinyi sbornik v chest' Nikolaia Pan'kova*, Ufa: Vagant.

Ostrovskaia, Elena Petrovna 2010, 'Leningradskaia buddologiia v nachale 1930-kh godov', *Pis'mennye pamiatniki Vostoka*, 2, 13: 231–46.

Paggi, Leonardo 1984, *Le strategie del potere in Gramsci: Tra fascism e socialism in un solo paese 1923–1926*, Rome: Riuniti.

Parvus, Alexandr 2009 [1905], 'What Was Accomplished on the Ninth of January?' in Day and Gaido (eds.) 2009.

Pavlovich, Mikhail 1922, 'Zadachi Vserossiiskoi nauchnoi assotsiatsii vostokovedeniia', *Novyi Vostok*, 1: 3–16.

Perkhin, V.V. 1997, *Russkaia literaturnaia kritika 1930-kh godov: Kritika i obshchestvennoe soznanie*, St. Petersburg: SPBGU.

Peterson, Mikhail N. 1923, 'Obshchaia lingvistika', *Pechat' i revoliutsiia*, 6: 26–32.

────── 1927, 'Iazyk kak sotsial'noe iavlenie', *Uchenye zapiski instituta iazyka i literatury*, 1: 5–21.

Petrov, D.K. 1910, '25 let zhizni Neofilologicheskogo Obshchestva', *Zapiski Neofilologicheskogo Obshchestva pri Imperatorskom S.-Peterburgskom Universitete*, 4: 1–12.

Pictet, Adolphe 1859–63, *Origines indo-européennes ou les Aryas primitifs: Essaie de paléontologie linguistique*, 2 Vols., Paris, Joël Cherbuliez.

Piotrovskii, B.B. 1930, *Semanticheskii puchek v pamiatnikakh material'noi kul'tury*, *Izvestiia gosudarstvennoi akademii istorii material'noi kul'tury*, 6, 19.

Pipes, Richard 1954, *The Formation of the Soviet Union, Communism and Nationalism, 1917–1923*, Cambridge: Harvard University Press.

────── 2010, *The Trial of Vera Z*, a special issue of the journal, *Russian History*, 37, 1.

Platonov, Andrei Platonovich 1978 [1929], 'Makar the Doubtful', in *Collected Works*, Ardis: Ann Arbor.

────── 1978 [1930], 'The Foundation Pit', in *Collected Works*, Ardis: Ann Arbor.

────── 1988a [1929], 'Usomnivshiisia Makar', in *Gosudarstvennyi zhitel'*, Moscow: Sovetskii Pisatel'.

────── 1988b [1930], 'Kotlovan', in *Gosudarstvennyi zhitel'*, Moscow: Sovetskii Pisatel'.

────── 1988c [1931], 'Vprok (Bedniatskaia khronika)', in *Gosudarstvennyi zhitel'*, Moscow: Sovetskii Pisatel'.

────── 1994 [1974], *The Foundation Pit*, Evanston: Northwestern University Press.

Platonova, N.I. 1998, 'Nikolai Iakovlevich Marr – arkheolog i organizator arkheologicheskoi nauki', *Arkheologicheskie vesti*, 5: 371–82.

────── 2002, ' "Bezzakonnaia kometa na nauchnom nebosklone". N.Ia. Marr', in *Znamenitye universanty*, St. Petersburg: Izd. Sankt-Peterburgskogo universiteta.

Plekhanov, Georgii Valentinovich 1923 [1892], 'O zadachakh sotsialistov v bor'be s golodom v Rossii (Pis'ma k molodym tovarishcham)', in *Sobranie sochineniia*, Vol. 3, second edition, Moscow: Gosizdat.

────── 1958 [1899], 'Pis'ma bez adresa', in *Literatura i estetika. Tom pervyi: Teoriia iskusstva i istoriia esteticheskoi mysli*, Moscow: Khudozhestvennaia literatura.

────── 1961 [1885], 'Our Differences', in *Selected Philosophical Works in Five Volumes*, Vol. 1, London: Lawrence and Wishart.

────── 1961 [1895], 'The Development of the Monist View of History', in *Selected Philosophical Works in Five Volumes*, Vol. 1, London: Lawrence and Wishart.

────── 1969, *Fundamental Problems of Marxism*, London: Lawrence and Wishart.

Plotnikov, I.S. (ed.) 1925, *Rol' orudiia v razvitii cheloveka*, Leningrad: Priboi.

Plotnikov, N.S. 2002, 'Filosofiia "Problem idealizma" ', in *Problemy idealizma*, edited by P.I. Novgorodtsev, Moscow: Tri kvadrata.

Pochta, Iu.M. 1993, 'Revoliutsionnaia Rossiia i musul'manskii mir (Sovetskoe islamovedenie v 20–30-e gody)', *Vostok*, 4: 81–93.

Podol', R. Ia. 2008, *Teoriia istoricheskogo protsessa v russkoi istoriosifii pervoi treti xx veka*, Moscow: Nauka.

Polivanov, Evgenii D. 1923, *Problema latinskogo shrifta v turetskikh pis'mennostiakh*, Moscow: Narodnyi kommunisticheskii natsional'nyi institut vostokovedeniia v Moskve, Seria turetskikh iazykov.

—— 1928a, 'Osnovnye formy graficheskoi revoliutsii v turetskikh pis' mennostiakh SSSR', *Novyi vostok*, 23–4: 314–30.

—— 1928b, 'Faktory foneticheskoi evoliutsii iazyka kak trudovogo protsessa. 1. Obzor protsessov, kharakternykh dlia iazykovo razvitiia v epokhi natural'nogo khoziaistva', *Uchenye zapiski Instituta iazyka i literatury Rossiiskoi assotsiatsii nauchno-issledovatel'skikh institutov obshchestvennykh nauk (RANION)*, 3: 20–42.

—— 1931, *Za marksistskoe iazykoznanie*, Moscow: Federatsiia.

—— 1974, *Selected Works: Articles on General Linguistics*, The Hague: Mouton.

—— 1974a [1927], 'Revolution and the Literary Languages of the USSR', in Polivanov 1974.

—— 1974b [1929], 'The Sphere of Immediate Problems in Contemporary Linguistics', in Polivanov 1974.

—— 1974c [1928], 'On the Phonetic Features of the Dialects of Social Groups and, in Particular, of Standard Russian', in Polivanov 1974.

—— 1974d [1931], 'Where Do the Reasons for Language Evolution Lie?' in Polivanov 1974.

—— 1974e [1931], 'Historical Linguistics and Language Policy', in Polivanov 1974.

—— 1991 [1929], 'Iz materialov "Polivanovskoi" diskussii v Kommunisticheskom Akademii. Fevral' 1929g. Arkhivnaia publikatsiia', in *Trudy po vostochnomu i obshchemu iazykoznaniiu*, Moscow: Nauka, 1991.

Pomorska, Krystyna *et al.* (eds.) 1987, *Language, Poetry and Poetics: The Generation of the 1890s: Jakobson, Trubetskoy, Majakovskij*, Berlin: Mouton.

Porokhovshchikov, P.S. (P. Sergeich) 1988 [1910], *Iskusstvo rechi na sude*, Moscow: Iuridicheskaia Literatura.

Potebnia, Aleksandr A. 1993 [1892], *Mysl' i iazyk*, Kiev: Sinto.

Priestland, David 2007, *Stalinism and the Politics of Mobilization: Ideas, Power and Terror in Inter-war Russia*, Oxford: Oxford University Press.

Primochkina, N.N. 1998, *Pisatel' i vlast'*, Moscow: Rosspen.

Procacci, G. 1974, *Il partito nell'Unione Sovietica*, 1917–1945, Laterza, Roma-Bari.

Protosova, S.N. 1938, 'Istoriia drevnego mira v postroenii Ed. Meiera', *Vestnik drevnei istorii*, 3: 298–313.

Rabinowitch, Alexander 2007, *The Bolsheviks in Power: The First Year of Soviet Rule in Petrograd*, Bloomington: Indiana University Press.

Rakitnikov, N.I. 2007 [1910], 'Intelligentsiia i narod', in Sapov (ed.) 2007.

Rakov, V. 1986, *Iz istorii sovetskogo literaturovedeniia: sotsiologicheskoe napravlenie*, Ivanovo: Ivanovskii gosudarstvennyi universitet.

Rakovsky, Christian 1980, *Selected Writings on Opposition in the USSR 1923–30*, London and New York: Allison and Busby.

—— 1980 [1923], 'Speech to the Twelfth Party Congress', in Rakovsky 1980.

Reid, Donald 2004, '*Etablissement*: Working in the Factory to Make Revolution in France', *Radical History Review*, 88: 83–111.

Reiman, Michael 1987, *The Birth Of Stalinism: The USSR on the Eve of the 'Second Revolution'*, New York: I.B. Tauris.

Renan, Ernest, 1947–61, *Oeuvres complètes*, 10 Vols, edited by Henriette Psichari, Paris: Calmann-Lèvy.

Reznik, Vladislava 2008, 'A Long Redezvous: Aleksandr Romm's Unpublished Works on Ferdinand de Saussure', *Slavonic and East European Review*, 86, 1: 1–25.

—— 2010, 'The Word as Culture: Grigorii Vinokur's Applied Language Science', in Brandist and Chown (eds.) 2010.

Riddell, John (ed.) 2012, *Toward the United Front: Proceedings of the Fourth Congress of the Communist International, 1922*, Chicago: Haymarket Press.

Ritter, Gerhard A. 1978, 'Workers' Culture in Imperial Germany: Problems and Points of Departure for Research', *Journal of Contemporary History*, 13, 2: 165–89.

Rosenthal, B.G. 1977, 'The Transmutation of the Symbolist Ethos: Mystical Anarchism and the Revolution of 1905', *Slavic Review*, 36, 4: 608–27.

Roth, Guenther 1963, *The Social Democrats in Imperial Germany: a Study in Working-Class Isolation and National Integration*, Totowa: Bedminster Press.

Rozen, Viktor R. (ed.), 1897, *Sbornik statei uchenikov Professora Barona Viktora Romanovicha Rozena ko dniu dvatsatipiatiletiia ego pervoi lektsii 13go noiabra 1872–1897*, St. Petersburg: Akademiia nauk.

Rozenberg, Otton O. 1991, *Trudy po buddizmy*, Moscow: Nauka.

Rubinstein, Annette T. 1995, 'Lenin on Literature, Language and Censorship', *Science & Society*, 59, 3: 368–83.

Ryazanov, N. [Riazanov, D.] 2009 [1903], 'The Draft Programme of "*Iskra*" and the Tasks of Russian Social Democrats', in Day and Gaido (eds.) 2009.

Said, Edward Wadie 1995 [1978], *Orientalism: Western Conceptions of the Orient*, Harmondsworth: Penguin.

San Juan, E. 2006, 'Edward Said's Affiliations', *Atlantic Studies*, 3, 1: 43–61.

Sapov, V.V. (ed.) 2007, *Anti-Vekhi, Intelligentsiia v Rossii; 'Vekhi' kak znamenie vremeny*, Moscow: Astrel'.

Saussure, Ferdinand de 1983 [1916], *Course in General Linguistics*, London: Duckworth.

Scanlan, James P. 1970, 'Nicholas Chernyshevsky and Philosophical Materialism in Russia', *Journal of the History of Philosophy*, 8, 1: 65–86.

Scherrer, Jutta 1989, 'The Cultural Hegemony of the Proletariat: The Origins of Bogdanov's Vision of Proletarian Culture', *Studies in History*, 5: 195–210.

Schleicher, August 1874, *A Compendium of the Comparative Grammar of the Indo-European, Sanskrit, Greek and Latin Languages*, London: Trübner.

Schmaus, Warren 1982, 'A Reappraisal of Comte's Three-State Law', *History and Theory*, 21, 2: 248–66.

Schrempp, G. 1983, 'The Re-Education of Max Müller: Intellectual Appropriation and Epistemological Antinomy in Mid-Victorian Evolutionary Thought', *Man*, 18, 1: 90–110.

Seifrid, Thomas 1992, *Andrei Platonov: Uncertainties of Spirit*, Cambridge: Cambridge University Press.

———— 2005, *The Word Made Self. Russian Writings on Language, 1860–1930*, Ithaca: Cornell University Press.

Selvanovskii, A. 1931, 'V chem "somnevaetsia" Andrei Platonov', *Literaturnaia gazeta*, 10 June 1931.

Selishchev, A.M. 1928, *Iazyk revoliutsionnoi epokhi. Iz nabliudenii nad russkim iazykom* (1917–26), Moscow: Rabotnik prosveshcheniia.

Semenov, I. 2003, 'Eduard Meier i ego trudy po metodologii i trudy istorii', in Eduard Meier, *Trudy po teorii i metodologii istoricheskoi nauki*, Moscow: G.P.I.B.R.

Senderovich, S.Ia. 2010, 'F.F. Zelinskii i Viach. Ivanov. Nachala i kontsy', in Lappo-Danilievskii and Shiskin (eds.) 2010.

Serge, Victor 1992 [1930] *Year One of the Russian Revolution*, London: Writers and Readers.

———— 2002, *Memoirs of a Revolutionary*, Iowa: University of Iowa Press.

Sergeev, V.S. 1931, 'Eduard Meier', *Istorik-marksist*, 21: 104–14.

Sériot, Patrick (ed.) 2003, *Contributions suisses au XIII e congrès mondial des slavistes à Ljubljana, aout 2003*, Bern: Peter Lang.

Shafir, Ia. 1924, *Gazeta i derevnia*, Moscow: Krasnaia nov'.

———— 1927, *Voprosy gazetnoi kul'tury*, Moscow and Leningrad: Gosizdat.

Shaitanov, Igor O. 2006, 'Klassicheskaia poetika neklassicheskoi epokhi', in Veselovskii 2006.

Shakhnovich, N.N. 2006, *Ocherki po isotorii religiovedeniia*, St. Petersburg: Izd. S-Peterburgskogo universiteta.

Shandro, A. 2007, 'Lenin and Hegemony: The Soviets, the Working Class, and the Party in the Revolution of 1905', in Budgen *et al.* (eds.) 2007.

Shanin, Theodor (ed.) 1983, *Late Marx and the Russian Road: Marx and 'the Peripheries of Capitalism': A Case Study*, New York: Monthly Review Press.

Shapiro, F. 1981, 'The Origin of the Term "Indo-Germanic" ', *Historiographia Linguistica*, 8: 165–70.

Shapiro, Joel 1976, *A History of the Communist Academy, 1918–1936*, Ph.D. Dissertation, Columbia University.

Sharadzenidze, T.S. 1980, *Lingvisticheskaia teoriia I. A. Boduen de Kurtene i ee mesto v iazykoznanii XIX–XX vekov*, Moscow: Nauka.

Shaw, W.H. 1984, ' Marx and Morgan', *History and Theory*, 23, 2: 215–28.

Shchedrina, Tat'iana G. (ed.) 2010, *Gustav Shpet i ego filosofskaia nasledie: U istokov semiotiki i strukturalizma*, Moscow: ROSSPEN.

Shcherba, Lev V. 1966, 'Pamiati A. Meillet', *Voprosy iazykoznaniia*, 3: 97–104.

Shcherbina, V.R. (ed.) 1993, *Aleksandr Blok: Novye materialy i issledovaniia*, Vol. 5, Moscow: Nauka.

Shearer, David Randall, *Aleksey Gastev, Russian Modernism and the Proletarian Culture Tradition: A Study in the Development of Social Thought in Twentieth Century Russia*, dissertation, Ohio State University..

Schieffelin, Bambi B. *et al.* (eds.) 1998, *Language Ideologies: Practice and Theory*, New York and Oxford: Oxford University Press.

Schirru, Giancarlo 2008, 'Filosofia del linguaggio e filosofia della prassi', in Giasi (ed.) 2008.

——— 2011, 'Antonio Gramsci studente di linguistica', in *Studi storici*, 52, 4: 925–73.

Shentalinsky, Vitaly 1993, *The KGB's Literary Archive*, London: Harvill Press.

Sheshukov, S. 1984, *Neistovye revniteli: Iz istorii literaturnoi bor'by 20-kh godov*, Moscow: Khudozhestvennaia literatura.

Shishkin, A.V. *et al.* (eds.) 2006, *Bashnia Viacheslava Ivanova i kul'tura serebrianogo veka*, St. Petersburg: Filologicheskii fakul'tet Sankt-Peterburgskogo gosudarstvennogo universiteta.

Shklovskii, Viktor 1924, 'Lenin as dekanonizator', *Lef*, 1, 5: 53–6.

——— 1966, *Zhili-byli*, Moscow: Sovetskii pisatel'.

Shishko, L. 2007 [1910], 'Rol' intelligentsiia v osvoboditel'nom dvizhenii', in Sapov (ed.) 2007.

Shishmarev, Vladimir Fedorovich 1937, 'N.Ia. Marr i A.N. Veselovskii', *Iazyk i myshlenie*, VIII: 321–34.

Shofman, A. (ed.) 1977, *Metodologiia istoricheskogo poznaniia v burzhuaznaia nauka*, Kazan': Izd. Kazanskogu universiteta.

Shor, R.O. 1926, *Iazyk i obshchestvo*, Moscow: Rabotnik prosveshcheniia.

——— 1929, 'retsenziia na V.N. Voloshinov. Marksizm i filosofiia iazyka', *Russkii iazyk v sovetskom shkole*, 3: 149–54.

Shpet, Gustav Gustavovich 2006 [1927], *Vnutrenniaia forma slova: Etiudy i variatsii na temy Gumbol'dta*, Moscow: URSS.

Shpil'rein, Isaak Naftulovich *et al.* 1928, *Iazyk Krasnoarmeitsa: Opyt issledovaniia slovaria krasnoarmeitsa moskovskogo garnizona*, Moscow and Leningrad: Gosizdat.

Shteintal' Kh. and M. Latsarus [Steinthal, H. and M. Lazarus] 1864, 'Mysli o narodnoi psikhologii', *Filologicheskie zapiski*, 1: 90–105 and 3: 248–73.

Shvartskopf, B.S. 1970, 'Ocherk razvitiia teoreticheskikh vzgliadov na normu v sovetskom iazykoznanii', in Kosomarov and Skvortsov (eds.) 1970.

Simmel, Georg 1997 [1911], 'The Concept and Tragedy of Culture', in Frisby and Featherstone (eds.) 1997.

Simon, Roger 1982, *Gramsci's Political Thought*, London: Lawrence and Wishart.

Simonato-Kokochkin, E. 2010, 'Le mythe de l'unification des alphabets en URSS dans les années 1920–1930', *Langage et société*, 3: 103–23.

Skribian, G.K. and E.M. Primakov (eds.) 1986, *Sergei Fedorovich Ol'denburg*, Moscow: Nauka.

Skorkin, K.V. 2011, *Obrecheny proigrat' (Vlast' i oppositsiia 1922–1934)*, Moscow: VividArt.

Slezkine, Yuri 1994, 'The USSR as a Communal Apartment, or How a Socialist State Promoted Ethnic Particularism', *Slavic Review*, 53, 2: 414–52.

——— 1996, 'N. Ia. Marr and the national origins of Soviet ethnogenetics', *Slavic Review*, 55, 4: 826–62.

Smilga, Ivar Tenisovich 1921, *Ocherednye voprosy stroitel'stva Krasnoi armii*, Moscow: Gosizdat.

Smirnov, S.B. 1970, 'Professor Tartuskogo (Iur'evskogo) universiteta D.N. Kudriavskii', *Uchenye zapiski Tartuskogo universiteta. Trudy po russkoi i slavianskoi filologii. Seriia lingvisticheskaia* 16, 247: 3–173.

Smith, Woodruff D. 1991, *Politics and the Sciences of Culture in Germany 1840–1920*, Oxford: Oxford University Press.

Smith, Barry 1995, 'On Drawing Lines on a Map', in Frank, Kuhn and Mark (eds.) 1995.

Smith, Barry and Achille C. Varzi 2000, 'Fiat and Bona Fide Boundaries', *Philosophy and Phenomenological Research*, 60, 2: 401–20.

Smith, Jeremy 1999, *The Bolsheviks and the National Question, 1917–1923*, Houndmills: Macmillan.

Smith, Michael G. 1998, *Language and Power in the Creation of the USSR, 1917–1953*, Berlin: Mouton de Gruyter.

Sobczinska, D. and E. Czerwiska 2005, 'Wilhelm Otswald and the German Monist League on the Social and Cultural Role of Science', in Görs *et al.* (eds.) 2005.

Sochor, Zenovia A. 1981a, 'Soviet Taylorism Revisited', *Soviet Studies*, 33, 2: 246–64.

——— 1981b, 'Was Bogdanov Russia's answer to Gramsci?' *Studies in East European Thought*, 22, 1: 59–81.

——— 1988, *Revolution and Culture: The Bogdanov-Lenin Controversy*, Ithaca: Cornell University Press.

Sokolov, Yury M. 1966 [1938], *Russian Folklore*, Hatboro: Folklore Associates.

Sparks, Colin 1996, 'Stuart Hall, Cultural Studies and Marxism', in Morley and Chen (eds.) 1996.

Spencer, Herbert 1864, *The Classification of the Sciences: to Which are Added Reasons for Dissenting from the Philosophy of M. Comte*, London: Williams and Norgate.

———— 1876, 'The Comparative Psychology of Man', *Mind*, 1: 7–20.

———— 1882, *Principles of Sociology*, Vol. 1, New York: Appleton.

———— 1884, 'Mental Evolution in Animals', *The Athenaeum*, 2945: 446.

———— 1897, *First Principles*, New York: Appleton.

Spenser, G. [Spencer, H.] 1866–9, *Sobrane sochinenii v semi tomakh*, St. Petersburg: Tiblena.

Ssorin-Chaikov, N. 2008, 'Political Fieldwork, Ethnographic Exile, and State Theory: Peasant Socialism and Anthropology in Late-Nineteenth-Century Russia', in Kuklick (ed.) 2008.

Stalin, Joseph V. 1953 [1913], 'Marxism and the National Question', in Stalin 1953–86, Vol. 2, Moscow: Foreign Languages Publishing House.

———— 1953–86, *Collected Works*, Moscow: Foreign Languages Publishing House.

———— 1954a [1923], 'National Factors in Party and State Affairs: Thesis for the Twelfth Congress of the Russian Communist Party (Bolsheviks), Approved by the Central Committee of the Party', in Stalin 1953–86, Vol. 5.

———— 1954b [1923], 'The Twelfth Congress of R.C.P.(B)', in Stalin 1953–86, Vol. 5.

———— 1954c [1925], 'The Political Tasks of the University of the Peoples of the East', in Stalin 1953–86, Vol. 7.

———— 1953d [1926], 'To Comrade Kaganovich and the Other Members of the Political Bureau of the Central Committee, Ukraine C.P.(B.), 26 April 1926', in Stalin 1953–86, Vol. 8.

———— 1954e [1929], 'Concerning Questions of Agrarian Policy in the U.S.S.R. Speech Delivered at a Conference of Marxist Students of Agrarian Questions', in Stalin 1953–86, Vol. 12.

———— 1954f [1930] 'Dizzy With Success', in Stalin 1953–86, Vol. 12.

———— 1954g [1931], 'New Conditions – New Tasks in Economic Construction', in Stalin 1953–86, Vol. 13.

———— 1954h [1931], 'Some Questions Concerning the History of Bolshevism: Letter to the Editorial Board of the Magazine *"Proletarskaya Revolutsia"*', in Stalin 1953–86, Vol. 13.

———— 1954i [1931], 'The Tasks of Business Executives', in Stalin 1953–86, Vol. 13.

———— 1972 [1950], *Marxism and Problems of Linguistics*, Peking: Foreign Languages Press.

———— 1976 [1938], *Problems of Leninism*, Peking: Foreign Languages Press.

———— 1978 [1936], 'On the Draft Constitution of the U.S.S.R.', in Stalin 1953–86, Vol. 14.

Stcherbatsky, Th. [Shcherbatskoi, F.] 2008 [1930], *Buddhist Logic*, 2 Vols., Delhi, India: Motilal Banarsidass.

———— 1969, *Papers of Th. Stcherbatsky*, edited by Debiprasad Chattopadhyaya, Calcutta: Indian Studies Past and Present.

Steila, Daniela 1991, *Genesis and Development of Plekhanov's Theory of Knowledge: A Marxist between Anthropological Materialism and Physiology*, Dortrecht: Kluwer.

Steinberg, Mark D. 2002, *Proletarian Imagination: Self, Modernity and the Sacred in Russia, 1910–1925*, London: Cornell University Press.

Steinthal, H. 1864, *Philologie, Geschichte und Psychologie in ihren gegenseitigen Beziehungen: Ein Vortrag gehalten in der Versammlung der Philologen zu Meissen 1863 in erweiternder Überarbeitung*, Berlin: F. Dummler.

Stites, Richard 1989, *Revolutionary Dreams: Utopian Vision and Experimental Life in the Russian Revolution*, Oxford: Oxford University Press.

Stocking, George W. 1987, *Victorian Anthropology*, New York: Free Press.

———— 1995, *After Tylor: British Social Anthropology 1888–1951*, London: Athelone.

———— (ed.) 1974, *The Shaping of American Anthropology, 1883–1911: A Franz Boas Reader*, Chicago: University of Chicago Press.

Stromback, D. *et al.* (eds.) 1971, *Biographica, Nordic Folklorists of the Past*, Copenhagen: Nord. Inst. Folkedigtning.

Sultan-Galiev, Mirsaid 1995 [1929], 'Nekotorye nashi soobrazheniia ob osnovakh sotsialno-politicheskogo, ekonomicheskgo i kul'turnogo razvitiia tiurkskikh narodov azii i evropy', *Gasyrlar avazy*, online at: http://www.protas.ru/magazine/go/ anonymous/main/?path=mg:/numbers/1995_may/05/2/.

Suny, Ronald Grigor 1993, *The Revenge of the Past: Nationalism, Revolution, and the Collapse of the Soviet Union*, Stanford: Stanford University Press.

———— 2001, 'The Empire Strikes out: Imperial Russia, "National" Identity, and Theories of Empire', in Suny and Martin (eds.) 2001.

———— and Terry Martin (eds.) 2001, *A State of Nations: Empire and Nation-Making in the Age of Lenin and Stalin*, Oxford: Oxford University Press.

———— and T. Martin 2001a, 'Introduction', in Suny and Grigor (eds.) 2001.

Susiluoto, Ilmari 1982, *The Origins and Development of Systems Thinking in the Soviet Union: Political and Philosophical Controversies From Bogdanov and Bukharin to Present Day Re-evaluations*, Helsinki: Suomalainen Tiedeakatemia.

Swift, Anthony 1999, 'Workers' Theatre and "Proletarian Culture" in Prerevolutionary Russia 1905–17', in Zelnik (ed.) 1999.

Tamazishbili, A.O. 2000, ' "Ssilaias" na Stalina … (K problem mifologizatsii roli politicheskogo rukovodstva SSSR v razvitii otechestvennogo vostokovedeniia', *Vostok*, 6: 88–100.

Tchougounnikov, Serguei 2005, 'Les Paleontologues du langues avant i aprés Marr', *Cahiers de l'ILSL*, 20: 295–310.

Teilor, E.B. [Tylor E.B.] 1868, *Doistoricheskii byt' chelovechestva i nachalo tsivilizatsii*, Moscow: Presnov.

Teilor, E.B. [Tylor, E.B.] 1872–3, *Pervobytnaia kul'tura*, St. Petersburg: Znanie.

Tenbruch, F.H. 1987, 'Max Weber and Eduard Meyer', in Mommsen and Osterhammel (eds.) 1987.

Thibault, Paul J. 1997, *Re-reading Saussure: The Dynamics of Signs in Social Life*, London: Routledge.

Thomas, Lawrence 1957, *The Linguistic Ideas of N.Ia. Marr*, Berkeley: University of California Press.

Thomas, Peter 2009, *The Gramscian Moment: Philosophy, Hegemony and Marxism*, Leiden: Brill.

Thompson, Edward Palmer 1991, *Customs in Common*, Harmondsworth: Penguin.

―――― 1991a [1967], 'Time, Work Discipline and Industrial Capitalism', in Thompson 1991.

Ticktin, Hillel and Michael Cox (eds.) 1990, *The Ideas of Leon Trotsky*, London: Porcupine Press.

Tihanov, Galin 1998, 'Vološinov, Ideology, and Language: The Birth of Marxist Sociology from the Spirit of *Lebensphilosophie*', *The South Atlantic Quarterly*, 97, 3–4: 599–621.

―――― (ed.) 2009, *Gustav Shpet's Contribution to Philosophy and Cultural Theory*, West Lafayette: Purdue University Press.

―――― 2012, 'What was "Semantic Palaeontology" and What Did It Have to Do with Literary Studies?' *Stanford Slavic Studies*, 39: 288–311.

Timroth, Wilhelm von 1986, *Russian and Soviet Sociolinguistics and Taboo Varieties of the Russian Language*, Munich: Otto Sagner.

Toddes E. and M. Chudakova 1981, 'Pervyi russkii perevod "Kursa obshchei lingvistiki" F. de Sossiura i deiatel'nost' Moskovskogo lingvisticheskogo kruzhka (Materialy k izucheniiu bytovaniia nauchnoi knigi v 1920-e gody), *Fedorovskie chteniia 1978*, Moscow: Nauka.

Tolstoy, Vladimir *et al.* (eds.) 1990, *Street Art of the Revolution: Festivals and Celebrations in Russia 1918–33*, Michigan: Vendome Press.

Tolz, Vera 2005, 'Orientalism, Nationalism and Ethnic Diversity in Late Imperial Russia', *The Historical Journal*, 48, 1: 127–50.

―――― 2006, 'European, National and (Anti-)Imperial: The Formation of Academic Oriental Studies in Late Tsarist and Early Soviet Russia', in David-Fox *et al.* (eds.) 2006.

―――― 2009, 'Imperial Scholars and Minority Nationalisms in Late Imperial and Early Soviet Russia', *Kritika: Explorations in Russian and Eurasian History*, 10, 2: 261–90.

―――― 2011, *Russia's Own Orient: The Politics of Identity and Oriental Studies in the Late Imperial and Early Soviet Periods*, Oxford: Oxford University Press.

Toporkov, A.L. 1997, *Teoria mifa v russkoi filologicheskoi nauke XIX veka*, Moscow: Indrik.

Trotsky, Lev Davidovich 1922, 'On the United Front', in *The First Five Years of the Communist International*, Vol. 2, London: New Park.

───── 1967 [1930], *The History of the Russian Revolution*, London: Sphere Books.

───── 1971 [1907], *1905*, Penguin: Harmondsworth.

───── 1971a [1922], 'On the Special Features of Russia's Historical Development: A Reply to M.N. Pokrovsky', in Trotsky 1971 [1907].

───── 1973, *Problems of EverydayLife and Other Writings on Culture and Science*, New York: Monad Press.

───── 1973a [1924], 'The Cultural Role of the Worker Correspondent', in Trotsky 1973 [1924].

───── 1979 [1918], *How the Revolution Armed*, Vol. 1, London: New Park.

───── 1979a [1918], 'The Creation of the Workers' and Peasants' Red Army', in Trotsky 1979 [1918].

───── 1991 [1923], *Literature and Revolution*, London: Redwords.

───── 2009a [1905], 'Up To the Ninth of January', in Day and Gaido (eds.) 2009.

───── 2009b [1905], 'Forward to Karl Marx, *Parizhskaya Kommuna*', in Day and Gaido (eds.) 2009.

Trubetzkoy, Nikolai S. 1969 [1939], *Principles of Phonology*, Berkeley: University of California Press.

Tuite, Kevin 2011, 'The Reception of Marr and Marrism in the Soviet Georgian Academy', in Mühlfried and Sokolovskiy (eds.) 2011.

Tukhina, I.V. 2000, 'N.Ia. Marr i F.A. Braun: istoriia vzaimootnoshenii (1920–5)', *Stratum Plus*, 4: 384–92.

Tylor, Edward B. 1871, *Primitive Culture*, New York: Harper.

───── 1881, *Anthropology: An Introduction to the Study of Man and Civilization*, London: Macmillan.

Ushakov, A.V. 1974, *Bor'ba partii za gegemoniiu proletariat v revoliutsionno-demokraticheskom dvizhenii Rossii (1895–1904)*, Moscow: Politicheskaia literatura.

───── (ed.) 1986, *Voprosy gegemonii proletariat v osvoboditel'nom dvizhenii Rossii perioda imperializma: Mezhvuzovskii sbornik nauchnykh trudov*, edited by A.V. Ushakov, Moscow: MGZPI.

Ushakov, Dmitri, 1935–40, *Tol'kovyi slovar' russkogo iazyka*, Moscow: Gosizdat.

Ustrialov, Nikolai Vasil'evich 1921, 'Patriotica' in *Smena Vekh* (online at http://www.wkzinfo.ru/russia/smena_veh_ustrzalov.shtml).

Vasenna, R. 2007, 'K rekonstruktsii istorii deiatel'nosti Instituta zhivogo slova (1918–1924)', *Novoe literaturnoe obozrenie*, 86: 79–95.

Vasetskii, N.A. 1989a, 'G.E. Zinov'ev: Stranitsy zhizni i politicheshoi deiatel'nosti', *Novaia i noveishaiia istoriia*, 4: 111–39.

───── 1989b, *G.E. Zinov'ev: Stranitsy politicheskoi biografii*, Moscow: Znanie.

Vasil'kov, Iaroslav V. 1998, 'Otchety F.I. Shcherbatskogo o rabote ego uchenikov v Buriatii i Mongolii v 1928 godu', *Orient almanakh*, 2–3: 106–12.

——— 2001, 'Tragediia akademika Marra', *Khristianskii vostok* 2: 390–421.

Venditti, M. 2010, 'Vnutreniaiia forma slova u G. Shpeta i u A. Marti', in Shchedrina (ed.) 2010.

Veselovskii, Aleksandr Nikolaevich 1873, 'Sravnitel'naia mifologiia i ee metod', *Vestnik Evropy*, 10: 637–80.

——— 1938, *Sobranie sochineniia*, Vol. 16, Moscow and Leningrad: Izd. ANSSSR.

——— 2004a [1870], 'O metode i zadachakh istorii literatury, kak nauki', in Veselovskii 2004.

——— 2004b [1897–1906], 'Poetika siuzhetov', in Veselovskii 2004.

——— 2004c [1899], 'Tri glavy iz istoricheskoi poetiki', in Veselovskii 2004.

——— 2004, *Istoricheskaia poetika*, Moscow: URSS.

——— 2006, *Izbrannoe: Istoricheskaia poetika*, Moscow: ROSSPEN.

Vickers, Brian 1988, *In Defence of Rhetoric*, Oxford: Clarendon Press.

Vinogradov Viktor Vladimirovich and Boris Aleksandrovich Serebrennikov (eds.) 1951, *Protiv vulgarizatsii i izvrashcheniia marksizma v iazykoznanii*, Moscow: Izd. Akademii nauk SSSR.

Vinokur, Grigorii Osipovich 1923a, 'Poetika. Lingvistika. Sotsiologiia (metodologicheskaia spravka)', *Lef*, 3: 104–18.

——— 1923b, 'Kul'tura iazyka. (Zadachi sovremennogo iazykoznaniia)', *Pechat' i revoliutsiia*, 5: 100–11.

——— 1923c, 'O revoliutsionnoi frazeologii (odin iz voprosov iazykovoi politiki)', *Lef*, 3104–18.

——— 1925, *Kul'tura iazyka: ocherk lingvisticheskoi tekhnologii*, Moscow: Rabotnik Prosveshcheniia.

Voigt, Johannes H. 1967, *Max Müller: The Man and His Ideas*, Calcutta: Mukhopadhyay.

Voitinskii, N. 1929, 'O gruppe "Vpered" (1909–1917)' *Proletarskaia revoliutsiia*, 12, 55: 59–119.

Vol'fson, M. 1931, 'Bogdanov i Marr', *Revoliutsiia i iazyk* 1: 28–32.

Vološinov, Valentin Nikolaevich [Voloshinov, Valentin Nikolaevich] 1973 [1929], *Marxism and the Philosophy of Language*, Cambridge: Harvard University Press.

Voloshinov, Valentin Nikolaevich 1926, 'Slovo v zhizni i slovo v poezii: K voprosam sotsiologicheskoi poetiki', *Zvezda*, 6, 1926: 244–67.

——— 1929, *Marksizm i filosofiia iazyka*, Leningrad: Priboi.

——— 1995 [1929], *Marksizm i filosofiia iazyka*, in *Filosofiia i sotsiologiia gumanitarnykh nauk*, St Petersburg: Asta Press.

Vucinich, Alexander 1976, *Social Thought in Tsarist Russia: The Quest for a General Science of Society, 1861–1917*, Chicago: University of Chicago Press.

Vygotskii, Lev Semenovich 2004 [1931], 'Istoriia razvitiia vyshikh psikhicheskikh funktsii', in *Psikhologiia razvitiia cheloveka*, Moscow: Smysl.

Walicki, Andrzej 1969, *The Controversy Over Capitalism: Studies in the Social Philosophy of the Russian Populists*, Oxford: Oxford University Press.

Wallerstein, Immanuel 1991, 'The Construction of Peoplehood: Racism, Nationalism, Ethnicity', in Balibar and Wallerstein 1991.

Wax, Dustin M. (ed.) 2008, *Anthropology at the Dawn of the Cold War: The Influence of Foundations, McCarthyism and the CIA*, London: Pluto Press.

White, James, 1998, 'Sources and Precursors of Bogdanov's Tektology', in Biggart *et al.* 1998.

——— 2001, *Lenin: The Practice and Theory of Revolution*, Houndmills: Macmillan.

Williams, Raymond 1977, *Marxism and Literature*, Oxford: Oxford University Press.

——— 1997a [1958], 'Culture is Ordinary', in Gray and McGuigan (eds.) 1977.

Wilson, J.A. 1976, 'The Evolutionary Premise in Folklore Theory and the "Finnish Method"', *Western Folklore*, 35, 4: 241–9.

Wood, Ellen Meiksins 1996, 'Demos vs. "We the People": Freedom and Democracy Ancient and Modern', in Ober and Hendrick (eds.) 1996.

Woolard, Kathryn A. 1998, 'Language Ideology as a Field of Inquiry', in Schieffelin *et al.* (eds.) 1998.

——— and Bambi B. Schieffelin 1994, 'Language Ideology', *Annual Review of Anthropology*, 23: 55–82.

Worthington, Ian (ed.) 1994, *Persuasion: Greek Rhetoric in Action*, London and New York: Routledge.

Young, Robert 1990, *White Mythologies: Writing History and the West*, London: Routledge.

Zabolotskaia, A.E. 1996, 'Konst. Erberg v nauchno-teoreticheskoi sektsii TEO Narkomprosa (1918–1919)', in *Minuvshee: Istoricheskii al'manakh* 20, Moscow and St. Petersburg: Atheneum–Feniks.

Zborovskii, I. 1932, 'G. Danilov. Kratkii ocherk nauki o iazyke', *Iafeticheskii sbornik*, 7: 211–18.

Zelinskii, Faddei Frantsevich 1894, 'O chtenii sudebnykh rechei Tsitserona v gimnazi-iakh', *Filologicheskoe obozrenie*, 8, 1: 143–66.

——— 1922a [1896], 'Tsitseron v istorii evropeiskoi kul'tury', in *Vozrozhdentsy*, Petrograd: Semnadtsataia.

——— 1922b, 'Znachenie oratorskogo iskusstva', in *Iskusstvo i narod*, Petrograd: Kolos.

——— 1911 [1901], 'Vil'gel'm Vundt i psikhologiia iazyka', in *Drevnyi mir i my*, St. Petersburg: Stasiulevich.

Zhirmunskii, Viktor Maksimovich 1932, 'Metodika sotsial'noi geografii (dialektologiia i fol'klor v svete geograficheskogo issledovaniia', *Iazyk i literatura*, 8: 83–117.

——— 1934, 'Problema fol'klora', in Krachkovskii (ed.) 1934.

——— 1936, *Natsional'nyi iazyk i sotsial'nye dialekty*, Leningrad: Gosizdat.

—— 1938, 'Istoricheskaia poetika A.N. Veselovskogo', *Izvestiia akademii nauk SSSR: Otdelenie obshchectvennykh nauk*, 4: 43–65.

—— 1939, 'Istoricheskaia poetika A.N. Veselovskogo i ee istochniki', *Zapiski LGU*, 45: 3–19.

—— 1964, 'Problemy sotsial'noi dialektologii', *Izvestiia Akademii Nauk SSSR: Seria literatury i iazyka*, 23, 2: 99–112.

—— 1969, Marksizm i sotsial'naia lingvistika', in Desnitskaia *et al.* (eds.) 1969.

Zhukova, E.E. (ed.) *U istokov NOT: Zabytye diskussii i nerealizovannye idei*, Leningrad: LGU.

Zinder, Lev P. and Tat'iana V. Stroeva 1999, 'Institut rechevoi kul'tury i sovetskoe iazykoznanie 20–30-x godov', *Iazyk i rechvaia deiatel'nost'*, 2: 206–11.

Zinov'ev, Grigorii Evseevich 1924 [1923], *Istoriia rossiiskoi kommunisticheskoi partii (Bol'shevikov): Populiarnyi ocherk*, Moscow: MKRKP.

—— 1926, *Leninizm*, Leningrad: Gosizdat.

Zinoviev, Grigory 1973 [1923], *History of the Bolshevik Party – A Popular Outline*, London: New Park.

Zubarev, L.D. 1997, 'Viacheslav Ivanov v teatral'nom otdele Narkomprosa', *Russkaia filologiia*, 8: 127–33.

—— 1998, 'Viacheslav Ivanov i teatral'naia reforma pervykh poslerevoliutsionnykh let', *Nachalo*, 4: 184–216.

Collected Documents

Dvenadtsatyi s"ezd RKP(b) 17–25 aprelia 1923 goda: stenofraficheskii otchet 1968 [1923], Moscow: Gos-izdat politicheskoi literatury.

GAKhN Biulletini (1926–8)

KPSS v rezoliutsiakh i resheniiakh s"ezdov, konferentsii i plenumov TsK 1898–1958 1953, Moscow: Politicheskaia literature.

Protokoły soveshchaniia rasshirennoi redaktsii "Proletariia" 1934, Moscow: Partizdat.

Protokoły odinatsatogo s"ezda RKP(b) 1936 [1922], Moscow: Gos-izdat politicheskoi literatury.

Tretii S"ezd RSDRP Aprel' – Mai 1905 goda 1959 [1905], Moscow: Gos. Izdat. Politicheskoi literatury.

XVI S"ezd vsesoiuznoi kommunisticheskoi partii (b): Stenograficheskii otchet 1930, Moscow: Gosizdat.

RKP(b), 'On the Policy of the Party in the Sphere of Artistic Literature (1 July 1925)', online at http://www.sovlit.com/decreejuly1925/ *VAPP*, 'Ideologicheskii front i literatura', http://www.teencity.ru/projects/myaeots/bibl_11/manifest/proletcult/proletcult3.htm.

Vosmoi s"ezd RKP(b) mart 1919 goda 1959 [1919], Moscow: Gos-izdat politicheskoi

Index